To Michael

All the Best Wishes and Good Health always — enjoy the reading —

Paul T Cook
Montauk
21 Aug '05

Cheers!!

FROM MONTAUK TO . . .

FROM MONTAUK TO ...

Paul T. Cook

VANTAGE PRESS
New York

Cover design by Susan Thomas

FIRST EDITION

All rights reserved, including the right of
reproduction in whole or in part in any form.

Copyright © 2004 by Paul T. Cook

Published by Vantage Press, Inc.
419 Park Ave. South, New York, NY 10016

Manufactured in the United States of America
ISBN: 0-533-14540-6

Library of Congress Catalog Card No.: 2003090634

0 9 8 7 6 5 4 3 2 1

In Memory of David Paul Cook

b. Honolulu, Territory of Hawaii, 2 February 1952
d. Woodbury, New Jersey, 7 October 1972

Contents

Preface	ix
Author's Note	xi
The Montauk "Fishing Village" the Way It Was	1
Effects of World War II on Montauk and Its People	39
Summer Experiences, Spare Time, and Friends	50
Montauk Public School—East Hampton High School	64
Training Command, Avionics, Air Squadrons, Commissioning, Deployments, NASA	91
Engineering Studies, Ship Installations, at Sea	155
A Change in Life—A Loss of Life	168
Passports Charlie?—Meeting in Ankara	173
Skiing in South Jersey? White Rain on Pahlavi! "Bitte, Thirty Pfennig"	181
Tavernas and Islands—Prayer Calls and Changes in the Sand (1979–80)	200
Life and Livelihood on the Nile	216
The Wurst Is Yet to Come!	277
Epilogue	291
Appendixes	
Appendix 1: A Cathedral of Holy Wilderness	315
Appendix 2: Naturalistic Observations	317
Appendix 3: Think and Complain No More	319
Appendix 4: Emotions	322
Appendix 5: What Is Smart?	326
Appendix 6: The Way the Twig Is Bent	328
Appendix 7: Tax-Supported Health Care	333
Appendix 8: Is a Good Education Essential for Success in Our Society?	335

Appendix 9: Perception: "It seems to be that way" 337
Appendix 10: Modern Communication Methods 340
Appendix 11: Ancestry Charts 343

Preface

Much has been written about Montauk, Long Island's history, about its Indian inhabitants, its being the first cattle ranch in the United States, the Montauk Point Lighthouse chartered by George Washington in the late eighteenth century, the pirates and bootleggers, Theodore Roosevelt and his Rough Riders camping there after the Spanish American War, Carl Fisher's developing of Montauk as the "Miami of the North," and more. The more modern history of the village relates primarily to Montauk's prominence in the area of fishing for sport and as an industry, the long white sandy beaches, the state parks, including the infamous Montauk Downs Golf Course, the wide open spaces in summer with comforting Atlantic Ocean breezes flowing over the Scottish-like hills that distinguish Montauk from the general flatness of the "Eastern End," the camping areas, and many motels and hotels for tourists and summer residents.

Very little, however, has ever been written on a complete life's story of a native of the Montauk "Fishing Village," as it was in the 1930s era. In fact, I am not aware of any biographical account written for, or by, anyone who lived on the shores of Fort Pond Bay in the Montauk Fishing Village. While the purpose of this book was to provide my children, and theirs, with a personal account of happenings in my life, it also serves as an interesting account to others about what it was like in the life of one young boy, raised in the remote, quaint Montauk Fishing Village in the 1930s. It follows with my teenage development and a description of my twenty-two-year career in the U.S. Navy, rising up through the ranks from Apprentice Seaman to Commander level, and, next, far from the shores of Fort Pond Bay, a second career of over twenty-three years with General Dynamics Corporation, progressing from project engineer to various positions of management in European, Near East, and Mideast countries. Descriptions of both careers provide details of interesting, exciting, and sometimes dangerous assignments and situations. Some of my experiences in family life are presented as examples of real-life difficulties encountered along the way.

Most New Yorkers are well aware that Montauk, New York, is located at the easternmost tip of Long Island, 120 miles (200 kilometers) from Manhattan. But it should be noted that there exists a town in Missouri with the same name, Montauk, also nearby a Montauk State Park, located on the Current River in the Ozark Mountains, 930 feet above sea level. What the two Montauks have in common is that both are "hilly," as the Indian name, Montauk, describes, and their economies thrive on fishing and tourism. Montauk, Missouri, is one of the most famous trout-fishing areas in the country. And, centuries ago, Indians inhabited both Montauks. A big difference is that Montauk, New York, is noted for fishing "in the sea" and Montauk, Missouri, fishing is "in the mountain waters."

Author's Note

A recent experience prompted me to provide my son, James Anthony ("Jim") Cook, and daughter, Patricia Anne ("Patti") Cook Moss, and their children an account of my life. I found while trying to gather information on my parents, and theirs, for the Cook family reunion in 1999 that the problems were soon apparent. Precious little was ever written on my parents' lives and experiences. Many gaps in the information that was available left us to wonder just how things really were when and how they lived. I am hoping that this account of what happened in my life will go a long way to minimize possible biographical gaps for the next generations.

    I want to thank Dr. Ursula Jahnecke for getting me through the various snags in the operation of my computer while assembling and finishing this work. I am certain that without her assistance I would still be struggling with some of the mysteries of how and why entire paragraphs would sometimes simply disappear from my screen.

FROM MONTAUK TO . . .

The Montauk "Fishing Village" the Way It Was
(1934–40)

The most memorable period of my early childhood was during the years 1934–1940 when living at the Montauk "Fishing Village." I think it important to differentiate for the reader that the Montauk Fishing Village was an area separate and apart from what one nowadays refers to as Montauk Village, the latter indicating the entire area of Montauk within the township of East Hampton, New York. The Fishing Village was located on the shores of Fort Pond Bay, essentially the area north of the railroad tracks that still exist as laid many decades ago. (See maps and sketch.)

When I was born, 16 July 1929, our family lived in Shepherd's Neck in a house next to the Gilmartins', on the side of the hill just below the Montauk Public School. I was given the first name Paul after the family doctor who delivered me, Dr. Paul Nugent Sr. of East Hampton. Thomas, my middle name, was given by my parents at the time of baptism, which took place on 1 August 1929 at St. Philomena's Church in East Hampton. My godparents, Augustus ("Gus") Pitts and Henrietta ("Hattie") Pitts, were of the very first to settle in the Fishing Village, along with several other families from Nova Scotia.

It is safe to say that as an infant, just three months after my birth, I may have been the cause, on October 22 1929, for my father to send in his request to resign as Montauk agent for the Railway Express Agency. I was already the fourth child, so I imagine it was incumbent upon my father to seek other employment with more salary and opportunity for advancement.

Dad had succeeded Pete Loftus as Railway Express Agent at the Railroad Depot where there was a small Western Union Office and Postal Facility with Hilda Tuma as Postmistress during the 1920s. While working at the Railway Express Agency, Dad learned of an opening for Postmaster in the Fishing Village for a Post Office to be established by the Postmaster General. He applied and was appointed. Dad received his appointment signed on 22 April 1930 by President Hoover and his Postmaster General.

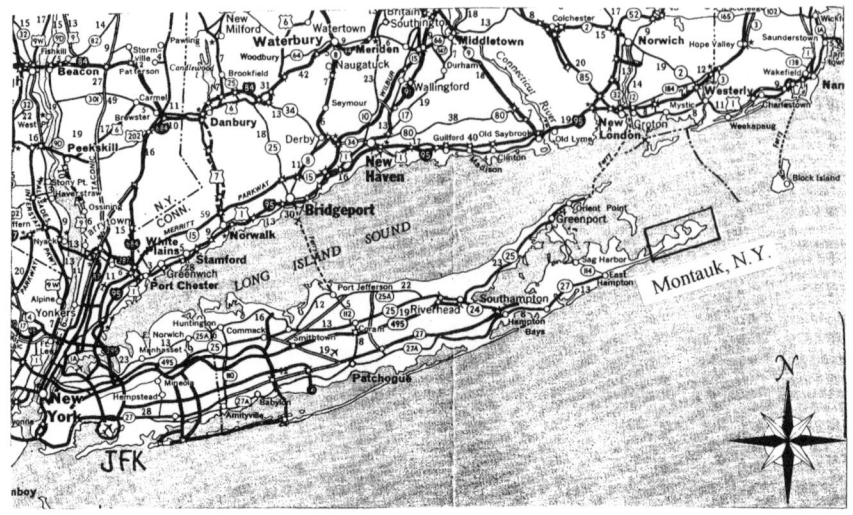

Montauk, New York, is located on the easternmost tip of Long Island, 120 miles (200 kilometers) from Manhattan. The land area inside the rectangle is Montauk and is enlarged in the map below. The Montauk fishing village was situated on the shores of Fort Bay until the U.S. Navy took over the land for a torpedo testing range during World War II. During the postwar period, the New York Ocean Science Lab was established there. Maps are provided courtesy of Avis.

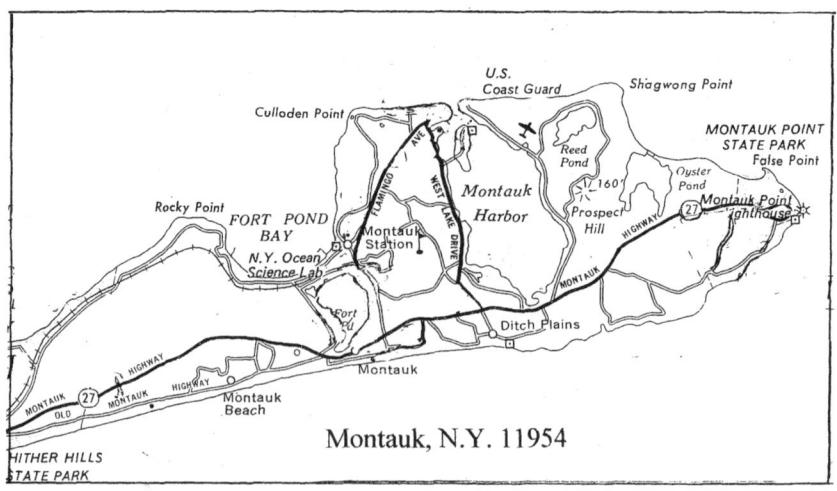

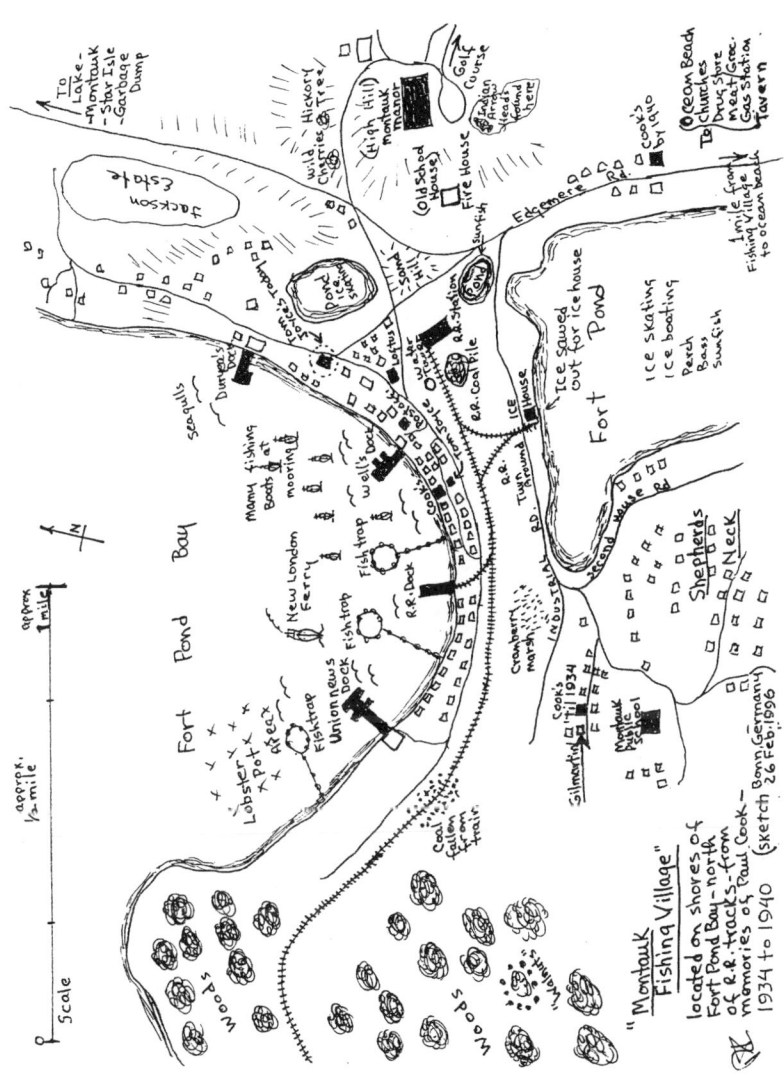

A sketch of Montauk Fishing Village from 1934–1940 drawn by Paul Cook.

In later years he received two further appointments by President Roosevelt, and his Postmaster General, James Farley, the last of which was signed on 21 March 1940. It was still the procedure in the U.S. until about the mid-1940s, postmasters were appointed by the President of the United States. After this time postmasters and clerks were employed under the civil service system. Our family members hold the three original certificates of appointment from Presidents Hoover and Roosevelt.

This first officially registered post office of Montauk, April 1930, was a two-room wooden building with a lobby located in the middle of the Montauk Fishing Village and adjacent to Jake Wells's Fish Company. It became the task of the postmaster at the outset to get the post office equipped with those items essential for postal activity, not the least of which were the mailboxes with combination locks for the permanent residents. Summer visitors got their mail under General Delivery, so when they came in they would simply give their name and say, "Anything in general delivery for [name]?" But the mailboxes for residents had to be bought and installed. They formed two sections of "wall" between the lobby and the office inside. From old papers left in our attic, records show that Dad arranged to purchase most of these boxes through Perry Duryea Sr. at the Fish Supply Company and later some through Pearson Construction Company, whose offices were located in the old Theater Building. I have receipts written on various and sundry pieces of paper, and forms signed by Perry Duryea and Albin Pearson. The installments were generally in the amounts of $20 each and totalled $340 during the period of March 17, 1930, through January 16, 1933. That last one was signed and marked "Paid in Full."

All Montauk residents, campers at Hither Hills, summer guests with homes at scattered locations, hotel clerks, individuals rich or poor, had to come to the Fishing Village to receive or send mail. And when the whistle sounded from the famous Long Island Railroad steam locomotive, bouncing and shaking around the curve at Rocky Point, everyone knew the mail was coming. All the kids ran to the rail station to see that great steam engine and to see the big clouds of steam hissing from the boilers.

Only in 1942 the post office operations were relocated from the Fishing Village to the old Theater Building between the liquor store and the original drugstore location. Then a new post office was finally constructed, in its current location, and dedicated on 18 March 1962.

Dad continued as Montauk's postmaster until his retirement after some thirty-five years of service. Many residents would come to the post office and ask him to help fill out various government forms, not the least of which was that of the Internal Revenue Service. Although this was not the work expected of a postmaster, Dad was always available and had the desire to help those in need. And it was to the post office so many came to get information about where certain people lived or where they could find one thing or another. It was a center for information and assistance. In memory of Dad's long and faithful service, a bench, with his name engraved, was installed at the sidewalk in front of the current Montauk Post Office.

After a few years of living in Shepherd's Neck, we moved into the Fishing Village, in 1934, nearer the post office, so that Dad could walk to work and, as well, enjoy the interesting and colorful, albeit sometimes difficult, living conditions that existed there. Dad bought our small house in the midst of the fishermen for a few hundred dollars and paid thirty dollars a month for the purchase, nearly equal in total amount to the purchase of the mailboxes for the post office.

The Fishing Village consisted of perhaps a hundred small wooden houses for fishermen families, primarily, as well as four docks and their accompanying wooden houses, known as Perry Duryea's, Jake Wells, Railroad Dock, and Union News Dock. These docks were all related to the fishing industry and where fishing boats tied up to fuel, take on supplies, unload fish, or carry sport fishermen, many of whom traveled from New York on special fish excursion trains. There were groceries sold at Jake's and at Loftus General Store, and food and drink at Trail's End Restaurant, Bill's Inn, Willard's Restaurant, Handrup's Roadside Inn, and the Union News Dock facility.

I was five when we moved to the village and at this time had two older brothers and a sister, Bob and Joe and Ruth (six, four, and two years, respectively, older than I). Two more sisters, Gladys and Joan, came to the family in the mid-1930s, during the years at the village. John was born later, in 1944, after the family left the village.

From the time of moving into the village, 1934, I am still able to clearly remember so many things about the Fishing Village because of my very close attachment to it.

I recall only two or three incidents before this time, while very young and in Shepherd's Neck. One day when four years old I was allowed to be in the school for a class visit. I was amused by the long hair of a girl sitting in front of me. Without responsibility for studying, I played with some of the ends of the long hair touching my desktop, and it seemed quite a natural thing to stick some of this hair into a hole in this little jar embedded in my desktop. How should I have known there would be something called ink in there?

The other incident was when I was perhaps three years old. I recall being in the living room, brightly lighted with sunshine. Having seen a cigarette butt lying in an ashtray on the windowsill, I wondered how far into my nose this cigarette butt would go. Being very curious, I put my thoughts into motion. It was far enough. So far that I could not get it out and my nose began to smart from the tobacco. A lot of tears from me, and a frantic mom who finally worked it out, all the while saying things like, "You shouldn't do that!", "Don't ever do that again!", et cetera. Of course, one does not ever do those things again with, or without, any warnings. The learning process!

In the Fishing Village there were more things to see and do than in Shepherd's Neck. There was never a dull moment to have to create diversions like dipping hair into an inkwell or stuffing my nose with a cigarette butt, and I was to experience very many new things around the waters of Fort Pond Bay as I grew older. My earliest days in summer at the ripe age of five saw me often walking a couple of hundred yards with Dad to the post office on a wooden boardwalk, which was built to avoid a walk in the sand among the various shanties along Fort Pond Bay shores. And in the post office I recall the chirping of little chicks coming from large, flat boxes lying on the package shelves. Curious to touch the little chicks, I would stick my fingers into the holes along the sides of the boxes made for air for the chicks to breathe. Sometimes they would peck on my fingers, but the tiny beaks did not hurt. It was usual in those days for some of the residents to buy chicks through Sears Roebuck or other catalog sources, and they would be mailed out through the postal service. Dad himself had bought Sears chicks, which were raised in our backyard, between the house and the shore. These were some of the nice things arriving at the post office from the steam train.

There was another aspect of mailing, sending out certain things, which I thought was very unpleasant to say the least. Many of the rich folks, or at least those with much more than the money in our family, were making use of the postal service to ship cylindrical containers filled with dirty baby diapers to the city (New York area) for laundering. The stinking barrels on a hot summer day were enough to gag a maggot. I did not at all understand at that time why these people did not do their own laundry so that everybody along the way from Montauk to New York City could breathe freely. But finally someone in the postal system thought better of allowing this service. I noticed in later years, while I was still living in the Fishing Village, the dirty diaper service came to an end. It was behind the times.

Some of our immediate neighbors in the Fishing Village, within a few hundred yards, were the families of Fred and Louis McDonald and Tom Joyce; the Worths (summer folks); Charley Larson; Algot Olson; John Nelson; the DeSantos; Mr. Chipperfield; Lyle Tuthill; Handrup's (Bar); Ecker's Trail's End Restaurant; Carl and "Babe" Erickson (with Chesapeake retriever kennels); Henry ("King") Shaver (with his dog, Furpel), a plumber and electrician when he felt like working; "Robbie" Byrnes; Vick (the Jake Wells Company cook and barber who cut our hair for fifteen cents with his hand clippers, producing a lot of ouches); and another Olson family (near Henry Shaver's shack, who would throw dishwater at all the kids during trick or treat at Halloween).

Speaking of Halloween, Jake Wells's grocery store windows would have comic strips pasted on by the older kids, who used a flour-and-water mix. There was always a lot of swearing and fussing by the workers who had to clean up the next morning. A lot of trick and little treat.

The Union News Dock was mainly for the excursion fishermen to board the boats and during summer for a steamboat that would regularly sail between Montauk and New London. This steamboat was for us a major attraction, and all the kids would run to this dock on weekends at the sound of the boat's steam whistle when still a mile or so out and when departing the dock.

On one occasion when the ferry approached the dock, a large sliding door had been opened anticipating the docking and a car whose brakes were not set rolled off into the bay. This caused tremendous commotion, since no one knew for sure if someone was in the car. Divers were sought from one of the boats with diving equipment. Two men operated cranks to pump air for the diver, who wore the bulky dive equipment in those days. After about one hour the diver managed to connect a line to the bumper of the car and a tractor, which drove up the beach until the car appeared through the water surface. It was a relief to all that only suitcases were in the car.

Now and then some man from "out of town" would gain attention on the Union News Dock by donning what looked like a straitjacket and then having someone tie his hands and feet. He would then jump off the dock into the water—a fearsome sight for a young kid to watch. Moments later the man came to the surface and climbed up on the dock to pass a hat around for coins in appreciation of his show. I am not too sure to this day how he managed this feat.

The fishing boats could be seen in the bay at the many buoys and pile mooring locations. Rowboats, hauled up and down from and to the bay on wooden rollers, could be seen all along the shoreline. Also present were those large piles of fish boxes with the fish vendor names such as Tuthill, Duryea, or Wells, in which the fresh fish with ice were shipped to the Fulton Fish Market on New York City's Lower East Side. And, of course, there were the stacks of lobster pots all along the shore. Scattered around the shore were many lobster pot buoys of various colors and designs denoting the owner. Each design and color was registered so that only the owner could raise the lobster pots and remove the lobsters. At times one could notice one or more broken wooden slats on a lobster pot. This was sometimes caused by a large eel, which could find its way into the pot and break some slats by the strength of its powerful movements. Subsequent to my time in the village lobster pots were made of metal, which precluded such damage and eventual rotting of the wooden slats as well.

The Railroad Dock was, as the name implies, the dock with tracks so that railroad freight cars could be run onto the dock in order for the fish boxes to be loaded. The sound of that old chugging crane engine still rings in my ears as the engine speed would vary with the load. We could tell without looking when the crane hooks were being just let down or at various stages of lifting fish boxes and how heavy they were.

One summer the Coast Guard training sail ship *Eagle* came into the bay and tied up at Railroad Dock. All the kids in the village were allowed to climb aboard and look around and talk to the sailors. We thought how brave they were to climb up to the yardarms to work the sails as they sailed into the bay and out again.

Wells's dock was for us sort of an institution. There was the dock for fish handling, fuel supply for the boats, crushed ice for boxing fish, a grocery store, kerosene for summer stoves and lanterns, a "punch board" for taking chances on various prizes (I remember that my dad won the only radio we owned on one of these punch boards), and, of course, just across the tracks was Wells's Ice House, which stored ice sawed out of Fort Pond during winter when this lake froze over. The ice house was located on the north shore of Fort Pond exactly at the end of the railroad turnaround tracks. This ice storage system became obsolete when Duryea established its ice-making plant at its current location. Some years later the ice house burned down.

Farther to the east coast was Perry B. Duryea's Fish and Lobster Company, which was generally considered the eastern limit of the Fishing Village on the shoreline of Fort Pond Bay. This was previously E. B. Tuthill & Company, Wholesale Dealers in Fish and Lobsters. Tuthill, established in 1882, also sold groceries, fishermen's supplies, paints, oils, naphtha, batteries, engine supplies, et cetera. In the late 1920s the Tuthills' telephone number was 11-R-1 Montauk. (How things changed with numbers today like 631-668-2350!)

Duryea's handled fish from the boats with catches from the sound and ocean as well as from the fish traps that lined the bay. Fish from the traps were brought in with large rowboats. Fish were sorted out according to type, for sale to "drummers" (agents for the New York City fish markets), and the others, considered "trash fish," were simply thrown into the bay for the seagulls to gorge themselves. A typical price for butter fish (a small fish the size of a man's hand) I recall was about fifteen cents a pound, but varying a few cents either way. The trash fish, such as the blowfish, today sell probably for two to three dollars a pound.

Our house was located only about one hundred feet from the water's edge at times, depending on the tide, with a shed and chicken coop between the back of our house and the shore. A garage for our old Chevy stood before the house, across a sand-and-gravel "street." The garage was large enough for the car and a chopping block where we split wood for the cast-iron cook stove. It was on this block where I cut the tip of my left thumb off with an ax while cutting lead weights off fish nets to sell the lead to a junk man who came around from time to time. Some of the lead we melted over fires on the shore and cast as sinkers for fishing. For sinker molds we simply pressed an old pyramid-shaped sinker into the wet sand, then poured the molten lead into the hole (formed by the old sinker). A loop of scrap electric copper wire was held in the lead just poured for only a few seconds, until the lead set. These sinkers were not as pretty as the ones the summer folks would buy, but we caught plenty of fish, off the piers, from the rowboats, and just casting off the shore for bottom fish using hand lines.

I do not recall ever having a real ball to play with when a youngster of about five to eight years of age. However, as with so many other things we made do with what we had. The nearest thing to a ball was a blowfish, which we had many of, since they were easy to catch. They would take any kind of bait, even from a six-year-old. The blowfish in its normal state is about the size of a large hand of a man. Often we would play a sort of ball game by using a blowfish. When you scratch the belly of a blowfish, it blows up to a round "ball" several inches in diameter. It would stay puffed up for quite a while, even with some kicking around. It may sound cruel at the thought of it, but you must remember the conditions. These fish were dumped overboard by the thousands, as trash fish. From my earliest memories as a child we grew up with all the sights and sounds of nature in the environment of the Fort Pond Bay. We grew up in pure nature. We were immersed in it and lived accordingly.

Times have changed in regards to what folks do with any kind of fish today. One eats the blowfish now as a delicacy because other fish are more scarce, perhaps, or because it is a fad; I do not know. Mussels and squid were never eaten in Montauk when I was a child. Yet these seafoods have always been eaten in Italy and Greece. Only now they have gained notoriety in and around Montauk because they are sort of "in." During my days in the village millions of mussels clung to the pilings, only to be smashed by the mooring of boats. Squid was used only as bait for more marketable fish.

Since there were no stores then in Montauk to buy clothing, or hardly anything else except most food, liquor, pharmacy prescriptions, and fish supplies, traveling salesmen would come around to the Fishing Village with suitcases filled with the very basic clothing needs. Styles and colors did not matter, only did it fit? One had samples of shoes and he would place our feet on a brown paper to trace the outlines for sizing. Strangely enough this was a pretty accurate system, so shoe deliveries on the next visit gave few problems. One fellow carried a medium-size suitcase with only a few items such as razor blades, shoe strings, and knives. Since he was a really colorful individual my dad bought an item each time so we could sit around the kitchen table and listen to the fellow's stories. This man always complained about his sore feet, because he hitched rides to get around, and I wondered years later if this was to gain enough sympathy for a sale.

In the midthirties, which I would say was the high point in Montauk for very wealthy vacationing summer guests, every few days my dad would send me, then about seven or eight years old, to the Montauk Manor with one or two special delivery letters (referred to as "specials"). It was worth the ten cents in tips for me, which I could spend immediately on a big cold Hires root beer to cool down from the walk up and down the manor hill. Most of the specials I carried were for Frank Molnar, a famous

Hungarian playwright. I guarded these letters with my life, as Dad told me they were very important and not to stop along the way. On the way back down the hill in late summer I would climb "the" hickory tree to gather a few nuts and also pick a few wild cherries a short distance farther down hill. Many other specials were addressed to guests at Gurney's Inn. In these cases Mom would drive me there and I would go into the lobby and get a signature and usually a tip of ten cents, occasionally a quarter if the addressee was in a very good mood.

Wild berries of all kinds were plentiful in many places "inland" from the Fishing Village, if any place in Montauk can be considered inland. Blackberries, blueberries, huckleberries, beach plums, cranberries, elderberries, wild cherries, wild strawberries, and grapes plus the hickory nuts were there for all of the Montaukers and the summer visitors. Mom would not only make assortments of jams and jelly, but she also canned fresh tuna fish and various fruit and vegetables when plentiful in summer. Bread and butter pickles were one of her specialties for canning. Apples and potatoes were bought by the bushels and stored for winter in a cool, dry space. The best cranberry picking was at a small marsh between Fort Pond and the railroad tracks, therefore very convenient for the Fishing Villagers. It is well to note that although we had a large family and little money, we were never in want for something to eat. If nothing else, there was always an endless supply of fish, lobsters, and clams during many months of the year. During school days, for lunch bags Mom always had to make a lot of sandwiches each morning, and this fare rotated around peanut butter and jelly, bologna, lettuce and tomato, and peanut butter and sliced bananas. At Montauk Public School small containers of milk costing four cents were available to drink with the lunches. Some of the kids from the village, too poor to pay for the milk, were given the four cents by the teachers out of their pockets. I ate hot oatmeal nearly every morning before school, except for very warm days.

During the years at the Fishing Village, there was one visitor, particularly during summer, who was always most welcome in our house, Charles Briand. "Charley" was a member of the Briand clan in the Fishing Village, but he was not a fisherman, rather a baker at the Montauk Manor. As mentioned, the blueberries were very plentiful in the summers of early Montauk. Our family often went out Sunday afternoons picking pansful of them. It was understandable that the wealthy guests at the manor should have the benefit of another one of the local "gifts," besides fish: fresh blueberries. Therefore, the bakery of the manor produced fresh blueberry pies as a choice for dessert on the dining room menu. But not all those pies found their way into the mouths of manor guests. It was as regular as clockwork that each time blueberry pies were baked Charley would appear at the door with one in hand for our family. I remember that wonderful taste of fresh blueberry pie from the manor bakery, and I remain a fan of this flavorful dessert. I remember also the person of Charley, a good friend of Dad through their friendly talks at the post office service window while Dad sorted mail. These "at the window" talks were a matter of course, as it was with so many of the villagers. Charley's appearance with eyeglasses with dark rims and thick lenses, and holding out the blueberry pies, stays clear in my store of great memories.

    Mom could recognize the fishing boats already on the horizon as they returned from sea. As they approached the fish docks, either I or one of my brothers would be tasked to go pick up fish for supper. Mom would say, "Here comes Tom [Joyce]," or "Here comes Lyle [Tuthill]," and "Go to the dock and get a cod [or mess of mackerel or a few flounders] for supper and don't take all day; your father will be home soon." Well we didn't take "all day," but our return never seemed to be soon enough. We just had to go to see the catches on all the boats or skip stones into the bay as we returned along the shore.

    As a hobby my dad built a boat from keel up, the size of a large rowboat. At a Greenport boatyard he bought an old used two-cycle engine with a large and heavy fly wheel, which produced *putt-putt* sounds never to be forgotten. Along with the boat, we helped Dad as much as he would allow us in building about twenty lobster pots. We set the pots in the bay at Rocky Point twice a week and collected the lobsters to sell to the yachts at anchor in the bay and to have some for ourselves at supper. The worst part of this operation, naturally, was baiting the traps (or pots) with absolutely rotten-smelling fish such as "daylights," which had sat for days in barrels on the shore between our tending the traps. Daylights were so called because you could hold them up to the sunlight and nearly see through them. The only relief from the smell was if there was a breeze or to steer the boat into the breeze while baiting the traps at the stern. I would go out sometimes with Dad or with one of my older brothers, which was a real thrill, especially when I was allowed to steer the boat out to our lobster buoys and back home again. Dad always insisted on measuring the lobsters with the measuring bracket and throwing the young ones ("shorts") back into the bay.

It was in the summer of 1937 that "Devil" paid us a visit at our house in the village on Fort Pond Bay. Devil was the nickname of a black porter who worked in the Pullman trains that came to Montauk in summer with hotel guests destined primarily for the manor and Gurney's Inn. Devil often came to the post office when Pullman cars arrived at Montauk, and Dad enjoyed talking with him at each visit. One day Devil was invited by Dad to go out with him in his boat to pull up some lobster pots and remove the lobsters. Devil could not swim, but there were life jackets, as required, available in the boat. Devil had never before been in a boat and certainly never in a boat to retrieve lobsters. The trip out to the lobster pots, near Rocky Point, the westernmost area of Fort Pond Bay, was uneventful. The action came when Dad pulled up one of the pots and took out the lobsters. The lobsters, especially when directly out of the water, were very active, and one commenced crawling in Devil's direction. Devil was beside himself and jumped over the side into the bay despite the fact that he could not swim. A life jacket did not enter his mind at this point, only departing from the boat faster than the lobster could crawl. Dad disposed of the lobster and pulled the baywater-soaked guest back into the boat. This was Devil's first and, I expect, last lobster-boat experience.

A Summer Morning's Close Shave in the Fishing Village

On a warm summer day during school vacation, it was not unusual for one of our group of young boys to suggest, without any better plan in the moment, to go over to Frank's house. We would sit on the sand and gravel, near his porch, until he would come out with daily regularity carrying his shaving paraphernalia. He would show up about nine in the morning with towel in hand, and top dressed in sleeveless undershirt. After several minutes in varied precarious leanings and unpredictable bodily movements, he managed the pouring of steaming hot water from a kettle into a basin. A leather razor strap was hung on a hook. The straight razor, brush and lather soap were placed on the railing. Then, with some difficulty, he hung a mirror on a nail, which had been earlier in summer laboriously hammered into one of the several stanchions which supported the roof of his small veranda. Frank Edwards was a man in mid-years and treated nicely by our elders as he was such a person. Yet, in our still childish minds, we came over to Frank's house to be "entertained." We all knew that something was not normal with Frank, but our immaturity led us to overlook the fact that he suffered from St. Vitas' Dance.

After wetting his face and brushing the whiskers with the soapy lather, Frank made some wild swipes with his razor on the strap, sometimes actually making contact with it. Then he commenced what we thought was the most daring of all, the shave itself. His head moved erratically and variously from side to side, and up and down. His right arm with straight razor in hand would make several uncontrollable sweeps in the air until at some point, which only he could imagine to be the right time, he made a rapid closure to his face to make a quick swipe with his razor. This process continued for at least twenty or so minutes, after which he rinsed his face and he never had so much as a visible scratch. This was considered, at the time, a sort of theatrical comedy for us youngsters, but as the years passed, I have always wondered about Frank's life-long hindrance and how he was granted adequate control, the mercy from the Almighty to actually survive this daily challenge.

Every spring a freight train with loads of soft pine lumber arrived at the Fishing Village. Just before the fishing season several workers from Wells's came to the big sand lot between Ecker's Trail's End Restaurant and the post office to set up for making hundreds of wooden boxes in which fish with crushed ice would be sent to the fish market in New York City. The somehow musical hammering of shiny eight-penny nails went on for many days for assembly of these fish boxes. Needless to say, I and the other young boys would gather to watch, and finally the fishermen would let us hammer a few nails as well. Before this box building was over we got good enough to make some of the boxes ourselves. It was great fun and we felt really good about having had a hand in their construction. And without our realizing then, it was a great opportunity to learn so much for use later in life. These fishermen, many originating from Nova Scotia, cared about the kids and had the patience to help develop our interest and abilities. When all the fish boxes needed were finished there was always some lumber left over and plenty of nails. The next step for us was to build small boats to paddle out in the bay. To keep water out of the cracks between boards we found leftover tar in cans used by the fishermen to tar their nets. With broken pieces of lobster pot laths (strips of wood) the tar was squeezed into the cracks and left to harden up some days. Then the launch and ecstasy of floating in one's own "ship." I nearly drowned in one of my boats after I had paddled quite far into the bay one Sunday afternoon.

A slow but steady leak developed through a crack poorly tarred, and the "ship" commenced to sink. It was a very lucky coincidence that my dad was out in the bay in his lobster boat and saw me as I yelled. "Putting" full throttle, he made it over to me in the nick of time.

In about 1934 the entire Fort Pond Bay was frozen over and most of the Long Island Sound, as I was told. We would panic, our mom especially, when we walked rather far "out to sea" over these masses of ice and at times jumped from one cake of ice to another during the spring thaw.

One summer about 1935 many ships of the U.S. Atlantic Fleet anchored in Fort Pond Bay. The memory of visiting the USS *Brooklyn,* at least to a degree, influenced my decision for a career in the navy. My dad, as postmaster, was invited one day to carry several bags of mail to the cruiser on the mail boat run and to be accompanied by the *Brooklyn*'s mail clerk. As I was often tagging along with my dad, at this young age, I, too, went out with the mail boat and boarded the ship. An extra treat was a very generous helping of "homemade" ice cream by the ship's cook in the galley. Ice cream continues to be my favorite dessert.

When the fleet was in, there was target practice for the pilots of the seaplanes aboard the cruisers. The ships would maneuver so that the stern came around to still the waters on the lee side; then the seaplane would be lowered to the water by a deck crane. When airborne, they fired at towed sleeves (targets), and after the firing practice the tow plane flew parallel to the shoreline of the bay (behind our house sometimes) and detached the sleeve for it to land on the beach. They then counted the holes in the sleeve, also noting the color of the holes. The bullets were painted with different-colored tips in order to see which pilot was getting the hits. This was very exciting for us, especially at the age of about seven at the time.

Another of Dad's hobbies was trapping small animals for fur, and for some extra money he sold the skins to Sears Roebuck. Muskrats, weasels, and foxes were trapped. One day very early in the morning after tending his traps, Dad brought home several of these animals and hung them in the garage before going to the post office. One of the weasels was still alive, shook loose from the hook, and ran toward my mom as she entered the garage. This put an end to the trapping hobby.

Many of the houses on the shore still had outhouses. Ours was no exception. It was not until about 1937 that Dad had enough money to install a toilet and build a cesspool. What a relief that was, especially in winters, which were generally damp, cold, windy, and not at all conducive to a walk "out back," particularly at night.

A bath was a Saturday night affair, with each of us taking a turn in a large galvanized tub near the warm kitchen stove in winter. With not any more washing than on Saturdays it was no wonder that I sometimes got only a C for a grade in school on the report card under the category of Hygiene. If we were ever graded in the summer, hygiene marks would have been higher, since we were then always in the water at some time each day.

The cast-iron stove was used not only for cooking but also for warming the house—a good reason that all the family activities took place in the kitchen. In summer a kerosene stove was used for cooking, as the temperatures of the cast-iron stove would be unbearable. We gathered firewood in the woods for when the cast-iron kitchen stove was used. My dad and older brothers and I would find fallen trees, saw them into lengths with a long two-man saw for the trailer, and tow them home. In the garage we cut the logs into smaller lengths, then split them to fit into the stove. With little money to buy coal, we had two uses for this same stove: for cooking and for banking a fire through the night. One way was to pick up pieces of coal on the ocean shore (just east of the Surf Club). This coal had washed ashore from a coal barge some years before, or it was waste from coal-fired ships. Nevertheless, it was used by the villagers. Interestingly, all these pieces of coal were rounded from months or years rolling along the ocean bottom and in the surf. The other and closer coal source was along the railroad tracks about a half-mile west of the railroad station on a curve in the tracks. Since Montauk was a coaling station for the (then) steam locomotives, the coal was piled high on the tender. As the train departed Montauk for Jamaica (where the steam locomotive was switched to electric) the coal would fall off the tender from the train vibrations at the curve and scatter along the tracks. Some coal chunks were so large that only one piece would fit into a bucket. Then at home we hammered the coal into smaller sizes to fit into the stove. And since this was the soft, bituminous coal, it was filled with gas pockets. It was not unusual for chunks to explode and blow the iron stove lids several inches into the air, including at times a pot for supper as well.

The kerosene for the summer stove was available at Jake Wells's place. For quite some time the kerosene was selling for ten cents a gallon, and I was given a dime and the empty jug to fetch this fuel. One day it became twelve cents a gallon and I had to go home for two cents extra, which made my mom very upset. Since she took in laundry from people at the Montauk Manor in order to help make ends meet for our family (now) of eight, she was sensitive to any "injustice," such as raising a price "two whole cents."

One day when we went to the woods for firewood my mom decided to go along to see what it was like. Our neighbor Tom Joyce went with us as well to help, since he needed firewood also. While in the woods Tom came running to my mom and said he had found a walnut tree. Excitedly Mom went over and started to fill her apron with walnuts. After we got home she called in neighbor Aggie McDonald to show her the big find. Aggie said, "Bea, these walnuts are just like the ones I bought at Jake's last week, with the Red Diamond brand on them." Only then Mom realized that Tom, the neighborhood fisherman/joker, had done it again. She had not noticed the Red Diamond stamp on the walnuts during her excitement in "finding" the nuts, which Tom had spread around on the ground. The thrill of finding the walnuts also distracted her from realizing that these nuts were under an oak tree.

Several comments have been made already about our fisherman neighbor Tom Joyce. He was involved in many ways in my life and the lives of all of us in the family, a steadfast friend and always a helpful person. But he never failed to seize upon the opportunity to play jokes on folks, particularly on Mom, because she took everyone more seriously and she thought when someone said or did something that he was also serious. Tom knew, to his delight, he could always get a rise out of her. This egged him on even more. Like the walnuts in the forest, which he "planted" there to make Mom think he had found a walnut tree. And when he was having dinner with Mom and Dad and a few other villagers one night at Wahlberg's Restaurant in 1937 he placed on the restaurant floor near the table a piece of molded brown rubber (an exact replica of what a dog usually drops in the call of nature). The Wahlbergs had a dog, and Tom wanted, of course, to have Mom believe that the dog did its thing just then. As one of the Wahlbergs came over with something to scoop up the "dropping," Tom reached down and said, "Never mind, I'll clean it up." He wrapped his handkerchief around the "dropping" and stuck it into his pocket, leaving all onlookers in shock and disbelief. Mom was so distraught she could not eat. Only months later could she laugh about it.

Another occasion involved neighbor Tom one spring day when I and one other of the family had scarlet fever. Being a very contagious disease, it was cause for the health department to put the customary yellow QUARANTINE sign on our front door. No one (outside the family) should enter the house, to avoid contracting this disease. There was a knock on the door, which Mom went to answer. As I was sick in my bed, I could not see but heard Mom: "Tom, you darned old fool!" It was Tom Joyce, standing six feet from the door, with a long-handled fish scoopnet in his hands, which he used to knock on the door, and he had our New York daily newspaper in the net. He had seen the QUARANTINE sign like everyone else, but for him the sign generated an idea, yet another act of comedy, by delivering a newspaper in a way so as not to contract the disease. Tom's humor was an integral part of the very fiber of the family of Montauk Fishing Villagers.

We, as children, learned to do without certain things and be satisfied with all the possibilities offered by virtue of the sea at our doorstep. Hand-me-downs were a way of life. There was a Mrs. Leroy Satterlee, wife of Dr. Satterlee, who lived in Montauk near the golf course, just around the corner from Harry Bruno's home. Mrs. Satterlee knew Dad well, naturally, as did most everyone in Montauk. She realized that we did not have much, in the material sense, so each year some weeks before Christmas she would visit our house in the Fishing Village. Mrs. Satterlee owned a shop in East Hampton, the Old Barn Book Shop. She sold all kinds of things besides books, including rather expensive gift items, some of which were toys. By the end of the summer season she had always accumulated a number of items that had been broken or damaged a bit. These items she brought to the house, because she knew that these fancy-looking and colorful gifts, despite some damage, brought a great amount of joy to us. Often what she brought was, in fact, my Christmas.

On one Saturday night, when I was perhaps in my sixth year, I had just been directed by Mom to "climb into the tub" (the galvanized metal portable tub used for scrubbing kids and clothes). Just as I set foot into this Saturday night special, in came Mrs. Satterlee with her box of joy. I made my way quickly behind the stove to avoid public view. While I was doing my best to hide myself and at the same time keep from getting burned on the hot stove, I remember well her comment to Mom: "Well, Mrs. Cook, that's a sure sign Paul is growing up when he doesn't want to be seen undressed." I thought it totally unnecessary under the circumstances for more woman talk, and all the while with her hand on the doorknob. She finally decided that my bathwater must be getting cold and so bid, "Good night, and Merry

Christmas to everybody." I should not want you to get the wrong idea. I really liked Mrs. Satterlee as a very generous and nice person. It was simply an embarrassing moment in the years when I began to realize that certain things should be private.

In later years, around 1940–41, Mrs. Satterlee gave me the job of cutting her lawn in summer for fifty cents an hour. Their house was on the way to the golf course where I caddied, so it was even convenient for me to handle both jobs in the same day. I recall it being said that Dr. Satterlee, owner of a short-wave radio, may have been the last person to have communicated with pilot Amelia Earhart, whose aircraft disappeared in her quest to fly around the world.

Summers in the village meant, for one thing, the "ice man cometh." When the word got around that the ice wagon was on its way along the sand-and-gravel street past our house we young kids waited anxiously. For as soon as the ice man cut and carried a twenty-five-pound block of ice into the house we lunged into the back of the wagon to pick up the small chunks of ice that had fallen during the use of the icepick to cut a piece from the much larger block. Today a child may scream if he cannot have a two-dollar ice cream when he wants it. We were quite satisfied with a "mere piece of ordinary ice" to counter a hot and humid day.

In winter, ice was not needed. The winters were cold enough to utilize the "window refrigerator," which was, in essence, a boxlike device (looking much like the size of a typical window air conditioner arrangement) sticking out from the house about one foot and with a sliding panel inside a room, to take items out or put them in.

Fresh milk was delivered each day by the milkman. Milk came in quart-size glass bottles delivered early in the morning to our doorstep from a dairy in East Hampton. Somehow the name Gould's Dairy stays in my mind. In those days before milk was homogenized, cream, lighter and a slightly different color, always rose to the top of the milk, about three inches high. Before you used the bottle of milk it was shaken in order to mix the milk and cream evenly. Anyway, in winter, with freezing temperatures, before the milk could be brought into the kitchen the cream would expand and rise up and out of the bottle, with the cardboard cap on the very top.

Perhaps it just seemed that winters were colder in the 1930s. The one of 1934 must certainly have been extremely cold, as I recall the bay being frozen over. I remember each winter in Montauk as having ice and snow, and as children we relished the idea of making our way through the snow drifts, sliding down the hills near the Montauk Manor, and gliding on the ice of the nearby ponds. It was mostly great fun despite the freezing feet and hands because of always inadequate gloves and boots. We did not know when to quit and usually got scoldings from staying out and away from the house too long. "Don't you know you will catch your death of cold?" was the basic phrase from Mom. And of course our reply to this was silence and all eyes on the floor, in a feeble attempt to obtain an ounce of pity.

Just like only one suit was available for hand-me-down (from oldest to youngest boy), there was only one bicycle, one pair of skates, and one snow sled in the family. Kids from another family would sometimes lend their sled to me. The Eckers were able to have more of some things like sleds, and I remember Eddy Ecker lending me his sled and sometimes his bicycle. But one day, when I was six, my oldest brother, Bob (then about twelve years old), allowed me to go down the hill with him. He would lie on the sled to do the steering, and I was on top of him. We got up to what seemed like an impossible speed so fast that when near the bottom of the hill we went clear across the road and slammed into a bank on the other side. Bob had either a badly sprained wrist or possibly a broken arm, which had happened to be on the front of the sled as we crashed. I was unhurt, but I was very much aware that Bob must have been suffering by the way he held his arm and wincing as he made his way back to our house. That was the last "two-man" sled ride.

On another occasion during this same winter I was with several others on a small pond located near the cranberry bog between the railroad tracks and the Industrial Road, which ran along the north side of Fort Pond. The pond was frozen over to the extent that some kids were ice skating and some had their sleds. One would hold the sled up with both hands, run a bit, then flop down on it to slide for some twenty or more yards on the ice. Great sport at a young age before learning to skate or before owning a pair of skates. It so happened that a young boy (from the Steck family) of my own age ran with his sled and went farther than usual, as I saw him and his sled disappear into an opening in the ice. One of the older boys, I believe his older brother, ran to his house across the railroad tracks and near the bay of the Fishing Village. In what appeared to be a very few minutes I saw Mr. Steck running so fast as I ever saw anyone run, literally flying across the tracks, and he then immediately dived into the hole in the ice where the boy went in. Mr. Steck found his son and ran ever so fast, carrying the boy in his arms, back to his house. During the ensuing moments we thought perhaps all was OK, since the boy was taken home. I was too young to comprehend the possible complications for the boy as result of water temperature, length of time in water, water swallowed, shock, et cetera. We learned later that day that the Steck boy died not long after the recovery from the freezing water. Mr. Steck had managed to call a doctor, but it was too late.

It is well to note that at that time, in the 1930s, there were no doctors in Montauk and no emergency squads. If one was lucky enough to own a telephone, he could call a doctor in an emergency, either Dr. Paul Nugent or Dr. Edwards, in East Hampton, the nearest town with medical facilities. As it was, at this time Dr. Edwards was contacted and he drove, they said, in record time from East Hampton to the Fishing Village. (The distance between Montauk and East Hampton is twenty-three kilometers.) In those days there was so little traffic, sometimes one could drive the entire way to Montauk without even passing a single car. But in this case forty-five minutes had elapsed, for whatever reasons, from the time of the call for the doctor to the time of his arrival at the village. It was simply too late. It may have been too late even before the call was made.

When I cut off the tip of my left thumb with an ax, as described, when chopping lead weights from fish nets, the subject of "doctor" never entered into the situation. Only until after I had received Mom's traditional verbal lashing, in this instance about why I should not play with an ax, was some attention given to my thumb, as the blood was all the while spurting out into the flood of tears already on the floor. The eventual household "doctoring" consisted of wrapping a large wad of toilet paper around the thumb with instructions to "hold it tight until the bleeding stops." Some hours later I dared to remove the paper and observed the wound drying up a bit. As we were often on and in the bay water during the summer months, I got to know early on in life what happens when you stick a large open wound into salty water. My thumb burned and throbbed for hours after I unintentionally immersed my hand into a bucket of sea water. Obviously, it yielded a relatively quicker cure. The fact that salt water is a good healing agent sort of fit in with what our priest once expounded on during part of one of his sermons at mass: "There is always some good that comes out of something bad." Actually, my thought ran in the reverse: *If I have to go through the burning process in order to realize the good of the salt water healing, I would be far better off quitting chopping lead weights from the fishermen's nets in the first place.* Well, it was great sport, melting the lead and making our own sinkers. The primitive alternative was searching around the boatyards to find a rusty old bolt or nut to use for weights on our fishing lines. Even at the ripe age of six or seven one can easily discern the better quality from this choice of sinkers. Now, however, already at this age, one also begins to learn the "why" in choice of source.

As I recall the services available in Montauk, such as medical, of which there were none, except for that of the pharmacist, Dick White Sr. and the supplies in his drugstore, it reminds me of the "law" in Montauk. The only law in Montauk, besides that of the commonsense respect given the other folks (do unto others as you would have them do unto you, as preached in religious services), was our one and only Bill Brockman, New York State Trooper. Bill lived with his family in Montauk, the Shepherd's Neck area near the public school, and he could be seen from time to time, nearly always in uniform, walking or cruising, seemingly ready for trouble. But nothing ever happened in those days in Montauk, especially in the Fishing Village, as far as I know. Oh yes, I remember that a stray dog was cause for some concern and it called for one of the few bullets ever fired from Bill's revolver in the line of duty. But on a somewhat higher level, above the concerns of the average native Montauker, Bill more than likely was privy to, or directly involved in, the periodic raids made by the state police on the gambling casino on Star Island. In any case, I always thought of Bill as our protector as he roamed the village in that impressive state trooper's uniform with the handcuffs and huge revolver on his side. Sort of reminded me of the friendly sheriff in a western movie when he made visits to a local bar (such as Handrup's, Willard's, Trail's End, Bill's Inn [Bill Belber's], or the Shagwong) and discussed with the barkeepers whether any shady characters were seen in the village lately. The post office and the bars were the most likely sources for any tips to the "law" on potential problems, and especially the bars, where one could conveniently tip a glass to prolong the inquiry, or prolong the inquiry to tip yet another, one for the road.

While "big-time" trouble among the inhabitants was not on the agenda during my days in the Fishing Village, it happened one day at about the age of six that I was taunted, pushed around, and hit with some stones by another of my age whom I will refer to simply as Butch. On the verge of tears I complained to my father that I could not go out anymore because of Butch roughing me up. Dad's answer was firm: "Just hit him with your fist if he pushes you around again!" This was and is not now my nature. But it came to pass on the very next day that I was accosted. I reacted immediately with a right fist into Butch's stomach. He was so surprised, and now hurting a bit, that he ran home and never bothered me again. We finished the rest of the days in grammar school on a friendly basis. (Years, many years, later, I was told by a former villager that Butch was serving time in a state penitentiary.)

The brother of Butch, whom I shall refer to as Joker, was another cause for concern. Joker was mute, for reasons I never knew. Actually, I liked Joker. Although he never wanted really to hurt anyone, he was bent on playing various scary tricks on his "friends." His greatest joy with me was on the docks. As I would sit on the edge of Jake Wells's dock, or at the Railroad Dock, with my feet dangling over the side, while fishing for snappers, Joker would creep up in back of me and make believe that he was going to push me into the bay waters. He knew that I had not yet learned to swim despite living on the water, and of this I had the greatest fear. An accidental push could have actually put me in danger of drowning. I learned how to swim only when twelve years of age during a summer job at the Montauk Surf Club, and then in the same year I already began to swim in the ocean and dive into the breakers. There were no such things as lifeguards in the village, and on the piers it was sometimes only Joker and me when he got his laughs. Well, you can imagine that after several of Joker's attempts to terrorize me I would be constantly looking over my shoulder, which frequently caused me to be slow in reacting to the nibbles on my baited hooks. It was very helpful sometimes when another kid would call out, "Watch it! Here comes Joker!" I tried, successfully, after some time to get Joker to sit beside me and also fish for snappers using one of my lines. This diversion from pushing to fishing sufficiently refocused his attention so that I was more able to cope with Joker's idea of fun. It was also a kind of training for me in learning about some of the anomalies in everyday life.

On the lighter side, a humorous incident on a summer day, concerning a young neighbor boy, Carlos DeSanto, about my age. Carlos, the son of a Portuguese fisher family, and I were playing around the shore behind our house but near the lobster boat that Dad had built. Dad had to fix something or other on the boat, and we commenced to watch what he was doing. It must be said that Dad acquired false teeth rather early in life and at times, to relieve his gums I suppose, he could and would occasionally make his lower teeth project out of his mouth without the use of his hands. He usually did this only in his off hours when around the house, and it was spontaneous, without forethought. While he was working on the boat, Dad looked up toward Carlos just for a moment, but it happened to be exactly when he made his lower teeth go most of the way out of his mouth. Carlos let out a yell and ran home screaming, as if he had seen a ghost. He was absolutely terrified. But we and others in the neighborhood, having witnessed this several times, could not help but have a good laugh afterward.

It was often on Sunday afternoons in the mid-1930s that we, as a family, would go to the beach on the southwest corner of Lake Montauk (not far from the small lake called Stepping Stones). At this time there were essentially no houses around Lake Montauk, except for those such as Wasey's on East Lake Drive, Ringwood's on West Lake Drive, and the few on Star Island. As youngsters we could wade far out into this shallow lake without danger. Most fun was to make tiny "lakes" in the sand at water's edge in order to have a place for all the minnows we caught with our hands. When leaving the beach for home we made a channel for the minnows to swim back out into the lake. Sometimes we were lucky enough with our little shovels to scratch around on the bottom of the lake and find some small hardshell clams and razor clams (almost the same size and shape of a normal unopened straight razor). Although there was plenty of water and beach area in the Fishing Village, not only was Lake Montauk a change of scenery, but also the beaches there were of pure sand and not with all the pebbles and stones like at the shores of Fort Pond Bay. As we grew somewhat older, the bottom of our feet got used to the stones and became hardened enough to walk the village beach without wincing. But this hardening was never enough to counter the cuts from pieces of glass or broken shells washed up on the shore. Many families in the village and boat crews simply threw all the garbage into the bay. What the seagulls could not digest went to the bottom and eventually wound up on the beach.

There was a lobster fisherman, Mr. Lawson, living on the west side of Fort Pond Bay, rather far from the center of the Fishing Village. The good lobster-trapping area was near Rocky Point, and this is where his small house was situated. He had a daughter, Helen. During all my six years in the village I never saw her mother, and I do not know actually if her mother lived. I only remember Mr. Lawson with his pickup truck, usually with lobster pots and buoys in the back and Helen in the front. It was a long walk for Helen from the Rocky Point area, but she often passed by our house along the beach, headed for Jake's store or the general store of Mr. Loftus. She was somewhat older than I, by a few years, but she always greeted me with, "Hello, Paul." Helen was to be pitied in my opinion for several reasons. She was for the most part isolated from the rest of the villagers due to the remoteness of her home, and she was not in any way whatsoever destined to become Miss Montauk from the point of view of beauty. But I must hasten to add that Helen was always friendly and polite to everyone. I don't know whatever happened to her in later life. The last time I saw her was in the Montauk Public School, repeating the seventh or eighth grade, in about 1939.

It was a routine after school on Fridays that catechism classes were held for all the Catholic children, and these classes stressed teachings of the church leading up to First Holy Communion and, later, Confirmation. We did not meet always in the church, only when a priest from East Hampton was available. Montauk was then only a mission church without a permanent priest. In fact, more often than not we met in a home of one of the parents, and it so happened this occurred many times, for me, in the home of Leonard McDonald or with one of the Pitts families. I don't know of any of the kids who relished the idea of another class after school about the mysteries of all the various things we were supposed to learn and having to sit on the floor in the process. There was never enough room for ten or more kids to be sitting anywhere except on the floor. It came to me, in any case, that there must be a supernatural being to make this whole world of ours somehow function despite the contradictions observed in everyday life. I made my First Holy Communion as planned, making my parents very happy. I liked the association with the church and what I believed it stood for. I was a few years later confirmed by the bishop from Brooklyn at Saint Philomena's Church in East Hampton. Almost as memorable as the classes for catechism themselves were the walks home from Leonard McDonald's house (or another) and while walking wondering, *What will I have for dinner tonight?* because by this time of day we were all very hungry. Well, this was much less of a mystery than the subject of religion, because we could be absolutely certain there would be no meat on Friday. The dinner would be either baked beans, baked macaroni and cheese, or fish with some vegetable. I had the good fortune of liking all of these choices.

It was before the 1938 hurricane, perhaps in 1935 or '36, when Dad had a broken leg. How? It was customary for a person with a car, hired and paid by the postmaster, to pick up the mail pouches from the daily trains[*] from New York City and deliver them to the post office. Dad would then empty the pouches and sort the mail into the respective mailboxes where everyone in Montauk had to come for their mail. One day when the

---

[*]The trains coming to Montauk originated at Pennsylvania Station (midtown Manhattan), but at Jamaica the electric engine was switched for a steam locomotive. Electric rails served only out to about as far as Babylon, Long Island.

pouches were to be picked up from an evening train, the Cannon Ball Express, Dad decided to go to the train. He got a ride with the pouch collector, but instead of getting into the car, Dad rode over to the train by standing on the running board. (In those days cars still had the "step" along the side of the car just under the doors.) When going around the curve into the area of the railroad station, the car was going at such speed that it threw Dad off and onto the gravel road. A leg was broken (I do not remember whether left or right), but he got around with crutches for a couple of weeks as he continued his work in the post office. Was this kind of accident, possibly this one and the countless thousands of others that occurred, the thing that doomed those sometimes classy-looking running boards? Or was it the fact that cars were being built lower to the ground and "steps" were no longer needed to "climb" into the car?

From the time of my earliest memories, in 1934 and '35, it seemed as though we went to Greenport every couple of weeks during several years for visits with Mom's parents, Vincent and Anna Santacroce; Dad's mother, Anna (Wells) Cook, and many aunts, uncles, and cousins. On a few occasions I went with my father to visit his father, William Cook, in Southold. William and Anna (Wells) Cook lived separately for most of my dad's life. These rides in the family car to Greenport would probably be of interest to anyone on studies in psychology on a theme of "the effects of many people in a small space," especially when most of the people would rather have stayed home than take this ride. In the earliest days of this routine there were as many as six persons in the car. Later years brought tears of joy when there were only five and sometimes only four. "How long more before we get there?" "Are we going the short way with the ferry, or do we have to go all the way around through Riverhead?" "He doesn't give me enough room!" "He hit me!" "She hit me first!" "If you kids don't be quiet I'm going to stop this car!" (inference of a whipping). Car is quiet. Five minutes later, "I don't have room for my feet!" "I have to go to the bathroom!" "I'm hungry!" "How long is it now?" "She's steaming up my window so I can't see out!" The car slows down. "You kids think I'm kidding about stopping the car?" (another inference of whipping, greater emphasis). There is suddenly silence except for the sounds of the motor, which is now missing on one of the cylinders as Dad steps again on the accelerator. Somehow with the arrival at Fifth Street, Greenport, the moods change into thoughts of either playing with the cousins, going to Gram Cook's for sweets, or going into Gramp Santacroce's grocery store and staring into the candy counter long enough with a pitiful look to draw on the generosity of Gram Santacroce. Actually, we enjoyed very much being in Greenport. It was the getting there that was a drag.

The greater portion of the Santacroce house living area was upstairs, above the store, which was at ground level. Also at ground level, behind the store, were the kitchen, large dining area, and grandparents' bedroom. There was a "bathroom" upstairs that I remember as only that, tub and sink. To answer the call of nature one had to use the two-holer outhouse in the backyard. It was equipped with paper from various sources, but the most desired was the occasional supply of fancy tissue wrappings in the store from certain fruits that were individually wrapped. Upon delivery of such produce, Gram would immediately remove all the tissue wrappings and take them to the outhouse.

On the very earliest of visits, when I was just old enough to remember anything at all, I recall being put in bed by my mother. The older kids were still out because "they are old enough to stay up longer. When you are older you can stay up longer also." When my mother would go down the stairs to be with her folks, I was alone in this big bedroom lighted by a single votive candle. My grandparents, Catholics as strong in belief as the pope, often attended daily mass, not just on Sunday. And when walking along the street, when the church bell rang they would automatically genuflect wherever they were. Votive candles were always lighted night and day, upstairs and downstairs. The light of the votive candle in my bedroom did not rest. In the heat of this warm summer evening, rotation of a large wooden-bladed fan hanging from the ceiling caused the candle's flame to dance so that many figures formed on the walls and ceiling. While imagining different objects and scenes I would eventually fall fast asleep.

From our Greenport visits there are many memorable scenes, which often come to my mind, but there was one in particular when we were at the Santacroce house. It usually occurred in the evening when I should be going up the stairs to bed. Nearly every evening, several of Gramp's Italian men friends would congregate in his office at the rear of the store. In this office were Gramp's rolltop oak desk, several chairs, and a potbelly coal stove in the middle of the office. A single lightbulb and a rotating fan hung from the ceiling. I loved to be there in a corner sitting on the floor. Simply being there, looking and listening. Typically, each of the men would get a bottle of Rheingold beer from the cooler box in which blocks of ice were used for cooling or Gramp would provide some red wine from his private stock. Each autumn when grapes were harvested he made his own dark red wine, enough to last the entire year. I was wonderfully excited being in

Gramp's office, especially in wintertime, when the potbelly stove with glowing coals made the room cozily warm and smoke from the black Italian cigars filled the air. All the men spoke in Italian about things I will never know, but one could imagine their conversations included the old days in Popoli, Italy, where they all had lived before immigrating to the United States. Sometimes, when they were so engrossed in talking to one another, Gramp would forget to adjust the damper slide at the bottom of the coal grate after starting the fire, and the coals began to roar with flames, making the potbelly turn red from the high temperature. One of the friends would call out, "Vincenzo, Vincenzo," [I suppose he was gesturing]. "Adjust the damper!" and Gramp would casually bend over from his strategically placed chair and close the damper enough to control the draft air.

Just as things began to get really exciting for me in the atmosphere of these evenings, Mom would show up at the door: "Paul, I thought I would find you here!" She more or less pulled me out, breaking my trance. Then the trek up the stairs to dreamland. While I understood not a single word of what these men were saying each evening, their kind mustached faces, with lines of experience from years of hard work, were a natural attraction. I felt that their facial expressions and their language of a faraway land were my invitation to sit among them.

Most of these folks got their first jobs in a brickyard that flourished at the time. While many of Gramp's friends had various jobs in Greenport over the years, Gramp Santacroce eventually saw the opportunity to establish a grocery store catering to the Italian community. He had the normal items available locally but dwelled on importing many special items from Italy, including salami, cheese, and black cigars. Being a good friend of the inhabitants and an honest merchant, Gramp built up his business also with determination and hard work. And he never let his friends down. Although he became more financially well off than his Popoli friends, he always treated them the same as before and never with a hint of arrogance. He sat with them each evening as equals in every way. On Sunday afternoons he and his Italian friends would play cards in a room that he had especially arranged for in a house next door to the store.

There was another scene with Gramp at lunch, which very often comes to mind. This was in the kitchen. There was a cast-iron stove (wood and coal) in the corner of the kitchen. Gramp's chair was between the stove and the kitchen table, against a wall. Just after he had lunch, consisting sometimes of a soup, like minestrone, and a glass of red wine, he would take a nap still sitting in the same chair. After eating, he would turn to his right, away from his dish, and put his right elbow on the edge of the stove and the left elbow on the edge of the table, but with his left hand on the glass of wine. Dressed in his vested suit and felt hat as always, he leaned back against the wall. After tipping the front of his hat slightly downward and taking a few more sips of the red, he would fall fast asleep. Woe to any of us who dared to make any noise in the kitchen area during this fifteen- or twenty-minute nap time every day.

I have revisited the location of the Santacroce store a number of times over the years. Each time as I stood in front of the store, which was deteriorating more and more and empty of life, I became very sad. It can never again be what it was for me. But the memories of those precious days will stay with me forever.

When, in April 1941, Gram Santacroce died, her wake was held in the large living room. This was the first time I had ever seen a dead person and the first time I experienced being at a wake. The wake was traditional for the Italians, staying up the entire night with the open casket, votive candles around the area, all the relatives and friends taking their time to pay their respects and to make sure several persons were always present. Everyone talked in hushed voices, occasionally taking a bite of food and some men sipping red wine. I could only think about how she would be missed, not only reminiscing about the penny candies she allowed me to choose out of the store candy counter as I pressed my nose against the glass, wide-eyed in anticipation. Gram was so very kind. And the large pot of tea she made every morning for us. She put a lot of milk into the pot; then we were each given several of those round Nabisco milk crackers to dunk into the tea. That was our simple but wonderful and unforgettable breakfast. Now this had come to an end. Yet the thoughts of those days will always be with me.

The time after this wake slipped by so quickly. It was only about one year later that Gramp (Vincent Santacroce) died, and it seemed to me it was definitely related to the loss of his devoted wife, Anna. They had experienced so many years together, good times and hardships, that it was as if he no longer had anything left to live for.

I visited Ellis Island a few years ago to see how it might have been when Gramp Santacroce and family entered the United States at this immigration site, now a museum. I found names of our Santacroce family inscribed on this very long wall that contains thousands of names of persons who immigrated to America, mostly through Ellis Island. In particular, I recall seeing "Vincent (Vincenzo) Santacroce," "Anthony (Antonio) Santacroce," and "Pasqual Santacroce." It was really a stirring moment as I stared at the inscriptions and realized that, e.g., Vincent Santacroce was my grandfather and because of him, his vision and courage to go from Popoli, Italy, in 1893 alone (wife Anna arrived later, in 1898) to a completely new and strange country, my mother, then I, were brought into this world, in New York.

The earliest ancestor of record on my father's side, through his mother, Anna "Annie" Wells, was William Wells, who settled in 1635 in Southold, Long Island, New York. Arrivals to America from abroad in those very early days were too scattered and recordless, for the most part, to establish a given site for an immigration monument such as on Ellis Island. However, the grave of William Wells is an exception in that it is clearly a private and singular monument to him. This and related family information are included in a historical account of the Wells family in the area of Southold, New York.

Mom and Dad both lived just a few blocks apart, and on the same street (Fifth Street) in Greenport, during most of their premarried life. They met when Dad went to the Santacroce grocery, where Mom tended the store with her parents. They married on 17 October 1923 in Saint Agnes' Catholic Church, Greenport, just around the corner from the store. On the marriage certificate Mom's middle name was spelled Elinore, whereas on all documents that I had ever seen it was Eleanor. In any case, she was always called "Beat" and "Bea" (for Beatrice) by family and friends in Montauk and Greenport.

When we went to Greenport and stayed overnight, we always stayed at the Santacroce house, because they had the space and facilities to handle our visiting family from Montauk. But naturally we always went down the street to Gram Cook's ("Annie" Wells Cook's) house to visit as well. We could always expect cake, pie, and candy and hear her words about, "How nice it is to see you," and such words, which were welcomed. She lived in three or four different houses over the years, but I remember most the house of earlier years, the one on Fifth Street, the same street as the Vincent Santacroce family. Gram Cook also had an outhouse, like so many families still, in those days. There was another feature in her house different from most. This was the hand pump in the kitchen for water. We had to go up and down with this long handle to pump water for any water used. As very young children we thought it was very much fun and always had to get a glass of water even though we already drank more than enough. The big tree on the side of the house that bore sweet cherries was yet another attraction, to climb in the late-summer months.

It happened often on the return trip to Montauk that we transported Gramp Santacroce's gifts consisting of a 100-pound sack of potatoes and/or a bushel of apples. Whereas the trip to Greenport was challenge enough, we now had to contend with even less room in the car on the return trip. During the Christmas season my mother would do her best to keep order among the children in the backseat by setting up a little contest for all to participate in to keep us quiet. As we drove along the highway we were to count the lighted Christmas trees seen in the windows of homes, one team on the left and the other team on the right side of the road. Whichever team saw the most trees was the winner. All well and good for the first half hour or so: "We have twenty-nine on the left!" "We have thirty-two on the right!" "You do not. We counted on your side, too, and saw only twenty-seven." "Yeah, but when you were looking at your side you didn't see our five other ones!" "Mom, they're cheating. That's not fair!" "Why don't you all have an apple. They're good for you and it'll give you something to do." "Mom, I was going to eat that apple and she took it from me." "Can't you kids find an apple you want out of that whole bushel? Why do you have to have the one somebody else has?" "Dad, how much longer is it to get home?" "Well, I can tell you it's going to be a lot longer if I have to stop this car!" (Another warning.) Silence . . . for a while. The boredom of traveling through the miles of potato fields and finally the sand dunes of Napeague puts us all asleep until we reached our driveway in the Fishing Village. Funny, now nobody wants to get out of the car. All too tired to move.

I had memory of a scene when I was seven that lasted over many years, but I could never relate it to anything significant, a vision of my father driving off in a car. The vision stayed in my memory. Only after my mother died in 1995 and when I obtained several papers as keepsakes I was finally able to tie in the vision with reality. Among the papers were five picture postcards with dates from 30 April through 8 May 1936, which my father had mailed to my mother, and each card was posted in a different town in the New York / New England area. (I noted that the postage in those days was a mere one cent.) Where Dad had stayed overnight he wrote just a few words to say in general he was fine and he hoped she and the children were OK. I learned that the purpose of this auto trip from Montauk via Connecticut and Massachusetts to Kennebunk, Maine was, as I read, to have a couple of days camping and fishing.

My memory from the age of seven was of seeing Dad in our old Chevy, waving good-bye to Mom while I stood beside her. I could see through the car windows some pots and pans and boxes piled up on the backseat of the car. I did not know then, and not even until fifty-nine years later, that I was watching Dad go on a vacation, alone. His postcards always began: "Dear Beat" (Beatrice) and ended: "Love to you and all the children."

To my knowledge this was the only real vacation, away from Long Island, that Dad had ever taken as long as he lived. Although he never outwardly expressed his philosophy on life, I can feel rather certain it was his conviction that his "vacations" were to be with his family, provide the ultimate in service to postal customers, serve the community as commissioner of the local volunteer fire department, participate in the church affairs, and last but not least enjoy his hobbies operating a ham radio, catching lobsters, and surf-casting for stripers on the shores of the Atlantic in Montauk.

There was one particular summer day when neighbor Tom Joyce decided to have his "yard" cleaned up. No one actually had what you would call a real yard in the Fishing Village. There were no boundaries. Among the variously scattered wooden houses, between the one and only tarred road running from the railroad station to the Union News Dock and the shoreline of Fort Pond Bay, there was only sand and stones in addition to the heaps of fishing nets, fish boxes, sharpies (rowboats), buoys, pilings, lobster pots, and the like. There was little to define a yard except perhaps to think that halfway to the neighbor's house was your "border." But Tom wanted to play a sort of game with the kids, and I became aware of this only after the fact.

About a dozen of us had gathered for this event at Tom's place because we heard we could get some money if we wanted to work in his yard to clean it up. But before starting, Tom had called each of us inside separately and asked if we would work for the amount he offered. And he stated, "Do not tell the other kids the amount I tell you!" My offer was five cents. I was then five years old.

After about an hour of picking up old cans, papers, and what seemed to be rubbish, Tom called in each of us again as we lined up and each of us was given a coin wrapped in a small piece of newspaper in payment for our work. Now, as I began to compare my five cents with the coins given the other kids I found that some of the others had ten cents and some fifteen cents. I thought that I had worked just as hard as the bigger kids who got more money. When I agreed to "work" for Tom, it never crossed my mind as a five-year-old to think whether the others would get the same amount. So I went to Tom to complain. Well, you see, Tom was a very religious man and attended mass each Sunday like many of the other fishermen in the village. He had recalled the priest's sermon in the last mass about the

Lord paying the laborer the amount agreed to, to work in the vineyard, and not more. Tom was playing out this theme with us. At the time I was very upset with him, because I had really done as much as the others. But at the same time it was one of those lessons learned in growing up. One has to establish, at the outset, what he believes his efforts and talents are worth before consummating an agreement with another party.

That five-cent piece bought me a large cold Hires root beer at Jake Wells's store, which was situated a few hundred yards east along the bay shore. After several wonderful minutes savoring this drink on that warm summer day, I began to skip stones into the bay from the shore while making my way back home. I have never ever forgotten working in Tom's yard. It was the first "job" in my life for pay.

Professional racing cars in Montauk? Something not very much talked about is an auto race that was held in Montauk one of the summers in the period (approximately) 1938 to 1940. While I cannot be certain of the exact year I am certain that an auto race took place because I was there along the road to see it. The "race track" was essentially the series of roads, including Essex Street and Fairview Avenue, that take you, even today, completely around the Montauk Downs Golf Course. I stood near the corner of Essex and Fairview, not far from the then home of Harry Bruno, watching and listening to these roaring cars with goggle-eyed drivers as they swished by the milkweeds, wild grapes, sumac, and blackberries. In the lull between cars there was always time to get a handful of ripe berries sweetened by the summer's midday sun.

Then there was the big hurricane at 2:30 P.M. on 21 September 1938. I was nine years old, in fifth grade at Montauk Public School. As we looked out the school windows from our desks during the storm, giant pieces of metal corrugated siding were flying through the air like pieces of paper. It rained as I had never seen before, and there was a roaring sound from the winds for a couple of hours. When the winds died down we went to the windows, looked down upon the Fishing Village about a mile away, and could hardly believe the destruction. The Fishing Village had a tidal wave that flooded the entire area, and all the houses were either off their foundations or floated away to another location. Piles of debris were everywhere, fishing boats torn from their moorings and many beached high and dry. The night of the hurricane and the next night all the public school kids who lived in the village were taken in by the families living near the school on the hill. I stayed with the family of Bob and Bert Tuma. It took several months before order in the village was restored. Until our house was returned to its place and repairs were made, our family lived with grandparents for a few months and we went to school in Greenport, although my dad had to work as postmaster and stay in Montauk during the weekdays.

When we first went to our house location in the Fishing Village two days after the hurricane, we found all the chickens drowned inside the chicken-wire-fenced area. However, our two ducks were swimming around as if nothing had happened. These ducks were brought to Greenport to fatten up for Thanksgiving, but the night before Thanksgiving someone stole them. They survived the storm but were prey to thieves.

Dad was in the post office sorting mail when the floodwaters rushed in. At one point he looked out a window and noticed telephone poles passing by. He realized he was not in a boat and that the post office was torn from its meager foundation and floating away. He grabbed all the registered mail and waded to our house to get to Mom and our two baby sisters. After some struggle they got aboard a train for higher "ground." The train tried to pull away to the higher woods area, but the tracks were washed out. Then most of the villagers went up to the Montauk Manor, where they stayed, so as to make plans for survival until the village could get back to normal.

When we lived in the village I can say that I *really* lived there. That is to say, rarely did I leave the village area except for riding the "Bluebird" bus to Montauk Public School, going to church on Sunday, or with my family going picking berries and grapes. Not until 1939 did I venture out alone *very far,* and that was to caddy at Montauk Downs Golf Club. I remember well one summer day as I was strolling along the road near Loftus's General Store a car stopped and the driver asked me if I wanted to make a dollar. (The most I had made at one time until then was maybe twenty-five or thirty cents picking up Coke and ginger ale empties along the tracks to get deposit money at Loftus's General Store.) This was a golfer from "up the island" who needed a caddy. As I never before had caddied, the man did not object but said, "All I need is for you to carry my golf bag. You look strong enough for that." Five hours later, after eighteen holes in the hot sun, I had earned $1.25. This started me on the road to being the avid golfer that I am today.

I was eleven years old when we moved out of the Fishing Village, in early 1940, to a house at 56 Edgemere Road, across from Bill's Inn (later the Windjammer). Our move came at this time because my mom got so nervous during each time there was a heavy wind, always thinking, *Maybe the water will come up again.* She wanted higher ground and the east side of Edgemere provided this security and peace of mind. Our family was to live here for the next fifty-five years, until my mom passed away in June 1995.

The Cook family house, located in the Fishing Village on Lease No. 11 of lands owned by the Long Island Railroad Company, on Fort Pond Bay, Montauk, was sold by Theodore and Beatrice Cook to Doris A. Strandberg on the eighth of November 1939 for the sum of $600.00. This house was further sold to Doris's sister, Mariam, and husband Robbie Byrnes, and on 7 March 1943 it was moved on skids to its current location on South Ilihu Place, Shepherd's Neck.

My activities changed dramatically, as they had to, away from the Fishing Village environment. I was depressed for some time, as I really missed all the things I had enjoyed and experienced there and the closeness and spirit of all the families in the village. My mom and dad used to say, "You can walk to the Fishing Village, Paul, whenever you want to." I could and I did, but only about one year later it was to be destroyed again. This time not due to storm and water, rather, because of the direct effect of the attack on Pearl Harbor. Not only did the attack on Pearl Harbor on December 7 in 1941 destroy that naval facility on Oahu, Territory of Hawaii, but also our famous and beloved Montauk Fishing Village. War was declared, and the U.S. Navy decided that the best location for a torpedo testing range was at Fort Pond Bay and its shores. In 1942 the Montauk Fishing Village commenced to become a page in history as it was totally vanishing before our very eyes. Many houses were towed on skids out of the Fishing Village to various other locations in Montauk, others simply wrecked in place in order to build this new naval facility. The only visible remains today on the bay's shores, aside from the bay and shore themselves, are Duryea's and the little white house of Tom Joyce, who was our neighbor during the 1930s. When you ride today from the rail station to Duryea's, you can see Tom Joyce's house relocated on the left side of Tuthill Road. Tom, the fisherman, neighbor, colorful friend, jokester, net mender, ice boat builder, always generous man, who helped save our baby sister during the hurricane flooding. Tom's little white house is his legacy to the people of Montauk and to those who love the sea.

If you should be so fortunate to visit this area today, continue past Tom's house on to Duryea's Dock and enjoy the superb sunset on Fort Pond Bay while you savor lobster or other items on the menu of Duryea's dockside restaurant. It is "elegantly informal." Sporty dress and paper plates, but with a Hollywood sunset. My companion, Ursula, and I did not realize that wine was not sold there, but you could bring your own. As luck would have it, Dick White Jr. and his wife, Rose, were there the same evening and shared a glass of theirs with us. Another great night to remember.

There is so much more that could be written about the Fishing Village, but suffice to say that my life on the shores of Fort Pond Bay was one of the greatest gifts I ever had and one that I will always cherish. If I had no other enjoyment in my future life I could just happily reminisce on my days "in the Fishing Village."

Wahlberg's Restaurant was operating already in the early 1930s more or less as a hot dog and hamburger stand, existing, it seems, for as long as I can remember. And it was located at the very beginning of the Old Montauk Highway, just west of the intersection with the state highway, near the Second House Museum. At some point in time, years after my navy career, I noticed that this business of Wahlberg's no longer existed. As I thought about this after each visit, it struck me that Montauk, the Montauk I knew, was actually becoming like a dream as when one wakes up one morning, and all of a sudden what you had experienced has simply gone up in a puff of smoke. I could not help dwelling on the thoughts about another one of those good things had disappeared from the Montauk scene. Just like the beloved Fishing Village because of World War II, just like the disappearance of the Surf Club because of hurricanes and finally fire damage, the disappearance of the original Golf Club House because of fire; like the use of the land meant for the second golf club (Hither Hills Golf Club), taken over by real estate interests to build and sell houses, the former public access to lakeshores eliminated because of private property exclusion, the loss of public access to the formerly unlimited supply of wild berries because of the real estate business, and more.

I was delighted to learn, on the other hand, only during a visit to Montauk in June 2000 that there has been a limitation placed on land use in that about 72 percent of the land of Montauk is being preserved as parkland. This is certainly a soothing thought about the future of this very special area of New York State. And I should add that time, fire, hurricane, and flood have destroyed some very significant features of Montauk, but disasters can never eradicate all the fond memories held by native Montaukers for the "old days" (which in my generation was the period before the mid-1940s).

Montauk, New York, Is Known Far and Wide!

Several years ago I was in a small group on a trip to South Africa. In a three-week period we traveled over most of the land from Johannesburg and Kruger Park to Swaziland, Port Elizabeth, Durban, and the Garden Route on down to Capetown. All extremely interesting. But in Durban a couple of incidents occurred that I remember as well as any other.

We were getting some sun on the beach at the Indian Ocean after having spent some hours at the food market, and lunch at the Middle East Club, which specialized in Indian food. A couple came along the beach and asked if I was from Montauk. I was taken aback for a minute, but I asked why. "The shirt," was their quick reply. Then I realized that I was wearing my light blue T-shirt with white letters modestly displayed across the chest, MONTAUK. I had bought it the year before in a boutique at Gosman's Dock at Montauk Harbor. This couple had visited Montauk several times, and they declared, "We just love Montauk." The coincidence was great. Halfway round the world and down under, from East Coast USA on the Atlantic Ocean to the east coast of Africa on the Indian Ocean.

It was not an hour later that a gentleman came strolling along the beach, saw the same shirt, and asked. "Is that Max Frisch's *Montauk?*" "Yes," was my answer, but required a bit more explanation. This man had read the book *Montauk,* which was written by a famous Swiss author, Max Frisch. Nearly every learned European, especially from Germany, Austria, Holland, Denmark, and Switzerland, has read this book, which is the account of a weekend spent in Montauk by Max Frisch in the early 1970s with a lady friend reporter. They stayed at Gurney's Inn and roamed on all the paths through the brush leading to water between the village and the point. Since I was living among Germans and knew their literary habits and was a native of Montauk as well, I was able to give this gent a complete rundown on the "shirt from Gosman's" and the relationship to the book.

The original publication of *Montauk* was written in German but later translated into English. There are copies of this book, in English, in the Montauk Public Library. Since I had three copies at home in English and one in German, I presented one of the English versions to Nick Monte, owner of Gurney's Inn, as a memento of Max Frisch's visit there.

On various occasions, as a result of wearing a certain other heavy sweater, in colder weather, with *Montauk* on the front while playing golf at various courses in Germany, I have been asked numerous times, "Are you from Montauk?" And the usual conversation takes place: "Yes, that's my hometown. Have you been to Montauk?" Occasionally some say they know of it or have been there, but more often it is because they have read the book, *Montauk,* by Max Frisch.

It was not only famous names who visited Montauk that put Montauk on the map, so to speak. "Gus" Pitts, for example, became a legendary figure for his knowledge of the sea and exploits with his fishing boats near the ocean's surf along the coastline of Montauk. There are others in recent history who stand out, but it has been the likes of Gus, and those of the Fishing Village era who provided the foundation for any successes that followed. I visited my godparents, Gus and Hattie, throughout the years whenever I made trips to Montauk during vacation or on business trips to New York. The last time that I visited with them was in June 2000. Gus was then ninety-five years of age and still driving his car about the village. Hattie, a bit younger, was a "picture of health," as described by her doctor. I am certain that the Montauk air and way of life have much to do with the relatively long life of most of the natives there. Gus had a multitude of stories to tell about the Montauk Fishing Village, especially in the early 1920s, the rum-running days. Gus's saga of running a high-powered launch out to sea at fourteen years of age to meet seagoing ships for the "cargo" during prohibition was really exciting. His experiences with incidents on and near the sea and as an expert fisherman have provided us with many not only interesting stories of the past but also important sketches of local history. One of the more amusing accounts of the earlier days was about Gus's father, Elias, who owned the first ever automobile in Montauk. Gus mentioned the name of this auto, but I remember only a part of it: Eastman. He described a trip to East Hampton from Montauk with this car. On the way, men on horseback passed them on the old road. At night the "headlights" had to be lit with a match, posing a difficult task at times and providing precious little light. Gus Pitts gained considerable fame as a striper fisherman through his expertise in boat handling close to the ocean surf. His boats *Marie* and *Marie II* (their daughter's name) were closely watched by other boatmen to learn where the fish were being caught. Gus knew the places and he knew the limits.

Effects of World War II on Montauk and Its People
(1941–46)

In addition to the disappearance of the Montauk Fishing Village due to the navy's torpedo testing range (TTR), the lives of the people of Montauk were affected by World War II in many other ways not only for the duration of the war, but also for many years to come.

Many young men either enlisted voluntarily or were drafted into the military when of age. I was only sixteen years old even when the war ended in 1945. My older brother, Robert (Bob) at 17, in December 1941, volunteered to join the navy when still a senior at East Hampton High School. After boot camp training in Newport, Rhode Island, he was assigned to destroyer duty in the Atlantic Fleet for convoys to Murmansk, where supplies were being delivered to Russia for the war against Germany. I remember being very proud of Bob, yet I always feared that something might happen to him. He often wrote letters, which were censored, about life and duties aboard the ship. What stayed in my mind most, at the time, was the lookout duty they had to stand, outside on the ship, going through the very rough and cold North Atlantic in winter. He wrote of his experience also on the USS *Tuscaloosa* where they were taking part in the North African Campaign, near Casablanca. The ship's guns were bombarding targets ashore day and night. They could get little sleep because of the noise and vibrations.

The *Tuscaloosa* was known as the "galloping ghost of the Atlantic" because it seemed to be active everywhere. Franklin Roosevelt rode the *Tuscaloosa* often when he was secretary of the navy.

Bob served on several ships in the Pacific as well, but the one that had to be most remembered was the USS *DuPage*. The *DuPage* was hit by kamikaze aircraft in suicide dives, killing a very large number of the crew. Bob's life was spared, as he had just gone down into the engineering spaces, where he had duty. I'm sure he had his moments of fear, but he never let on in his letters. After one of the invasions, in which his ship participated, he went ashore. There he picked up a Japanese bayonet off the beach at Iwo Jima and sent it home to me as a souvenir from the South Pacific. My son, Jim, now has this bayonet in his possession.

My brother Joseph, "Joe," joined the marines when he came of age and trained at Parris Island. I recall him writing that Tyrone Power (movie star) was in his company, but that he had to train like everyone else, side by side. Joe was later assigned to a marine aviation night fighter squadron stationed at Eagle Mountain Lake, Texas.

My father was exempt from military service for a combination of reasons: his age, forty-one, and being the father of seven children, and Montauk's postmaster in the post office that, at that time, was located in the old theater building (next to White's Drug Store). Therefore he was given duty as a warden, whose job it was to see that certain of the wartime regulations were followed by the folks in the section of Montauk assigned to him. One of those duties was to ensure that all the lights were turned off, or blacked out, in his area when air-raid sirens sounded. I remember a number of drills held. One I recall vividly, when I was in school in the eighth grade. The siren went off, but we students did not know if it was for real. The teachers at school also did not know, for a considerable period of time. For some reason or other we just had the feeling that this particular warning was serious. But after some frantic phone calls between the school and military authorities, it was announced "only a drill." This drill really got our attention, because what if there were really something involving an attack of some sort? Actually, I do not remember what we were told we should do if planes attacked or if ships bombarded Montauk, but I believe it was to disperse and go directly home. It inspired me, for situations in the future, to try to have a clear, well-thought-out plan for emergencies. Realistic drills will train participants to react automatically, in order to keep fear and indecision from taking control of a situation.

Our pharmacist, Dick White Sr., was also exempt from military duty since he was the *only* pharmacist in Montauk and source of medical supplies and medicine in the civilian arena.

One of the persons who we thought would never be drafted was Henry "King" Shaver. Everyone knew King as the capable electrician/plumber, also one who, you could imagine, was allergic to soap and water, as it appeared that he wore the same clothes until they stood up alone. Well, he was drafted into the army. One day he showed up in Montauk on home leave. Few of us could recognize him at first sight, as he was really "shaped up" by the army, clean-shaven, with new teeth and a pressed uniform. It did not take long after the war to find King in his usual habitat and even discarding the false teeth made for him by the army. Yet everyone liked King. He was, despite his toiletry habits, actually a very likable person. King was an integral part of Montauk.

Of the Montaukers in military service, three war casualties came early on. Bertil Olson, a son of the Algot Olsen family, neighbors of ours from the village, was killed when his plane, in which he was a gunner, was shot down over Germany. Another neighbor, Edward McDonald, son of Louis McDonald, was killed in service with the army. And Linwood Townsend of the Coast Guard was killed during a landing in the South Pacific.

On the homefront, rationing became a routine on several items that were scarce because of the need to supply the military. Items such as sugar, butter, and gasoline are what come to mind. But since we lived with a fishing fleet at our doorstep and there was an abundance of potatoes, apples, berries, and the produce from "victory gardens," no one would have ever starved. Everyone with any ground at all was encouraged during the war to plant vegetables or other food plants as support for production of food. In back of our house, 56 Edgemere Road, on a plot of ground with about four hundred square yards, we planted corn, peas, string beans, tomatoes, rhubarb, onions, carrots, peppers, strawberries, radishes, and sometimes pumpkins, watermelons, and squash. When we planted corn, squash, watermelon, and pumpkin seeds in the "hills" (mounds), for fertilizer Dad put a whole fish (dead of course) into the ground, about ten inches below the seeds. These plants always, without fail, grew extremely well. I suppose he got the idea from the Indians, who used fish for fertilizer.

We also had about twenty or so chickens, for eggs and poultry meat. I remember the "chicken for meat" idea ended when Dad was chopping the head off one of the chickens for a Sunday dinner. Despite the chop, the headless chicken continued to run around the backyard for some minutes. This took out some of the enthusiasm from one sector of the victory garden (the poultry department).

In place of real butter my mother always bought the white margarine and the little pouch of yellow coloring powder that we mixed to make the margarine look yellow, like the butter. It was a fun thing to do and we vied to get the "job." Little did we know then that avoiding real butter was actually healthier by today's standards relative to cholesterol. Our family, by the way, continued to use margarine all the time even after the war ended.

We Boy Scouts held waste paper drives for the war effort and stored the paper we collected in the Montauk Public School basement. Every few weeks it would be picked up and our scout troop was paid a few dollars per ton, which we used for troop activities. We also collected scrap aluminum, which we piled high at "the Circle" between the tall office building and Montauk Highway.

Many of the men and teenage boys, like my brother Joe (before he joined the marines) and myself, were assigned lookout watches in a guardhouse built on top of the Montauk Public School. These watches were manned around-the-clock for a couple of years. We had to report the sightings and sounds of any and all aircraft. This information was provided over a special telephone line direct to the air defense center (perhaps Mitchell Field; I don't recall the airfield) on the west end of Long Island. Our call-sign at Montauk was "Dudley 71." Typical report: "Dudley seventy-one . . . two . . . high . . . westbound," or "Dudley seventy-one . . . three . . . low . . . northbound." This was, of course, at a time before any radar installations were possible.

On a midsummer day two other boys and I found a yellow rubber military life raft that had drifted up to the beach and the three of us happily paddled our way out into the relatively calm ocean. After about two hours of this fun, a blimp came toward us and descended to a pretty low altitude. "Hey, this is neat," someone in the raft mentioned. When we got back in from our "trip," I was severely admonished because the navy had a report of "survivors" in a raft on the ocean off Montauk and a blimp was sent to investigate. The navy and the Coast Guard were always on the lookout for survivors on the ocean.

Torpedo Testing Range and Big Reed Pond

During 1942 and 1943 the army, navy, and Coast Guard developed their facilities at a furious pace. The navy had their TTR at Fort Pond Bay (where our Fishing Village used to be). This facility had several large warehouse-type structures, piers for the boats (to retrieve torpedoes that were tested and fired into the bay); the rail yards, a seaplane hangar, and facilities for Kingfisher and Seagull aircraft, which were used in torpedo testing operations. And up the hill the Montauk Manor was used for barracks to house the sailors. Across the street from the front of the manor, a hospital was built (and torn down after the war). The officers' quarters were located in the tall office building near the circle. The commanding officer of the entire TTR was a former submarine captain, U.S. Navy Commander Hodgkiss, whose family lived in one of the "Fisher houses" on the road just to the west of Montauk Downs Golf Club entrance. His son, Kingman, and I became friends and spent time together fishing and shooting.

I had asked Kingman if he wanted to go fishing, and of course I was referring to surf casting at a place on the ocean beach. Being new in Montauk he automatically thought of freshwater fishing because that was all he had ever done where he lived previously. When we met he had his freshwater gear and he was very eager to go. His father was going to drive us in any case, so I asked him if he would get a second freshwater rod and reel for me to use. Now the only place I had seen people try for bass and perch was in Fort Pond. But I told Kingman we could go to a more secluded place, and I thought just on a hunch to try at Big Reed Pond near the Deep Hollow Ranch. I had never in my young life fished there before. It was really a gamble on my part to even suggest Big Reed. Commander Hodgkiss dropped us off on East Lake Drive and we walked to Big Reed. Within just a few minutes we were ready, and we both cast at the very same time. I could not believe what happened. As soon as our lures (plugs) hit the water there was a lot of splashing and we commenced to reel in. Each of our lines had a beautiful bass, about sixteen inches long. I began to wonder if anyone had ever fished here before, and if so, it must have been long ago. These fish were hungry and not shy about the lures. We were so excited about the catch that we started immediately walking all the way back to King's house, not so far from the entrance to the golf club. When we explained to different folks how big the fish were and where they were caught, most of the reactions were expressions of doubt and disbelief . . . like our story was a fisherman's lie about how big the fish was that got away! But the reality of this wonderful teenage experience is the kind that lives on forever.

The army had installed several giant coastal defense guns on the cliffs on the south coast, near the Montauk lighthouse. An integral part of this gun system was the network of fire control towers that were made to look like houses.

The Coast Guard had gradually increased their surveillance of the shores by adding more patrols, and with dogs. It was off-limits for anyone to be on the beaches after sunset, as the guard had authority to shoot what moved. Indeed there were stories of cows being shot in the Hamptons areas. On moonless nights sightings were especially difficult.

Submarines

Any sightings of submarines or their periscopes were to be reported by fishing boats crews who were, in reality, a working part of the coastal defense. One fisherman reported an incident where his boat commenced to go backward even while having forward throttle. He realized that his net had caught on to a submarine going in the opposite direction, and he cut the lines to the nets. I believe it was not a foreign sub at that time. There was, however, one sub in particular, not detected or, shall we say, not recognized in June 1942. This was the German submarine (U-boat) U-202.

German U-Boat Landing near Montauk

Just west of Montauk is Napeague, only a two-mile stretch of sand dunes until about the midforties. Along the shores of the Atlantic, except for Frank Eck's small restaurant and the U.S. Coast Guard (USCG) station, it was barren. On 14 July 1942, a German submarine, the U-202, landed a team of four saboteurs not so far from Frank Eck's and the CG station. A flag had been seen on occasions flying upside down in front of the restaurant. Perhaps a signal to the U-boat as being the right location for landing? It was a belief that Frank Eck, of German descent, was instrumental in somehow assisting the landing in this remote area.

When on the beach, the saboteurs encountered a Coast Guardsman on patrol duty who faked acceptance of a bribe from the Germans and quickly informed his superiors at the Napeague Coast Guard Station. This together with information from the observant railway agent in Amagansett, and the FBI, led to the saboteurs being tracked. The four Germans in this Long Island landing were Georg Johann Dasch, forty-two (leader); Ernst Peter Burger, thirty; Heinrich Heynck, thirty-three; and Richard Quirin, thirty-five. The leader, Dasch, told the young Coast Guardsman, "Take a good look at my face. You're going to see a lot more of it." How wrong he was!

A similar landing of four other German saboteurs from a submarine, the U-584, took place three days later, 17 July 1942, on the Atlantic coast of Florida. The leader of this group, Eduard Kerling, twenty-nine, had with him Werner Thiel, thirty-seven; Hermann Neubauer, thirty-three; and Herbert Hans Haupt.

All eight of these "Germans" were actually living in America before the war, but they had the notion to assist their fatherland after U.S. involvement. The details on names of the German saboteurs and the short story to follow were provided me by Col. Rudolph "Rudy" Nottrodt, U.S. Army, Ret., residing near me here in Bonn, Germany. It was of the greatest coincidence that this information became known to me. I had been talking to Rudy about where I came from and at one point mentioned that German saboteurs landed near Montauk in 1942. Immediately he said, "Yes, I know all about that. In fact, I knew some of these guys personally." I was eager for more information from his knowledge on the subject and here is a summary taking the case of Herbert Haupt as part of the story.

Rudy, oddly enough, was a boyhood (teenage) friend of several Brown Shirts (members of a Hitler Youth group), including Herbert Hans Haupt, at the Haus Vaterland at the German American Bund Headquarters in Chicago, where they met regularly. Rudy says, "It was kind of like the Boy Scouts," as far as he was concerned at the time. When the war really got under way there were different thoughts among the Brown Shirts. Many enlisted in the U.S. military services. But Herbert Hans Haupt of Chicago and the other seven would-be saboteurs from various other U.S. cities decided to make their way to Germany. Actually, Rudy, also at Haus Vaterland, was put in confinement and questioned at length, but finally in 1944 he agreed to enlist in the U.S. Army to show allegiance. Rudy distinguished himself, rising to the rank of colonel and ultimately in charge of three POW camps with 6,000 German prisoners in Leghorn, Italy.

Herbert Haupt was instructed to register for the draft. But then in 1941 he left Chicago and made his way through Mexico and on to Japan. From there he obtained passage on a blockade runner to the coast of then-occupied France. At an estate in Brandenburg, near Berlin, Haupt, along with the other saboteurs, was trained in sabotage against the United States. In July 1942 he embarked on the U-584, with three others, at a French port and was transported to the Florida coast. Haupt made his way to Chicago to "get his bearings." One of his mistakes was that he checked in with the FBI, because he said to them, "I heard you were looking for me" (because of the draft). Haupt thought this would throw the FBI off in suspecting him. The FBI played along with him, knowing more of the situation than Haupt had given them credit for. Dasch had become an informant by contacting the FBI and disclosing the sabotage plans, because he felt slighted that Germany had not accorded him due recognition of his services. The FBI had been tracking Haupt and all the others as well.

On 27 June 1942 all eight of the saboteurs were arrested. Haupt had a travel case with him that had a false bottom containing $9,950 and in his pocket a stolen, or forged, identification card of one Larry Jordan. Jordan had also been a Brown Shirt in Chicago and was also a friend of Rudy Nottrodt. Jordan and Haupt had been very close friends but were sharply divided on the war issue and country allegiance. Larry Jordan was serving honorably in the Pacific theater and his allegiance was toward America.

Herbert Hans Haupt and most of the other saboteurs were executed on 8 August 1942 in the electric chair and buried in Potter's Field near Washington, D.C. One not executed was given a prison sentence only, on the basis that his involvement in sabotage was considered "not voluntary."

I remember well when the landing near Montauk occurred. I learned about this the very next morning while I was caddying at Montauk Downs Golf Club. The next day I walked from our home on Edgemere Road, Montauk, all the way to, and through, Hither Hills and on the beach to the spot where the Germans had landed. I knew that it happened and stood on the spot. But it was only now, in the year 2000, that I had the occasion to meet and talk with Colonel Nottrodt, who personally knew about the saboteurs, and get an "update" with details nearly sixty years later. It was of interest to think about this special relationship among Rudy, Jordan, and Haupt, all of whom were members of families who for a better life had emigrated from Germany in the late 1920s and were subjects of the same Haus Vaterland in Chicago. The background of each was essentially identical, but each had a different destiny. Rudy pointed out that Jordan and Haupt were very close friends and both Catholic, Jordan practicing, but Haupt never attended mass. Jordan never entertained the idea of participation for Germany in the war and served honorably in the Pacific. Haupt, seeming to lack any semblance of social order, was an adventurous and ill-fated soldier of fortune. Rudy, Colonel Nottrodt, at eighty-two years of age reflects today on how it might have been for him in Chicago, but also how life has been good to him during his army career and in his current days of retirement with his French-born wife, Mona.

Air-to-Air Gunnery Practice

Several days a week, fighter aircraft would fly along the ocean coastline and make practice firing runs on towed target "sleeves," firing to the south. During each of these firing runs, a lot of empty .50-caliber shells would fall from the aircraft and land mostly in the water but often just anywhere over the town. For the kids, a shell was a collector's item, but the falling shells were potentially dangerous to humans if they landed on one's head. We had one shell hit the roof of our house and it went in about one inch. Some shells hit car tops and left substantial dents.

One day we saw from our house, 56 Edgemere Road, a parachute floating down from overhead and immediately noticed a Thunderbolt P-47 taking a nose dive downward to the surf at the ocean. This P-47 was in line with Edgemere Road as we looked to the ocean from our house at 56 Edgemere. There were no buildings at that time to obstruct our view. The crash made a hellish fountain of water rising high above the sand dunes. In the meantime, the pilot bailed out and came down a few hundred feet behind our house, bruised but not seriously hurt. Dad called the local army office, and soon an army officer came with a jeep and picked up the pilot. We went down to the ocean and found pieces of aluminum and various aircraft parts strewn around the beach, even though the plane crashed about one hundred feet offshore. For many weeks pieces of the plane washed up along the ocean beach. I observed that each piece of the fighter aircraft that I found had the smell of fuel despite its saltwater bath over a period of several days.

Gold Star Banners

In each home where one or more sons (or daughters) were in the military, the mothers hung a banner that displayed one star for each child. Bob and Joe, my two older brothers in service, were the two stars in our banner. These stars also were an indication that there were possibly two bedrooms empty. We had two army officers and their wives come to our home and rented the two empty bedrooms. They had kitchen and bathroom privileges and could use any of the vegetables (during summer) in our victory garden. Each room rented for seven dollars per week.

United Service Organization (USO) Facilities

In the basement of the Catholic church a USO (United Service Organization) facility was established to provide a place of recreation and pastime for all the servicemen in Montauk. Dinners and dances were arranged, and there were reading materials, games, drinks, snacks, and many volunteers of the community to talk with on a daily basis. My mother often cooked Italian-style spaghetti dinners when it was her turn to contribute, and my sister Ruth would join the other young ladies to dance with the soldiers and sailors stationed there. One of my contributions to the USO was making all the posters each week for the schedule of events at the USO. I was given all the art materials with which to work in order to make the posters as colorful and interesting as possible.

At times some members of the East Hampton High School band and orchestra formed a group to play dance music for servicemen at various locations, including the TTR in a building near the railroad station of Montauk. I was leading this dance band one night because the group asked me to do so. I normally played the drums in the marching band and in the orchestra so I did have some rhythm but was certainly not any expert in the technical aspects of music. When a sailor came to me and asked if we could play a rhumba, I said,"We don't know it." I had not the least notion how to lead a rhumba. I felt especially bad later when my classmate musicians told me, "Of course we can play a rhumba!" There were now and then these kinds of goof-ups in the younger days. But the dance band actually made the soldiers and sailors quite happy. There was precious little other social entertainment available in Montauk aside from the USO and occasional affairs such as this kind. Sammy Kaye and his orchestra did play for the servicemen on one engagement in the old tennis court building below the manor. And it was also in this same building where movies were frequently shown by the navy and "smokers" (boxing matches) were held among navy boxers. The local civilians of Montauk were allowed to attend these movies if they were escorted by a navy man who would vouch for the guest (as a security gesture).

Entrepreneurship

On the normally clean ocean beach at Montauk there accumulated a lot of crude oil from accidents on the many ships under way or presumably from torpedoed tankers offshore. As the summer vacationers from the city walked along the beach their feet would be pretty well tarred. Since I worked summers at the surf club during the last couple of years of the war, I was in a good position to know the problem and seek a solution. I bought new empty six-ounce prescription bottles at the pharmacy and filled them with kerosene, as kerosene was the quickest and easiest way to wipe off tar. When the club guests came to me I cleaned their feet, asking nothing in return, but they were so grateful for getting their feet cleaned I got very generous tips. After a while, though, I just sold the "customers" a bottle of the "magic potion" for twenty-five cents, which they thought was very cheap, but I was paid only twenty-five cents per hour to work at the club. What I earned selling several bottles each day was almost as much as I received for working the eight hours.

World War II Ends, 2 September 1945

At fifteen years of age, I was just beginning my senior year of high school and I remember the still-warm summer day, September 2, 1945. While in White's Drug Store, I heard that the war with Japan was finally over. (Germany had unconditionally surrendered already on 8 May 1945.) I was so overjoyed that I went directly to tell the news to my father in the post office next door in the old theater building. I was so filled with emotion that I could hardly speak, as if my breath were taken away. He kept saying, "What is it, Paul?" I finally managed to say, "War is over, Bob and Joe can come home." He hugged me to share his own happiness and relief.

Summer Experiences, Spare Time, and Friends
In Montauk (1941–46)

I just now happened to glance at my right wrist and saw the scar that always reminds me of a day with laughing and crying. It was early in the spring, when one could find a good breeze off the water for kite flying. This was a very popular sport. Somehow and somewhere we would find sticks or limbs from small trees for the necessary cross pieces, acquire strong wrapping paper for the body of the kite, then tie on a tail with pieces of rags. Flour-and-water paste was used to glue the edges of the paper around the strings tied to the four ends of the stick frames. Then of course a long string was needed to fly the kite. Most convenient was the use of a saltwater fishing rod and reel with a few hundred feet of line, an easy way to let out the kite and to reel in as desired.

One of those spring days, my brother Bob, a junior in high school at the time, built a kite. He wanted, or I should say needed, my assistance to hold the kite and run with it against the wind while he also ran in the same direction controlling the line. This was in a small field in back of our house at 56 Edgemere Road. We had gotten no farther than about twenty feet or so when I tripped and fell. I had looked up to be sure the kite was at the correct angle into the wind. What I had tripped on was a metal pipe that had been hammered into the ground, months before, as a stake to tie down something. The top of this pipe was "mushroomed" by the hammering, causing very sharp and ragged edges. That is what my wrist landed on. I could see about a half-inch into this two-inch-long cut. The blood spurted out everywhere, and this made me kind of sick to my stomach. I was holding the wrist tightly because it hurt so bad, and fortunately, that helped some to reduce blood flow. My mom did not have the car, so the summer neighbor, Mrs. Worth, volunteered to drive me to East Hampton to Dr. Nugent. She really floored the gas pedal, but my tears were running faster than the car. It surely seemed a whole lot longer, but I guess it was not more than fifteen minutes after I left the house that Doc Nugent had my arm in his hands and was telling me, "It's just a scratch!" An overexaggeration to my point of view. But, of course, he was doing his best to pysch me out of any fears. I was afraid that he was going to put some medicine on this gash that would burn terribly and, between sobs, I asked if it would hurt. "Not much," he said. He was mostly right, it did not hurt much, but it was not something I wanted a second time. He put a normal piece of tape across the wound to sort of close the cut and did no stitching. It healed in a couple of weeks without complications, but it left a scar, a reminder of the kite that almost got airborne, the fun in trying, and the interrupting tears.

I served as an altar boy for several years, until my last year of high school. I felt very comfortable serving mass as well as helping around the church for various activities, such as the annual church fair in summer, softball games, and in St. Patrick's Day plays in March.

A real-live pig, among many other items, was being raffled off, at twenty-five cents a chance, to raise money for the church maintenance expenses. I bought a raffle ticket really only as a contribution of the twenty-five cents to the church. Well, my luck was to win this pig and my unluck was that my mother said we could not take care of a pig in our yard. What to do? The priests in the rectory, located in East Hampton, offered me twenty-five dollars for the pig, which I quickly accepted. They were happy to have fresh pork which was scarce during the war, and I had an easy twenty-five dollars. A farmer in the Hamptons who donated the pig for the fair in the first place agreed to slaughter it as a further donation to the church.

One year our Montauk mission priest, Father Brady, "demanded" that I take part in a St. Patrick's play to be performed on the stage of the East Hampton movie theater. He said I fit the part because I was big enough and I knew how to play the bass drum. I found out too late that I was to play the part of the Swedish bass drummer in *McNamara's Band,* which also required that I sing these words to the familiar tune: "Oh . . . my name is Unkel Yulius and from Sweden I do come," et cetera. It further required that I sing with a Swedish accent. There were many practice evenings in East Hampton, and Father Brady was convinced finally that we (the trombone and trumpet players and myself) were ready, along with the excellent pianist, Michael Smolling. We wore our high school marching band uniforms, except that I had to wear an old felt hat to emphasize the part of the old Swede. Our little musical was a hit, with a full house. I will never forget Father Brady with his sometimes tough, but oh, so gentle style to draw out what he wanted from a person.

Scouting was also important to me and I attended all the meetings and jamborees held. I became a Life Scout and missed Eagle by one merit badge, Camping. I had had plenty of camping experience, but the badge required thirty consecutive days. I could not do that because of my need to work in summer, and sports took all my other spare time. A few of the scouts simply "camped" out in their backyard and became Eagles. I did not see sense in that. The way I looked at camping and the way I thought the rules were, one had to be in the woods or somewhere away from normal living. Anyway, I really enjoyed all that I learned in getting the merit badges and believe it good for any boys to be involved. On one of the jamborees, Virgil Conway and I teamed up for the semaphore signaling contest and also making a fire without matches. We won.

I continued to caddy at Montauk Downs during this period for a couple of years, which earned me a few dollars a day in summer months. A typical eighteen-hole round brought one dollar to a caddy plus between ten cents and fifty cents for tips, depending upon the generosity of the player and his mood, which varied with the number of birdies, pars, or bogies. Occasionally some players would give only the required one dollar without tips, and this was referred to as a "flat." Naturally, all the caddies would try their best to avoid these kinds of people. On the average, eighteen holes paid $1.25.

The thought of golf brings to mind a "discovery" made between the (new) Montauk Highway and the Old Montauk Highway about halfway between the Second House and Gurney's Inn. I was with two or three others, who could have been Pete LeBlanc, Eddy Ecker, and/or "Virg" Conway. We were simply roving around town and happened to walk through this area. There were a lot of pipes of various sizes lying around to carry water, obvious evidence of earth removal here and there, plus a wooden shed with a danger sign on it, indicating explosives. I could only wonder, at the time, what had been going on and why the work was unfinished. I found out many years later that this was the planned location of an eighteen-hole golf course, Hither Woods Golf Course, a second course for Montauk after the existing Montauk Downs Golf Course.

My father had a need to look at various properties when arranging for the location of the present-day post office. In the process he acquired an index map of the Montauk Beach Development Corporation, a 15 October 1926 engineering plan of Montauk showing the surveyed property lines and other areas. Included on the map is the layout of the Hither Woods Golf Course (see p. 3). But you could also imagine this planned golf course location when you drive from "downtown" Montauk toward Gurney's Inn on the Old Montauk Highway and about halfway to Gurney's look on the right-hand side. Today you will see many homes that were built after the early 1940s. If a golfer, especially, you would appreciate the foresight of Carl Fisher even more so when you drive into and around this area of homes, which he had selected for golf with "hill and dale" so perfectly suited for a natural course. The planned course area includes streets today with names of Washington, Lincoln, Cleveland, Madison, and Davis, to name a few. Not to lose sight of is the fact that there would have been, in addition, an ocean view. The Club House for the Hither Woods Golf Course was planned to be situated directly off the "Old Road" (Old Montauk Highway).

I have often wondered, with the Montauk Downs Golf Course classed by the *U.S. Golf Digest* as one of the top public courses in the United States, what it would be like with two "top-class" courses in Montauk. I can visualize Hither Woods, with its natural terrain and ocean view, as a dream for the avid golfer. And its fame today would be even greater with the likes of Tiger.

One summer I worked for a few weeks on a sport fishing boat, the *Candy,* owned by Captain Schwarz, who hired me as his first mate. In this instance, *first mate* meant, "Here are the hooks and here is the bait," but sometimes he let me steer the boat when he had something else to do. One day he told me to hold the course he set, and with very low speed, as he wanted to put the anchor over in order to do some bottom fishing off the Montauk Lighthouse. Well, he threw the anchor over and he shouted to me, "Cut the engine," which I did immediately. But Captain Schwarz forgot to tie the end of the line to the cleat, so the anchor and a brand-new line, just bought, were lost. Naturally we began to drift, but toward shore and with the engine stopped. He had always told me, "Don't do anything unless I tell you to do it." I waited for him to tell me to do something, but all I heard was cursing as he rushed to the helm. Then he could not get the engine started right away. I learned more new words. Finally, when only about a hundred yards from the shore, the engine coughed and sputtered into life and we went back to the yacht club.

A more pleasant trip on the *Candy* was with a party of four or five people from Hollywood, including movie star Carol Landis, all presumably to go fishing. Whereas they did, in fact, fish and catch a few bottom fish, they were more interested to swim in the rip tide directly off the lighthouse. They all shed their outer garments and in they went. It was a task to bait the hooks for Carol Landis without sticking a hook in my fingers now and then. She would say, "How sweet of you to put the bait on." I told her, "It's my job." She was a pleasant distraction from the likes of Captain Schwarz. When they were leaving the boat, she declared how helpful I was to her and gave me her autograph as she said good-bye. It was at this point that I decided to leave the *Candy,* because I wanted to remember this day, the best of the times, and not have to spend my future on a boat with an error-prone captain with a "rich" vocabulary.

My job at the Montauk Surf Club as locker boy in the men's locker room was really very enjoyable, at a place where I met a lot of people who came just for the summer on vacation. Most of them had more than the average in terms of wealth, and during the last three years of the war many of the guests seemed to be wealthy refugees from Europe. I knew that things in our society were about to change when one of these European women lay near the pool in the sand naked, except for a sandal over her lower parts. The club staff was in a frenzy as to what to do, but a manager, Gigi, a restaurant owner from New York City, was familiar with the ways in Europe and simply stated, "Leave her in peace." She was the only one in the club at peace, as she was oblivious to all the curious taking a path past her well-tanned body.

My job was such that I had plenty of time to also be on the boardwalk with the lifeguards and to sit around the pool and talk with the guests. One of those guests, of my age, I remembered (wrongly) in the years to follow as "Alfredo" Toscanini (so that "Al" lingered in my mind). But as it turned out "Al" was the nickname of another friend at the Surf Club. I had mixed up the names and faces. Nevertheless, the nickname of Al stayed with me for the next five decades. At the time of first meeting him I commented, "Toscanini. That is the same name as the famous conductor whose concerts I often hear on the radio." "Yes," he said, "that is my grandfather." I was impressed getting to know the grandson of Arturo Toscanini, but also impressed with his kindness and fine personality. I tried in the years that followed to make contact with "Al" because he was such a nice fellow. But my chances at the outset were slim, and became less and less, as I had entered the Navy in the year after graduating from East Hampton High School. During the ensuing years I was very often underway, somewhere in the world. While I had little time to do any searching whenever passing through New York City on business trips I did inquire of people with connections to the music world about my long lost friend "Al" Toscanini. I had no positive leads and I was even told by one source that Arturo Toscanini never had a grandson. This, I could not believe. I remained puzzled for years as to what happened to this friend, and about his matter of factly expressed relationship, with Arturo Toscanini.

It would happen by sheer coincidence, fifty-six years later in Bonn, Germany, while visiting in the Schumann Haus, where the famous composer, Robert Schumann, spent his last two years, and where he died in 1856. I had arbitrarily picked out a book from the Music Library and found it contained the life story of Arturo Toscanini. I was very surprised, and became actually excited, to read that Arturo Toscanini, in fact, had a grandson, but was named "Walfredo" and that this grandson was of my age as well. It had to be him. I checked further in my computer at home on the internet for "ArturoToscanini" (in Google) and found further evidence through several references to his grandson, Walfredo. That now convinced me. He was listed, for one thing, as a Senior Consultant in an architectural firm in New York City and an address given for the firm. I wrote a letter to him in November 2002 and just a few weeks later, in December, I received Walfredo's reply confirming the summer days spent at the Montauk Surf Club, and recalling names of common friends. I was to be reminded that it was "Wally" for Walfredo and not "Al" for Alfredo or other names. Little wonder that some inquiries were met with dead ends when asking about "Al" Toscanini. Well, all is well that ends Wally! We began to correspond. It is "Dear Walfredo" now, to avoid any further misconceptions as I have found with the casual use of a nickname, so common in America. I sent Walfredo a cluster of photos I had taken when working at the Surf Club and it was very useful in that he was able to identify clearly where he appears in the photos. and also who "Al" was. The "Al" in question was really Alessandro Treves. Naturally at this point in time I felt how great it would be if I could also make contact with "Al" as I came to realize through clarification from Walfredo that it was "Al" who had invited me to visit him in Manhattan in 1946. The photo cluster not only solved an identity problem but served well for nostalgia on the summers in Montauk.

After Walfredo and I had exchanged several postal and FAX letters during the weeks following first contact, Walfredo indicated he would investigate the whereabouts of Alessandro "Al" Treves. A few days afterwards, Walfredo informed me that he had talked with a lady with the family name of Treves but she was not related to Al. However, she did know him and said that he was probably living in Monaco, and as a side note he had been good at *fencing*. Walfredo suggested I check in the internet telephone book for a phone number for Alessandro Treves. After surfing through many places on the internet without luck, I checked next with an international operator in Bonn, the home of Deutsche Telecom. I gave this operator what little information I had. I was astounded on how quickly a connection had been made, as within seconds there was a response on an answering machine. But the voice was in Italian, therefore I did not understand what was said. There was the usual "beep" denoting "leave your message now." I did. I left a short message stating my hope that this is the correct number for Al Treves, gave my name, where I am living and my phone number, also if I have the correct number that we had met each other in 1945/46 during the summer days at the Montauk Surf Club.

Nothing happened that day or the next. I thought it was probably the wrong number or another with the same name who had no interest or connection with the Montauk Surf Club. I dwelled on the thoughts of the Italian language. If I had only been able to learn Italian, even coerced to learn when young. My mother was born in Greenport, New York, but in the Italian family which had only a few years prior immigrated to America with three of their nine children from Popoli, Italy. She had always spoken Italian with her parents and all the other Italians in the neighborhood. However, the philosophy of these immigrants in those days was for the children to speak English, not the "old" language. As children we would be amused because of the way our grandparents spoke with their badly broken English. We had to hide our snickering since my mother chastised us on more than one occasion for "making fun of their speech." During many hours I could not help to wonder why the immigrants could not see the value of learning another language in a very natural way, and not having to go through the drudgery of language in a classroom.

On the second day, the ring of our phone brought me out of this wonderment and back into real time. A cheerful sounding male voice in English announced, "This is Alessandro Treves, are you Paul Cook?" Another really exciting contact with acquaintances for the first time after fifty-six years, first with Walfredo Toscanini, in November 2002 and only a couple of months later, Alessandro "Al" Treves, in mid-February 2003. During two relatively brief exchanges on accounts of our lives during this very long intermission, Al (Treves) confirmed that he *had* lived at a Central

Park West address when I visited in 1946. I was certain that I had made a visit to a Central Park West apartment, but the problem was that I had thought it was to Walfredo, who I had been referring to as "Al." In order to relieve the acquaintances at the Surf Club of stating his longer real name, Alessandro Treves, he said, "Just call me Al." For reasons unclear to me I had remembered Walfredo as "Alfredo" and therefore placed the nickname "Al" on him. Without contact, the longer the time passed, the more imbedded was this false impression. This situation had occupied my mind for so many years that I became obsessed with learning what ever happened to these two teenagers, of my own age, with whom I became acquainted at the Surf Club during the Montauk summers 1945/46.

Alessandro "Al" Treves was, in fact, not only *good* at fencing, but *outstanding*. He was on the fencing team from the United States in the 1952 Olympics at Helsinki; he was World Military Fencing Champion 1953, and NCAA Champion in 1949–50. In 2000 "Alex" Treves was entered into the Rutgers University Sports Hall of Fame. (Al and Alex were both used as his nicknames.)

As of this writing I am looking anxiously forward to the possibility of Al, Wally, and I meeting together to reminisce and wistfully recount events of our lives. With respect to nicknames I am reminded that when very young my grandmother Cook called me Paulie (which I did not like, but I tolerated it for the goodies she always had for us); at an early teenage I was referred to as Cooky. In later years, that is early on in the navy, it was P.T.; in some years to follow, the sound of this abbreviation turned into Petey, then I was named Pete because new friends, in hearing Petey, thought my real name was Pete. When I became commissioned in the navy it was always a call by rank. During my post-navy years it had become always Paul, except for more recent years in Germany I was tagged with Paul-Heinrich by a golf group with whom I played during several years. The actual name, Paul Thomas Cook.

At various times on weekends as well, for extra work I cut lawns of the neighbors, at the summer homes of Ms. Agnew, Dr. Satterlee, and Harry Bruno. I also washed windows, chopped wood, painted, worked as a soda jerk at the drugstore, and stock-clerked at Sear's Market, mostly all for twenty-five to thirty cents an hour. I still caddied some. It was a rule at home that I give half of what I made to my parents as a lesson in life, more than as an indication of their dire need for the money. But it was of course useful for the household expenses.

While I worked for some months at Sear's Market, stocking the shelves with all the cartons, cans, and bottles, plus doing other odd jobs handling the produce as needed, I learned that Dick White needed help during the summer in the drugstore. The work at Sear's Market was not really hard or dirty work, but I thought it did not require so much talent and I longed for something to do from which I could learn and have tasks in which I could be more creative. There was another factor that became the catalyst for my deciding to look elsewhere. At Sear's Market in the meat department sauerkraut was sold as well. This sauerkraut was delivered in, and left on display in, a wooden barrel. Each time a customer ordered kraut, Charley, the butcher, would roll up his sleeves and dig deep into the barrel, grasping a large handful of kraut. And, depending upon the amount ordered, he would again lunge into the barrel, always coming up with his hairy forearms dripping with remnants of this sauerkraut. The sanitation aspect of this operation was of no small concern to me and I found it necessary to give wide berth to the smell emitted from that barrel. I applied for the job at the drugstore across the street.

I went to the druggist, Dick White Sr., and simply told him I would like to work at the soda fountain. He knew I was already working at Sear's, so he asked how much I was getting paid there. It was really twenty-five cents an hour, but I told him thirty cents, not only because I wanted to be paid more, but also because I thought work at the soda fountain surely would be a challenge to the self-analysis of my budding creative abilities. He said, "OK, you can start next week!" I was into the job as "soda jerk" for about one week when Dick came to me and, in a friendly voice, said, "Paul, you're doing a great job. But I want you to know that I know you got paid only twenty-five cents at Sear's Market." And he simply walked back to his drug station in the store, never again mentioning anything about this. He knew instinctively that I got the message, which I presumed he meant "be honest even for only five cents."

There were always a lot of interesting people coming into White's Drugstore because everybody had to go there for something, and among the "everybody" were many important or "just plain rich" folks. It was the only store in Montauk at that time where one could buy the items offered. Besides toiletries, patent medicines, and drugs for filling prescriptions one could buy anything from newspapers, film, and bathing suits to sandals, stationery, and sunglasses. Then of course, at the soda fountain where I worked, all kinds of ice-cream creations, sodas, milk shakes, and some sandwiches were available.

One typical summer afternoon in 1942 I had all stools filled with customers ordering various ice-cream sodas and sundaes, banana splits, and milk shakes. Everything was going well until I got an order for a large buttermilk. Well, I had not even heard of buttermilk and I had to say that we didn't have it. "Could I get you something else, like a vanilla milk shake?" He agreed despite his look of disappointment. Normally when serving a lot of customers I would not have time to really see much of the person because of concentration on scooping and mixing, et cetera. But on the buttermilk deal I took longer to look at this man to find out what he would accept. As I finally saw his face, I spontaneously said, "You look just like Fred Allen!" (Famous comedian of radio and stage.)

His reply: "I am Fred Allen. What is your name?"

I told him, "Paul Cook," and as I did, he wrote on a slip of paper: "For Paul, from a satisfied customer [signed] Fred Allen."

There was quite a commotion in the store for a while because of this celebrity in our midst. After Fred sipped his milk shake, he really appeared satisfied and he casually walked to the door.

"Good-bye, Mr. Allen," I said. "Thanks a lot for your autograph."

"It was a good shake. Bye, Paul," and out the door he went.

One evening as I was working the soda fountain at the drugstore, a local man, Mr. Verhaegen, came in for his usual, almost daily, glass of ginger ale. As I was about to prepare the ginger ale, Dick White came over to the fountain from the drugs area and insisted that on this occasion he would take care of the customer. Dick gave Mr. Verhaegen a glass of drink. After about five minutes, he slid off the stool at the counter and hurried out to his car. Dick, I learned, had given him a glass of citrate of magnesia, which looks and tastes very similar to ginger ale but is normally used as a laxative. Most of their joking around had always been bantering in words. In this instance, action spoke louder than words.

I had bought a Kodak camera for taking photos of family and friends, and because the cost of extra prints became too much for me I decided to buy the necessary items like enlarger, pans for developing, dryer, and glossing machine. So, where my older brother Bob had had his chemistry set in our cellar and performed such noble experiments as generating the smell of rotten eggs with the burning of sulphur and powdered iron, I set up shop for print making. Bob had, by this time, joined the U.S. Navy (early 1942). Joe's hobby interests did not require cellar space, and the families of mice running to and fro were enough to keep my sisters out of harm's way, so I had the whole place to myself. Further, as I needed darkness except for the red light, when my mother needed anything for cooking she would just call down and say what she wanted brought to the kitchen when I came up for air. Quantities of apples, potatoes, onions plus the products of home canning such as tuna fish, jams, jelly, bread-and-butter pickles, fruit, cranberry sauce, and the like were stored in the cellar.

Dave Edwards, a photographer, had opened a photo shop in Montauk located just a few steps east of Sear's Market, and he was nice enough to show me how the development of film and printing was done and how enlargements were made. It was great of him to do this, as I had an enormous amount of fun while producing my own prints and at a price I could afford. Dave married Betty Darenberg some years later and moved his business to East Hampton. The photo shop became Johnny's Fish and Tackle Shop. I still have a number of the prints I had made during the mid-1940s in my cellar photo lab.

When I think of developing during these years, it reminds me of the day when, in August 1944, I had just come up from the cellar and my mother and father were preparing to leave the house. I asked where they were going. My mom replied, "Paul, I'm going to the hospital to have a baby." I did not even know that she was pregnant. I was both embarrassed and shocked at the same time. While this might sound impossible, that I could not realize the development of my youngest brother, John, during all the months of this pregnancy, I must explain. First of all, Mom was not slim but built rather on the plump side. Changes due to a pregnancy would naturally be less obvious than otherwise. But more important, my ignorance emphasized an important point in the life of our family. Mom and Dad, and their parents, very rarely talked about anything personal, and it was the case that they stuck to this practice even to the day she walked out the door to have John. My parents had not said a single word to me about the coming of a baby. I was still in a state of shock as they left the house. I kept saying to myself, *A baby! Jeez! It's been seven years since Mom had Joan! And how come I did not know about this before?* By this time, at fifteen years of age, at least I had been given the father–son briefing, so I knew how babies were made. But it had been only a few years earlier that I thought my sisters Gladys and Joan arrived in early morning in a sling hanging from the beak of a stork. This was so typical that we were shielded from all sorts of information that, in my mind, would have been extremely interesting, if not actually necessary or useful. Why was this?

I think that probably parents of most families in the past generations put a lid on anything that had the slightest tinge of sex, scandal, failure, or misbehavior in order to spare anticipated embarrassments. I had heard of stories in the years of my youth, for example, of a young lady running out of the bathroom screaming about bleeding to death because she was never informed of the natural process of a woman's menstrual period. Or as teenagers already many wondered where the stork finds the babies. While the flow of information has fortunately come a long way since those days, it seems that the pendulum on sensitive subjects has perhaps swung sometimes too far in the other direction. But, how much is too much is debatable. At least these days everybody seems to know when a baby brother is on the way months before his birthdate!

Montauk was still very sparsely populated early during this period of the war years. Whether it was shooting a rifle at rats in the dump or at bottles and cans or at loons (ducks) sitting in the bay or hunting with shotguns for ducks or deer in season, it was a usual thing to have a rifle or shotgun. Ammunition could be purchased at a local fish and tackle shop and in the hardware store in East Hampton. We had many enjoyable days with these guns, particularly when duck hunting at Oyster Pond, despite the early and cold morning hours. Even from the back of our home on Edgemere Road we shot at "targets" placed on the hill in the back. When skunks came to the garbage can we fired at them with the shotgun. There were some rats under our house in the crawl space, and they seemed too clever to get caught in the steel traps set for them. I developed a plan. I placed kernels of corn from some dried ears just outside the crawl space to entice the rats. After several minutes two or three of them came cautiously out for the corn and I fired both sides of the double-barreled twelve-gauge shotgun at them. The result was rat splattered all over the side of our cedar-shingled house. Mission accomplished. Unfortunately, I had not considered what the repercussions would be from my "successful rat elimination operation," that is to say, with the use of my double-barreled twelve-gauge shotgun toward the house. Mom came running out. Having heard, and now seeing, what I had done, she immediately and emphatically forbade me to use the guns anymore. "But, Mom!" The guns were not used again.

Ice skating was very popular in winter on Fort Pond just across the road from our house. During these years it seemed that there was always ice thick enough to skate and for ice boating. At any given time fifteen or twenty kids had the whole pond to themselves either just skating or playing ice hockey with tree branches and a flat stone. When it was especially cold, a fire would be built on the edge of the ice and a rubber tire sometimes thrown on for more heat and a lot of smoke. I had hand-me-down skates, which required a couple of extra pair of socks to make them fit. Some of the fishermen with the experience from Nova Scotia had made ice boats and we begged for rides that were thrillingly fast. The ice also served as a shortcut to walk across between Shepherd's Neck and "downtown" instead of taking the long way around on the Montauk Highway or the Industrial Road past the railroad turnaround.

When summers rolled around there were always the rodeos to look forward to at the Deep Hollow Ranch. It was exciting to hear the names of the cowboys called out on the public-address system. They hailed from Wyoming, Texas, Oklahoma, and various other cattle states. But there was always representation from Montauk as well. The Dickinson family, sons Phineas, Frank, and Jack, were regular participants. I vividly recall one of the rodeos (roughly 1940) during a bull-riding contest in which Frank was participating. It seemed things were going OK when suddenly Frank was thrown into the air, and he came down in such a way that a horn of the bull ripped his nose open. A nasty ride, to say the least. I can still see him in the bandages he wore for quite a long time after the rodeo.

During my visit in June 2000 to Montauk I made a stop at the Deep Hollow Ranch just to look at what changes may have taken place. I struck up a conversation with a "cowgirl," that is, a very nice-looking lady named Diane, dressed in western attire, as if in a rodeo. This in itself got me to reflecting on the old days when I described briefly to Diane a rodeo I attended and the bull-riding incident with Frank. She said, "Were you really there and saw that?"

I answered, "Yes, I could not forget it!"

"That was my father, Frank. I am Diane Dickinson Leaver."

"Are you really?" I was astounded. I had never met Diane before, nor had I any knowledge of Frank's children, and I had no idea that a Dickinson was still nurturing the Deep Hollow Ranch. This was for me, and her, quite a coincidence, as fifty years had passed since I had seen any of the Dickinson family. I went to East Hampton High School in the 1941–42 timeframe on the very same Montauk schoolbus as Jack, Frank's younger brother.

Diane then explained more about the ranch and how it had been built up and maintained as a real working ranch. I was very happy to have decided to simply drop in. It was obvious to me that things were going just fine, in the meanwhile, "back at the ranch."

During this period of my life, the majority of my spare time in Montauk was spent with my immediate neighbors Pete LeBlanc Jr., Eddy Ecker, Virgil "Virg" Conway, and Kingman "King" Hodgkiss in scouting, hunting, skating, walking the ocean shore, fishing, caddying, and riding horses Western style.

Montauk Public School—East Hampton High School
(1941–46)

I finished my eighth and final year of elementary school in June 1942 in the Montauk Public School where I had started first grade. I had just turned five years of age in July before the start of school in September 1934. There were at that time only four classrooms, which meant that two grades were taught by the same teacher in each of the classrooms. This allowed us to learn the subjects of each grade twice in each classroom, which in the long run gave us more learning by repetition. There was also a small but very nice library, which I often used. It was well known that in most cases the students from Montauk when entering high school in East Hampton had a very good education. In the entire Montauk Public School there was a total of about eighty to ninety students in any given year during my time. In the first and second grades my teacher was Ms. Schmidt, third and fourth Mrs. Parsons, fifth and sixth Mrs. Mulford, and seventh and eighth Mr. Farrell, who was also the principal of the school.

The school had a large auditorium, which was used for sports, Wednesday assemblies, music classes, and plays, plus various public meetings as needed. Another room was used for displays of materials for learning and as a lunchroom during inclement weather. I remember the teachers always telling us to chew our food (sandwiches brought from home) forty times. I thought in later years that it was obviously good for our digestion process, but on second thought, it also gave the lunchroom teacher on duty a certain period of peace and quiet, as it was rather impossible for us to talk very much during this "forty times chewing" process. Half-pints of milk were delivered each schoolday and available for four cents, which not everyone was able to afford. In some cases I remember teachers paying for the milk for the less fortunate.

During the assemblies all the students and teachers gathered in the auditorium and the first item on the program was the principal winding up the

Victrola by hand and setting the pickup needle on one of those large phonograph records of some music, such as a John P. Sousa march. After this, everyone stood with hand over heart reciting together the Pledge of Allegiance while looking toward the American flag. Then there were recitals of poetry "by heart," a bit of singing by an older student, sometimes reading of some literature, announcements by some of the teachers, group singing of songs such as "Home Sweet Home," "My Bonnie Lies over the Ocean," "Row Row Row Your Boat," "Old Man River," or the likes of these. Often an interesting documentary film was shown with a sixteen-millimeter projector about how an item was manufactured or about mining coal or iron, et cetera. And the assembly ended with the Lord's Prayer, with all participating. The Catholics were not obligated to use the ending most used by the Protestants, and there was never any question about the use of prayer.

I vividly remember the "Christmas plays" in mid-December each year in the auditorium at the Montauk Public School in which all the students, in grades one through eight, participated. In a performance such as a Gilbert and Sullivan operetta every one of the (then eighty) students was involved, most in costumes of cloth or crepe paper created by the teachers and mothers. The music accompanying the strained voices of the stage-frightened kids was always that of the piano played by our music teacher, Mrs. Mulford, who also taught the fifth and sixth grades. A large lighted Christmas tree stood to the right of the stage, and beneath were presents, each of which was destined, after the stage performance, for the student whose name appeared on the "To" tag. The auditorium was always filled with the families of the students and many others of the village, as it was a sure source of comedy and as well a moment of pride for the parents seeing their young ones perform. There were always the missed cues, a forgotten line requiring anxious prompting from the wings, a costume accidentally ripped fallen to the stage floor and the young performer looking wildly about wondering what to do about it, or perhaps one voice of a singing group still singing further when the song was actually finished. The Christmas plays were, at the time I was in grade school, something not to be missed, the event of the year.

I was in the first grade in 1934 and it was the time in my life when Santa Claus was quite real or, let us say, an unsolved mystery. However, on the evening of my first experience with a Christmas play in December 1934, after performing as a Chinese coolie with several others similarly dressed in red-and-yellow crepe and wig pigtails, the Santa Claus mystery began to unravel. Upon completion of the operetta came time for the arrival of Santa Claus from "the North Pole," whose act it was to hand out the gifts from under the tree to each child. Santa's first words to all were, "Ho Ho Ho! Hello, everybody. I just came in on my sled from the North Pole to give you presents. I am in a hurry now because I have to go to many places with my gifts, and my reindeer with sled are waiting outside for me." The presents were then handed out to each as Santa called the names on the "To" tags. Now it was my turn. I was quite pleased to get my present, but I had a question for Santa: "Santa Claus, how can the reindeer pull the sled when there is no snow outside?" I never got a direct answer from Santa, only another, "Ho Ho," and, "I am very busy, Paul." But it was at this moment, for me, that the Santa Claus story began to unfold.

God, patriotism, work, and obedience were integral parts of our education and upbringing. If anyone was chastised by a teacher at school, the parents usually took for granted that the teacher must have had good reason and backed them up. There were not really any serious things happening and not any kind of misdemeanor terribly often, but something like acting up during class was cause for "the ruler" in Mr. Farrell's classes. You had to stand up in the front of the room, and he would give you the twelve-inch wooden ruler and say, "Now hit your hand three times" (or ten times, depending). Of course one could hit lightly, but standing in front of your peers you had to show you were not scared and actually hit harder than the principal would have done. There was also a piece of rubber garden hose hanging in the basement near the coal-fired furnace. This was "a threat" that the students always considered best to avoid. An incorrigible cousin of ours, Freddy, was sent to my mother by her sister, Aunt Mary, who lived in Bridgeport, Connecticut. Cousin Freddy lived in a tough neighborhood and was really always in big trouble. My mother thought she could help Aunt Mary by having Freddy stay with us for several months. The first week, he was caught smoking in the rest room at school and the principal whacked him on the head. Freddy settled down somewhat in school, but it turned out he was too far gone in regards to discipline and more than Mom could handle at home, so she sent him back to Bridgeport. A few years later, Freddy became a ranger in the army, was sent to Korea, and was killed in action.

In September 1942, at the age of thirteen, I started high school, ninth grade, which meant a fifteen-mile bus ride every day from Montauk to East

Hampton. High school opened up a whole new life for me, as I began to meet more new people my age and engage in new and interesting activities. It was almost like being in a large city compared to the village of Montauk. I enjoyed the more advanced subjects of high school and started right away playing all the sports . . . football, basketball, and baseball. And I met a girl in my class, Ruth Osborn from Wainscott, whom I liked very much, and we were together as often as time and distance allowed. In my high school days a girlfriend ordinarily meant having Cokes and hamburgers together, going to a show, attending the school dances, or walking the ocean beach, and for me it was, in fact, this kind of relationship. In reflection on those days it was no surprise that I was confronted with a big problem, because we were of different religions. Although I still liked her very much, because of my upbringing I thought it just would not work out, i.e., in our ultimately getting married. I told her as much, and the next morning she placed a big box of all the things I ever gave to her upon my desk in front of the whole class. What an embarrassment! But I was convinced I had done the right thing. She ridiculed me from time to time during the remainder of the senior school year. (The strange thing is that three years later, when nineteen years of age in the navy, I married a Southern Baptist, against my parents' advice. My decision ultimately, after twenty-four years of marriage, led to a divorce because of problems directly related to our deep convictions and differences in religious beliefs and practices.)

Each afternoon after school we had practice for the sport of the season and in each case the practice ended about six-thirty or so. But since the school bus left East Hampton for return to Montauk about 4:30 P.M. I had to find a way home and it was usual to take the one and only train at 7:30 P.M. (the "Cannon Ball Express": it was not a cannonball and certainly not express). Because I was playing varsity sports and no school bus was available, the school was obligated to get me home. The school had enough funding to pay me thirty-three cents for the cost of each train ride, and that was my only source of money during the school months. If I missed the train for any reason my options were (1) to hitchhike to Montauk, which was difficult since only three or four cars ever went to Montauk at that time; (2) to stay overnight at a schoolmate's home; or (3) to walk fifteen miles home. Most often I took the train; however, many nights I hitched rides or stayed with friends in East Hampton. But still, several times I walked the entire fifteen miles to Montauk, arriving there near midnight. On nights without moonlight, and without streetlights much of the way, through miles of only sand dunes and scrub pines, I could only know exactly where I was by having one foot on the pavement and one on the sand alongside the road. Many of the times during the four years of high school I purposely did not take the train when I could have, because I needed money occasionally for the hamburgers and Cokes, or movie, et cetera, for when Ruth and I could be together. Two nights of train money was needed for the hamburgers and Cokes and three nights of train money to include a film.

When I did get home in Montauk after school, by any of the methods, I still had homework to do, and often there were chores around the house such as emptying ashes or chopping wood for the cookstove in the kitchen, the heater in the living room, and the small stove in the basement for making hot water. Many times I was still up at 1:00 A.M. doing homework, and I can hear my dad now saying, "Paul, when are you going to bed? You'll never be able to get up in the morning."

"Pretty soon," was my answer, but it was not always the case. When morning came, the school bus could be seen, through the front window of our house on Edgemere Road, across the lake (Fort Pond). At this point (when the bus could be seen), there were only ten minutes left before it arrived at our house. I don't know how many times my mom would call up the stairs, "Paul, the bus is coming!" That meant that I had something less than ten minutes to come down, eat something, and dash out as the bus brakes squeaked it to a stop. And on those days Mom would be standing in the doorway with my books and coat as I grabbed them on the run.

I enjoyed the sports very much and I'm sure that it was good for me physically, and mentally as well. I cannot say that I excelled in any one of the sports, but I did my best and learned lifelong benefits of teamwork. Besides the varsity letters that I earned for each sport, I did receive one award to be especially proud of, and that was the Paul Yuska Award, a trophy on which my name was inscribed for 1946, my senior year. Paul Yuska was a very good sportsman, especially in football, but he was killed in a hunting accident. The Paul Yuska Award was established in memory of him for the "most active participant in varsity sports."

The teachers and coaches in the East Hampton High School were of relatively high caliber in my opinion, and I liked them all, except for a bit of reservation on the Latin teacher, Miss Fitzgerald, as she forced me to sing "Adeste Fidelis" in front of the class. I never had a singer's voice, but because I was an altar boy and had to regularly use Latin, she thought of no better way to demonstrate the usefulness of this basic language. While I knew the words very well, I absolutely did not have the courage, from a musical aspect, to do such an injustice to the hymn. She had to practically drag me up front. As if her insisting were not bad enough, all the kids in the class had looks on their faces with a mixture of pity and attempts to keep from laughing. Somehow, with thoughts of Father Brady (who made me sing in the St. Patrick's show), I got myself together by imagining myself at the altar as if at Christmas mass. I had to look outside through the windows often to avoid glimpses of any classmate's expressions. As was part of the lesson . . . *veni, vidi, vici!*

Another of many memorable situations in high school occurred in a history class of Ms. Ebell just prior to the 1944 presidential elections. Ms. Ebell was very popular and an excellent history teacher, very near retirement age. As far as I knew, she was a spinster or widow. In any case, a very nice "little old lady." Our assignment for this class was to arrange debates between political parties (Democrat and Republican). Each of us was to select the party of our choice and debate another student of the opposite party. When it was my turn, as a Democrat in support of Franklin D. Roosevelt, my opponent at one point insisted after five minutes of discussion that my candidate, FDR, was much too old to run again for president. I became rather exasperated, because I really believed in FDR, and therefore reached subconsciously for an example to convince my opponent, the class, and the teacher that my candidate, despite his age, was a very capable person for the job. Then it came out of me so spontaneously: "It doesn't matter how old anybody is if they can do the job; just look at Ms. Ebell. She's old, but she's also a great teacher!" Needless to say, the class roared with laughter, and so did Ms. Ebell, and for at least five minutes. Ms. Ebell was so taken with this and while still laughing herself to death she felt compelled to go the principal's office, where other teachers were to tell them what happened. This class was not the same for the rest of this day's period, and this story was told dozens of times by Ms. Ebell to others in the years to come.

One other incident I must mention involved Mr. Stowell, our high school music teacher. As I was walking in the hall one Monday morning I happened to run across Mr. Stowell, who said, "I want to see you in my office." I had not the slightest idea what he wanted or if I had done something wrong. I had nothing to do with the music department. All my classes were strictly academic, and I played all the sports. But I went after my last class of the day to his office and he told me to take a seat. He got right to the point: "Cook, how would you like to play the bass drum? I think you would do a good job. How about it?"

"But I never played anything musical and do not know a thing about music except to turn on a phonograph."

"I will teach you how to play the drum."

Well, it sounded more like an order than a request, so I took it on rather seriously and decided I had better say yes. "OK, Mr. Stowell. How and when do I start?" Arrangements were made and after a few weeks I found that I could at least beat this drum with acceptable timing and eventually played it very well. What I did not know at the outset is the fact that Mr. Stowell needed someone big enough to carry this bass drum and I was the only one he could find, and available, to carry it.

After Mr. Stowell saw that I was a bit more than big enough to carry the bass drum, he put a snare drum in front of me one day in a music session. I learned to play the snares in the orchestra with some degree of success, and the tympani and cymbals as well. I must say again, even if I have already done so, that I really did not understand the music (notes) very well on the music sheets and had to keep looking at them all the time in order to come in with my percussion instruments at the proper time. Fortunately for me, classmate Sorenson played the snares very well and could cover my snare errors now and then. A highlight of error came one evening when our orchestra performed in a concert for the residents of East Hampton in the movie theater (or Guild Hall, not certain). We were playing a classic, "Lustspiel," and I had to handle the tympani and cymbals. All the while I was doing fine and very intent in counting the measures, et cetera, for when something had to be done in the percussion section. In the middle of this piece, it seemed to me all of a sudden there was complete silence (no instruments heard), and this silence really got my attention. I looked up toward Mr. Stowell, conducting, and he was repeatedly and frantically pointing toward me with a great deal of emotion. I had miscounted some bars along the way and I suddenly realized that seven quick crashes of the cymbals were needed like five seconds ago. I grabbed the cymbals quickly and gave the seven crashes so fast that my classmates recognized the error, began to laugh, and could not properly blow their wind instruments. A stern glance to all by Mr. Stowell brought order once again. It was most probably the case that few in the audience ever knew what had happened and if they did, they would not let on. The city fathers and the proud parents knew their kids were performing for them.

Another big event of my senior year in high school was the senior play. This was a stage production of *Best Foot Forward* in the Guild Hall, East Hampton, October 12, 1945. I was cast as the manager of the movie star. While the play was written as a musical comedy, there were moments during the play when impromptu events resulted in comic acts not in the script. It must be said at the outset that I had just come from playing in a football game in which East Hampton "battled" the Sag Harbor team in Sag Harbor. During the game I was carrying the ball, as halfback, and at some point I was tackled in such a way that my face went on the ground precisely on the thirty-yard line. Since the lines were marked with white lime, my eyes began to burn and it became difficult to see through continuously flowing tears. This was my condition when I went onstage. Although I remembered my lines quite well, it was not always clear just where I was on the stage because of the tearing from the lime. In one instance I was to go to the "actress," but I could not see her. Then I heard one of the cast in a loud whisper: "Paul, over to the left!" I managed to turn as directed and saw only a blurred figure, but as luck had it, it was my "actress." That was "my" best foot forward.

In 1946 our senior class, as a group of about twenty teenagers, made a trip to New York City to discover what else was in the world. Two of the high school teachers who had planned the trip were our chaperones. It was really an eye-opener for most of us, as we had not really very much experience out of eastern Long Island and certainly not in a midtown New York City hotel. We stayed at the Commodore Hotel on 42d Street, which has been in the hands of Hyatt many years now. Guy Lombardo and his Royal Canadians played for many seasons at the Commodore in the Roosevelt Grill. Guy Lombardo was remembered by everyone on New Year's Eve since his music was always aired at that time on the radio. We attended a radio show of Lowell Thomas, the famous newscaster; a movie theater film along with special stage show with Ella Fitzgerald, when she was about eighteen years old, and a Radio City Music Hall show including the Rockettes. And we "from the sticks" were being served by proper waiters. It was great and memorable. Oh, yes! Someone had brought along a quantity of balloons. These were filled with water and selectively dropped from the twentieth or so floor of the Commodore Hotel windows to unsuspecting pedestrians on the sidewalks below. Complaints to the management filtered on down to our chaperones and, from there, inevitable scoldings to the perpetrators.

I had applied for enrollment in a few colleges, where I could possibly have afforded it, upon graduation from high school in June 1946. Months went by without a word because of the flood of applicants, mostly from the multitude of veterans from World War II. While waiting for responses, I took postgraduate courses, starting September 1946, in advanced levels of calculus, trigonometry, radio theory, and laboratory. Then after six months I decided to get on with things because I still had no reply from a college. So I made preparations to join the U.S. Navy, which promised an electronics education equivalent to a year of electronic engineering schooling. This was not the start in life that I had really wanted, or planned, rather college. The very sound of "navy" rang out in pleasant memories of the Fishing Village, so it was a subconscious catalyst. Dad convinced me that it was, under the circumstances, a good method to get under way in life. I would learn a trade in a growing industry. In the years to come, I never had reason to regret this decision.

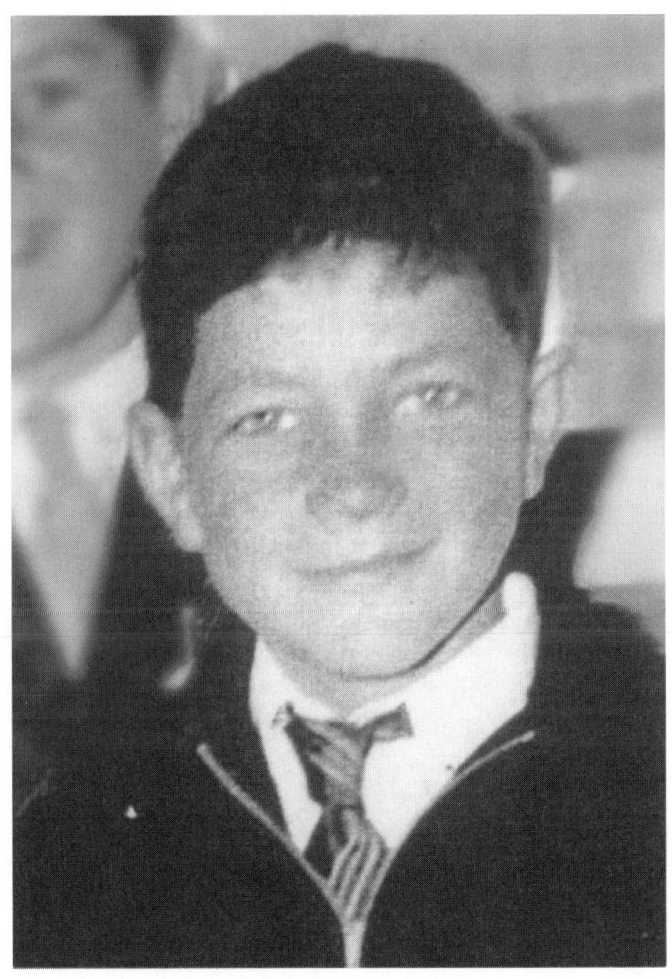

Paul Thomas Cook at age 9 in August 1938.

Shown here is a westward view of the Montauk Fishing Village from the mid-1920s. *Photo courtesy of Montauk Library Historical Archives.*

This is a southwest view of the Montauk Fishing Village from the mid-1930s. *Photo courtesy of Montauk Library Historical Archives.*

Pictured here is Duryea's dock, where fish and lobster were processed for local market as well as for shipment to New York City, as seen in 1934. *Photo courtesy of Montauk Library Historical Archives.*

An example of one of the houses in the village, this is the only original house still on the shores of Fort Pond Bay. Relocated several times due to hurricanes and floods, it is now located on Tuthill Road between the Montauk rail station and Duryea's. *Photo courtesy of Marge Winski.*

Fish Boxes, lobster pots, dock and boats were all typical sights in Montauk Fishing Village during the 1930s.

Fishermen sorting fish caught in Fort Pond Bay was a typical scene in the 1930s.

Robert "Bob" Cook, age 14, worked aboard Captain Lyle Tuthill's boat, *Julia,* **during the summer of 1939.** *Photo is provided courtesy of Robert Cook.*

With a special catch (sturgeon), Captain Tuthill stands alongside the Railroad Dock waiting for the fish to be loaded for their trip to the Fulton Fish Market in New York City. *Photo courtesy of John Tuthill.*

Seen here is Captain Lyle Tuthill aboard his fishing boat *Julia* in 1939. *Photo courtesy of Robert Cook.*

The Fishing Village shore in the aftermath of a hurricane, 21 September 1938. Montauk Manor is on the hill.

Train, near Railroad Dock, could not take villagers out since tidal wave from September 1938 hurricane washed out tracks westward.

Fishing boats were left high and dry as the floodwaters receded.

The original club house of the Montauk Downs Golf Course.

After the original club house burned down, a more modern one was built.

From the left: Paul Cook, Virgil Conway, Frank Tilden, and Eddy Ecker with Carlton Farrell, their scoutmaster, and their principal at Pospisil's Camp.

From the left: John Pfund, Frank Tilden, Paul Cook, and Virgil Conway at Pospisil's Camp in February 1943.

The Boy Scouts of America Montauk Troop held its awards meeting in the auditorium at Montauk Public School, circa 1944. Back row left to right: Carlton Farrell, Colby Pilbro, Eddy Ecker, Bill Conway, Frank Tilden, Vincent Grimes, Bob Darenberg, Paul Cook, John Pfund, Virgil Conway. Front row left to right: Ed Pugh, Bill Lycke, Pete LeBlanc, Dicky Darenberg, Alex Joyce, unknown, Bernard Farrell, Edgar Grimes.

Pete LeBlanc, Ed Pugh, Eddy Ecker, and Paul (taking this picture) playing ice hockey on Fort Pond in 1943.

Paul holds striped bass, his lucky catch, surfcasting, circa 1946.

Alongside Virgil Conway, Paul poses with one of his kittens outside the Cooks' home, circa 1942.

Paul rides Lucky, one of the horses from the stables on the old Montauk Highway, to a water-stop at his home on Edgemere Road.

Walfredo Toscanini (right) holds a conversation afloat a raft at the Montauk Surf Club, circa 1946.

Al Treves heads for the surf.

Walfredo Toscanini (right) and Lois Brenner (center) pushing away from the sides.

Lifeguard Frank Tilden (left) with Locker Attendant Paul Cook.

The Cook family in 1946. From left to right are Robert Theodore, age 22; Gladys Jane, age 12; Joseph William, age 20; Ruth Marie, age 19; Paul Thomas, age 17; Mom—Beatrice Eleanor, age 43; Dad—Theodore William, age 45; John David, age 1; and Joan Cecilia, age 8. (*Photo by Dave Edwards, Lighthouse Photos, Montauk, NY.*)

Training Command, Avionics, Air Squadrons, Commissioning, Deployments, NASA
U.S. Navy (1947–61)

Great Lakes, Illinois; Corpus Christi, Texas; Memphis, Tennessee; Whidbey Island, Washington; Kodiak, Alaska; Treasure Island, San Francisco, California; Oahu, Hawaii; Brunswick, Georgia; Patuxent River, Maryland; Guantanamo Bay, Cuba; Roosevelt Roads, Puerto Rico; Lages, Azores; Halfar, Malta; Rota, Spain; Suda Bay, Crete; Naples, Italy; Blackbush, England; Nice, France; Palma, Majorca; Tripoli, Libya; Nancy, France; Munich, Germany; Sigonella, Sicily; Wiesbaden, Germany; Kindley Air Force Base, Bermuda; Harmon Air Force Base, Canada; Thule, Greenland; Argentia, Newfoundland; Keflavik, Iceland; Port of Spain, Trinidad; Belem, Brazil; Recife, Brazil.

Since I had taken and passed the "Eddy Test" given by the navy late in 1946, I was already officially designated Apprentice Seaman Electronics Technician Mate (ASETM) as I was being sworn into the U.S. Navy at 90 Church Street in the Federal Office Building, New York City, on 11 February 1947. An Eddy Test consisted of a day-long test covering many disciplines, including mathematics, trigonometry, science, physics, electricity, and logic, and general topics such as geography, culture, and history. I was given a set of orders to report to the Great Lakes U.S. Naval Training Center just north of Chicago, Illinois, on Lake Michigan. My orders also read that I was in charge of the twenty-five other recruits from the New York City area during travel by train from Grand Central Station to Dearborn Station, Chicago, and then on to the naval training center. At seventeen years of age I saw this as a tremendous responsibility, since I myself had never before traveled so far outside the New York area. The assignment of this responsibility came from the fact that I was the only high school graduate of the group and was designated ASETM.

I had expected the worst from these particular recruits since they were from the places in Brooklyn, Queens, and the Bronx that had a name for "trouble." I was a bit afraid that one or more of them might try something or other, such as jumping the train when stopping at a large city along the way, which they had talked about. Although very concerned, I did my best to give the appearance of not letting their talk bother me. Eventually they settled down when they realized that their taunting did not get the reaction from me that they expected.

After being sworn in we were given meal tickets for lunch at the Seamen's Institute on the waterfront just before leaving New York City. It was a relatively short walk, and as I approached the institute what I saw already made me wonder what I was getting into. Two bloodied merchant seamen were being carried horizontal, i.e., a seaman at their feet and another holding these seemingly unconscious guys at the shoulders. It was quite obvious that they had been in a brawl somewhere, either in the city or on their merchant ship. This was a sort of introduction, I thought, to being around sailors, ships, and the waterfront. It impressed me to the point that I could not eat after I got into the mess hall of the institute. I felt quite sick to my stomach, having seen those bloody bodies carried in such a way that I thought, *This is the way it is going to be?* Well, of course the navy life turned out in quite a different way. Yet on that day, with the trip to Chicago still in front of me, I was one very apprehensive young sailor.

Our training at Great Lakes Naval Training Center (boot camp) began by all the 120 recruits of our company, from all over the eastern half of the United States, standing in a large room and lined up like so many rows of corn and each standing in a numbered block painted on the floor. We were immediately informed it was a "deck" and not a floor that we were standing on. We were ordered to remove all our "gear" (our clothes) and put it in the cardboard box provided. What we would be wearing in the future would be provided by the navy. Our gear (clothes and any other unnecessary belongings) would be shipped to our home addresses. Then immediately after this, each recruit passed by two hospital corpsmen (one on each side) who injected us with various immunization shots. Several recruits felt faint and collapsed on the spot. Then came basic physicals by doctors including the usual military checks such as, "Turn your head and cough." The next process was to pass by the "small stores" counter, still naked, and receive our ration of "general issue," or GI, clothing, from socks and underwear to shoes and trousers and shirts. Sizes were not of the utmost importance to us at this point, rather just to get something on our bodies and that the items be "big enough." All these items of clothing were literally thrown toward us, to be caught up into the baglike mattress covers to be used later to cover our bunk mattresses in the barracks.

When we got to the barracks assigned we had to fold all the items received from small stores in a very particular way and stow them into our seabags, which would be lashed to the ends of the bunks. This folding and rolling of clothes was to be the nemesis of us all during three months of boot camp, as the chief petty officer in charge of our company seemed never to be satisfied. A routine commenced immediately beginning with a 0430 reveille, at which time the wooden "decks" were scrubbed in the barracks, our bunks had to be made ("tight," no wrinkles), and we marched off to "chow" (a meal) in the mess hall. All day there were various drills (marching, rifle, semaphore flag signals, knot tying, seamanship, live firing, fire fighting, physical training exercises, boat rowing, sports, et cetera).

What I had learned as a Boy Scout, as a native of the "Fishing Village," and from my activities in high school all contributed to my preparedness in the U.S. Navy. Semaphore signalling and knot tying I had learned from scouting, seamanship and rowing were part of my early life on the water, and I was a very active participant in the high school sports program. This has made me a believer in having all children, to the greatest extent possible, engaged in youth programs in and out of the normal schooling process. The benefits can be great, somehow, somewhere, in later years.

It turned out that I was the only high school graduate in the entire company of 120 recruits (seventeen to nineteen years old) and was therefore assigned as the Recruit "Acting Chief Petty Officer," or ACPO. With this, I was given a bunk now in a separate room along with three others who were deemed part of the recruit staff. It was a very, very unusual experience for me in that during the night, on a number of occasions, some recruits would come to my bunk crying. They had never been away from home before and, being extremely nervous, were unable to cope with their new situation. Several had nervous crying problems, but others experienced bedwetting. Out of the 120 recruits there were seven or eight who could not psychologically manage the military environment and were given medical discharges. Once again, like on the train from New York, as ACPO now, I knew I had to maintain my composure and do my best to be strong enough mentally and physically to cope with other recruits' problems, which could just as well have been my own. But I learned that when given responsibility I somehow had also been given the strength necessary, through the navy's faith in me, to do the job.

At any given time at boot camp there were about ten companies of recruits, and there was always competition in marching drills, boat races, et cetera, at the battalion and regimental levels. My company won regimental and battalion flags for both marching and boating. During the marching drills the ACPO wore a .45-caliber pistol at the waist while all the other recruits carried rifles. This was a decided advantage in being ACPO. I had to learn the handling of the rifle, dismantling and remantling, and firing at the range, but in marching drills the "badge of authority" for the ACPO was the forty-five.

After completion of recruit training we were ready for OGU (Out Going Unit), which was a status of waiting during a week or so to be assigned to a specific ship, air squadron, or naval station. Since I was already designated ASETM it was, to me, a matter of course that I would be going to the electronics school that happened to be also located at the Great Lakes Naval Training Center, where we just finished recruit training.

One morning a boatswain mate posted a list of twenty or so names on the board, just received from the Bureau of Naval Personnel, Washington, D.C., for assignments to various ships and squadrons. This list also included ten names for the electronics school. My name, oddly enough, was not on the list, but it was supposed to be, or so I thought. So when the boatswain said for all those assigned to the electronics school to fall in and march to the school, some two hundred yards' distance, I put my seabag on my shoulder and marched off with the others to the school. I was assigned a bunk and set myself up for classes. After the third day, at noontime, there was an announcement on the public address system, "Cook, lay down to the MAA [Master at Arms] shack, on the double." I could not imagine what I was being called for and with such urgency or if I had done something wrong. As I entered the MAA "shack" (office), I reported to the chief petty officer at the desk as I had learned to do in our recruit training: "Cook reporting, sir!"

The chief jumped upright from his seat shouting, "Cook! Where the hell have you been? Do you know where you are supposed to be? In Corpus Christi, Texas! Three days ago! Get your seabag, put on your dress blues for travel, pick up your train tickets and meal tickets at Personnel, and get to Dearborn Station in Chicago for the next train to Corpus Christi via Houston." This came as a very big shock to me.

It was also a very hot day, just before the 4th of July weekend. When the chief told me I had to go to Personnel, I thought it would be quite all right if I used the bicycle that was standing idle just outside the office window. Well, this was another wrong assumption on my part, and it was not to be the last. At this point the chief could hardly maintain his composure from the thought of my having the nerve now to use his two-wheeler and he only sputtered something to the effect, "Get your ass out of here and walk!"

My name was not destined to be on the list for Shipboard Electronics School. On the day after I packed up from OGU, another list had been posted and with only one name on it for that day: "Cook, Paul Thomas ASETM transfer to the Aviation Electronics Technician Mate School, Ward Island, Corpus Christi, Texas." What had happened was that one of the sailors scheduled to attend the aviation school became sick and a quota for this week had to be filled. The only sailor available and eligible, academically, was me. The navy moved me like a pawn on the chessboard. I was now destined to become an aviation electronics technician and not shipboard electronics technician. I was suddenly in the aviation branch of the U.S. Navy. This transfer occurred just on the first of July 1947. My state of shock was compounded by the fact that through summer friends in Montauk I had arranged a date with a girl in Oak Park, Chicago, for the 4th of July. Since I was literally whisked out of town to Texas, I had no way to contact her to explain the situation. The fickle finger of fate had irrevocably diverted my life's path. As it eventually turned out, to a life on the international scene.

The first really repulsive experience in my budding career occurred in the men's room of Dearborn Rail Station in Chicago. A civilian man of middle age approached me, very closely, and asked if we could not "get together." I had not even so much as read fiction about gays, but now I was boldly accosted by a person whom I had observed lurking between the urinals. I was at the moment scared but was also filled with the strongest feeling of aversion. There was never anyone who told me what I might expect on such occasions, much less what to do about it. But in retrospect I see that such despicable acts require no special training. It is simply a matter of immediate rejection and departure.

The military were often sent traveling long distances by train in pullman (sleeping) cars in those days. The porter put my seabag in the baggage car of the train. I was assigned a sleeper bunk and I was on my way to Texas, which was most of a two-day trip. I got to like the service in the dining car as I ordered what I liked and all I had to do was give the porter some of the meal tickets given to me at the personnel office. After a twenty-four-hour period of travel, I began to realize that the meal tickets were about finished with still many hours to go. I had paid little attention to the prices against the worth of the meal tickets. When I reached Houston I no longer had meal tickets and, unfortunately, had no money. The fifty-dollar-per-month from the navy pay was spent travelling on a two-week home leave to Montauk during the time between boot camp and OGU.

It did not dawn on me that I had to change trains at Houston since the train from Chicago continued on to Galveston. But when I did learn that I had to get a train to Corpus Christi and was about to do so, I realized that I did not have my seabag. It was still in the baggage car of the train now under way to Galveston. I, furthermore, realized that I had also left my sealed orders of transfer and my wallet in the compartment at my bunk in the pullman car. My problems were compounding. I had assumed wrongly at the OGU about the school. I used up all my meal tickets with another day to go. My seabag, wallet, and orders were on their way to Galveston. And this girl in Chicago? I had just time to talk with the station agent in Houston about my belongings in the train bound for Galveston before the train for Corpus departed. The agent said he would send a telegram to the station agent in Galveston and do his best to retrieve all my belongings and send them to the naval station in Corpus. He was very kind and told me not to worry. Ten days later, in fact, all the items were sent to me at Corpus.

In the meantime, on the train to Corpus from Houston I met a group of marines from Cherry Point, North Carolina, who shared their meal tickets, so I did not have to go hungry. But the worst was not over. As I arrived in Corpus Christi, Ward Island, late in the evening, I was directed to the Officer of the Day (OOD) at the Aviation Electronics School. The OOD was at a desk looking down, reading a newspaper. As trained, I said, "Cook, reporting for duty, sir."

The OOD continued to read his paper but raised his hand to receive my set of orders (automatically, I supposed, for all the many recruits who must be checking in for school). After about five seconds: "Your orders, Cook!"

"I don't have any orders, sir."

This got his attention, as he now dropped the newspaper on the desk and looked up. "Where are your orders?"

"They're on a train to Galveston, sir."

The OOD was now wide awake and trying his best to keep under control. "Let me see your ID card, Cook!"

"It is in the train, too, in my wallet, sir. Everything went on the train to Galveston." Since all the navy clothing we wore had our name in stencil, I could only show the OOD my name, as stenciled inside my hat and shirt, "Cook, P. T."

His final words to me that night on 3 July 1947: "You will be restricted to the base until we have a copy of your orders and ID card in hand."

I was assigned a bunk in one of the barracks. My only clothes for the following week were those that I wore, woolen dress blues, in the July heat of Texas.

On the first night in the barracks it was difficult to sleep because of the problems and I wondered where all of this would ultimately lead. Had I made a huge mistake in entering the navy? Would I have gotten into these kinds of problems if I had gone to college or in any other direction in life? Perhaps I should have waited even more months after high school graduation for an answer to my requests for entrance to colleges. After all, I did, in fact, receive a letter from Oneonta State Teachers College just four weeks after joining the navy stating: "You have been enrolled in the Fall Term at Oneonta State Teachers College." I could have fallen through the floor when I received this letter. There was nothing I could do about it. I was in the U.S. Navy, for better or for worse, until twenty-one years of age. Actually, I would have preferred to attend a college or university with emphasis on sciences, so the letter from Oneonta was received, in afterthought, with mixed emotions. I told myself several times that I must forget this whole thing because I was now property of Uncle Sam and I had to get on with the navy's Aviation Electronics School.

But also on this first sleepless night I had occasion to visit the "head" (rest room/toilet), and on such occasions we were always directed in boot training to wear our GI wooden shower shoes, with canvas overstraps. These shower shoes were usually referred to as "go-aheads" because you could only walk in them when going forward. If you stepped backward they would usually come off. Without my seabag these shower shoes were one of many items I had to do without for several days. This night as I walked into the head, at each step I imagined that someone had failed to sweep out the candy wrappers or whatever from the day before. After "lights-out," only the red night-lights were left on, and they provided only the dimmest light to see anything but where you are going. I was not bothered. Not until the next morning at least. It was only then that I saw the carcasses of about twenty giant cockroaches. I had never seen a cockroach before in my short life, and the thought that I had stepped on these creatures during the night made me quite sick. I began to imagine that during the night they would be crawling on my bed, inducing further sleeplessness. I recall sending a letter sometime later to my parents and drawing a sketch of a roach on my pillow. The roaches were everywhere. They even ate all the glue off the postage stamps in my locker. This was my very first encounter with cockroaches, but it was not to be the last in subsequent assignments. I abhor the sight of them to this day.

In the first five months in 1947 I learned a lot in a very very short time that was to stay with me for a very long time. Never assume or take for granted anything; listen to persons of experience and keep control over important personal belongings.

I had just gotten through a pretty hectic period of learning what life in the U.S. Navy was all about and now had some "off-base free time" away from the avionics school routine. One weekend I met up with an older sailor, Frank, also a student in this school, who suggested that we go to a certain outside bar and restaurant in Corpus Christi. He indicated it was an interesting place. Interesting it was. During the first hour or so we were sitting at a table on a dirt floor, peacefully having a drink and snack. To my left were some civilians, one of whom threw some ice cubes at this guy at a table to my right, apparently to annoy him. Then one of the ice cubes accidentally hit me on the left side of my head. I looked at this fellow throwing the ice, and noticing my reaction, he started to throw ice at me. The older acquaintance of mine made a comment to the ice thrower. All of a sudden the latter turned his table over. It seemed that this was a signal for several others to do the same thing. My reaction then was to clear out, and while doing so I saw the owner of this establishment pointing a .38-caliber pistol toward the middle of the crowd. I found my way to the perimeter of this entire scene as SPs (Shore Patrol) from the naval air station commenced to stream into the chaos. This was not my cup of tea and it was another one of those lessons learned, to be more selective in choice of entertainment.

One would think that I had had enough of this older sailor, Frank, from our acquaintance at the ice-throwing contest in Corpus. But some weeks later, he suggested we visit his hometown, Georgewest, Texas, and spend the weekend. We hitchhiked northward from Corpus and were lucky to get a ride to our destination. Georgewest turned out to be a real-live cowtown. It was like in the movies: wooden graying buildings with false fronts and unpaved streets with rising clouds of dust from the few cars and horses. I got a room in a hotel that could have been used for a *Gunsmoke* program, later a popular long-running western TV show. Beside a single bed in my room were a nightstand with basin and pitcher and a slowly rotating overhead fan hanging from the ceiling. The bathroom was down the hall for all the hotel guests. Frank contacted me to say we would go to the barn dance that night. This affair was really in a barn, straw, cowboys, and the stomping feet of horses nearby. We were in this barn no longer than an hour when a fight started, it seemed, over some girl sought by two cowboys. In no time there appeared the badged sheriff, gun in hand. The next morning saw me on the highway, thumb out, for the next ride back to Corpus Christi. Frank and I remained friends, as he was actually a likable guy, but the friendship continued mostly on base, at the swimming pool, or when lifting weights.

I continued study of aviation electronics at Ward Island, Corpus Christi, until the end of 1947, when the entire school was relocated at the Naval Air Technical Training Center (NATTC),[*] Memphis, Tennessee, and there continued the one-year-long course until graduation in mid-1948. I was then promoted to Aviation Electronic Technician Mate (AETM) Third Class. This rating name was changed shortly after to be known as Avionics Technician (AT), so I was then an AT3.

Immediately after completing the avionics school, mid-1948, I was assigned as an instructor but, of all things, an instructor in Aviation Crash Fire Fighting School. Instructors were very scarce, and four were needed at the U.S. Navy's Airman School, also located in Memphis. For one and a half years I was on a team of instructors who set fires to discarded aircraft

---

[*] The NATTC is located near the town of Millington, which is about twenty miles north of Memphis, and adjacent to the NATTC is the naval air station (NAS). Since hardly anyone outside of Tennessee recognizes the name Millington, the standard address for both NATTC and the NAS is Memphis.

and taught hundreds of young airmen, every week, how to fight aircraft fires and how to retrieve crewmen from the burning aircraft. These airmen sailors would be assigned to aircraft carriers and naval air stations or wherever naval aircraft operated. We presented a week-long series of classroom lectures and demonstrations followed by participation at the "fire mat," where we poured gallons of oil and gasoline on the aircraft, then set it off with a torch. There was a really big and hot fire engulfing the aircraft that produced a huge plume of rising black smoke visible for a few miles. Each student was required to go into the fire area with an instructor and systematically douse the fire, using various methods. Sometimes in fear, the students would drop their hose, leaving the instructor alone to handle the fire. We had been so thoroughly trained that we did not have serious mishaps, but the lone instructor had to really concentrate on the task to ensure safe extinguishment. I knew that fire fighting was not the job of a trained electronics technician, yet it was important, in my mind, to have all personnel well trained in fighting fires, especially when operating aboard aircraft carriers at sea.

But after the one and a half years of fire-fighting instructor duty, there was an inspection team from Washington who learned that avionics technicians were being used as "fire fighters." We were immediately reassigned to the Airman School for duty as instructors. I was assigned as aviation physics instructor, which I liked very much. I continued instructor duty in physics until near the end of 1950, when I was promoted to AT2 (Avionics Technician Second Class).

I had made a decision, by myself, in high school that it would be unwise to think in terms of mixed marriage. Although I was advised now, by my parents, that it was not a good thing for me to marry a girl of a different religious faith, I thought that I knew better in this case. At the ripe age of nineteen, still very much Catholic, I was married on 10 June 1949 to Mildred Pauline Maddox, a Southern Baptist, in Memphis. This religious difference was to become a definite hindrance to our relationship as the years passed.

We had met at the USO in Memphis, Tennessee, and continued to see each other there, at picnics, at her sister Dorothy's home, and naturally at Milly's own home, where her mother lived mostly alone during this time. Milly's father operated a drag-line machine very often in foreign countries. Later he worked his dragline in various areas around Memphis with help from prisoners as oilers on the machines. These prisoners were picked up each day from the Shelby County Penal Farm. The mother and father were "many miles" apart in that she was an extremely religious Southern Baptist and he seemed never to have wanted any kind of religion or a "normal" family life. He was always drinking excessively and most probably died because of it before retirement age. I really just tolerated the visits to Milly's home when her father was around, because of my experiences in the unsettling atmosphere there. But of course I had my mind set on marriage with Milly, not only a very nice person but also an attractive Miss Memphis, who had just won a competition in a hairstyling contest.

I had often gone on liberty (free time after work) into Memphis, several nights each week, like most of the sailors from the training center and naval air station. The main transportation was by bus from Millington to Memphis along Highway 51. Sometimes I would hitchhike or get a ride with one of the more senior petty officers who had a car. Milly did not always know when I would, or could, come to Memphis, but it might have been nearly every night after we had known each other for a year or so. Well, one of those nights, when I arrived in Memphis I went to Milly's home and she and her mother nearly dropped on the spot at the sight of me. Why? On the front page of the Memphis newspaper, the *Commercial Appeal,* on that day there was an account of an accident in which a man was killed. It read something like this: "Avionics Technician Paul Cook, an instructor from the naval training center, was killed last evening in an auto accident on Highway 51 near the Loosahatchie River." I had not seen the newspaper yet, so was unaware of the article. It happened that there was another Paul Cook, avionics technician, at the training center and of course Milly and her mother thought that I was the one who no longer existed!

After marriage, with me an AT3 with about $150.00 salary per month, the first of many places we lived during my navy career was at 1223 Tutwiler, Memphis, Tennessee. I had one month's rent of forty-nine dollars paid in advance and two bags of groceries on the wedding day. There was no reception, flowers, or rice. We were to live a very sparse life financially for several years. Even some of the furniture, such as it was, tables, bed frames, and lamps, I built myself. Without a car, our transport was by foot or bus during the first two years of marriage.

It was in my earliest days of assignment in electronics schooling at Memphis that I had read about the possibility of a certain quota of enlisted men being considered for a special program for entrance into the U.S. Naval Academy. It did not simply require filling out an application. One would have to face a board of senior officers for interviews, take tests in various disciplines, have personnel records reviewed, and undergo medical and dental examinations to go through. The usual path for entering the naval academy was by selection in one's home district through recommendation of senators and congressmen. I had no special connection in Montauk with which to facilitate such an approach.

As it turned out, after all the interviews and tests were given I was one of about 50 airmen out of the 10,000 at the naval air technical training center who were selected for final consideration for the academy. I was very upbeat about the whole program, since I had made it this far. All I had to do now was take my medical and dental exams. I sailed through medical without any problem. The very last step was dental, and I would be home free, so to speak. I lay back in the dental chair, and as the dentist began the checkup I began to hear this "hmmm, hmmm" sound. From my experiences with doctors it meant, generally, the doctor was not certain at the moment what to make of the situation or had found something that pointed to bad news. Without discernible comment the dentist walked across the room and opened a page in the "dental bible," resulting in one more but emphatic "hmmpf!" I supposed this meant trouble, but it did not really register; that is, the severity of his now-discernible words was devastating. The book he quoted stated that "candidates for the Naval Academy must, among other things, have four opposing molars." I was missing two molars in this area. All of a sudden I was disqualified for the academy.

I kept thinking all the weeks after this dental episode that because of missing two miserable teeth I was being chastised out of this naval academy program despite my qualifications in all other respects and requirements. I thought further that if I had entered the academy by the normal political or other route and broken these two teeth in a football game I would not be thrown out of the navy. Why me? But I did not give up so easily.

There was another kind of officer program that I applied for in the following year. It was the so-called Seaman to Admiral Program. If selected, I would go through the Officer Candidate School (OCS) in Newport, Rhode Island. Again I went through all the required steps of tests, interviews, and examinations. Again dental was the last step. I tried this program because I was informed that the requirements in dental were not as stringent as for the academy. The dentist (a commander), after referring to "the dental bible," said that I could pass on this program if I got a bridge to handle the molar problem. The academy wanted all natural teeth; this program allowed bridges. OK. The commander fitted me with a bridge after a few dental sessions, and this bridge contained a considerable amount of gold, as he was quick to remind me. It was not usual to do so much dental work with gold in the navy because of costs. Now I was set to go. But wait. It's not over yet.

When I went home that evening, I had taken the bridge out of my mouth because it was a little uncomfortable, as I was not used to such things. I wrapped it into some tissue and laid it on a shelf in the bathroom. I went to work the next day and was into my routine teaching. At some point I suddenly realized that I forgot my gold bridge at home and I got very concerned because this was my "ticket" to becoming a commissioned officer. I got a buddy to take over my class and I nearly "ran" home, which was near the base. I went into the bathroom. The tissue was gone. I went white, I am told, as I asked my wife what happened to my teeth. She did not know what I was talking about. "The gold bridge I wrapped in tissue and put on the shelf last night. Where is it?"

"I did not know about your teeth. I just cleaned the bathroom and threw all the waste into the garbage can this morning."

I ran to the garbage can in the backyard. Empty. The garbage truck had already been there, and by now I understood that my gold bridge must be in the city dump!

It was quite clear that my only recourse was to make another visit to Dental. I got an appointment about two weeks later, and again I lay in the chair awaiting a dentist. But it was to be yet another case of misfortune for me that I was looking up into the face of the same dentist commander who had fitted me with the gold bridge just days ago. When he asked what he could do for me my answer was, "I lost my bridge and I came to get fitted for another one to be in the OCS program."

I will never forget his look as he towered over me and what he said with a tone of disgust: "Yes, Cook. I'll fit you for another bridge. In about five years, after I take care of another thousand men who really need teeth just to chew their food. The navy budget doesn't have enough money to keep supplying you every week with gold fixtures." I simply "crawled" out of the Dental Clinic as the realization of what this all meant to me sank in.

I talked to my division officer. I made trips to the Personnel Office and libraries, inquiring about various officer programs. The only possibility for me now was through the LDO (Limited Duty Officer) Program, referring to one coming up through the ranks and being a specialist in some field such as, e.g., electronics, supply, engineering, avionics, et cetera. For me that meant that I would have to have ten years of service at the time that I would be commissioned, if selected. This was 1949, so ten years meant it would be *possible* for me to be an LDO in 1957, because I joined in 1947.

Our first child, James Anthony (Jim), was born on 28 March 1950 at the Naval Hospital Memphis (Millington), Tennessee. Jim brought a lot of pleasure, and of course those days were mixed with some anxiety because of our inexperience as parents. We had just begun to learn how to handle a baby, so there were times of not knowing what to do in certain circumstances. For example, during the first week poor Jim had diarrhea continuously for several days. We brought him to the hospital. The doctor learned that twice as much powder as prescribed was being used for Jim's milk formula. We did not realize that we had purchased a "concentrate" instead of the "normal" version at the commissary.

I remember carrying Jim on my shoulders, which he loved, as we walked into the village of Millington for groceries or went to the base theater for a movie. We had to walk or take a bus everywhere we went.

After marriage and having Jim we moved into navy housing in Millington. Television was in its infancy and since money was not plentiful in a sailor's pocket, I told my wife we could go to the base theater for only ten cents each, but I would first find out what was playing. I phoned the base operator, thinking that she would probably know. When I asked, "Could you please tell me what is playing at the base theater tonight?" she answered, "Call *Northside seven-seven-seven.*" I presumed she did not know and gave me the number to call to find out. This large naval station was split into two parts by a public road running east and west, so that there were the north side and south side of the naval station. Therefore, I dialed 777 on the north side. The fire department answered the phone, and I was promptly asked where the fire was. I imagined I had dialed the wrong number and apologized to the fireman on the phone. I redialed 777 Northside, and again it was the fire department. I was chastised for calling this number, meant only for emergencies. I called the base operator once again and told her she gave me the wrong number to find out about the movie. She told me that she had given me the name of the movie. I said to her that I did not get the name of the movie but was told to call Northside 777.

"Cook, *that* is the name of the movie, *Call Northside 777.*"

In an effort to bring in a little more money into the household, I accepted a job involving the selling of vacuum cleaners. A man, Mr. Bell, told me if I would go around knocking on doors and get a man and wife to agree for an appointment with him in their house for a vacuum cleaner demonstration, he would give me ten dollars. I had to do this in the evenings, because of my work at the training center. Well, I did get Mr. Bell quite a number of appointments, and he did pay me the ten dollars each time. However, for every place where I got an agreement I must have knocked on the doors of thirty houses. And all those who answered the door were not so pleasant. In fact, doors were rather frequently slammed in my face. After a very few months I was getting rather irritated and downhearted at averaging only ten dollars every one or two days. This was each evening for two to three hours, after a long day instructing at the base.

Interestingly enough, the success rate of Mr. Bell was exceptional. He was a genuine showman in the scientific approach during his vacuum cleaner demonstrations. The two demos with the most mouth-gaping results were the one with the steel ball and the other with a piece of pure white cloth filter material. He had obtained a steel ball that was just a bit too large to actually get sucked up into the hose. He first let the couple hold the ball in their hands. "Very heavy!" was always the exclamation. Mr. Bell knew his physics and especially the Bernoulli's Principle, the same principle that gives lift to an aircraft and brings two ships slamming their sides together if too close to each other when moving on the seas. This steel ball would have been sucked up to the mouth of the hose and stayed there with practically any vacuum cleaner.

He would next ask the couple if they thought they were sleeping on a clean mattress. "Well, of course," was the typical answer.

Mr. Bell would then say, "If you agree, Mr. and Mrs. Jones, going into your bedroom, I will show you that this vacuum cleaner will pick up a lot of dirt from your mattress."

The housewife's jaw drops in disbelief now, as Mr. Bell places his pure white filter cloth at the intake of the cleaner. He went along the seams all around at the edges of the mattress and finally removes the filter. What was pure white is now an absolutely black filter. Again, nearly any vacuum cleaner filter of that type will usually come out no less black. As long as I was associated with Mr. Bell, he scored 100 percent in sales with these demos. He had told me in the beginning, "If I can get into the house when both the man and wife agree to an appointment, I will make a sale."

One evening in a grocery store while I was waiting in a slow-moving line to cash one of Mr. Bell's ten dollar checks, a man in back of me struck up a friendly conversation. He got around to asking what I did. I told him about the navy and that I sold vacuum cleaners in the evening to make a bit more money. "Here is the check for yesterday," I said as I displayed it to him.

Almost immediately he asked if I would like to work for him on some evenings and on weekends: "If you can sell a vacuum cleaner, you can sell anything." He understood that I was getting the "foot in the door" for Mr. Bell.

From then on, for the next year or so, I did make considerably more than the ten dollars every couple of days. The new work was selling furniture and appliances on Summer Avenue in Memphis. The name of the store was Railroad Salvage.

Railroad Salvage started out in business selling items damaged in shipments on the railroad. When the amount of damaged items became so scarce, the owner supplied his store with middle-priced new furniture and appliances intended for middle- and lower-income families. This in itself was quite all right, naturally, but he wanted to keep the "connection" with the idea of salvaged items so that the customers could believe this was what they were getting and therefore must be less expensive. What he did was have about one-half of the store assigned to "salvage items," but they were not really salvaged. One of the regular salesmen, not part-time like myself, carried around with him a hammer and a screwdriver. He would slam his hammer on the edge of a select chair, table, or chest or door of a machine or scratch it with the screwdriver. This purposeful damage did not distract from the usefulness of the item, but it was enough to mark the item in big red grease pencil: "Damaged $25 Off." But even after the damage, the price to the customer was still the normal price used even if the item were undamaged. I tried my best to sell only the new items that did not get the hammer. But even then, knowing how this store's management operated, I finally decided that it was not for me. I learned so much about people and ways of life, with both the door-knocking routine and the salvage store, where the customers were being railroaded.

Jim was very curious about things and investigating even at a young age. He had a great imagination. One day he spread the two tips of a lady's hair pin and stuck them into a 110-volt socket. Although he burned his fingers badly because of the current running through the hair pins, which got as red as a toaster element, it was fortunate that he was not between the high side of the voltage and ground. Another time when a couple of years older, he wondered what would happen if he stuck his finger inside the guard piece of an electric fan. After running water from the faucet over his very bloody hand, I was greatly relieved to see that his fingers were still there, although with deep cuts and profuse bleeding. In both cases a doctor visit afforded care to the wounds.

There was not too much opportunity in my earlier life for formal recreation for financial reasons (I never had any skiing, tennis, trips to special places, et cetera, et cetera, only picnics in a park or a show occasionally). But I always managed to make a trip home with my family to see my parents in Montauk once a year, despite our meager resources. And there was hardly ever an uneventful round-trip to Montauk. The most eventful was early on in the late summer of 1950. I had not yet owned a car because of the obvious reason: lack of funds. However, on this occasion a sailor acquaintance, George, offered to rent me his car for $200 to drive to Montauk. Things went quite smoothly from Memphis through most of Tennessee and Virginia, but on a rainy afternoon in one of the towns my wife, Milly, exclaimed what a beautiful house there was off to the right. I looked. But I looked a bit too long, as I noticed too late that a car ahead of us had braked for a traffic light. As I crashed into his rear, the engine hood of my rented car popped up and steam commenced to rise from the radiator. Being unfamiliar with the surroundings, I did not know which way to go or what to do at the moment. I was thinking that I needed to get to a garage to assess the damage. What I knew for sure was that the radiator was leaking water and the hood stayed opened up because of the broken latch. Under these conditions I could not get on a highway, not for long. As it turned out, a local man who had apparently seen the accident suddenly appeared with a handful of baling wire. He said, "Son" (I was only nineteen years old), "yore gonna need this ere wahr!" He further, with a heavy southern drawl, informed me that according to his experience the amount of radiator water leakage would require I stop about every fifty miles to refill the radiator. And as he wired the hood for me to stay put, although still precariously open, he said, "Son, take 'er easy and you'll git there."

Well, I took it easy and stopped about every hour, as he predicted, for water refill, when the steam started to hiss out again. This program was easy enough to manage until I ran out of water in the middle of Manhattan. Anybody who has ever driven in midtown New York City knows full well that gas stations are not to be found, at least not at all where you need one. I was somewhere between 35th and 42d Streets when the steam from the overheated radiator signaled me to stop. Aside from no service stations, there is also no obvious place to get water and, in addition, if there is water, what do you put it in? I walked a few blocks until I came upon a parking lot. Near a wall was a discarded empty, rusty five-gallon can. I picked it up and walked until I saw a bar and grill. I dared to go in and headed for the rest room to fill the can. The bartender started to shout at me, "What the hell are you doing walking in here with a rusty old bucket?"

My main thought was of water for my car, to get out of the city, but as I looked around I now noticed this was a very nice bar and restaurant and the customers were well dressed. My defense: "I did not realize what a very nice place you have here. I urgently need water for my car radiator. I am in the navy and on home leave to see my folks in Montauk."

"Oh, you from Montauk? I go fishing out there every summer. OK, hurry up and get your water, but get that damn bucket out of here!"

I finally got to Montauk and then spent a few days of my leave trying to find some garage not too busy with summer tourists to weld my radiator to stop the leaking. With this ultimately accomplished and our visit with my parents over, we headed back to Memphis. Two days later in the Great Smoky Mountains near Chattanooga, Tennessee, while driving in the rain around a right-hand curve the car began to slide, on the wet blacktop, to the left and went into the oncoming lane. We rather severely slammed into the side of an oncoming car, demolishing the car I had rented. Jim was sleeping on the backseat of our car, and my wife was sitting in the front on the passenger side. Jim was thrown onto the floor in the back, unhurt. My wife and I were bruised but mostly badly shaken. The cause of the accident was clear. The tires on the car I drove were completely bald. Inexperienced, I had paid no attention to this when I agreed to rent the car from the sailor, George. As we went around the curve on wet pavement, the bald tires simply did not hold and we crossed the line. I began to think this situation out. George surely knew there was no tread on those tires, yet he let me take the chance with my family on 2,000 miles of driving. Another lesson in life: make sure of all the safety features about a car as well as things and situations in the home or at work.

The sheriff who arrived on the scene of the accident could not have been more helpful to us. He had the car towed away to a garage in the nearest town. He took my wife and son, Jim, and me, along with all the items we had in the car, to his office.

Next the sheriff arranged a bus trip for us from there to Memphis. The box containing all our personal items was too large to handle on the bus, so he had it sent by freight to our home address, which at that time was in a navy housing area at the training center in Millington. Jim was still young enough that he needed to drink milk from a baby bottle. I bought a can of evaporated milk in a nearby store and diluted it with an equal amount of water. He drank it hesitantly but eventually emptied the bottle. We had to wait for some time in a hot, dirty, and fly-ridden room to take the Greyhound bus. We were also uncomfortable having to travel in the same clothes we wore in the car. Our clothing appeared especially dirty because the grime from the accident showed up so much more on my white uniform and the white shorts that my wife wore. When we finally walked into the bus, the other riders must have thought that I had been on a drunk with my wife and had not properly cared for the baby.

Upon our return to Memphis the owner of the car came to our home and asked how badly the car was damaged. He was referring to the radiator and hood damage about which I had written him from Montauk. I had not time yet to inform him that his car was not only damaged now but demolished. But when I told him about the latest accident, his quick reaction was, "I'm glad it's demolished and not just damaged. I needed to get another car; that one was too old. Now the insurance company has to buy me another car." Not a word about whether anybody was hurt. And he still demanded the $200.00 despite the case of his renting me an old car, with bald tires. What a miserable trip, but certainly one to learn from!

Then late in 1950 I was transferred from Memphis Naval Air Station to Whidbey Island Naval Air Station, Washington State, into a patrol squadron (VP-4), whose mission was low-altitude mining and bombing but was also capable of electronic countermeasures and radar photography. The squadron had twelve Lockheed P2V-W Neptune aircraft, and I was assigned for duty as aviation electronics technician for maintenance and repair of radar, navigation, and communication equipment and as a flight crew member for radar and electronic countermeasures operations. This was my first assignment for air squadron operational duty.

I was accompanied on this transfer to the state of Washington by Milly and young son Jim. We flew from Memphis Municipal Airport in a civilian Boeing Stratocruiser and landed in Minneapolis, Minnesota. As we started up again and began to taxi, one of the engines caught fire and I could only think that I was in the wrong place, on the inside. It was a bit scary. I was thinking that I should be on the outside to put the fire out. Anyway, there was also a very bad snowstorm, and we finally had to take a train the rest of the way to Seattle. We could see nothing but the white of snow most of the trip.

After a very long train ride halfway across the United States actually, we arrived in Seattle, then took a bus to Oak Harbor, the nearest town to the Whidbey Island Naval Air Station. At the time, there was only one hotel in Oak Harbor. The Oak Harbor Hotel, as it was called, was a big white wooden house with only a few rooms for rent. When we went into this house, I inquired about space and was shown a rather large room with a high ceiling and fireplace. The lady owner said rather curtly, "Here is the room, there's a crib for the baby, there's the fireplace, and if you want to keep warm, there's a pile of wood and a chopping block out back where you can split the wood!" Well, there was absolutely no choice in the matter, so I set about to chop enough wood to warm the place up. This situation required that I find a house as soon as possible for the family in the town nearest the naval air station. With a bit of luck after a few days, I talked with someone in a coffee shop who knew of a small house for rent. We moved in within the week. At this point in time my navy pay was only about $250 a month, so there was not too much we could buy or pay for rent, but the rental was very low-priced and, let us say, within our means. There was nothing to spare after buying the essentials for food and some clothing. It must be said of course, at this point in life of beginning a career I did not expect very much, so I was not in want of anything more than the essentials necessary to live. I was then only twenty-one years old, and it was always in the back of my mind that I would plan to take advantage of every opportunity for further study. I had already completed the first leg of my unwritten program for advancement with successful completion of the continuous fifty-two-week electronics school in Texas and Tennessee. Also, through home self-study I had successfully passed written exams for the first and second years of college-level education with the USAFI (U.S. Armed Forces Institute), Madison, Wisconsin.

After some few months living in Oak Harbor and daily flying operational training flights with the squadron, we found a better house in Coupeville, Washington, about five miles farther away from the air station, and about the same time learned that my squadron was going to have to deploy to Kodiak, Alaska, for several months. This unforeseen deployment came about because of the loss of several aircraft in the air wing due to weather conditions as well as action involving the Korean Conflict.

But before leaving Whidbey Island Naval Air Station there were still several important operational and training flights to accomplish. In one of the operations it was necessary to fly a hundred miles or so west and out over the Pacific, then return toward the coast at very low altitude over the ocean and, also flying very low along the Hood Canal, on to Seattle. The mission was to see if we could penetrate our coastal radar coverage and then lay aerial mines in the harbor. We were low enough that we were not detected but so low that there the underside of our aircraft was always white from the salt spray of the ocean. I was never, ever comfortable on these flights, and especially because the flights were made in fog and the darkness of night. The farmers with dairy farms along the Hood Canal were also not so comfortable, because their cows became nervous and did not produce as usual. Another factor that kept me uptight was, as a radar flight crewman, I had to keep radar contact with our accompanying P2V patrol plane while in the dense fog that lay along the canal during this period and to be sure we stayed together in formation without colliding. Needless to say more, as I am still here to write about it.

A deployment from the Seattle area to Alaska meant that the families had to stay behind, as the flight crews would be operating out of the air base on Kodiak Island.

Flying out of Kodiak for missions along the Siberian coast during the Korean War was a dangerous duty, both in the sense of squadron aircraft being shot down as well as the very bad weather of ice, snow, heavy winds, and mountainous terrain all around. Three patrol aircraft and their crewman were lost during operations there during this period. It was rather depressing to know that one particular bunk, next to mine, was the same bunk slept in by three different crewmen who were killed in aircraft losses. No one, at least as long as I was stationed at Kodiak, would ever sleep in this bunk again.

I was also one of those in the Avionics Branch responsible for maintenance of electronics equipment for my aircraft. But there were hours of relaxation, as well, in between flights. We were able to fish for salmon, silver salmon at this time of year, in the Buskin River, which flows alongside the Kodiak Air Base. Dolly Varden trout were also found in the streams not far from the base. Often we would dine on freshly caught salmon cooked on a hot plate in the hangar instead of eating in the mess hall. Some salmon that we caught were kept in a deep freezer provided by the recreation department so that we could ultimately take them back home upon completion of the Kodiak deployment.

But aside from the danger of flying, there were the duties of Shore Patrol (SP), similar to the Military Police (MP) in the army and air force. All the petty officers had to perform this duty in accordance with a rotating duty list. About every two weeks I spent a day and evening in the town of Kodiak as an SP, primarily to keep watch on the sailors to stay out of trouble, but also it had been arranged that the SPs support the local sheriff when the need arose. There were always about five SPs each day assigned and operated out of the sheriff's office. We would patrol the street and the bars to make our presence known to the sailors as a deterrent, I suppose. When not actually on the street we had to sit on this bench, and when the sheriff and his deputies needed an assist the first one on the end of the bench had to go. All the guys would slide down to fill the vacancy and the one who was then on the end of the bench went next. It was sort of like Russian roulette. In two instances I was very lucky to "have an empty chamber."

A call came in that a merchant ship had docked and a group of rowdy drunken crewmen were terrorizing the main drag, which consisted of one bar after another. It was not my turn to go out. The sheriff and three SPs were left lying unconscious on the street while the merchant crewmen still had their wits about them to quickly return to the ship.

In another case, the sheriff was called about a disturbance at a private house up the hill from the main street. He was accompanied by an SP from the end of the bench, not me. During the approach to the house to quell the disturbance, the occupant fired a high-powered rifle at the doorway and tore off an arm of the sheriff. The latter was sent to Seattle in critical condition for hospital treatment. In other words, at such an outlying post at that time, in 1950, the SP's duty was not the usual routine of merely picking up the drunk sailor, so he does not disgrace the uniform.

I witnessed a "polar bear club" in action for the first time in my life at the waterfront in Kodiak. At least I believe they were members, or they were very drunk. I saw about ten men only in ordinary bathing trunks jump off the end of a pier into the icy bay on a late November day. I was dressed in my winter navy pea coat, and it was too cold for my comfort to even stand out there and watch these "bears" splashing around in water near freezing. Some years later at a ski resort in Vermont there were men and women with only bathing suits rolling around in the snow after coming out of the sauna. It was hard for me to understand what joy anyone has in this sport. A cold shower is too cold for me.

When my Alaskan tour was completed late in 1951, I was assigned to the Fleet All Weather Training Unit Pacific (FAWTUPAC) at Barber's Point Naval Air Station, Oahu, Territory of Hawaii. There were various types of training being accomplished, but much of it was involving dive bombing. The types of aircraft on Oahu during this period were Hellcats, Avengers, and Dauntlass, primarily, but also Beechcraft, helicopters, and DC-5s, P2Vs, MARS, and B-27 aircraft. The P-80 jet was just being introduced in 1952 for jet pilot training flights at Barber's Point. I was now promoted to Aviation Technician First Class (AT1) and responsible for repair and maintenance of radar altimeters for all the aircraft and for the Training Program for the aviation technicians in FAWTUPAC.

My transfer to Oahu from the mainland was aboard one of the MARS seaplanes (the *Caroline* MARS). These were the largest seaplanes then in the U.S. Navy. Our MARS taxied the water out of Alameda Air Station, California, and made its takeoff run in the direction of the Oakland Bay Bridge. There was a crash boat zigzagging in front of us to break the water, as was routine for a seaplane, or "flying boat," takeoff. Then all of a sudden four JATO (Jet Assisted Take Off) bottles on each side of the flying boat "exploded" into propulsion state and the MARS finally started to lift. This explosive sound from the ignition of all eight JATO bottles truly scared the hell out of all of us traveling for the first time in a MARS. I was sure we would fly under or, worse, into the bridge, as our altitude was still nearly zero feet. Then water started to pour into the aircraft, where we were sitting on benchlike seats; which gave us the thought that we would sink before getting airborne. This water was also something normal for the MARS, but we did not know it. As it turned out, we became safely airborne and at a reasonable altitude over the Bay Bridge and finally were on our way to Hawaii. The flight took some thirteen hours, smooth but noisy, and the food was a box lunch sandwich and apple. It is well to note that I could never stand to eat mayonnaise and all the sandwiches had it. I tried to trade my sandwich for an apple but found no takers. So for the many hours I had only an apple and a coffee, which left me very hungry by the time we eventually got to the air station several more hours later after our landing. The evening landing in the Keehi Lagoon, Honolulu, was so smooth, I did not realize that we had landed. This was one of the last flights of this type aircraft. (There were, I believe, only three MARS aircraft built: *Hawaii* MARS, *Caroline* MARS, and *Philippine* MARS.)

Following my transfer to Oahu, Milly flew with son Jim in a DC-5 transport out of Travis Air Force Base, California, to Hickham Air Force

Base on Oahu. I was informed that the cabin pressure was such that it caused Jim very much ear discomfort on most of the flight to Hawaii and of course he cried often during the flight. I was, unfortunately, unable to help provide comfort, as I was required to fly in the military aircraft with the rest of the squadron personnel during our transfer. I met Milly and Jim upon arrival of their flight at Hickham and then went to a small hotel in Honolulu to live until finding an apartment.

Our first rental for living on Oahu was an apartment in a private house in Honolulu at 2325 Liliha Street, across from St. Francis Hospital, in the Puunui District. The big white house had been owned by a rich Japanese family, and it was sold after a son had drowned in the swimming pool. The owner was a Chinese man, married to a full-blooded Hawaiian woman. Some of their grown children also lived in this house. One son was the superintendent of highways on Oahu. Never can I forget that nearly every day when he came home from work with his pickup truck there was a pile of fresh pineapple in it because he was always cutting roads through the pineapple fields. I found it difficult to eat any canned pineapple after having this fruit fresh from the field. We had use of their kitchen when the family was finished with their dinner, which was OK, but what was not OK was the massive number of large cockroaches that scampered all over the kitchen when we went in and turned on the lights to cook and eat. The family was extremely nice to us, but the "crawly" conditions prompted us to move out and live temporarily, for some months, at the Halawa Vets Housing area, which was directly across the Kamehameha Highway from Pearl Harbor.

Living in Honolulu, in any case, required the use of a car. With the limitation of funds I purchased a 1930 Model A Ford coupe with rumble seat for a total of ninety dollars and paid the former owner forty-five dollars in two payments. The Ford ran like a top and clicked along every day between Barber's Point and Honolulu at about forty miles per hour over the thirty or so miles each way. Then one day housing became available at the air station at Barber's Point, so we moved there because it was so near work. But the car was still necessary in order to go to various places of interest around the island, to shop, and to go to the Tripler Army Hospital, located in Honolulu.

Our second child, David Paul, "Dave," was born at Tripler Army Hospital, Honolulu, on 2 February 1952. It was in this Model A Ford that I drove the wife to Honolulu for David's birth. As I was driving up the steep hill to Tripler, the engine blew a head gasket, so there was not enough power to go the entire way up. Luckily, another car with a sailor came along and took us up the rest of the way to the hospital. Later that day I bought a new gasket, borrowed a couple of wrenches, bought a jar of petroleum jelly, and repaired the engine myself when I got back to the air station. I had no money for garage repairs. While my wife was in the hospital with David, it was necessary for me to not only work but also take care of Jim, who was only two by then. Some days I brought him with me to work at the electronics shop, and sometimes a neighbor, Mrs. Rorex, wife of a chief petty officer, cared for Jim, because she had a son the same age as Jim. Another of many instances of having very little money now as well for food, I bought a big sack of rice and several cans of tomato soup, which we lived on for several days.

"Creepy crawlies" (various bugs and spiders) were not only in Puunui's Liliha Street at my first residence in Honolulu when it was still the Territory of Hawaii. The U.S. Navy's housing area near Oahu's Barber's Point as well would have been, and may still be, the delight of any self-respecting entomologist. I was offered and gratefully accepted an apartment that had just become available through the transfer of another navy family back to the mainland. The apartment was located in the section of housing referred to as Mongoose Manors. A delightful name, we thought, with *manors*. The name had a nice ring to it. It was aptly named, we found, because mongooses were everywhere, night and day.

The mongoose is a small carnivore with a pointed head, long tail, thick hair, short legs, but over a foot long, and weighs typically about five pounds. The suricate is of the same family but smaller and looks more like a mixture of cat and monkey at first glance. But this relative also has an appetite similar to the mongoose. The gold-spotted mongoose was introduced to the Hawaiian Islands many years ago to control the rats. It did diminish the rat population and, by the way, all the snakes as well. The mongoose is often portrayed fighting the cobra and is almost always victorious because of its agility, speed, and timing. Unfortunately, the mongoose did not mind its manners, as it also seriously depleted populations of native birds and mammals. For people, the mongooses simply became pests, but mostly because people cannot remember whether the plural spelling is *mongeese* or *mongooses*. The latter is correct.

It would have been just fine with me if the mongooses had in the meantime extended their glory, even if with the help of their cousin suricate, by devouring all the scorpions, six-inch-long centipedes, and giant spiders. Storage buildings on and near the base were notorious for the scorpions under the boxes and in dark corners. It was usual to carry a hammer to a storage room when shifting boxes around, since it seemed to be the best antidote for these creatures. In Mongoose Manors, there were in the apartments, in particular, spiders and centipedes. The first time I saw one of those long centipedes with many one-inch-long wirelike legs, I nearly flipped, as I grabbed a shoe and frantically squashed it into the next world. And one of the neighbors who had been living there for some time told me, "If you see one of those centipedes, there is always a second nearby, because they live in pairs." We looked everywhere we thought possible and could not see any trace of one. Lo and behold, some weeks later as I opened a seldom-used side door there was number two on the floor in the doorway just under the door when closed. Strangely enough, this second centipede was dead. I was told that if one of the pair is missing for a long period of time the other will just die. I did not know how much truth there was in this, but it seemed as though it was the case.

One of the sailors in our squadron who lived in the barracks got up one morning for a big surprise. As he put on his socks he was bitten by a centipede that had crawled into one of his socks. His foot got so swollen that he could not put his shoe on this foot for some days. It was said that these centipedes were not deadly poisonous, but they could scare one nearly to death. The hunt was on for the second one, starting with all the socks in the barracks.

Up until this time of my life I had never seen such large spiders as in this housing area. They were not only huge and ugly, but they also actually appeared to gallop, instead of moving along with the normal gait of spider walk. From this assignment I went on in life believing I had seen the largest spiders that exist.

Now I must relate, while discussing creepy crawlies, that I was even more shocked one day more recently while on a safari observing a rhinoceros in South Africa. As we were looking at a rhino from rather close range, our guide sensed a possible danger from this animal and motioned us to get back to the vehicle quickly. In my haste, moving in the direction of the vehicle, but mostly with an eye on the rhino, at one point when I looked again toward the vehicle I found myself with my face only six inches away from an enormous spiderweb spun between tree branches. In the middle of this web, directly at my eye level, was a truly gigantic spider several inches overall in size with brightly colored body and very long black legs. I must have let out some sort of scary cry of fright, as the rhino commenced to turn and trot in the opposite direction. When I managed to allow my legs to move normally again, I showed the guide and the others in our small group just why my uncontrollable sounds diverted the rhino. The guide, seemingly unconcerned, responded, "Oh, yes, there are lots and lots of these beautiful creatures around here. But they won't hurt you if you don't bother them." My proximity to this spider was purely unintentional!

Since I very often worked at nights maintaining the aircraft equipment in order for the aircraft to start their early-morning flights, I was in a position to use several hours during the days for my personal time. It was then that we were able to drive around the island of Oahu to all the various sights familiar to the tourists. Many of these hours were on Waikiki Beach, which at that time had only three hotels, the Royal Hawaiian, the Moana, and the Liliukelani on the east end of the beach, with Diamond Head in the background. The keyhole at Kokohead was also a pleasant place where the waters were calm for the young ones, Jim and David. We often visited one of the closer beaches to us, at Nanakuli, when living near the base. It was noted for some rough surf, although not so rough as the north side of the island. One day with three others from my squadron I got a large rubber life raft, such as those normally stowed in aircraft for emergencies, and we paddled rather far out into the ocean off Nanakuli to catch a good wave. We were coming in toward the beach with good speed and a lot of excitement atop a giant wave when all of a sudden, it seemed, our wave simply collapsed straight down instead of rolling in smoothly up on the beach. The raft went flying into the air with the paddles, and I, like the rest, found myself falling head-first into the sandy surf. We were spitting out sand the rest of the day.

David was still very much a toddler all the while in Hawaii, but Jim got around in the close neighborhood to play with a few of the young ones. Both David and Jim loved to sit in the rumble seat of the 1930 Ford. I did not go out on the highway with them in the rumble seat, only slowly around the housing project at the base area. They knew not to stand up, because it would be dangerous for them. So things went pretty smoothly in this respect. After about one year someone offered me $150 for the Model A, and since I had paid only $90 for it I thought I had a good deal. Well, in a way it was. However, for $200 I bought an old slant-back Buick, which was quite an upgrade in style, but I learned that the cost of operation and repairs made short work of my paycheck. I wished I had not sold the Ford. In fact, as an afterthought, I wished that I had transported the Ford to my next duty station, because such a car became increasingly more valuable as a good-running antique. Unfortunately, by the time I had let this lesson sink in I was to be transferred back to the mainland. Before Hawaii became a state, one always referred the States as the "mainland" when living in Hawaii. I sold the Buick to a neighbor just before transfer from Hawaii. During the ongoing Korean War period, there was another shortage of instructors at the Naval Air Technical Training Center in Memphis, and a call was put out for all available trained instructors. I was on the list.

The transfer from Barber's Point Naval Air Station, Oahu, Hawaii, to another tour of instructor duty in Millington (Memphis), Tennessee, in 1953 was neither wanted nor unwanted. The navy needed more instructors at the avionics school and I was one of those selected because of my past experience. I had no choice. I also had no choice of the method of transportation for my family and me when departing Hawaii. There was my wife and two young sons, Jim and David at that time. The least expensive, and available, mode of travel was the navy transport ship *General Morton,* so we were assigned to this transport for the portion of journey to San Francisco, then by train on to Memphis. The ship ride was not so terrible for a few days, except that I, as a senior petty officer, was obligated to supervise certain groups of men on tasks in various parts of the ship while under way, This meant of course that I could not always be directly with the family. The real difficulty started when the ship was twenty-four hours out from San Francisco. The weather became stormy, and that, together with the normal swells prevalent off the California coast, caused the *General Morton* to roll heavily. Nearly all the women and children were sick, as well as some crew members, and many were confined to their bunks. When in the dining room on this rolling ship much of the food, dishes, and tableware would slide away onto the deck. Because David was still under a year old he had to be in a high chair for feeding. The ship rolls were so heavy that I had to hold the high chair with one hand and try to eat with the other. But under such conditions, this one day and night, it was rather senseless even to be in the dining room. I nearly got sick, not because of the sea but the odor from so many passengers' heaving in an enclosed space. This was one trip I wished I had had a priority status in order to be able to get a flight, instead of ship passage, out of Honolulu.

Riding a train between San Francisco and Memphis produced no sea swells from storms; however, it was quite a chore to keep David and Jim from boredom over a full two-day period. Pullman cars were not available to us, so it was *all the way* in a coach car, *day and night.* It was difficult to get any sleep because of having to keep an eye on David and Jim, who wanted to constantly go up and down in the car. We were walking zombies as we arrived in Memphis.

So in 1953 I was once again on instructor duty but this time at the new Class A Aviation Electronics School. For three years I taught A/C (Alternating Current) theory from atomic structure and on through to tuned circuits and motors and generators to hundreds of young sailors who would eventually go out to the fleet and squadrons around the world to maintain and repair radar, navigation, and communications equipment.

It probably would not have been so bad if I had waited for responses from the colleges and universities after high school graduation and actually attended Oneonta State Teachers College. But how could I have known? I really enjoyed teaching. It was so gratifying to have young men, and eventually women (WAVES) as well, come into the classes with little or no knowledge of electricity and after some months go out into the air squadrons and eventually be able to repair sophisticated electronic equipments.

In 1953, when I was able to purchase my first car in the States (the old Ford Model A was bought on Oahu when Hawaii was not yet a state), it was a used 1950 Chevrolet, financed with Geico. I paid them something like fifty dollars a month for twenty-four months. There was never a trip to Montauk and return with this Chevrolet without something going out, fuel pump, water pump, fan belt, flat tires, overheated radiator, and the like, but this was common with most cars in those days. And what money I had planned for motels and food usually had to be shared for repairs. On one occasion the gearshift would not go into reverse. When it first occurred I was near a highway with graded banks on each side. I had to turn around to go in another direction. Since I could not back up, I drove the car partially up one of the banks on the side of the highway, then let it roll backward, turning the steering wheel around until I could drive forward, to go in the opposite direction. When I finally found a garage to correct the problem, the mechanic lifted the hood, jerked on one of the rods (I do not know to this day what rod or why), and said I could go now without problem. He did not charge anything, and I never had the problem again. I suppose some good mechanic familiar with the older (1950s) cars would understand what the probable cause and solution were in this case. The earlier models were a far cry from today's vastly improved autos.

Our third child, a daughter, Patricia Anne, "Patti," was born 18 January 1954 at the Memphis Naval Hospital, Memphis (Millington), Tennessee, the same hospital where Jim was born in 1950. And so our family remained at three, Jim, Dave, and Patti.

Early on in this marriage I felt sort of incomplete in attending my church alone, but it was there that I found the inner strength necessary to attend to my navy obligations and provide for the family food, clothing, and shelter and be close to the children in the ways of a father. While there are cases of mixed marriages, where religion is concerned, that get on well, I felt, more and more, that I should have followed my initial instinct. But I always felt the obligation to be good to my family and support them as a whole, in every way, to the best of my ability, guiding the children, teaching, and helping them to understand right from wrong in my own way. Visiting our blood relatives to maintain family ties was important to me as well as, for example, supporting Little League baseball with Dave and Jim over many hours. I remember taking Patti with me to town (Memphis) and going to the Peabody Hotel for an ice-cream sundae. She was about three or four years old and dressed up so cute by her mother. Patti handled herself as a real young lady as she ate her sundae, and I was very proud of my young daughter. In those days, as today, there were several ducks in the lobby of the Peabody Hotel, and it was often referred to as "the hotel with the ducks."

I was out in the backyard of our apartment in Millington one evening repairing a small hole in the bottom of a cooking pot when Jim, four years old at the time, watched closely as I made this minor repair with a screw, nut, and washers. In order to check if the hole was completely closed, I was holding a flashlight behind the pot to see if the light would shine through. If so, it needed further repair. I explained to Jim why I shined the light as I was doing it. He stood and watched the entire time without a word. Then he looked up at the night sky with many stars shining and said to me, "Dad, is the sky up there full of holes?" His imagination led him to believe that the sky was like a pot and all the stars were light coming through the holes. I was truly astounded that such a young mind could possibly go that far in trying to analyze a rather complicated situation.

I was always very interested in trying to develop new ideas on how to present a lesson in ways making it easier for students to understand the subjects more quickly and thoroughly. Each week there were evening remedial classes for those students who wanted to attend in order to "bone up" on any points that they were not sure about. And each week there were different instructors taking turns as "duty night instructors." When the word got out that AT1 Cook had the night duty, the classroom was so full that there was standing room only. One of the devices I had developed was a Motor-Generator Training Device (MGTD), in order to demonstrate exactly how a generator, or a motor, functioned. The materials I used came from the salvage yard where old electronics equipment was discarded. Powerful magnets, which were essential items in the construction of the MGTD, were obtained from the magnetrons of discarded aircraft radar. Wires and switches were no problem in salvage, and the wood and Plexiglas were available in the carpenter shop. In the end, because this device was so useful, I built several for each of the four rooms where this alternating current theory phase was taught. For this I received a commendation from the Commanding Officer, Naval Air Technical Training Center.

During this tour of duty we first lived in navy housing just west of the base but then found a house in the country about twenty minutes east of the base. Here we could become very well informed about life as it was in the countryside of Tennessee. Although we were "military poor," the cost of having a black woman iron and clean house was so inexpensive that we hired a really polite and efficient lady called Mabel. She would talk to us nearly the whole time that she was in the house. And from these conversations we learned so much more about the lives of the country folks, black and white. Those who picked cotton would assemble at the general store near our house, then go out into the fields, also nearby. Before starting out, however, it was normal for most of them to buy an RC and a Big Moon Pie. Royal Crown cola is a drink similar to Pepsi and referred to as an "RC." A "Big Moon Pie" was, in fact, a small American type pie with various fillings—apple, cherry, peach, et cetera. I myself had an RC or a Dr. Pepper with a Big Moon Pie on many occasions. (RC and Dr. Pepper are essentially unknown to Europeans unless they have tried them during visits in the States.)

I must say that all the black folks were very peaceful and polite in the farming area where we lived. I would also talk with the men who gathered at the general store inside or out on the veranda when they were not in the fields. I guess it was here where I learned to understand what they were saying, that is, the way they talked with that very strong southern accent and slang. But when they would talk and laugh at the same time with their shrill voices, it was a real challenge to know what they were saying. Often I visited the cotton gin and watched them at work, then the baling of cotton amid the joking and laughing with one another. Most often I was left without the slightest idea what they were saying, but I had great pleasure seeing and hearing them in such a happy state. I really believe that they, in fact, were happier than most others who had far more material assets. Naturally, they had a need for an upgrade in their standard of living, yet I placed that need in perspective to the development of my own life. In the beginning we had precious little resources, but in time, with visions of better things, we worked to make the best of life.

While I was still assigned to this long tour of instructor duty we found another house in the countryside not so far from the last, near the general store. The house was not anything more special than the last except for the monthly rent, which was cheaper. We acquired a large dog for some reason. I suppose because in the country "everybody" had a dog. Ours, Rover, was a very large one, a mixture of Doberman and German shepherd. Life went on as usual, the same peaceful country living, until one day a farmer came to the house and said, "Your dog is eating my chickens." I was really shocked. I could not imagine this. I never saw our dog do anything out of the ordinary, except when inside the house, knocking nearly everything off the coffee table by a swing of his huge tail. "How do you know my dog is eating the chickens?" I asked.

"Just come out and I'll show you!" he firmly replied.

I thought it safe enough to go out since he had no shotgun in hand. "Look under your house!"

And there they were. Sure enough. Thirteen of the farmer's prize pullets lay dead in the crawl space under the house. Rover had killed the pullets and then simply dropped them in his favorite sleeping place. I had to promise to get rid of my monster, as the farmer called our dog, or pay for the pullets. The man from the dog pound picked Rover up the next day.

One of our neighbors decided to paint houses for a living. He was not a professional in the sense that he had formal training, but he one day decided to buy some brushes and a ladder and went around looking at houses that were in obvious need of paint. Then he convinced some of the owners of the need and that the price would be right. As he knew we were always in need of more money, he asked if I would help. "Yes," was my immediate answer, "on weekends and some evenings during the period of Daylight Savings Time, when it stays light longer." I had already quite a bit of experience painting houses, which I had rented, and navy buildings. Thereafter, for a couple of years, on weekends and after work sometimes, weather permitting, the "painter" and I would pick up the paint at the general store and proceed on to the paint jobs. It was a lot of work for the pay, but I had more money to buy the family necessities such as clothes and food. There were also routine car expenses and the costs involved with annual visits to my parents in Montauk.

I was promoted to Avionics Chief Petty Officer (ATC) in November 1955 while at the Naval Air Technical Training Center, Memphis. I was then assigned as the building chief and responsible for the new Class A School Building with 110,000 square feet (approximately eleven thousand square meters) of classrooms and laboratories and responsible for the disciplining of the several hundred students in study.

When I look back on this job I always think about a situation, on the lighter side of things, related to discipline. During one period of about three months, there arose a problem with some culprits leaving trash on the grounds during smoking breaks. No matter how much we tried, we never could find the guilty students, as there were hundreds of men out there at each break for smoking and coffee, et cetera. Most of the trash happened to be paper and in particular empty packets that held a "Jell-O sugar" popular at the time. One day, while I was talking to my master at arms about this problem, a young third class petty officer, who was listening in, told me that he could solve the problem. Both my MAA and I were rather taken aback by the petty officer's confidence in being able to solve this mystery. He wanted permission from me to have all the students in this section fall into ranks in the outside smoking area. Permission was granted. Then the young petty officer ordered each man, as he passed by, to stick out his tongue. In five minutes the problem was solved. Nearly all the empty packets had contained a strawberry sugar powder. Each of the culprits had a red tongue. End of problem.

In another instance I was called in one day by the school's phase officer. Each major section of the avionics school had a commissioned officer in charge of the instructors and students, and these officers were called phase officers. It was not often we engaged in conversation, as there was always a lot to do and most talking was done in the classrooms, so I was curious what this phase officer wanted. "Chief Cook, your master at arms has caused me a big problem. What kind of a man do you have for an MAA?"

I said, "I have had him working for me for many months, and he has always done a fine job. What happened? What did he do?"

"The commanding officer, Captain Diffley, called and said one of our people, Petty Officer Culpepper, was using very foul language at the officers' club. Why did you send him to the officers' club? We cannot have men like this working here."

I interrupted the phase officer, asking, "But, sir, just what did he say? I cannot imagine Culpepper talking using foul language."

"Well, if you must know, he asked the secretary in the officers' club for a piece of ass!"

It became then immediately clear to me, and I began to explain: "We ran out of ice for making iced tea for the smoking break, so I sent Culpepper over to the officers' club. They have the only ice-making machine on the base which is working. You know, sir, that Culpepper is from Alabama. And when anybody from that far south asks for a piece of ice, well, you can't be sure what he's going to get."

When I joined the navy, I decided, on my father's advice, to get an education in electronics. I was seventeen years old and at that age to enlist a parental signature was required, which my father provided. When one joins under these conditions (seventeen being underage), the sailor serves what is referred to as a "Kitty Cruise." The contract ends when the sailor turns twenty-one. My thought was that upon completion of the Kitty Cruise I would get out of the navy and then go to college. It just so happened that the Korean War was under way in the meantime and I had to stay in the service, which meant another four years in the navy. Then with further thought under the new conditions I said to myself that if I could become a commissioned officer I would stay in. If not, then I would get out and still have time to get into the college routine. As it turned out, I did receive a commission of ensign in June 1957. I was then very proud that I was able to make the grade, coming up through all the petty officer ranks, starting from apprentice seaman, and being earmarked as a "mustang" ensign. It was routine at that time that the mustang be sent to the Officers Candidate School (OCS) in Newport, Rhode Island, for several weeks. We were not candidates in the real sense, because we already had been given the commission. However, the navy felt that perhaps these mustangs might need some social training or orientation in the world of officer rank. I never felt that I did not know how to act, or how to eat, in the presence of the "higher social level." But this school was jokingly referred to as the Fork and Knife School, an indication that the attendees needed to learn manners in the various aspects of an officer's life. It was never a problem for me to integrate among people of any level, or country, before or after this orientation at OCS.

One morning in July 1957 I was walking near the Newport base chapel just before attending mass. It happened that President Eisenhower, whose summer home was there at Newport, was strolling in the same area. I demonstrated my knowledge of military etiquette with a sharp salute and, "Good morning, Mr. President!"

He responded, "Good morning, sir!" Dwight David "Ike" Eisenhower was the thirty-fourth U.S. president, 1953–61, and one of the very select few with the rank of General of the Army. I was impressed by his very friendly and caring response to my expected military greeting.

Subsequent to my commissioning in Memphis, Tennessee, and the orientation in Newport, Rhode Island, I was transferred to the naval air station in Brunswick, Georgia, for duty as student in the Naval Air Observer (Controller) (NAO[C]) School, for a period of about six months. With very lifelike mock-ups in laboratories we were taught the operation of a shipboard CIC (Combat Information Center) and CIC live operations in aircraft with the Super Constellation WV-2. The aircraft operations included the controlling (vectoring) of fighter aircraft for intercepts of "enemy" aircraft.

Graduates of the NAO(C) School came out designated as naval air observers (controllers). The position in a WV-2 squadron for an NAO(C) was, typically, in a flight crew as a CICO (Combat Information Center Officer). When on the ground, between flights, he would be assigned a position according to other training. I should be assigned as an avionics officer because of all my avionics background.

The family lived in a home at the water on St. Simon's Island near Brunswick. The house was really very nice and, like most of the homes on St. Simon's, had been given a name by its owner. The name was written on a small sign planted on the lawn near the driveway. Ours was named The Singing Surf, because of its proximity to the ocean and the sounds of the waves that variously pounded the shore or gently rolled up and receded, depending upon the weather conditions. Actually, the surf was not normally heavy, but with a stiff wind would be choppy and stormy-looking. Jim, Dave, and Patti had very nice friends, of the neighboring Crihfield family, who were about their age, to play with. Ray Crihfield was also promoted to ensign in Memphis at the same time as I was, and we were both assigned duty in early warning squadrons. But he went directly to Argentia, Newfoundland, and I to Patuxent River, Maryland. The Crihfields live in San Diego now and their children, Joey, John, and Cheryl, are all living and working in the San Diego area.

St. Simon's was one of those places I did not want to leave. It was very pleasant. Near the beach, Spanish moss hanging from all the trees, it was quiet with generally good weather the year round. I recall only one time in the winter when there was frost on the ground, and we never experienced any snow when we lived there. The only drawback, but only on some days, when the wind blew the wrong direction, was the terrible odor from the wood pulp mills in Brunswick. If you were blindfolded and being driven along the coast in Georgia you could surely know when you approached Brunswick.

About twenty years later when revisiting the South, I stopped in at St. Simon's Island to stay overnight in the Prince Hotel. We were advised not to remain because we might have "to stay for several days." The tide was rising steadily because of an approaching hurricane and the island would be flooded, with no way to drive back to the mainland. So we proceeded on up north to stay ahead of the storm.

Upon graduation from the NAO(C) School, Brunswick, as a naval air observer (controller), I was assigned duty with Airborne Early Warning Squadron Two (VW-2) with twelve Super Constellation Radar Aircraft, at Patuxent River Naval Air Station and Naval Air Test Center, located at Lexington Park, Maryland. This is about an hour's drive southeast of Washington, D.C. I was assigned the duties of the avionics officer of the squadron and as a flight crew member in the capacity of an airborne Combat Information Center Officer (CICO) qualified for control of fighter aircraft intercepts.

The Super Constellation aircraft, besides being used for some years as a popular passenger aircraft, was also configured as an early warning aircraft and filled with a lot of electronics equipment, including a large search radar underneath with an appropriately large radome and a large height finder radar atop the aircraft, also with large radome. The aircraft were affectionately referred to as Willy Victors, WVs, Connies, or Super Connies. Whenever we landed at some civilian airport, people were curious and asked, "What kind of aircraft is that?" or, "What are those big 'bumps' on the top and bottom of the plane?" We often told them that the big dome on the top was our "bar" and the one below was our "swimming pool." They were nearly so large.

Upon arrival at Patuxent we were almost immediately assigned an apartment in officers' housing next to the base. All three children, Jim, Dave, and Patti, now attended the Lexington Park school and continuing to do well. Again here I got a dog because I thought it was good for the kids and in general, I guess, because many families there had a dog. I bought an English setter that was a really nice and gentle one. I always liked the looks of a setter, either English or Irish. Things went on rather well for several months until one day came a knock on the door and a familiar comment from a neighbor when we were living in the countryside near Memphis: "Your dog is . . ."

I waited anxiously, thinking, *What now?*

"Your dog is drinking my milk."

"What do you mean? Your milk?"

What happened, as explained by the neighbor, was this: She was up very early that morning and watched as our dog, and another dog of the area, knocked over her two glass bottles of milk that were placed there on her porch in routine morning deliveries by the milkman. As soon as the bottles were broken by the manipulating dogs, they commenced to drink the milk. In fact, for the past several days the bottles were broken and the milk gone and the neighbor could not imagine what happened. If she had not seen it with her own eyes she would not have believed it. She had the idea that some kids were pulling pranks. To avoid another dog problem I gave this setter to friends of mine, the Pruitts, who had a farm in Columbia, South Carolina.

Initially, in February and March 1958, squadron operational training for me included a total of sixty-four hours flying out of Patuxent River to a nearby operating area over the Atlantic. Then the first real departure from home base was with the Fleet Training Unit at Guantanamo Bay, Cuba, during the period 7 to 11 April 1958. It was in this time that Fidel Castro was leading his revolution against the then Cuban government. The officers in my flight crew had planned one evening to leave the naval base and take a bus for a visit into a nearby town. It was fortunate for us that we missed the boat from the airfield to the main base, because the group that did go on that bus in town were made captive by Castro's men and held for a month in the mountains nearby. So we learned that it is not always a bad thing when one "misses the boat." There was a second training period at Guantanamo Bay for my crew during 5 to 9 May 1958.

My first real deployment as such with Squadron VW-2 was for three months' operational duty with the Sixth Fleet in the Mediterranean. The crews of these early warning WV Super Constellation radar aircraft when deployed normally consisted of about twenty men, seven or eight officers and the rest petty officers of various ratings who were capable of nearly any repairs necessary no matter where the aircraft may be. Commander Dixon was the plane commander. The Aircraft Bureau number was 137890. We departed from Patuxent River, Maryland, on 11 August 1958 and landed at Lajes, Azores, the same day, then continued on the twelfth of August to Halfar, Malta. On the thirteenth of August we flew to the NATO airfield at Suda Bay, Crete. From there we commenced flying twelve- to fourteen-hour barrier patrol flights over units of the Sixth Fleet during the Lebanese Crisis. In this period of operations we slept and ate on an LST (USS *Tallahatchie County*), moored at the shore of Suda Bay just a few kilometers below the airfield. At the time, in 1958, there were no personnel facilities at the NATO airfield in Crete. There were also no special medical services available for us on Crete, and because of this on one occasion I had to be flown, accompanied by our flight surgeon, to Naples to an eye doctor. I had spent so many long hours on the radar scope in CIC operations, and with so little sleep, that my eyes became infected. After one week of treatment and rest in Naples I was restored to duty.

The flight to Naples for eye treatment was actually the first time I had ever been in Italy, and I just knew many things would seem very different to me. After we checked in at the hotel and I looked out the hotel window I had a surprise. What was staring me in the face was a huge ESSO sign, the likes of which are visible everywhere in the USA. There I was with my 8mm movie camera and excitedly expecting to bring home typical Italian scenes because this was where my grandfather and grandmother Santacroce came from. The ESSO sign severely dented my expectations on this day of arrival.

After having only limited shower hours because of water supply limitations in the ship at Suda Bay, I thought it would be nice to take a long hot bath in the very generously sized bathtub in this Naples hotel. As I commenced to enjoy the luxury and looked around at the way things are done in Italy, I put my hand on a cord that was hanging on the wall near the tub. It was no more than three minutes later that a maid appeared at the opened door of my bathroom. While I thought that I should become small enough to go into the drain with all this water, I realized that she had already asked me at least three times if I were OK. "Yes, yes! OK, OK!" was my answer to this now half-smiling would-be savior. I learned after this most embarrassing incident that the cord on the wall was to be pulled whenever help from the maid was needed. At the time I needed help only after she appeared in the doorway.

The next surprise on this same first evening in Italy was when I went to use the urinal. The surprise came when I went to flush the urinal, which I learned later was something they called a bidet in Europe. This unit was rather highly pressurized, with the result that I had to change into a dry uniform in order to join up with the flight surgeon for dinner.

While I was at Suda Bay, there was precious little to do for entertainment when not flying. A couple of times some of us took a boat across the bay to a very small town and simply sat at a table outside in the warm and sunny air to have beer and some local food. We were warned not to eat or drink any dairy products, as they were not pasteurized. Beer, Metaxa brandy, Domestica wine, and Greek coffee were some of the drinks "blessed" by the flight surgeon as being safe.

I recall that one day I carved my initials into a big tree by the roadside on the way to Cania. In 1997 during a visit with friends in Crete I thought about that carving done thirty-nine years prior and wondered if I could find the tree. The whole area between Suda and Cania had changed so very much, I could not even tell which road I was on when there in 1958.

Just about the only other pleasure in off time was going swimming in the bay and diving off a small floating platform built by the *Tallahachie County* ship's personnel. This was a pleasure up to a point. One day I dived off the platform and when I came up from the dive just a foot away in front of me was the head of a water snake about six inches out of the water repeatedly moving its head left and right, then forward and backward. My swim back to the float might have been a world's-record ten yards.

In our squadron there were three or four relatively new young pilots with the rank of Lieutenant Junior Grade who were on their very first deployment anywhere. Good pilots, but just now about to gain experience in various modes of navy life. I must explain first that when the commanding officer or captain of a ship leaves his ship to go anywhere, for example, into town, an announcement is made on the PA system by the officer on duty that the CO or captain is leaving the ship by stating the name of the ship and "departing." We were during one period on the LST USS

Alameda County, which was moored at the shore of Suda Bay with the bow door lowered on the beach. The captain decided he wanted to go to visit Chana. An announcement was made, *"Alameda County,* departing." One of the new pilots, who had been fast asleep on the tank deck after a long flight, heard this and jumped out of his bunk, grabbed his hat, flight suit, and shoes, and only in his underwear ran off the ship onto the beach. As he went past me I wondered where he was going so fast. *Is there a fire or what?* I thought. When he finally stopped well clear of the ship, I asked him what was happening. "I'm not about to go to sea aboard this ship!" He really thought the ship was about to depart the mooring and go to sea.

On the twenty-first of August we departed Suda Bay and returned to the Royal Naval Air Station Halfar on Malta, where we were based for further flight operations with the Sixth Fleet. We American officers lived at the British Halfar Wardroom, where we slept and dined and participated in the social events of the wardroom.

We got along very well with the British, and I recall enjoying several invitations at the homes of some officers who had families living nearby the base. On one occasion I brought with me the items needed for making popcorn at one of the homes. I did not know what else to bring because not much was available at the base except certain items at the small American PX. Well, these families had heard much about popcorn but never seen it made, nor had they eaten it. It was a great hit. Thereafter, I received many more invitations and always brought a gift bag with popping corn, butter, salt, and vegetable oil.

Sunday evenings were especially interesting in the Halfar Wardroom, as we had to put on dress white uniforms for dinner—which included (only on Sundays) ice cream. The British wives were always present on Sunday evenings, and after dinner Tom and Jerry cartoons were shown. If you can picture it, as Tom (the cat) would be chasing down Jerry (the mouse) the veteran officer flyers would jump and shout for the mouse to go here or there to avoid the cat. It was really amusing. Drinking took up much of the spare time in the off hours while telling tales of the latest happenings during operations. Although the table settings were rather elaborate, the quality and quantity of food were not something to write home about. There were more pieces of chinaware and glassware and more knives, forks, and spoons at each place setting than I ever remember having in our kitchen at the Montauk Fishing Village. I certainly knew "how" to eat, but I did not know here, at first, which utensil to use or for what, because there were so many pieces. I glanced around the table and always hoped that one of the Brits would be slow enough that I could follow his lead in order to eat correctly. The extent of the silver, china, and glassware in this environment surpassed anything that the Fork and Knife School in Newport had ever indicated. The very first evening meal was only a small boiled potato, a piece of corned beef, and a few leaves of cabbage, and I thought a simple fork and knife would have been fine. I lost several pounds during this deployment, which I attributed partially to this factor. But the entire setting and atmosphere were really "royal," and I thoroughly enjoyed the assignment.

As I mentioned, the British treated us very well; but not the Maltese stewards in the wardroom. The British officers frequently told us that the Maltese could not be trusted: "Don't leave anything out in your room or it will be gone before you know it." After living there a few weeks and observing what went on I gained a different perspective on the situation. Nothing was stolen from the American officers, and, in fact, the Maltese stewards provided us with very good service. Why? Without realizing that we might be doing something out of the ordinary, we were treating them like anyone else, as normal human beings. Even as we took a cigarette out for ourselves, we quite naturally offered a cigarette to the porter if one stood nearby. The Brits would not have dreamed of doing such a thing. I will describe a very good example of what it was like in Malta and typical of a reason that I believe the Maltese sought independence from the British. One day in the wardroom during midafternoon coffee I heard a British officer saying, "Porter, bring me coffee!" while he picked up a cup and saucer from a table. As the porter responded with the coffee, the officer looked into the cup and said, "Porter, this cup is dirty!" and never looking at the porter, but looking straight ahead, simply dropped the cup on the ceramic tile floor, and of course it broke into a thousand pieces. Then he pointed to the floor where the shattered cup lay and ordered, "Now! Clean it up!" It was never a question in my mind, after having lived several months with the British, as to why the British did not hold on to this colony or some of the others.

If you ever visit Malta you will notice immediately rock walls around nearly every one of the properties. It was really interesting for me to learn that all the soil on Malta came by ship. In years past when a ship arrived in port it was required to carry in a certain amount of soil for the purpose of developing agriculture. Therefore, with the soil so important, rock walls were built around each plot of land so the soil would not erode or wash away. In the fall of the year at harvesttime one can see thousands of pumpkins, one of the items grown, sitting atop these rock walls.

In Valleta, Malta, there is a rather famous old church. Most famous probably, because during World War II a very large bomb, dropped by the Germans, went through its roof and did not explode because it was a dud. I can imagine that all the parishioners inside the church at the time became even a whole lot more believers in God that their lives were spared. This dud bomb still rests in the church as a "miracle" reminder.

I did not realize that there were so many catacombs on Malta. In fact, I had never before heard that any existed there. I made a tour through them and in the process thought a lot about the past history of this island. For example, Saint Paul was shipwrecked at Malta in A.D. 67, the reason the bay is called St. Paul's Bay. Also, the fine cathedral in the ancient walled city of Medina is in his honor. In the midst of this atmosphere of religious history, I imagined many of the stories of the early church and accounts of the saints and Crusaders of the centuries past. Accidents such as that involving Saint Paul in the bay named after him, where I stood on many occasions were some sort of reminder, a very recent reminder, of what seemed like just days before.

I experienced two harrowing situations on this 1958 Med deployment. The first occurred on the evening of 6 October while returning from an operational flight from the Lebanese area with intent to land at the NATO airfield at Suda Bay on the western end of the island of Crete. I heard the navigator over the intercom informing the plane commander that our airfield was dead ahead and it was time to descend for approach to land at Suda. I noticed on my radar in CIC that the west end of Crete was still some thirty minutes away, so I questioned the navigator, but he was convinced that he was right. I took my copies of navigation charts to the navigator to try to quickly explain to him the situation. The problem was that there were two charts that covered the island of Crete and each chart looked similar in that the landmasses were almost the same and there were airfields at the west end of the landmass on each chart. The navigator had the chart for the eastern half of Crete and was looking at data for the airfield at Herakleion. He should have had both charts on his navigation table. It would have been a recipe for potential disaster in this mountainous area if the pilot had followed the navigator's instructions. The pilot would have been using erroneous landing patterns and altitudes in a "lookalike area." I went immediately from the navigation station to the cockpit and quickly informed the pilot of the problem. He added power, reconfigured for the climb out, and proceeded on to the correct airfield, Suda Bay.

After the last of the operations involving the Lebanese Crisis, we left Suda Bay and returned to Malta for a few weeks of local fleet operations.

Near the end of our Med deployment, we then made a familiarization flight to Fuerstenfeldbruck, Munich, Germany. Our plane commander had made a good choice of location in this instance, since the Oktoberfest was in full swing and we had the opportunity to experience for the first time what it is like when tens of thousands at the fairgrounds are drinking a lot of beer from one-liter glass mugs (*Masse*), everyone looked happy, and many were singing. We were astounded as we observed there were no drunken brawls as would be more usual if such an event took place in the States. In 1958, the dollar was exchanged for four Deutsch Marks (DM 4), and this actually allowed us to rent a hotel room and be able to participate in the Fest. However, after the Fest on the last evening we realized we had spent whatever we had and had no money left for a taxi. We had to walk all the way back to the hotel not knowing the way from the fairgrounds. It was very late at night, and since we spoke no German it was very difficult to explain to a passerby what we wanted. Most of the people we approached seemed not at all familiar with our hotel, but most probably because they did not understand what we wanted. Finally, about three in the morning, we managed to get to the hotel, located just north of the Marienplatz.

Again, near disaster took place in the flights over the North Atlantic as we were returning from the deployment area to our home base, Patuxent River, Maryland. The incident occurred on the evening of 10 October 1958 on the flight of our aircraft from Malta via Blackbush, England, and Keflavik, Iceland. Halfway between Ireland and Iceland I noticed on my radar a disturbance indicating a very severe storm dead ahead about ninety miles. I notified the Plane Commander (PC). His response was that everything looked OK (a visual from the cockpit). In spite of his response I recommended a ten-degree change in heading to avoid the storm. "It's OK up ahead, Paul, no problem," came from the cockpit.

As we were now getting very much closer I recommended a necessary forty-degree change in heading to avoid the storm. The radar returns were very strong, even with the radar gain control set lower, indicating very turbulent weather. I had also checked my height-finding radar returns to coordinate the readings with the surface search radar. The storm was confirmed to our altitude as well as directly in the direction of our flight path. I was performing my duty in reporting a potentially dangerous situation. The PC ignored the information from CIC. At this point the PC said, "We will continue on the present course; it doesn't look so bad." He misjudged the usefulness of the radar and my experience in analyzing the readings as well.

I informed my CIC crew of ten men to "buckle up tight" as I judged this storm to involve extra severe turbulence. No sooner said than the aircraft shook violently and a giant blue ball of St. Elmo's fire rolled from the cockpit, inside the aircraft, all the way back to the tail section. We had entered a snowstorm and had also been hit by lightning, which not only severely damaged the nose radome but also burned up all the coils and other sensitive front-end electronic parts in all the radar, navigation, and long-range communications equipment. The UHF transceivers were usable only within reasonably close range of a base or another aircraft. The automatic direction finders were malfunctioning.

Some fifteen minutes later we flew into clear weather and eventually observed the lights of Keflavik Airfield in Iceland, which was our scheduled refueling stop. As we went into the operations center to file the flight plan for the remainder of the trip, we were given clearance to continue from Iceland to Patuxent River but only at an altitude of 4,000 feet. Only aircraft with radar (such as our Super Constellation or other military patrol aircraft) would be allowed such an altitude, primarily because of the bad weather forecast along our route but also because of the 8,000-foot mountains on the south coast of Greenland (Cape Farwell).

As CIC officer, I began to say, "But we don't have any more radar—"

The PC gave me an elbow in the side indicating to "shut up," a full navy commander, the PC, against an ensign CIC officer. I obeyed for the moment, as a military requirement. I should comment at this point that during the deployment in the Mediterranean there were several occasions when this PC got aboard our aircraft for operational flights when he had had too much to drink. This had always bothered me, and now things with him and his decisions were going too far. I would wait until we got back, with any luck at all, to home base, then would report to the commanding officer, "I refuse to fly any further flights as a crewman with this PC."

We got airborne and only after about one hour out of Keflavik, at 4,000 feet in another snowstorm, the number 3 engine caught fire. Some seconds of an aircraft fire, when airborne, are enough to get one's complete attention, but this engine fire burned considerably longer until finally the fire extinguishers were activated. With more luck the fire was extinguished. The propeller on number 3 engine was feathered and we were now with only three engines. The PC was asleep in a bunk as the first pilot was attempting to contact oceanic control for change of altitude to get on top of the storm and to avoid the 8,000-foot mountain peak on the southern tip of Greenland. However, after many attempts, communications did not work because of the lightning damage earlier that evening.

The PC was awakened and given the particulars. His reaction: "We have to get on top of the weather. Since we cannot contact anyone, we'll just climb up through the flight levels until we get into clear weather." This meant, of course, climbing up through several flight levels with no way of knowing the locations of other aircraft at these levels.

With luck, again, we got into the clear at 12,000 feet. There was a partial sigh of relief. But then the navigator revised his original estimate of distance we could fly, given the fuel used in climb out and the three engines, which reduced speed, along with headwinds. The navigator informed the PC that we could not reach our home base at Patuxent River, Maryland, but with our remaining fuel we could reach the airfield at South Weymouth in Massachusetts. Only thirty minutes later the navigator again revised his estimates with less fuel and stated that we must land at the first airfield available in Newfoundland. As we approached land and communicated, now with short-range UHF transmissions, with Argentia, the pilot reported no landing possible because of snow-covered runways. The same for Halifax, Nova Scotia. The skies, fortunately, along the coast were now clear and we descended to very low altitude, one could say with a bit of truth at treetop level, to conserve fuel. With yet additional luck we finally landed at Brunswick, Maine, after that twelve-hour, thirty-minute flight from Keflavik on 11 October 1958. The flight engineer, in measuring the fuel in the tanks, reported that the tanks were, in essence, empty. We were supposed to all meet at the NAS Brunswick Officers' Club for dinner. I just flopped down on my bed, still in my flight suit, thinking that after a half hour or so I would shower and dress for the club. I was so tired that I was still lying on the bed in my flight suit in the same position the next morning. It is quite difficult to describe the kind of relief experienced by the crew being safely on the ground after a total of 17.5 harrowing flight hours (during a twenty-four-hour period) between Blackbush, England, and Brunswick, Maine. Our PC, with twenty-five years of flying experience, had lost his feel for air-safe conditions and disregarded his CIC officer's recommendations. This and the potentially disastrous situation developed by our navigator over Crete on 6 October did not have to happen.

All the wives of the officers and men in our crew were waiting at Patuxent River that 11 October evening for our scheduled return, to greet one another after the three-month deployment, and a formal dance at the officers' club was planned on this night. Obviously, for me, for all of us, there was no meeting and no dance.

We returned to Patuxent after engine repairs on 12 October 1958. I met with the commanding officer that same day to inform him that I refused to fly in the crew with this PC. After the commanding officer heard my story, which was backed up by our flight surgeon, who happened to fly with us on several occasions, this PC was grounded, as was the navigator. I felt no remorse. It could have saved lives. When it became time for the PC to be transferred to another assignment some months later, he personally came to me where I worked as the squadron's avionics officer, apologized, and said that I did the right thing. It seemed that he had become another person. In fact, I learned that he was assigned to a transport squadron and successfully completed his tour of duty before finally retiring from the navy.

All during the month of January 1959 I was flying out of Argentia, Newfoundland, on the North Atlantic Barrier Patrol, which was maintained for several years for early warning against approaching Soviet bombers flying toward the United States. These flights were in some of the worst weather conditions of high winds, snow, and icing, plus freezing surface temperatures for an aircraft ditching or bailouts, if they were necessary. At least two aircraft (Radar Super Constellation) with crews that I remember were lost in these operations.

Thinking of ditching the aircraft if necessary, and/or bailing out of one in icy waters of the North Atlantic reminds me vividly of the training sessions at the base swimming pool at Patuxent River Naval Air Test Center. With life jackets and "poopy suits" donned, we had to periodically train by jumping off the rather high diving board and learning to go through the motions of survival, automatically, after hitting the water. A poopy suit is an all-enclosing waterproof jump suit with only the face exposed to the elements. Its purpose is to protect the body from extremely cold water, especially in the northern latitudes where our squadron would often operate. It was on one of these sessions that I landed in the water from the high diving board and instead of coming up from the bottom of the pool in the normal way, with head up and out of the water, my entire body was upside down. There was absolutely nothing I could do to get upright. I pulled the cord on my right side to discharge the CO_2 into my life jacket, but nothing happened. I thought (and it was quickly) to pull the cord on the left side to inflate my life jacket. Still nothing happened. Water was now continually seeping inside the poopy suit through the only opening, at the face. Because of this, the water inside my poopy suit at my head and shoulders and air inside near my feet kept my body upside down. I am still very much grateful to two of the officers in my crew who recognized the excessive time with my head underwater and pulled at my feet to haul me out. The problem was caused by the training officer himself. There was only one CO_2 cartridge in my life jacket, on the left side, and it was empty. It had not been replaced after the last use. The other, on the right side, had been taken out by the training officer for a soda water dispenser on his private bar at home. A check was made on all the life jackets and the "lifesaving sessions." It was found that only one cartridge was being used for training and the other went to his bar. The training officer was summarily dismissed from this assignment.

    Although Newfoundland, Canada, can have wonderful weather in summer, anyone who had to fly there in winter will remember mostly the days of high winds, cold, and snowstorms. At the height of a storm the wind would make a dismal howling sound, day and night, as it swirled around the window frames and corners of the officers' quarters, which were located on top of a hill. I was sometimes awake at night because of the howling winds, and this in turn reminded me of the winds in which we would have to fly early the next morning. It meant rough and bouncy flights for several hours while on station patrolling the barrier between Argentia, Newfoundland, and the Azores. When we were completing the barrier patrols it was sometimes not possible to land at Argentia because of extreme conditions. This meant flying back across the Atlantic and landing at the Azores for crew rest. When we did land at Argentia in stormy winter weather there were actually times when we could not stand up and walk up the hill on icy roads to the officers' quarters but had to crawl for some distance on hands and knees.

    On one of the nicer early-winter days on my first trip to Argentia, I took a bus ride to the post exchange and when through decided to walk back to the officers' quarters. Since I had not been there too long and was not well acquainted with the area I had to ask someone where the quarters were located from where we were standing. He pointed to a distant spot and said that they were "there." The ground was covered with several inches of snow; everything was white. I commenced to walk in the direction given and after about twenty minutes I reached quarters. A friend asked me where I went and I said, "To the PX to buy a few things and I walked directly back here for some exercise."

"You mean you came directly back here from the PX?" He pointed in that direction. "You just walked across the lake!" The lake had just barely frozen over at this point in the season, and I had no idea there was a lake. It was snow-covered. I had luckily reached the other side by missing any weak spots of thin ice.

During the period 19–24 February 1959, I was assigned to a crew (all volunteers) for a secret mission. Only the squadron commanding officer and our plane commander, it seemed, had any idea where we were bound, except for the fact that it would be cold enough to require special winter clothing. We landed at Quonset Point, Rhode Island, on 19 February 1959 to pick up a navy captain and a lieutenant. The Captain, McWethy, was the commander of Submarine Division 101, which included the USS *Skate*. The lieutenant was the *Skate*'s navigator. We proceeded on to Harmon Air Force Base, Canada, for further information, and it was there that we crewmen found out the next stop was the U.S. Air Force base in Thule, Greenland, above the Arctic Circle. Also, we learned that we were going to gather the necessary data about the ice pack for the USS *Skate,* which, a few weeks later, would be making the first winter exploration by a submarine at the North Pole.

The takeoff out of Harmon was to be a most unusual experience for most of us in the crew. There was a very big snowstorm in this part of Canada during our short stay there. The runways had been cleared a few times, but then as we taxied to the end of the runway for takeoff the wind began to blow so hard that the deep snow that lay on the ground began to blow around in such a frenzy that visibility became zero.

For our purposes this blowing snow was worse than a snowstorm. Because the runway lights and other normal markers were covered with snow, freshly cut pine trees were placed at about five-hundred-foot intervals on each side of the runway. The tower personnel advised the pilots that this wind condition would last for some time, but since we needed to get on with this trip they advised the following: "Now and then the wind will subside enough so you will be able to see the pine trees on the sides of the runway. When you can see three trees distant, put on full power and go." We waited on the end of that runway for at least forty-five minutes and wondered just when the pilots would ever see three trees and what if we got to rolling along and blowing snow started again before we got enough speed for takeoff? For those of us in CIC at the rear of the Super Connie aircraft, it was more anxiety-ridden because there were no windows in the electronics operation center. When airborne we were pretty much in control of the tactical situations. But in this particular situation, we were in the dark, in more ways than one. It finally happened that even with some more blowing snow the pilots managed to "eyeball" the three necessary pines for a safe takeoff. I believe that is one of those longest fifty seconds rolling down a runway that I remember. Nine flight hours later, farther north from Harmon, we were once again safe on the ground. Now at the USAF base, Thule.

The temperatures in Thule were extremely cold. Special clothing was provided to us, including thermal underwear. Parkas with fur-lined hoods projecting out from the face for protection were also provided. Despite these precautions we were forbidden to walk to the hangars or to the officers' club. We had to use the air force vehicles provided. And because of lack of hangar space for our visiting aircraft, the Super Constellations of our squadron were parked in the subzero temperatures outside overnight. They could not be started in the usual way. Each engine needed about forty-five minutes of heating by special heater-blower units in order to get warm enough to turn over.

At our base in Thule we lived in small "houses" that actually were constructed like reefers or refrigerators, completely insulated from the subzero temperatures. The handles on the doors were made of plastic instead of the usual metal so that one's hands would not stick to the handle and be permanently damaged. The toilets had a closed loop system like that of a submarine, we were told, so after using the toilet one had to follow a very special procedure for flushing. If you used an improper sequence in operating the various valves, switches, and foot pedals, the contents in the toilet would summarily fly straight up into the air, instead of through the piping system. It was said that one makes that mistake only once.

We did, in fact, successfully chart the pressure ridges and leads in the ice pack from our Radar Super Constellation aircraft in support of the first winter exploration of a submarine, the USS *Skate,* at the North Pole. It was a series of not only long and tiring flights requiring utmost concentration but also flights at very low altitudes for extended periods over the ice pack. The mission on the return flight from Thule, via Spitzbergen and Iceland, was to chart the ice pack to its southernmost edge. The pilot, copilot, crew chief, and I (as CIC officer) of the flight crew received letters of commendation from the Commander, Submarine Division 101, Atlantic Fleet, for the success of the mission.

A very interesting thing we did on this trip was to "fly around the world in nine minutes." One asks how this is possible when it takes the astronauts about an hour and a half to orbit. Well, it depends where you orbit. We did it around the North Pole in one complete turn through all lines of longitude. My one other around the world was on a pleasure tour in various countries over a three-week period.

After another operational training period at Guantanamo Bay, Cuba, during 4–9 March, I started my second three-month deployment to the Mediterranean. Lt. Cmdr. Dave Rowlands was the plane commander of Radar Super Constellation Aircraft, Aircraft Bureau number 145937. We flew out of Patuxent River and headed for Lajes, Azores, on 25 March 1960.

The approach to the Azores brought on another thriller that I could have done without after some of the experiences on the previous deployment. When we were approximately a hundred miles or so short of reaching the Azores, our navigator gave the pilot a change in heading to 045 degrees (from existing 090 degrees, which we were on). It was my feeling, as CIC officer on watch, that we should have continued straight on the 090-degree heading. While the navigator was ultimately responsible for the navigation of the aircraft, in the early warning Super Constellations with all the electronics capability, the CIC officers usually did back up navigation both for crew training and to relieve boredom on long flights. On every flight over the water I maintained a jump plot navigation exercise on the DRT (Dead Reckoning Tracer) charts.

The jump plot procedure was as follows: From the beginning of the flight, with a range and bearing from radar, we established a "reference" (a known point of land that had a very recognizable characteristic, as seen with the radar). As the aircraft proceeded, in this case from Maryland to the east over the Atlantic, just before that reference point of land on the radar would disappear, we marked where we were, a geographical location, on a navigation chart. At the same time, we located a ship on radar that was about 50 to 100 miles out in the direction of our flight path, got a range and bearing on it, and then transferred that point to the nav chart as well, which gave us the actual geographical location of that ship. With respect to the speed of the aircraft, any merchant ship at sea is going so slowly that it can be considered as an island, for all practical purposes, not moving. Farther on, we would pick up another ship on radar in the direction of our heading and plot it on the navigation chart giving that ship's actual location. And so it went across the entire ocean. From my experience in Atlantic Ocean crossings I knew it was an accurate-enough navigation method that we were never more than about fifty miles off-course, maximum, before reaching the final destination, across the entire Atlantic. And when we were only fifty miles away, the radar we had could easily detect specific islands such as in the Azores. It is necessary to understand something about this jump plot method of navigation in order to realize the problem that developed and the solution that saved the day. Our navigator, instead of using the usual methods of navigation (such as the sextant), was trying to use the jump plot method on his navigation station radar scope. When our aircraft was at a point about a hundred miles from the Azores, what he saw on his scope appeared to him to be a massive amount of sea return (actually, many heavy rain clouds were in the area at the time) and not a clear and distinct picture of the five islands of the Azores. With this, he thought we were too far south off course and consequently gave the pilot a change in heading to 045 degrees. After about forty-five minutes more flight time there was absolutely nothing on the radar scope ahead of us on the new heading. I had asked the navigator why he changed the heading, and he said we were too far south. Then the pilot called me in CIC and asked what I had for a position. I told him my jump plot showed us within fifty miles of the Azores at the time we changed heading. Commander Rowlands said to me, "Paul, give me a heading to where you believe Lajes to be located. If we continue in our present direction we'll never make it to any land." I gave a new heading of 180 degrees, due south from the current position. After about half an hour, way down on the bottom of my radar scope I detected five tiny blips of radar return. I reported the same. The pilot said, "It's our only hope." As we continued southward, the blips became stronger and eventually I saw and recognized the five blips and their shapes as the familiar radar returns for Lajes. Once more, a safe landing. Had we continued on the 045 heading, which turned out to be in the direction of the Portuguese mainland, we would not have had sufficient fuel to reach the next possible landing field at Rota, Spain.

While at Lajes this one night we went to the officers' club for dinner. They always had very good steaks, and on this night there was bingo, which we decided to play after dinner. As we entered the bingo hall, I paid for two bingo cards and received two tickets, which were needed to pick up the cards inside. The serial numbers on my two tickets were 145937 and

145938. I could hardly believe the coincidence. Of the twelve Super Connies in our squadron, two of the aircraft had precisely these Navy Bureau numbers, and I was actually in the crew of aircraft with bureau number 145937 on this deployment. Further, on the first bingo calling I had bingo and won a magnum of champagne. Had this something to do with the fact that we had a safe landing at the intended location, Lajes, and not a ditching in the waters northeast of the Azores?

On the twenty-sixth of March we made a four-hour-and-thirty-minute flight to Rota, Spain, where we stayed overnight. Then on 27 March 1960 we went to our deployment base at the naval air station in Sigonella, Sicily. The majority of the flights during this deployment involved operations with units of the Sixth Fleet ships and aircraft, and during this period we averaged about eighty flight hours per month, with a flight approximately every third day. But in the meantime there were a few "familiarization" flights that allowed us to land in various countries to become familiar with the airfields that we would use from time to time for refueling and emergencies. Some of the tourist locations were of course interesting for us as a change from remote military settings.

The first of these trips was on 2 April 1960 to Nice, France, for three days. I recall the hotel, Hotel Ruhl, which was within walking distance for a beach and cabana area where we three CIC officers went to swim. Two oddities for us were quickly experienced. One was the millions of stones, not sand, on the beaches. This could be cast aside not as a criticism but as fate from Mother Nature. Montauk, Long Island, was blessed with miles of white sandy beaches. The other experience was gained after the swim. We inquired about showers to wash off the salt, and we were directed to a location underneath the boardwalk along the beach. As we stood under the showers void of all clothing, there suddenly appeared only several feet away from us several women under showers also naked but completely oblivious to anything or anyone around them. They began to observe our reactions, which were a mixture of surprise, embarrassment, and confusion. We asked ourselves if we went into the wrong shower space. Or did they? None of the above. The ladies began to grin and chatter and most probably declared that we must certainly be some of those Puritan American tourists. We learned that this integrated washdown was quite normal in France and a portent of things to come in many other parts of the world.

We three officers of CIC rented a small car to drive up and around the mountainous curves to Monaco from Nice in order to see the palace complex of Prince Rainier, Monte Carlo, the harbor with expensive yachts, and the like. Just as we arrived we saw the changing of the guard in front of the palace. We walked quite a bit to see more closely how things were there in Monaco. I never have forgotten a rather simple scene on a very narrow street. Only one person was there slowly walking on this little street, perhaps contemplating, with both hands clasped behind his back, a Catholic priest with black cassock and with black beret. This "picture," I thought, really belonged to the Monaco scene.

Some years later when hearing of the tragic death of Princess Grace (Kelly), I reflected on my visit to Monaco and the road that took us up to Monaco from Nice. It was the path Princess Grace took before plunging into the depths by failing to negotiate one of those many curves of that very road.

On 11 April we flew to Naples, Italy, after more fleet operations out of Sigonella. I got to know more about my mother's parents' country by having more time on this trip to observe the people, foods, and customs in general. And actually I had tried in a short time before this deployment to learn a few words of the Italian language so that I could at least get through some basic situations. But on one occasion I really got stuck when I went out of the city to look into the countryside. When through with my minitour I hailed a taxi and asked him to take me to the NATO Headquarters. Well, we went back and forth for the longest time with the driver trying to understand where I wanted to go. I thought the term or acronym *NATO* was on everyone's mind because most of the European countries were members and surely they must all know NATO. Perhaps fifteen minutes later a man walked by and saw that the driver and I had a problem. The driver asked the passerby, who seemed to know a little bit of English, to find out where I wanted to go. He asked me.

I said, "Nay tow."

He told the driver, "He wanna go 'Nah tow.'"

The driver: *"Si, si,* you wanna go Nah tow!"

It sounded to me as though we were all saying the same thing and it was hard to figure out why there was such a problem. I learned this to be a common problem. Misunderstandings, for example, develop between Americans and Europeans simply with the mispronunciation of one vowel. I was saying "nay tow" how *NATO* is pronounced in America, and this sounded very different, especially at that time, to the European who has always said, "Nah tow." It was certainly not the biggest of issues, but those fifteen minutes of helplessness for me with that driver in a remote location and strange country left me with the hope that one day we could all speak the same language. It could serve to facilitate not only clear directions for a driver but also international problems solved on much higher, more important levels between governments.

One evening as several of us were walking on the sidewalk from the hotel to a restaurant a few blocks away, two women walked up to two of the pilots of our crew in front of us. The women put their arms around these two and chatted for perhaps less than a minute, making certain provocative comments, then departed as quickly as they had appeared. Too late, the two pilots found that they were minus their wallets.

On this same evening I saw an American sailor in an alley with an Italian civilian and a canvas travel bag on the pavement between them. The Italian with his wallet in hand appeared as if he were going to pay the sailor for something. Suddenly the Italian shouted, "Police," the sailor ran, and the Italian as well, but in the opposite direction. What had happened? The sailor was selling several cartons of cigarettes on the black market and the Italian feigned acceptance of the cigarettes for some amount of money. Instead of carrying out the purchase, the Italian shouted, "Police," even though none were around, to scare the wits out of the sailor. He knew that the sailor would not want to be caught by the police and ultimately be turned over to U.S. Navy authorities. The Italian picked up the bag with the cigarettes and ran without paying anything.

We made one other trip to Nice, France, on 21 April 1960, but mostly as a result of having to refuel at the international airport. But we stayed there overnight and then went to Palma, Majorca, on 22 April for two days' rest and recreation. We had a difficult time finding a hotel in Palma because of many tourists, I suppose. We had a chief petty officer (aviation electrician mate) who was a real comedian, and on this trip his talents were used to the fullest extent to obtain rooms for the seven officers of our crew in the Princess Hotel. One of the talents of this chief was to be able to babble on in a nonsensical manner, which sounded like some foreign language but in fact was no language at all. It sounded as though he were really talking about something, but it was absolutely nothing that anyone could understand. This chief was of medium build, bald-headed, and about forty years old. He was to play the part of an important political leader from a nonexistent country such as depicted in a *Mission Impossible* movie. All the officers were to act as part of his entourage and walk as porters behind him into the hotel to carry "all his baggage" (which really belonged to each of us). We approached the desk of the hotel and the chief started his act with very serious-looking facial expressions. Naturally the desk manager could not understand a thing. Then our plane commander stepped up to the desk, purposely acting nervous and playing fear of our leader to convey fear to the manager, to explain that our leader ordered eight rooms for himself and his porters. When the desk manager started to reply that there were no rooms, the chief would start loudly babbling his private language, giving the impression that he had already stood waiting too long and wanted immediate attention or he would call Generalissimo Franco. Only the word *Franco* was actually understandable by everyone. It was like someone suddenly put a gun against the head of the manager, and paper started to fly. We had all we could do to keep from laughing, as the chief was so funny and he kept a straight face the entire time. The end result was that we had very nice rooms, including a suite for our "leader," who was the electrician petty officer. It became apparent that the hotel had to cancel somebody's reservations in order to satisfy the special needs of this political leader from . . . where?

There were several more operational flights with the fleet, and one of them required us to land at Wheelus Air Force Base in Tripoli, Libya, on 5 May 1960 after a sixteen-hour flight operation in the area. We had been a few times before at this base in Libya, but it was always considered unsafe to visit in town. We idled the hours away on base in the cafeteria and at the Officers' Club, a film, and PX, where we could buy cigarettes very cheaply. Pall Malls were "the" cigarette at the time.

On Sicily itself some of the things that stand out in my mind, aside from the operational flights, were varied and of interest to me. For example, when the flight crews took the normal route to go to the airfield, which was located some distance from the base where we lived, we had to cross railroad tracks. Most of the time there were no trains passing through. On the other hand, there were several occasions when we were in a hurry to get to the airfield and a train would be on its way. The real problem was not the train itself but a little old lady who controlled the gates to warn drivers of a train passing. She would invariably lower the gates about fifteen minutes before the train was anywhere near the rail crossing, and there was no way to convince her that our passage was important. We had to wait. The alternative was to take a route that was very long and therefore of little advantage. This woman lived in the tiny house near the crossing and her sole function was the operation of these gates, which she took very seriously.

On the drive to the airfield and to almost any other point all that one could see, it seemed, was fields of artichokes. And you would get the impression that these artichokes were very valuable or a lot of theft was experienced. There were men frequently seen either on bicycles or on motorscooters, patrolling their areas with shotguns. I was never a threat to these folks, as the artichoke is one of those food items that I can do without.

The first opera that I ever attended was with several officers of our squadron at an opera house in Catania, Sicily. We enjoyed *Rigoletto,* which was performed in an opera house of a wonderful and elegant old world style. This created a memorable atmosphere, an unforgettable pleasant experience. I could not ever critique such an opera performance, as I do not have the expertise in this field. But I can say that, to me, the singing sounded very good, the costuming was fabulous, the stage settings fitting and elegant. Of the operas that I have attended in the years since 1960, none has ever measured up to my memory of *Rigoletto* in Catania. We did gain a certain amount of culture on a number of occasions in the very transitory navy lifestyle.

Our flight crews also had quite a show of nature, as Mount Aetna blew its top while we were stationed at Sigonella. In fact, it used to be some kind of sport flying directly over Aetna each time we came in for a landing from operations. Of course, after the eruption such flights were banned. It was quite a bit of luck that Aetna didn't blow during one of the many passes of our aircraft over its top.

Then on the eighteenth of May 1960 we were heading toward home, ultimately the Patuxent River Naval Air Station, when we lost an engine. Its propeller was feathered and we went down for a landing at Wiesbaden Air Force Base. I believe it was a case of "throwing a piston." In any case, we needed a new engine and had to wait until one was flown from a storage depot in the States. So we had nine free days to sightsee, except when the engine arrived the mechanics and electricians of our crew had to work changing the engine. It seemed the air force personnel based at Wiesbaden did only what they had to. Our crew actually did the entire engine change, including the massive propeller, by themselves and outside on the tarmac, not inside a hangar. Altogether it was a big job and they did very well. The CIC crew had little to do with the mechanics of the plane, only the electronics, so we had all the days off. I went for the first time to Rudesheim and some other small towns on the Rhine. It was all new in this area of Germany for me, so it was very interesting, also in Wiesbaden itself. While in

Wiesbaden, we were staying in the von Steuben Hotel (military), which was later taken over by Penta Hotels.

When I enter the air force PX today in Wiesbaden, not far from Penta, my memories go back to 1960, because the very same buildings and shops still stand as before. And it was here that I bought a Telefunken (or Grundig) stereo console, which I brought back to our home at Patuxent.

On the twenty-seventh of May 1960 we flew to Rota, Spain, then on to Lajes, Azores, and to Harmon Air Force Base in Canada, all on the same day. Once again, before finishing an Atlantic crossing we had some excitement about halfway between the Azores to Canada. It was quite obvious on our radar that there was a cold front along a line running north and south about a hundred miles long. There we could expect some very bumpy weather at our altitude, which was between 5,000 and 6,000 feet. There would normally be a change in course to avoid storms, but with a 100-mile front the diversion would have been too great, considering fuel and destination. So we were all set for this bump, which came like running into a brick wall. The aircraft shook violently and all loose items flew upward and then down onto the deck. That in itself was not as terrifying as the smell of fuel fumes. With the violent shaking up, we all had visions of ruptured fuel tanks. We went into emergency mode to the extent that all radar, communications equipment, and unnecessary electrical circuits were shut down. The flight engineer with flashlight commenced his process of damage assessment starting at the cockpit area and working toward the after section of the aircraft. This process took quite a bit of time. In these situations time is very much relative. As the plane could blow up because of fuel leaking in the aircraft, five seconds were an eternity. Actually, it took about ten minutes of searching through the entire length of the darkened aircraft, only with the aid of this flashlight. The fuel fumes persisted all during this time without any word from the flight engineer. Because of his silence we thought further that there may be one of those insidious hidden ruptures or cracks of a fuel tank. At last! There, at the very back of the plane. The plane commander had purchased a motorscooter in Naples, and it was now lying on its side from the violent turbulence. There was the smell of fuel running out of the scooter's gas tank. We were in one moment very relieved that it was not a fuel tank rupture, but in the next moment came the aftershock of what if? What if, I thought, what if during this frontal turbulence we had simultaneously another instance of St. Elmo's fire inside the plane as we did on the flight to Keflavik in 1958? Well, we had to tell ourselves it did not happen and we were still here to tell about it. The only thing that can be done when you survive is pass on lessons learned to preclude accidents and near misses. Always defuel and purge a fuel tank of such an item, or better yet, leave it on the ground.

We happily arrived back at home base, Patuxent River, on 28 May 1960.

The next deployment, away from operations in the local area (off the Virginia Capes), was in Keflavik, Iceland. On 8 September 1960 we departed Patuxent for Iceland via Argentia, Newfoundland, where we stopped overnight. On 9 September we landed in Keflavik to take part in a two-week antisubmarine operation. The winds were very strong during this period and flying was often made more difficult because of cross winds during takeoff and landing. We were housed in Quonset huts, World War II vintage, and the temperatures inside our hut were nearly the same as outside temperatures. I recall ice forming on the inside of the windows and the only place to get a little warm was within two feet of the single potbelly stove in the middle of this Quonset hut. In Iceland there were no fences around the base and the Icelandic police had authority, it seemed, throughout the entire area of our base.

There were as always, wherever deployed, places of interest to visit. On one occasion we, three or four officers, walked into the town nearby and found ourselves attracted to the waterfront where some of the fishing boats had just come in from a few days at sea. The catches of fish they unloaded were mostly large halibut. Then continuing along the waterfront we came upon a small pier where several young boys, about eight or nine years of age, were fishing with simple hand lines. Memories again of my own youth stirred my desire to try my hand at fishing, and the boys gave me one of the fishing lines. In no time I had caught three or four fish about eight inches long and very good-looking for pan frying. I could see myself in Montauk at the Fishing Village, twenty-five years prior, doing precisely the same as these boys. I left there with a very good feeling.

We returned to Patuxent River Naval Air Test Center, Maryland, from Iceland via an overnight in Argentia on 26 September 1960.

It was during this period that I was promoted to lieutenant senior grade. On a very cold autumn day after the return from Iceland, all the officers who had just received promotions were summarily thrown into the outdoor unheated swimming pool at the Patuxent Officers' Club, new blue uniforms and all. It was a mighty cold initiation, but a warmly proud day for me.

In late January 1961 the Portuguese government requested assistance from the U.S. State Department to locate their hijacked passenger liner the *Santa Maria*. Galvao, in an attempt to overthrow the government of Salazar, had taken control of and hijacked the ship. Galvao had already killed some of the ship's crew in the process. Our squadron was assigned to fly to the Caribbean, staging out of Roosevelt Roads, Puerto Rico, and patrol as necessary to find the ship.

We had to first be able to take off out of Patuxent River, but the heavy snowfall required the runway be cleared of snow. Since the time for clearance of the entire runway would have taken too long it was determined that we take on only enough fuel to fly to Jacksonville, Florida, and there fill the tanks. The lesser fuel load at Patuxent allowed for a much shorter takeoff, consequently less time for runway clearance. We departed home base at Patuxent River on 26 January 1961, headed south, and after the Jacksonville fuel stop landed at Roosevelt Roads for a briefing on the *Santa Maria* hijack situation.

Our first landing in Brazil, which was in Belem for the purpose of refueling, was really an interesting part of this operation. As soon as the three Super Constellations from our squadron landed there in Belem, our aircraft were immediately surrounded by dozens of heavily armed Brazilian marines. We crewmen had no idea what was happening and why we were being held, sitting on the hot tarmac in our flight suits for most of the day. Finally, after the squadron commander had talked for hours with these people, we were informed of the problem. A message was originally sent from the U.S. Naval authorities and U.S. State Department requesting permission for "Landing of VW Aircraft." Permission had been granted. The military authorities in Brazil, however, had interpreted that as "one aircraft." The intent of the original message was meaning "VW-type aircraft." So as we landed three of these rather large and strange-looking early warning aircraft, the military in Brazil got very nervous and put us under arrest. Kind of scary, since we had come to help the Salazar government and suddenly found ourselves, albeit for only a day, looking down the barrels of these guns.

After the Belem incident and early during the search process, we landed at Port-of-Spain, Trinidad, for refueling. We were informed that a boat with the dead purser from the *Santa Maria* had been found at the shore. After several more days of searching, the *Santa Maria* was finally located fifty miles east of Recife, Brazil. Our navy aircraft orbited the ship until U.S. Naval destroyers arrived with Brazilian marines who boarded and regained control of the *Santa Maria*. Our aircraft remained in Recife for several more days, until all the passengers were safely ashore at Recife's port. I have some 8mm movie film of the passengers coming ashore and a Brazilian newspaper with the story (in Portuguese). Galvao, the hijacker, found asylum in Brazil after being taken from the *Santa Maria*.

Our flight crews stayed at the Hotel Boa Viagem, located on the ocean front, a very nice hotel. Here at the Boa Viagem, aside from the *Santa Maria* story itself, the memorable moments were breakfast. There was such a huge selection of fresh fruit, including pineapple, papaya, and mango, that every morning I ate mostly an assortment of fresh fruit with yogurt, along with coffee and toast. It was really great. While at this hotel we learned that one of the very many newspaper reporters from other countries was so intent on being the first to cover the *Santa Maria* hijacking story that he had hired a small aircraft to fly him over the ship and bailed out with parachute. He landed in the water near the ship, but the U.S. Navy plucked him out of the sea to keep him from getting on the ship. This reporter was also unlucky, because he wound up with a broken leg from the jump from the aircraft. His little parachute adventure gained him almost as much news as the *Santa Maria,* during the last days of this sea saga.

After the *Santa Maria* was secure from the hijacker, Galvao, we had a chance to look around the city of Recife and see how the people lived, what was in the shops, and how the food was. As we walked along the streets the most noticeable sight was the large number of persons lying on the streets and sidewalks with huge goiters around the neck, almost the size of their heads in many cases. It was really difficult to view, and I wondered just why so many were afflicted with these goiters and what anyone might be doing about them, if anything.

Much of the flying after 1960 and until 1962 involved North Atlantic barrier patrol flights and support of the NASA Recovery Forces in Project Mercury, to which I was assigned as the SARAH officer. SARAH (Search and Rescue and Homing) was special equipment installed in our patrol aircraft for the sole purpose of locating a Mercury capsule after splashdown in the ocean from a suborbital or orbital space flight. It was my responsibility to not only operate this equipment in my flight crew but also train all the operators in the other flight crews involved in Project Mercury recoveries. I was very happy on two occasions to experience success in this project after many many months of training exercises. The first was in locating the

Mercury capsule MA-3, which was the first long-range (unmanned) test from Canaveral into the South Atlantic. With the use of SARAH, after splashdown, I vectored our pilot toward the signal I received and after about another three minutes of flight the MA-3 capsule was visible from the cockpit. The head of the recovery forces for NASA, Milton Windler, was aboard our aircraft on the flightdeck to observe firsthand the SARAH locating capability. Smoke pods were dropped from our aircraft at the landing site as locators for the naval ships that came in shortly after for retrieval of the capsule.

In support of an unmanned orbital space flight our crew was deployed to Lajes, Azores, to be on station in the South Atlantic in the event that it might be necessary to search for a capsule in an abort area. During the period 22–27 April 1961 we flew thirty-six hours for this mission. No abort was necessary. One of the incidents I recall on this assignment occurred one early morning on the flight line. It was customary especially at Lajes to provide box lunches for the flight crew, and this meant about twenty box lunches would be placed by a driver from the mess hall near the nose wheel of the aircraft. This particular morning there were no lunches and there was this hassle between our flight engineer and the duty cook at the mess hall. The cook said he had sent the lunches out to flight line. But we had none. What had happened was some Portuguese kids came over the base fence earlier in the morning and stole all the lunches. Yes, we got more rations, but this time with direct delivery.

Once again in Argentia, Newfoundland, from the fifteenth to the nineteenth of May 1961 for flying the North Atlantic barrier patrols.

In June 1961, I was transferred from Squadron VW-2 (AEWRON-2) at Patuxent River to another squadron (AEWTULANT) also based at Patuxent. This was the Airborne Early Warning Training Unit Atlantic, also with twelve Super Constellations and carrying out some of the same missions as AEWRON 2, where I had just served for some years. I was again assigned as avionics officer, airborne CIC officer, and responsible for the SARAH training for NASA capsule recovery operations. In the three months following my transfer, we had operations in the Virginia Capes area. But then we were again assigned North Atlantic barrier patrols out of Argentia, Newfoundland, and Lajes, Azores, during 17 to 26 August 1961. From September 1961 through February 1962 there were local operations with the fleet and with NASA except for the 27 to 30 November 1961 in the Azores.

On the twelfth of February 1962 we landed in Bermuda for a nine-day stay to cover the abort area in the South Atlantic for possible recovery of the first manned orbital flight. It was during this Bermuda deployment that I experienced the second situation in which I had such a good feeling of success working with NASA. It was when John Glenn made the first manned space orbit, on 20 February 1962. Our flight crew, staging out of Bermuda, was assigned to the abort station where, if an abort were necessary, the Mercury capsule with Glenn would splash down. As SARAH operator I, as well as the rest of the flight crew, was at the ready for its recovery. As we all know, there was no need to abort. The flight went as planned in perfect orbit. A little known fact, perhaps only important to the members of our squadron, is that I was the person to have received the first signals from Glenn's Mercury spacecraft as it passed over our aircraft on the first American manned orbital space flight. It was because of this that the commanding officer of our squadron, AEWTULANT, Capt. Louis J. Papas, USN, held a special dinner for this occasion with all officers present at the officers' club, Patuxent River, Maryland. James Webb, director of NASA, had commended our activities and ships of Flotilla Four, Atlantic Fleet, to the chief of naval operations for successfully performing in support of Glenn's space flight operations.

During the period we were in Bermuda I made a number of observations that were of interest to me and there were some interesting experiences as well. Here is a medley of some memories on this island. I met several of the other astronauts, including Virgil Grissom, who later died in a capsule mishap. Also on this visit to Bermuda I witnessed my first cricket match, but I must admit I still do not entirely understand the rules and scoring of this game. And in Hamilton I had one of the best Cordon Bleu dinners in a small restaurant that I believe had a Hungarian-oriented kitchen. The British-looking "Bobbies" were interesting to see, in their tall helmets, directing traffic on this small island far away from London. I learned that a bicycle could take me from one end of Bermuda to the other in the course of a day. (U.S. military personnel were not allowed to rent motorscooters in Bermuda when we were there because some inebriated sailors a few months earlier had played Evil Knievel and raced a few of them off the piers into the bay.) And all the drinking and household water at that time, maybe still today, came from rainwater that was caught in those huge concrete encasements that covered the sides of the mountains. Water was also caught on the roofs of individual homes and other buildings and stored in water cellars. I learned that Bermuda is the northernmost coral island in the world. And I thought that Bermuda was one of the cleanest, most orderly places I had seen and in a warm sunny atmosphere surrounded by the most beautiful sparkling green-watered coves. But I also noted that I had not the money to take advantage of any lengthy stays in its luxury.

Another type of operation our squadron was involved in was range clearance. There were many research and development tests conducted in the upper atmosphere by sending various payloads up by rockets fired from Wallops Island, Virginia, in Chincoteague Bay. Before the rockets were fired all the ships, boats, and aircraft had to be cleared out, in about a ninety-degree sector from Wallops Island, out to the east over the Atlantic Ocean. About an hour before the scheduled firing time one of our squadron aircraft had to get on station and fly a barrier flight pattern, continuously flying north and south on a fifty-mile line just west of Wallops Island, and report to the fire control station at Wallops whether the range was cleared. It was the job of CIC, where I was the CIC officer, to inform the flight deck of headings to fly our aircraft to stay on the barrier we patrolled so that we remain just west of Wallops. Whenever there would be a firing, "Notices to Mariners" would be sent out to inform ships at sea that the range area was restricted during a given day at certain hours. Likewise pilots flying into this general area would be warned of restricted areas for rocket firings when filing their flight plans. So there always should not have been any ship or aircraft in the range area. However, invariably there was a sailboat, a pleasure yacht, or a small private aircraft "tooling" (traveling) through the range and we had to put a hold on the firing.

One night there was a rather exciting moment when our own Super Constellation aircraft had drifted slightly off course so that our flight path brought us practically over the rocket firing pad at Wallops. I had noticed this drift and tried to call the flight deck to warn the pilot and copilot. However, they were for some reason communicating with someone else just seconds before the firing and I could not get through on the intercom. All of a sudden, back aft in the CIC radar and communications section, which had no windows, we felt the aircraft lurch and there was just a second of a hellish roaring noise. Immediately after, the pilot called me: "Cook, what the hell are you trying to do . . . get us all killed?" I reminded him that the lines between the cockpit and CIC must be kept absolutely clear and everyone especially attentive near the very time of the scheduled launch. The difference in ranks suppressed my true urge to say more. Because of their vantage point in the cockpit the pilots had an even scarier moment, which I thought they had earned. They were also shaken by the sudden and immense brightness as the rocket flame zooming upward pierced the night sky just a short distance from the nose of our aircraft. We always said, "Any flight that you can walk away from, is a good flight!"

I had heard about the Electronics Technical Officers School [ELTO] that was located at the Naval Air Technical Training Center (NATTC) in Memphis (Millington), Tennessee. This was where eligible avionics officers could study for one full year to acquire an education equivalent to two years of college electronic engineering. I applied for this and was accepted in early 1962. This was my departure from the operating early warning squadrons at Patuxent River and faraway places to a purely academic scene for one year.

It was about this time that there began a building up of domestic tensions, around the 1960s and on into the 1970s. The bubble seemed to have burst, so to speak. The Vietnam War certainly had its very bad effects on not only the soldiers suffering there but also with the teenagers revolting and using drugs, irrespective of family conditions, good or bad. A general revolt of the teenagers, antiestablishment, and drugs were the scene. Naturally, problems within many families became more prominent, more so difficult in a confused national atmosphere. Within all this I felt I was being deprived of the normal navy social life, and reciprocating to my fellow officers and their families became less and less. Milly did not believe at all in drinking or being around it and, in fact, did not want alcohol in the house. Inviting navy friends, whom I flew with in good times and bad, was not thinkable. She was not interested in attending many social functions at the officers' clubs. I had to attend "Command Performances" alone, as well as go alone to my church. Milly had all the morals anyone could possibly have, and I certainly could never put her down for that. But many activities in various aspects of what I considered "normal life" simply did not exist between us or for me personally. Life continued.

Engineering Studies, Ship Installations, at Sea
U.S. Navy

Memphis, Tennessee; Philadelphia, Pennsylvania; Baltimore, Maryland; Panama; Acapulco, Mexico; Point Mugu, California; Port Hueneme, California (1962–68)

My transfer from Patuxent River, Naval Air Test Center, Lexington Park, Maryland, to the ELTO School at the Naval Air Technical Training Center in Memphis (Millington), Tennessee, took place in early 1962. My family, wife and three children, lived in Raleigh, Tennessee (near Memphis), and we stayed there one full year while I was attending ELTO School. With a Federal Housing Administration (FHA) loan I had purchased a newly constructed home for only $19,500. The house was a really beautiful two-story structure with four bedrooms, living room, dining room, kitchen, three full baths, and two-car garage and on a half-acre of land. We still had the 1956 Buick Special that was purchased in Memphis when I was stationed there the last time, just before my commissioning in 1957.

For one solid year I was a student in ELTO School. The lectures and labs had significant depth to include, e.g., the actual design, construction, and testing of various electronic circuits as student projects. Upon the successful completion of the ELTO School, I was assigned for duty with the Naval Air Engineering Laboratory (NAEL), Philadelphia, in the Ship Installation Division. My specific assignment was as the NAEL representative at the Maryland Shipbuilding and Drydock Company (MS&D) in Baltimore, Maryland. This required a household move from Memphis to the Baltimore area. For two years, mid-1963 to July 1965, I was responsible for progressing the installation of the new $200 million Typhon Weapon System (TWS) aboard the 15,000-ton USS *Norton Sound* (AVM-1), a former seaplane tender in service during World War II. This involved daily visits throughout the entire ship and reporting weekly on the TWS installation progress to the chief of Naval Ship Systems Command in Washington, as well as to my immediate superiors at NAEL in Philadelphia. Copies of my reports were sent to all organizations with whom I worked in very close coordination. Westinghouse Defense (manufacturer of the TWS), the John Hopkins Applied Physics Laboratory, the shipyard superintendent, the USN Bureau of Weapons, and several other participants related to the project. This was one of several very satisfying and enjoyable assignments during my naval career.

I rented a house in Harundale, which is the next town from Glen Burnie, Maryland, just south of Baltimore and the MS&D. In Harundale the first shopping mall in America was built. The location of our house was very good in terms of closeness to the MS&D, schools, and shopping, as well as being a very nice neighborhood. Jim and Dave were getting interested in Little League baseball, so we spent many hours at the baseball fields during this time. Patti, I recall, had a very nice girlfriend in the Tribble family just down the street from our house. From this vantage point, near Baltimore, we were able to more easily visit Montauk to see my parents, to visit my brother Joe and his family in Brunswick, Maryland, and to visit my sister Gladys and her family in Virginia Beach, Virginia.

During one of the AVM-1 sea trials after the TWS installation was completed, the ship encountered a hurricane in the Atlantic off the Virginia coast. It was certainly not intended; however, the storm served as another test of the ship's ability to withstand the rigors of such a storm, especially in view of the newly installed five-deck-level tower that contained a large segment of the TWS. During this storm, with the ship severely pitching, rolling, and yawing, I was required to climb up the five deck levels of the tower to determine the condition of the system with respect to the effects of the various forces exerted on the system by the storm. On my hands and knees, and hanging on every inch of the way, I managed to make the necessary observations and to report that all was well above, way above, in the upper decks. I had recalled President Kennedy saying once that "the sea is so great and my boat is so small." This was never so true as then. At one moment we could look down from the decks of our 15,000-ton ship into fifty-foot troughs and several seconds later look up the same distance to the wave crests. And when the ship pitched with the stern high, the ship's screws turned in thin air, causing the entire ship to shudder from vibrations of the loadless propulsion system. There were, without question, moments of concern by all aboard from this tossing about. The experience of being on a ship in a hurricane, for many of us being the first time, forever planted in our minds the tremendous power of the sea and the respect it must be given.

After all the scheduled tests and trials had been completed, the captain decided to make a port visit at Miami, Florida. It was not only to provide a little rest for all the crew and shipyard personnel who had worked so hard to get the ship ready. It was also a chance to "show the ship" with its new superstructure, five additional deck levels containing this new TWS weapons system. The AVM-1 was built in the early 1940s, a rather old ship, yet it was a perfect platform for the testing of this new equipment. Because of the radical approach in the TWS antenna system, this new weapon system's exterior completely changed the silhouette of the AVM-1, giving the ship a look like something of another world. Reporters and photographers were in abundance at the pier as we eased into our berth. They had a field day. The next morning the *Miami Herald* had a giant photo of the ship, covering half the front page, showing an equally giant headline: "1980 Ship with 1890 Problem." What had happened was the accommodation ladder, an integral part of the ship to be lowered for personnel to board and leave the ship, was so rusted at the pivotal joints that the deck force could not make it budge. This ladder had not been used for some three years, for it was never needed during this time. The ship's crew could not leave the ship, and those who had waited on the pier, the reporters, the mayor, and anybody who was anybody, could not get aboard the ship in a timely manner. That is, it took some hours to correct the problem. By then, the newspapers had more story than they had hoped for. The port authority had planned a social hour for the officers of the ship, and although rather late, because of the ladder, the social hour did take place, with a very jovial exchange of quips about the old and new of the USS *Norton Sound* (AVM-1).

On the way back to Baltimore the ship anchored overnight in the bay off Norfolk, Virginia. I took this opportunity to go ashore by way of one of the ship's boats and visited in Virginia Beach with my younger sister, Gladys Sage, who had just given birth on 18 January 1965, some weeks before, to son Matthew, the fourth of five children. I was the first, outside the immediate family of Bob and Gladys, to hold little Matthew.

Actually, the AVM-1 was the only U.S. Navy ship at the MS&D. Most of the ships there at MS&D were freighters or tankers coming in for overhaul or repairs but mostly repairs. I learned that a merchant ship stays in port or in a shipyard only so long as absolutely necessary, the reason being money. The shipowners do not make any money unless their ship is moving, carrying goods from point A to point B. In port, they are the ones who have to pay. It was further interesting to this end that the MS&D was noted for their quick turnaround capability in repair work. I had witnessed the patching up of a twenty-five-foot gash in the side of a merchant ship, making it seaworthy, in just twenty-four hours. This merchant had had a collision with another in the Chesapeake Bay. In this case the MS&D guaranteed the shipowner he would have his ship out in twenty-four hours. And so it was.

MS&D also had an interesting room in their superintendents' building that was called the Chain Locker. In reality a chain locker is a compartment in the forward part of a ship where the anchor chains are stored. The MS&D Chain Locker was a very comfortable, cozy mahogany-paneled space with easy chairs. It was in this chain locker that the ships' captains and chief engineers were welcomed with open arms to have their daily whiskey or other related choices of refreshment. Anything to please the masters of the merchants. Well, I must say that in my position, progressing the navy's ship and being one of only two naval officers in the yard during most of the AVM-1 overhaul, I was given the same privileges as those from the merchant ships. However, my main interest in the infamous Chain Locker was primarily in listening to these seafarers and hear all the stories, real or imagined. It was one of the very important marketing tools in the shipyard.

One of the highlights for me at the MS&D was the drydocking of the U.S. Navy's old sailing vessel the *Constellation*. I watched as it was towed into the dock and as its bottom gradually became exposed. From time to time I watched the *Constellation*'s bottom being cleaned, then treated with antifouling paint and again watched when it was towed out toward its resting place in Baltimore Harbor. Another part of U.S. Naval history witnessed in person. I expect that I have the only home movie film made of this drydock visit by the *Constellation* and have had it put on a video tape.

In mid-1965, with the AVM-1 overhaul and Typhon Weapon System installation completed, I was assigned to the ship as the electronics officer and assistant combat information center officer (ACICO). I had been an avionics officer of two squadrons and an airborne CIC officer. Now I held similar positions but aboard a ship, in the surface navy. I could not help to think back to 1947, when I joined the navy as ASETM, programmed for electronic training and shipboard duty, and one day just out of boot camp in Great Lakes, Illinois, I was summarily transferred to aviation because the navy had to fill a quota in the Avionics School in Corpus Christi, Texas. Now, as fate would have it, I went full circle and got duty in the surface navy, not as an electronic technician mate but as the electronics officer of a ship with all the technicians in my division. My assignment to the ship as ship's company was due, in part, to the fact that I had complete familiarity with every part of the ship, having progressed every aspect of the overhaul during the previous two years, including the engineering spaces as well as those of all the electrical, electronic, and weapons systems. The USS *Norton Sound* (AVM-1) sailed from Baltimore to its new West Coast home port, Port Hueneme, California, after transiting the Panama Canal in the summer of 1965.

I was not only impressed with the Panama Canal operation, my first and only time through it, but we also had the chance to stop at the U.S. Military Base in Panama for a couple of days and get to tour and learn all about Panama City and the whole area within about a twenty-mile radius. In the years that the canal was built, with what engineers had to work with it was amazing to me just how all that work was accomplished. Of course we read about all the problems, the accidents, the deaths from disease and the like. Yet it is difficult to comprehend how the tremendous daily obstacles were overcome. The perseverance and determination of the leadership in that canal work had to be just great. One of the more interesting stories that took place in Panama City, or nearby, was about this Catholic church that had a golden altar. Many years ago the town was about to be overrun and sacked, as the story goes, when someone had the bright idea to coat or whitewash the altar. It was saved.

During our passage through the canal en route to the Pacific Ocean we passed a Japanese naval destroyer bound for the Atlantic Ocean. As we were both sailing very low speed, nearly stopped, we got to exchange a few words with some of their crew standing at the rails. We asked, in English, from where they were coming. It took several minutes to understand anything they said. But finally, we learned they had departed the U.S.Naval Shipyard, Long Beach, California, a few days before. But some of what they said, at least what we heard, was like "rongabeech." I remembered that during World War II a famous password for the American soldiers to use was *lollapalooza* because the Japanese cannot pronounce the letter *l* and it comes out like an *r*. Hence the response from these Japanese sailors was "Rongabeech," not "Long Beach."

The commanding officer (CO), Captain Arthur, of our ship, AVM-1, had a retired naval officer friend who was now the manager of the La Brisis Hotel in Acapulco, Mexico. Captain Arthur decided that a four-day rest-and-recreation stop at Acapulco was in order before we continued on to the new home port at Port Hueneme. So contact was made by ship's telephone and rooms were arranged for the twenty or so officers who were not on watch and could go ashore. Dress whites were the uniform of the day for the reception planned for us at the hotel. We went ashore by launch, as we had anchored in the bay. The greetings at the door of the Las Brisas Hotel were made by a bevy of young ladies whom the manager had invited for the occasion. Each held two frozen daiquiris, one for each officer and one for the lady holding it. There was music, some dancing, and then a fabulous dinner in a private dining room. Quite a departure from the routine of many months in the shipyard and the shipboard activity. Each hotel room had a pink jeep that we used to travel about the area, and each hotel room had a private swimming pool, all overlooking the bay where our ship lay at anchor. Something that was very new to most of us at this time was the individual bar and fridge in each room. We thought that this friendly manager really fixed us up with comfort. It did not dawn on us that we had to pay for anything taken out of the bar. The bills were more than any one of us could afford, but somehow we managed the payments by pooling resources.

We got to see all the city and noticed quickly one side of the street with richness, the other side in poverty, a scene to become very familiar in further travels to other countries later in my career. Another experience for me was about what and where to drink, any kind of drink. When I went back to the ship the next day, I got so sick that I thought the end was near. I had had a drink with some ice cubes at some bar, and since I always drank slowly the ice was nearly all melted before the drink was finished. In this particular instance, because I had no more money to spend, I purposely prolonged the time of drinking this and only one, a highball, "7&7" (Seagram 7 and 7Up). Bad water used for making the ice cubes produced another victim of Montezuma. For five days I could only lie on my bed in my stateroom and the ship's doctor paid a visit twice a day telling me it would be over soon. It was not soon enough for me. Thereafter, I never took any water, or anything made from water, when in Mexico.

When we reached our new home port, Port Hueneme, I continued as the ship's electronics officer but also took on full Combat Information Center (CIC) responsibilities, safe navigation, air intercept control, tests for missile firings, and other related work. Most often I was able to live at home, in Camarillo, California, but frequently during three years, until

1968, I sailed on the ship for operations in the Pacific Missile Test Range (PMR) off the California coast from Point Mugu. The massive Typhon Weapons System (TWS) manufactured by Westinghouse and installed in the ship at Baltimore, in short, never did perform properly, and it was scrapped in 1966. The majority of the TWS installation was removed at the Long Beach Naval Shipyard (LBNS); however, all test equipment was kept aboard for use in other follow-on test projects at the Pacific Missile Range. The fact is, even during the installation of the TWS in Baltimore there were already such new developments and big advances made in electronic components and systems it was pretty well known that TWS, ultimately simply referred to as "Typhon," would soon be superseded. The successor to TWS, or Typhon, became known as the AEGIS system. However, it must be said that what was learned from the Typhon was significant in the development and testing of the AEGIS Weapons System, which has been operational in our fleet now for a number of years.

Aside from the continuous operational requirements on the Pacific Missile Range and the ongoing equipment maintenance requirements, there were always the accompanying personnel problems to deal with. I had already learned before this time that people in military or civilian life are going to be the source of most problems in any organization, self-inflicted or through inexperience. I myself am included as you recall certain difficulties from the first months of my navy career. My assumptions and inexperience, as an example, were cause of grief to me, as well as to some of my immediate superiors, when I had just finished boot camp at Great Lakes Naval Training Center. A piece of electronic equipment, an engine, or a pump can give problems as well; however, the maintenance and repair are accomplished with simple logic and proper equipment. They are without all the intangible variables of the human being. The engine does not talk back to you. The pump does not decide how it should be used. The electronic gear does not decide to change its frequency after you set it. If all that a civilian manager or military officer had to deal with were broken down equipment, life could be more of a breeze.

People are the cause of the large majority of time-consuming and costly problems. I have often stated that I believe 90 percent of all the problems in an organization relate to personnel. The costs are not only financial but often the lives of men and women. What follows immediately here are a couple of examples, but you can probably recall several instances in previous chapters of other very good examples of "people" problems.

At one point in time there were nine men from our ship who had been hospitalized for injuries caused by motorcycle accidents. Repeated sessions were held with the sailors on board our ship dealing with the dangers of motorcycles and recommendations to put their money into other hobbies. Many obviously did little to heed this, and a lot of man-months were lost due to their indifference to advice, not to speak of their permanent scars and disfigurement.

One day I took over command duty on the ship because the officer scheduled had something important to do on this day. I thought I would have an easy night, tied up in port. Around midnight, I was awakened by the officer of the deck and informed that one of sailors had been killed just a few miles from the ship. The sailor had used full throttle from a standstill. His bike wheeled, and it threw him up in the air. He came down with his throat upon a metal street sign post. In effect, he hung himself. He died immediately. The worst part of this of course was the trauma in his family, but we also lost a trained electronics technician. A senseless loss. The entire night I spent making reports to the local police, the Bureau of Personnel, and the Red Cross to notify the family.

From time to time each officer had to take assignments as defense attorney in a Court-Martial (CM) to defend someone accused of a wrongdoing. We used the Uniform Code of Military Justice (UCMJ) as "the bible," or guide, to perform the task. I think about all the hours and days I had to spend on some of these assignments because some character in the crew had decided to perform a misdeed. The charge against a seaman in one case was that he had stolen a large can of ham from the chief petty officer's mess on the ship. Actually, a witness on duty on deck saw this accused seaman with a ham as he stowed it, presumably to pick it up later. This witness gave the can of ham to the officer of the deck (OOD), who in turn gave it to the chief master at arms (CMAA), who simply put it into a storage area and locked it up. This appeared to be an open-and-shut case. After some weeks of preparation by the prosecutor (the ship's legal officer), witnesses, and myself, the court-martial took place. The accused was found not guilty because I had found a paragraph in the UCMJ that deals with "Chain of Custody." There was a lack of signatures given when the ham was handed over from the witness to the OOD and CMAA. There was no "proof" that the ham in the storage locker was the same ham seen by the witness.

Several days after the court-martial was over, the commanding officer of the ship, Captain Behl, called me into his quarters. He had received the written review of this case from the naval district legal officer, who agreed with my defense argument in this CM. "I see, Lieutenant Cook, that the seaman was found not guilty. We all know that this guy stole the ham. You didn't have to do such a damned good job as defense attorney"! (He knew well, of course, that I had to do what I did.) But this was not the end of it for me, because all the "bad guys" now pleaded for my help. More of the people problem!

During our ship overhaul at the Long Beach Naval Shipyard about the year 1967 a pool of several officers began driving every day from Camarillo to Long Beach, a distance of ninety miles. After just a couple of weeks we found this to be a very grueling run. For the rest of the overhaul we went home on weekends and stayed aboard the ship on weekdays.

During the week I often visited cousin Barbara Piccozzi Whitmore, her husband, Victor, and young daughter, Susan, their only child at the time. They lived in Los Alamitos, not very far from the ship. On a couple of occasions I was baby-sitter for Susan while Barbara and Victor went out for a show. I did not see any of this family again for thirty years, until Barbara visited Bonn in 1998 and then at the family reunion in 1999 at Jamesport, Long Island, which Susan and brother Peter also attended. Victor was divorced many years before.

What I thought a lot about was a night when I was command duty officer and invited Vic and Barbara for dinner in the wardroom. After dinner I had coffee served. With cups of coffee in hand we walked out of the wardroom outside alongside a rail and watched some activity in the yard. Suddenly the yard steam horn blasted away, denoting there was a change in work shifts. The sound was so loud and penetrating that Victor, a rather nervous soul, literally threw his coffee into the air from fright. I had to hold my expressions of amusement, because that sound really was terrible. After some weeks in the yard and living on the ship we were more or less used to it. The horn had pierced Victor's routine of a very quiet home life in the suburbs of Los Alamitos.

On 1 December 1966 I was promoted to lieutenant commander (LCDR) and had the dubious distinction of being the third-youngest LCDR in the U.S. Navy who had come up through the ranks at that time. I was proud of attaining this goal, having started out as an apprentice seaman (ASETM) in February 1947, then advancing up through seaman second class; seaman first class; aviation technician third class; aviation technician second class; aviation technician first class; chief aviation technician; ensign; lieutenant junior grade; lieutenant senior grade, and finally to commander level in the course of nineteen years.

New Year's Eve Ship's Log Entry

It is a tradition on New Year's Eve that the officer on watch aboard ship write the official log entry in verse. I was the command duty officer during the evening of 31 December 1967 on the USS *Norton Sound* in Port Hueneme. Collaborating on the verse were Lt. Ralph Robie and Chief WO Charles Owens. This verse in the official deck log was reprinted in the local newspapers the next day.

The Port Anchor is out, 15 Fathoms at Hawse

USS *Norton Sound* (AVM-1)
0000-0400 1 January 1968

I'm moored in Port Hueneme for the Holiday
In southern California, USA
The U.S. Navy CB Center is my host
Home of the Seabees on the West Coast.

On my portside is number five pier,
To starboard the Pacific Ocean is near.
My bow is east and is proud to state
It was first to greet 1968.

To shore for my power, the shift has been made;
Steam from the beach for some heat is an aid.
Cold is my iron, no steam to propel,
Fresh water arriving direct from the well.

Winds, cold winds, appeared from the east
They are called Santa Ana, like a terrible beast.
In summer they're hot, in winter they're cold
But in any case they are all very bold.

Not today did it happen but two weeks ago
When the Holiday started, Santa Ana did blow.
It was felt at the time that an extra bight
Would be better made then than when my sailors were tight.

So here I ride doubled with standard moor
Offshore wire and surge, both aft and fore,
To prepare for a Santa (not Santa Claus)
Port anchor is out, 15 fathoms at hawse.

Present are various Naval Ships
Tonight they are free from tracking blips.
Massilion Victory rides at Pier 3
When cargo is loaded, underway she'll be.

No Ops to support, no targets to tow
Leaves AVRs nowhere to go.
Through the fog I see the tugs are here
To join in greeting the brand-new year.

Blues are the uniform and would you believe
I'm proud that my skipper has much on his sleeve.
It's also nice that all should note
That he's the Senior Officer Present Afloat.

* * *

During the three years that we were in Camarillo we lived in three different rented houses. All were nice, but the third was best, and it was there we lived the longest during my duty aboard the *Norton Sound* and until after I retired from the navy in late 1968. From this house one could view miles of flower and vegetable farms. Large orchards of lemons and oranges were in the vicinity. Camarillo was essentially a residential town—that is, no factory or industry—and situated among the farms. Oxnard, between Port Hueneme and Camarillo, had an air force base, and one was kept aware of this by the frequent jet takeoffs and landings. This AFB was turned over to civil aviation several years after our departure from Camarillo.

Jim and David picked lemons in their spare time for about fifty cents a box. And, I recall that David also harvested peppers and broccoli, because when he came home he said he had eaten both of these vegetables raw from the fields. At the time I could not imagine this and thought it one of the strange things teenagers were doing then. Years later I experienced at various cocktail parties given by Americans, in the states and overseas, hors d'oeuvres being precisely that, raw vegetables. I must say that compared to many of the canapes I was given during very many receptions and parties, I began to accept the vegetables in the raw.

Everything seemed to grow well in California, particularly the lawn grass, which had to be cut without fail each week. And here one would learn that there must be more snails in California than anywhere. They were especially evident in the evening when I walked on the lawn and near the hedges. Each step meant the crunching of another snail in shell. I wondered in later years, and now, if those snails were edible. My first dinner of snails was experienced in Egypt at the home of a German couple. Frankly, I did not know what we were being served until after I had eaten one. It tasted somewhat like the snail shellfish, with which I was familiar. So if the lawn snails are edible it seems I may have been too slow in realizing it.

Jim had invited his high school girlfriend to our home for a dinner he would prepare. He did very nicely in all aspects of preparing the program and the meal, Italian spaghetti. All went well until he carried the food from the kitchen to the dining room—and the spaghetti dropped on the floor. He must have been more than embarrassed of course, and we felt so sorry for him. You cannot imagine just how much.

Jim played football at Camarillo High School and was good in sports as well as studies. He also played baseball at Claremont Men's College and was good at it also. Unfortunately, he was beginning to not take these things too seriously. It seemed the teenagers during these years of the late 1960s were rebelling against the establishment in almost all aspects, and this was extremely difficult for parents to understand and cope with. David was also intelligent and often ran several miles in track and it appeared he was doing OK, but he was apparently drawn into the wrong atmosphere when he started Simi College. Disaster struck hard in his life, which was ended a few years later, with the effects of LSD put in his drink by someone as a prank. Patti, too, was good in school, but this antiestablishment attitude began to grow with her and too many of the young folks. For so many years I wondered what I or their mother did or did not do that might have made such a difference. But there seemed to have been a national teenage "virus" of rebellion. And when Jim and Patti finally settled down to complete their higher education and raise fine families, I was so proud of them and especially relieved and happy that they now were successful and happy in their lives.

After twenty-one and a half years of naval service I decided to retire from the navy in August 1968. A primary reason was that, at the time, it was not possible for a "mustang" to ever be promoted to captain in the navy or become commanding officer of a ship or squadron. Only a year or so later the rules were changed, but that was too late for me. I voluntarily retired from the navy. In any case, I never regretted the decision, and it happened that I was offered and accepted a good position with General Dynamics Corporation only two weeks before retirement.

In a ceremony on the hangar deck of the USS *Norton Sound,* at Long Beach, in August 1968 I was presented with my retirement certificate by the ship's captain, Capt. George Lewis. All the ship's company personnel were in formation as I spoke my farewell words to them. Also present were my wife, Milly, and my children, Jim, Dave, and Patti.

On the fifteenth of September 1968, I commenced employment with General Dynamics Pomona Division, in Pomona, California.

A Change in Life—A Loss of Life
General Dynamics, Port Hueneme, Pomona, Philadelphia
(September 1968–Fall 1972)

During several months prior to my retiring from the navy and in anticipation of retirement, I had sent résumés to at least fifty firms without receiving any positive results. Those that did respond stated in so many words: "You have a great background, but we cannot effectively utilize you at this time. Will keep your résumé on file." However, one day at breakfast in the *Norton Sound* wardroom, I was informed by the executive officer, Cdr. Jim Ford, that he had arranged a meeting for me with the engineering head at the Pomona Division of General Dynamics, in Pomona, California, about an hour drive south of Port Hueneme. I was very surprised but also elated that something seemed to be falling into place.

Since we had no planned operations the following day, I was granted the day off to attend the meeting. Well, it was a case of Commander Ford having already recommended me and I was essentially hired before I ever arrived at Pomona. This was a step in my learning about civilian life that the large majority of people hired in responsible positions are usually hired through recommendations to the firm by a person who is well known and trusted by them. Note here that General Dynamics, just a few months prior, had been one of the firms that had also informed me that "they could not use my services," et cetera, et cetera.

After a few years of experiencing civilian procedures I began to understand the reasons for firms sometimes ignoring résumé submissions or treating them lightly. I observed literally hundreds of résumés being circulated among the various departments whose directors simply glanced at and initialed them because they had little or no time to process the paperwork. But more interesting was the general comment that I frequently heard: "Anybody can write a résumé, but we don't really know the man."

My first assignment with General Dynamics was as a project engineer with the Pomona Division. Pomona is about midway between Los Angeles and San Bernardino. Since I had a lot of experience on the USS *Norton*

Sound involving missile systems and radar testing, I was given the job, over a several-month period, of developing a document containing the physical and electrical characteristics of all the systems being designed for the advanced AEGIS Missile System, a U.S. Navy project on which we were bidding. There were well over a hundred engineers working on the proposal for the AEGIS system, and we worked sometimes until ten in the evening. During this time my family was still living in Camarillo, so I spent the weekdays in a motel in Pomona and drove home on the weekends. The night hours did not affect me so much, since I had to stay in Pomona anyway during the week and I had something to do to keep me busy. The big outlet for "entertainment" was for several coworker engineers to get a booth in Orlando's Restaurant and order giant hamburgers and beer or cocktails and tell sea stories.

I quickly realized one of the major differences between military and civilian procedures relative to studies and the associated reports. In the navy, when I made any recommendations or studies the results of my work went up through the chain of command and perhaps weeks or months later I would find out whether my reports were useful or wanted. In my first week at work at General Dynamics I was given a study project about where a certain radar should be installed on the *Norton Sound* and why and how it should be installed there. In just a couple of weeks my study was finished and it went to my supervisor. It was nearly a month later when I wondered about the reactions to my study report. I had to find out for my own curiosity. I thought perhaps it might have been so bad that it was simply discarded or ignored. I went to my supervisor and got the nerve to ask, "Whatever happened to my study report, Charlie?"

"You mean the one of the *Norton Sound* radar location?"

My reply was a kind of nervous, "Yeah, that one."

"Paul, that went to print and distribution the week after you handed it to me."

The point is, in my comment on this subject, that personnel were hired on by the company as experts in their field and it was expected that what they produced would be accurate and immediately usable. What I learned from this was that any job I would be given in the future must be always done very thoroughly and accurately, as much as humanly possible, the first time around.

But while the big proposal effort was continuing in the Aegis project competition, General Dynamics was fortunate to have received a contract, in another area, from the Naval Sea Systems Command, Washington, D.C.

This was to train ship crews in the operation of the new weapons systems being installed during the modernization of all DLG-6 Class missile destroyers and to be involved in the follow-on "at sea trials." The contract further required that General Dynamics have responsibility to observe and report on the progress of all ship installations and all testing during the modernization overhaul work at the Philadelphis Naval Shipyard. I was selected as the manager of this project work, on-site, in the shipyard.

I had the good fortune first of all in having been assigned this important work, but also because I liked this job very much. It was challenging and so interesting to be involved in so many disciplines within all areas of the ships' modernizations. I charted the progress of several ships over a period of five years and sent weekly reports to the Bureau of Ships (PMS-378), the shipyard commander, and each captain of the ships being modernized. The average time for completion of each ship was one and a half years. With my method of progressing I was able to predict for these authorities the ship completion date with an accuracy of within two to three weeks. This was valuable for the authorities concerned for lots of reasons, such as deciding whether to add night shift work to complete PERT events, knowing when to transfer sailors to man the ship, when the ship could join the fleet for active duty, and cost control.

During the Philadelphia assignment I authored a book, *OSPIPS* (On-Site Physical Inspection Progressing System). It described in detail how one man can go through an entire ship each day looking at specific key items and record data points to develop a simple graph of curves to determine the completion date of a major ship overhaul in all categories, including engineering spaces, weapons installations and testing, living quarters, builders' trials, and the like.

The family lived in Wenonah, New Jersey, which is just across the Delaware River from Philadelphia. A very nice brick home was purchased with use of the money from the sale of the house in Raleigh, Tennessee. Although I was very successful in my job, it was very interesting, and our living conditions were excellent, the personal or home life especially during the latter part of this assignment became very difficult stemming from years of the effect of religious differences between my wife and me. In hindsight, some asked me why I did not arrange separation earlier. I thought only that it was my responsibility to try to maintain a "home" for the children's sake. But all of these many years of differences certainly had a profound effect on the three children.

The teenage problems in general prevailed after the move to New Jersey. Jim was on his own in California, and there was little contact. Patti had married a free spirit, and they went on to California. David insisted on commencing college on his own in Simi, California, although I thought at the time it was not a good idea, because of his rather shy nature, being three thousand miles away from home. But then came the cruel situation involving David, attending Simi College, when someone placed LSD in whatever he was drinking. David was a good student, observed healthy eating habits, and ran track for sports, but he was obviously out of his element that evening with a group of idiots. After many months in and out of mental wards there came the tragic ending. In 1972 it happened. One day when David was out of the hospital ward he simply disappeared. We had no idea where he was. I had searched for Dave almost the entire night, and I also went to the police to inform them of the situation so they could be on the lookout for him. The police came to the house on the next morning for me to go with them to identify a body. David had been hit by a train in Woodbury, New Jersey. This was the worst happening I experienced in my entire life—that is, having to make an identification in the hospital morgue of my own son after he was hit and killed by a train.

I so often think of young people who believe they can handle themselves even if they don't actively participate, as they say. But just being near the drug scene sometimes proves to be deadly! And during the many trips I made to the mental wards of Pennsylvania Hospital, to visit David, I always saw dozens of high school and college-aged young men and women crouched in the corners or someone staring into space. Their problem, according to the resident doctors, was "only" marijuana. When I hear one say that marijuana is not harmful I think about these young, nice-looking, "intelligent" men and women in the mental wards in Philadelphia.

As I write today in 2002, I am very happy to say that both Jim and Patti are happily married and doing well in their chosen professions. Patti is a licensed professional counselor (LPC) for drug- and alcohol-related problems, living with her husband, Jimmy Moss, and sons, Dallas and Zachary, in Lynchburg, Virginia. Jim (son James Anthony Cook) was an art professor at Elmira College and visiting professor at Cornell University, living with his family, Ellen and children Theo and Lila, in Ithaca, New York. Jim is now a professor in the art department of the University of Arizona in Tucson. Both Jim and Patti, I should add, brought themselves around from the world of free spirits and attained their master's degrees through their own determination and will. I am especially proud of them for that.

It was some months after the death of David that I separated from Milly and lived in an apartment in Marlton, New Jersey, until finishing my assignment at the naval shipyard in Philadelphia. I obtained a divorce in September 1973.

While still assigned in Philadelphia however, I was sent on a special assignment with a military-industrial team to Turkey. The purpose: to survey the Turkish Naval Shipyards, at the request of the Turkish government, for their capability relative to the construction of a new class of fast patrol boat configured with weapon systems designed and proposed by General Dynamics. My task was to evaluate the electronics capability in the shipyards, and we would prepare a final report, on all disciplines, in Ankara before leaving the country. In the latter months of 1972 the team assembled and flew to Istanbul and on to Ankara. Charlie Pearson, my superior based in Pomona, California, was also selected as a member of the team, and in this particular situation we were given equal status as team members. This relationship was to become a problem near the end of the survey, as will be related in the following account of happenings.

Passports Charlie?—Meeting in Ankara
Istanbul, Ankara (Autumn 1972)

The Boeing 737 out of Istanbul had just reached cruise altitude as we settled in and I thought about our arrival in Ankara, where our colleagues were waiting. Charlie and I of General Dynamics Corporation, Pomona Division, were members of the military-industrial team to survey the naval shipyards. We were to check the capabilities for construction of a specific ship of new design. The country was under martial law at the time, and we would generally be with military escort during our work, which was planned for several weeks. We were about thirty minutes into the flight when I just happened to think of my passport. "Where is it?" I was saying to myself, but aloud.

"Where is what?" said Charlie.

"My passport. I don't have my passport! Do you have the passports, Charlie?"

"Hell, no, I thought you had them!"

We realized only then that the passports must still be at the customs office at the airport in Istanbul.

Upon our departure from the United States I was tasked with carrying, along with my personal baggage, an oil painting of a ship encased in a wooden crate with metal bands around it. I was to deliver this painting to the Turkish chief of naval operations at Naval Headquarters in Ankara. When Charlie and I landed at Istanbul International Airport, on a Pan Am flight that originated in Los Angeles, we encountered a problem with the customs officials in that they wanted me to open the wooden crate. The situation was chaotic, as none of the customs officials could speak English and we, of course, spoke no Turkish. We understood only by their gestures that the crate must be opened and they expected me to open it. Without tools, this was impossible. The stalled discussion continued at length, with both sides getting very impatient. They took our passports. We had yet to transfer to a domestic flight to get on to Ankara and time was slipping by. Finally, someone motioned us to follow him across the hangar deck and we went, along with several of these customs officials, until we came to a small office with a young woman who spoke English. She apparently had some level of authority above these customs officials. "What is the problem?" she asked in English.

I had to answer in a way to gain her full attention: "You understand that Turkey is under martial law. In this crate that these men want opened is an important oil painting which I must deliver to your chief of naval operations in Ankara. If we're kept here any longer we'll miss our flight and the CNO his painting as well."

Almost immediately the young lady informed the customs officials that we must be set free to go to the domestic terminal. They were so impressed by the order that they, all of them, could not wait to get their chalked initials on the crate signifying it was OK to continue. I quickly thanked the lady for her understanding, and Charlie and I departed the area immediately.

Charlie and I rushed over to the domestic terminal with the crate and other baggage, and as we finally reached the domestic counter the agent informed us in very broken English that the plane for Ankara was ready to taxi. We saw the plane with doors closed and the ground crew maneuvering their vehicles off to the side. I went to another agent whom I heard speaking good English and I quickly explained to him our problem. Calmly he asked us to take a seat and said he would handle the situation. *How?* I thought.

He went out to a car with waiting driver and sped out to the front of the plane. Soon a cabin door opened and a stairway was let down. The agent went aboard the plane and in a few minutes came out with two unhappy-looking persons, who were brought back to the waiting room. He then took Charlie and me out to the plane. As we rode out I asked who the persons were who came off the plane. "It doesn't matter. I needed two seats for you! Have a good flight!" With a great sigh of relief Charlie and I took our seats. The steward stowed our baggage and the crate, the plane taxied to the runway, and we were off.

So in the confusion and rush at the airport in Istanbul we could think only of getting to the next flight with the painting and forgot completely about customs taking our passports. Just minutes before landing, Charlie said, "What are we going to do without passports in a country with martial law?" Despite the many hours thus far traveled and the waiting, we had become wide awake thinking about when and how to retrieve the passports.

As we disembarked the plane in Ankara there was a small group of

U.S. and Turkish naval officers waiting for us. I told the U.S. Navy commander from the embassy that our passports were at Customs in the international airport in Istanbul. "Christ! How did that happen? You have to have passports." We gave him a quick rundown. He slowly calmed down and said he would now have to accompany us nearly everywhere, since we were without passports. It was no time now for us to think anymore about passports, as the survey work would begin the very next day. Until the survey report was completed, there would be no chance for time out to search for the passports in Istanbul.

The painting was delivered and we went about the task assigned, traveling in a group to the various shipyards and related facilities throughout the country. Our survey took us for inspections at the Turkish Naval Shipyards and to other naval facilities bordering the Bosporus. One of the very interesting activities at the Golcuk shipyard was observed in a metal-forging shop. Dozens of workers were continuously pedaling foot bellows to maintain high temperatures in the coal fires that heated the glowing hot metal pieces on which they were working. Although this was a very much outdated method, it soon became obvious to us that their methods were sufficiently effective to accomplish their tasks in producing various parts needed for the ships.

It was noted in other shops where more technical (electrical and mechanical) expertise was necessary on equipment that the father and son system was predominant. The son learned from his father; then his son taught another of the next generation. In my own interpretation, I assumed that this was not only a good system of learning, on the job, but also lent itself to good security with military equipment and systems. In general, the Turks amazed me by how quickly they seemed to learn and how they were able to accomplish so much with so little of the more modern equipment.

One day Charlie and I were taken on a ride in one of their FPBs (Fast Patrol Boats) from a navy port into the Black Sea. This was an unusual opportunity for us foreigners to experience, because it was during the cold war and Soviet naval ships were patrolling the waters rather close to the Turkish shore. It was also unusual because Turkey, at that time, was under a state of martial law. We came within visual contact distance of a Soviet naval vessel, then returned to inland waterways.

We stopped at one pier along the way and moored for a couple of hours to tour a typical village. Memorable, aside from the boat ride itself, were the tree-ripened figs, deep purple in color. These were the best I have ever eaten, although the figs of Crete and Malta were noteworthy. Ever since Grandpa Santacroce gave us dried figs out of his Italian grocery store in Greenport I have always liked figs, dried or tree-ripened. But those in cone-formed newspapers sold to us by the vendors on the street in that Turkish village were, in any case, the best.

I observed in Turkey that hardly any fruit goes to rot. All the fruit that may not be consumed on the market is made into juice, which is bottled and made available in nearly every village, certainly in every village we visited. Juice, not cola, is what we saw and what we were given anytime we were invited.

When we had finished our survey inspections, arrangements were made for the team to ride the Orient Express from Istanbul to Ankara. Each of us had a sleeping compartment for this train trip, which started about 9:00 P.M., and we arrived in Ankara at 7:30 the next morning. We spent some time in the lounge car in order to get the flavor of this historic train. That part of the ride was an experience to remember. The space was so filled with the strong aroma of Turkish cigarette smoke that you could hardly see the face of a man in the next booth. To breathe deeply would surely have affected your lungs as if you had smoked a pack of cigarettes in the space of half an hour. The odor was what finally drove us back into our sleeping compartments. And of course we were told of the story about Marlene Dietrich losing her silk stocking on this train. Whether the tale was true or not, no one reported finding it during our trip.

For a few days after returning to Ankara, briefings were given to the CNO and staff at Naval Headquarters. While waiting for the briefing and gazing out the nearby window, I noticed a large company of soldiers marching in the compound below. At one point a ranking soldier, perhaps a noncommissioned officer (NCO), apparently did not approve of a soldier's actions in ranks. I saw the NCO, with the butt of his rifle, hit the soldier in the head. He fell to the ground. The others marched over and around him. That must have been an example of Turkish army discipline, of which we had heard many stories. It has been said that the Turks are known to be especially tough fighters.

Near the end of the project our team prepared the final report in the Buyuk Ankara Hotel, using one of the hotel rooms as an office and workspace.

Finally came the time that Charlie and I needed to retrieve our passports in order to leave Turkey for return to the States. Charlie said, "Paul, you fly to Istanbul, locate the passports, return here, and then we'll fly out starting from Ankara." I must explain and emphasize at this point that

Charlie was my boss in California, but on this particular job in Turkey we were both on an equal footing on the survey team, each with a specific responsibility. All the while, though, his attitude was that of still being my boss on the team and he used every occasion to let me know the relationship. *Well,* I thought, *OK, I will go and in the meantime I will have a bit of free time to look around the ancient and still-exciting city of Istanbul.* Until now there had been no time for sightseeing. Since I needed funds for this trip to Istanbul, I went to the survey team leader, Steve, who was much senior to either Charlie or me. Steve knew the situation about the passports, naturally, and said, "Paul, why don't both you and Charlie go to Istanbul to find the passports, stay a couple of days for R and R, and just continue on to the States? The report is finished, no need to return here." This sounded great to me, and very sensible.

Another team member, Bernie, who had heard my conversation with Steve, accompanied me back to Charlie's room. And this was crucial for me, as probably no one would have believed Charlie's reaction. When I told him that we were both going to Istanbul for the passports and continue on home after the weekend there, one would have thought that I had stabbed him with a jagged knife.

"You don't make no goddamn decisions. You work for me and I tell you what to do."

He proceeded to call me many things and insulted me terribly. He didn't believe me that it was Steve's order and not my idea at all. His lambasting upset me so much that I left his room and went to my own with Bernie tagging along. I told Bernie that I would quit General Dynamics if I had to keep working for such a person. It became obvious, soon afterward, that Bernie had informed Steve of the situation. Steve came to my room, and I had to repeat to him what went on.

Steve said, "Paul, we all know Charlie is an ass; take it easy."

"I don't want to be in the same room with him, so I will not attend the admiral's cocktail party tonight."

"Paul, you don't have to go to the party, but don't quit General Dynamics. You are doing a fantastic job and we want you to stay."

Well, I really stayed because of Steve, who, technically, was one of the best engineers in the company and a likable fellow.

That night I decided to go up to the fourteenth floor, where there was a restaurant, and bar lounge. It was only about 7:00 P.M. and since life in Turkey did not get under way until about 10:00 P.M., the entire floor was void of people except for a few waiters preparing for the evening and a bartender. I ordered a gin and tonic and sat on the open balcony overlooking the city. I was at peace and quite happy to just be alone after this incident with Charlie. An hour or so passed as I nursed the drink and had a few cigarettes. Suddenly the elevator door opened. Two women walked into the lounge, took seats, and ordered a drink. They had my attention because by coincidence I had seen them in the lobby of the hotel the night before. One of them on the previous night had looked at me and I at her, glances at a safe distance and quickly forgotten. Another half hour passed on the balcony with the ice melting in my gin and tonic, but I finally walked over to the two at the lounge with at least something to say: "Didn't I see you ladies last night in the lobby?" I sought nothing but conversation and company on this distasteful day with Charlie.

Since I really came up to have dinner I asked if the two ladies, Christa Anders and Gila Kessler, would care to join me. It seems they had already had dinner in a local restaurant and just stopped in at the hotel for a drink before returning to their apartment. But they consented to have wine at my table while I had dinner. I learned that Gila was secretary to the German ambassador in Ankara and Christa, working for Deutsche Bank in Madrid, was on vacation visiting her very close friend, Gila, who had also worked before in Madrid. We had a enjoyable evening, including a few dances after dinner.

Christa had mentioned that she and Gila would leave the next day by bus for sightseeing in Istanbul. To their surprise I took flight tickets from my pocket, saying that I was bound for Istanbul as well. "Could we meet there and see the sights together?" After a few minutes of private discussion, the ladies agreed it would be a good thing to be accompanied by men in this period of martial law. Women going alone on the streets at night in Turkey was not really appropriate.

The next morning as I entered the breakfast room on the ground floor the only table with an empty seat was a table where several team members were seated. To my displeasure and confusion, Charlie was there and he greeted me as if nothing had happened. He even used almost complimentary expressions in welcoming me to the table. Steve had had a very serious talk with Charlie. We would fly together to Istanbul.

Charlie and I were booked into the Istanbul Hilton Hotel. Christa and Gila had reserved rooms in the Park Hotel a few blocks away. Charlie and I enjoyed the first evening there at dinner while escorting Gila and Christa, and we also managed to retrieve our passports through the help of the U.S. Naval attaché and Turkish naval officers with whom we had the pleasure of working during the survey. Having the passports again was really a great relief, and we were then able to enjoy the rest of the weekend worry-free. We did the usual sightseeing in Istanbul the next day, and in the evening Charlie took Gila to dinner and I dined with Christa at the Hilton.

The following day, we met again for lunch at the Hilton balcony overlooking the Bosporus. This was a highlight of relaxation but also of comedy, as Gila was describing to us how rich Charlie must be. I had to stop eating as I asked Gila, "Why do you say that?"

"Well, he said he lived in a marble home with a large swimming pool and near a golf course and he lives there all alone! It sounded almost like an invitation to me."

"Gila," I said, "tell me once more exactly what did Charlie say."

She repeated the same words, and as she did so, I suddenly understood what had happened. Charlie, a Texan, had a drawl so thick you could cut it with a knife. He actually lived in a mobile home and as he said "mobile" this would sound to a non-Texan like "marble," denoting great and grandiose for the wealthy. Most of these mobile home parks in California do have swimming pools, and many are near a golf course. "Charlie is not a rich man, Gila."

Gila, Christa, and I never laughed so hard and long as at this moment, with Gila thinking that Charlie must be very rich.

The time came for Charlie and me to leave for the airport, and it now became apparent that I had more than a passing interest in Christa. I asked for her address and a small photo, which she gave me hesitantly. After all, we would be an ocean apart and perhaps never see each other again. She had also some thoughts of men being untrustworthy through some past experience. I was not divorced but separated and living alone in New Jersey while still assigned as manager of the Field Office at the Philadelphia Naval Shipyard. Although still working for Charlie, I was 3,000 miles away from his office in California. This arrangement suited me just fine as far as that relationship was concerned.

I wrote to Christa two or three times with no answer from her, and after many weeks I received a scathing letter with her wrath about how all men are alike. She had not received any mail from me. Actually, she had just moved to another street, La Habana, and had given me the old address at La Florida, which I used to address her letters. With the then inefficiency of the Spanish post, my letters were not forwarded to her new address but returned to me in New Jersey via ship. Ultimately Christa received my letters and her faith in me was restored. The next year, I flew to Madrid to visit her and to meet her friends, and months later she came to the States and visited some of my friends and parents. Fate through the various happenings in Ankara and Istanbul had brought us together.

Skiing in South Jersey? White Rain on Pahlavi! "Bitte, Thirty Pfennig"
Philadelphia, Seattle, Pomona, Tehran Revolution (1972–78)

I returned to Philadelphia to find that I had now not only the prospects of a new personal relationship but also an added assignment, which was to interface with the commanding officers of two Iranian destroyers that were being overhauled in the shipyard and to be outfitted with missile systems built by General Dynamics. The Imperial Iranian Ship DDG-7 (IIS *Babr* DDG-7) and the IIS *Palang* (DDG-9) were to be commissioned into active service on the twelfth of October 1973, commanded by Cdr. Esfandiar Mokhtari and Cdr. Shoa Majidi, respectively.

Since I had already plenty of experience in progressing the U.S. Navy ships undergoing modernization, I had developed a routine that allowed me the time to assist the Iranians without affecting my work on the U.S. ships. However, this meant a very active period for me until the Iranian ships were commissioned in one year's time. It turned out that the Iranian officers were requesting my assistance at some time every day and in the last few months before the commissionings I was most of the time in the office of the Iranian division commander. I assisted him in the preparations for the commissioning ceremony and for the gala on this occasion at the Cherry Hill Inn, Cherry Hill, New Jersey. The rehearsals for the ceremony were taken very seriously and gone over several times. In the final dress rehearsal they used me as the "Iranian ambassador to the United States" (because the ambassador himself was not available). I dressed in my finest dark suit and wore a pair of horn-rimmed sunglasses (such as used by the ambassador) in order to really "play the part." Many of the ship's crew thought that the ambassador was actually there. The commissioning ceremony went off without the slightest problem. My relationship with the officers and crew was extremely good. It will be interesting for the reader to learn of the following relationship, with these same Iranians, as result of passing time and politics.

In August 1973, during a few weeks' vacation, I visited Christa in Madrid to learn more about her and her friends. During this time we traveled to Portugal and Morocco. The downside of the Morocco trip was that in August the heat was scorching, but it was the only time I could have taken vacation from my work in Philadelphia. We also saw Christa's family in Krefeld, Germany.

In late 1973, Christa came to Marlton, New Jersey, likewise to meet friends of mine. We paid a visit to my parents in Montauk then and again in 1974. Between visits, it became obvious that marriage was in the making. One thing Christa demanded was a ski trip each year. This meant that I should learn how to ski. I had never entertained the thought of it, nor had I the time, with so little vacation given American employees compared to the Europeans. The fact is that I had never had a vacation in the real sense in all my years, up to now at the age of forty-four. Before and after marriage, all my time off was directed toward visiting my parents and other relatives.

I learned how to ski, of all places, in Pine Hill, New Jersey. Pine Hill is a small town in South Jersey and I expect that most people would wonder how anyone could possibly learn to ski in the "flatlands" in the south. It so happens that there is a "big hill" in Pine Hill, just across the Delaware River from Philadelphia. There was an Austrian man living nearby who saw the need and began to give lessons to beginners like myself. The ski run from the top of the big hill took only about three minutes, but the training here was good enough to learn how to snow plow, how to fall down, and, importantly, how to get up again with a pair of skis.

After several weekends of training, I felt that I could do it alone. The big moment came one sunny Sunday afternoon. I plowed down the hill with ease, but when nearing the bottom I had to maneuver to stop. Since the sun had warmed the air, the snow had melted some, and my right ski failed to negotiate the turn in the wet snow. The result was that I went headlong down, flattened out and quite embarrassed in front of weekend onlookers from half of South Jersey. On top of this, a young skier not more than seven or eight years old came to a rather professional stop and in so doing thoroughly sprayed my goggles with wet snow, so as to completely obscure my vision, asking, "Can I help you, mister?" As I wiped the snow from the goggles with my gloved hand and regained my vision and some composure, I also gained the determination to really learn this sport. After a "no thank you, I'm OK," I told myself, *If this young kid can learn to ski properly, so can I!*

I had my first real outing with a good friend, Herb Olson, at Snow Mountain in Vermont. Herb had told me that he had a lot of experience in the Rocky Mountains, so I felt comfortable being with him and his daughter, Melody. On the very first run down the slope Herb fell and broke a leg, which meant he was sitting with a cast the whole week long as I struggled along with some help from Melody. But I learned a lot about the ski world. Subsequently I skied in Washington State, Canada, Iran, Greece, Austria, and Germany.

I played tennis wherever we traveled, including the Near and Mideast until the last year of my Cairo assignment, in 1986. There it became obvious that it was a bit dangerous in the heat of the desertlike temperatures. Two of our friends had died on the courts in Cairo, and it was then that I decided golf would be my exercise and fun sport.

With the assignment ended in Philadelphia, I was given duty at the U.S. Naval Shipyard, Bremerton, Washington, near Seattle. There was one more ship, of the class modernized in Philadelphia, that I would progress for the U.S. Navy on a General Dynamics (GD) contract. This was the nuclear-powered missile frigate USS *Bainbridge*.

The transfer from Philadelphia to Bremerton was via my VW Bug along Interstate 80 for the most part. When in New Jersey I had purchased a new 1971 VW for $1,900, and it was very adequate for my needs. I had already made many trips to Washington, D.C., where I had to do some marketing work for General Dynamics, while still working at the Philadelphia Naval Shipyard. Now I was to drive in this VW across the United States to Bremerton and a new start in life. It was to be used later through the years in Greece, Egypt, and Germany, where it was finally sold.

During the cross-country trip, in Iowa on Interstate 80, there was a thunderstorm of immense strength and so much rain, really heavy rain, that it was impossible to see more than a few feet ahead. We had to stop for quite a period until it became dark, then found a hotel in Walnut, Iowa, for the night. The next impediment was at Cheyenne, Wyoming, where there was a snowstorm, in early June 1974, with a foot of snow on the highway, which required us to stop. The highway was closed for over 150 miles. We were lucky to find a hotel, as there were numerous autos in the same situation. After a day of waiting for the snow plows to do their job, we were able to continue. Upon entering the state of Washington, it seemed that the state was one huge forest, as we saw nothing but beautiful large trees. We were quick to find an apartment near the water and a tennis court.

Having met in Turkey late in 1972, and after my separation, then divorce in September 1973, Christa and I were married on 31 December 1974 in a community church in Bremerton. The only persons with us were the two witnesses, Capt. Bruce Newell, U.S. Navy, commanding officer of the USS *Bainbridge,* and his wife, Ingrid. A close friendship had been established with them while I was working on his ship. There was a rather tragic ending to this relationship, as Ingrid was killed several years later in an auto accident in Virginia on the Beltway and Bruce then retired as a rear admiral from the navy. He became an Episcopalian minister. Unfortunately, after many years of my assignments in the Near and Mideast we lost contact with Bruce, who we presume is with a congregation somewhere in the States.

The work at the Bremerton Naval Shipyard was enjoyable, and many good friends were made among the naval officers, especially since I was, so to speak, one of them as a retired lieutenant commander, USN. Because my days always ended at 4:00 P.M., we often went to one of the many state parks after work in summer for picnics. Fresh salmon was grilled over charcoal. A few times we met on the Hood Canal and obtained oysters ourselves from these waters, also for grilling in nearby parks. It was really a nice time not only for the outdoor atmosphere but also for the friends we met and with whom we maintained contact over the years. The skiing was superb on the slopes of Mount Rainier, and we had the experience of skiing at Whistler Mountain at Alta Lake, British Columbia, when the Whistler Mountain ski resort was just in its infancy. Only cabins were available at the time, 1974, and fireplaces were the source of warmth. On the third day of skiing at Whistler, Christa injured her shoulder. So I skied with acquaintances from New Zealand each day until early afternoon. I built a fire each morning to keep the cabin warm until I returned. The ski friends joined us for Christmas Eve, which made for a nice evening despite the skiing accident.

Being German, Christa, like all the other German folks living in the area, constantly shopped for dark bread, unsalted butter, wurst, and the likes of other German-type foods that they missed. In this way, however, many new German friends were met in the various shops and markets in Bremerton and Seattle. Helmut and Tina Lehr were among the best of these friends, and we became very close. Helmut ran an auto repair garage in Bremerton primarily for European cars, and it was here I brought my VW upon arrival in the area. I had mentioned to Helmut that my wife was German. The next day Tina came to the house with flowers for Christa, a typical German gesture, and our friendship began. They had three young sons, Michael, Dominik and Andy. Later in 1976 after my transfer to Pomona, California, the family moved to Oberstdorf, Germany, where they had lived before going to the United States. Helmut and Tina wanted the boys to attend school in Germany when they became older. During the late 1970s and '80s we often visited the Lehrs on winter vacation in Oberstdorf and skiied there and in Kleinwalsertal, Austria. By the mid-1990s each of the "boys" had been through college and they were working in various parts of the world.

While in Bremerton we were visited in 1975 by Christa's parents, who were making their first and only trip to the United States. Since the VW was too small for extensive sight-seeing trips through the states of Washington and Oregon, we bought a used four-door Chevrolet Caprice with air-conditioning for about twenty-five hundred dollars. Although the car was a few years old, it was in very, very good condition. We toured for their benefit and ours, just about every sight of interest in Washington State, including the state capital, Olympia, Mount Rainier, Mount Olympus, Grand Coulee Dam, Lake Roosevelt (formed by the dam), Leavenworth (city built with many German-style Fachwerk houses and where German language is predominant), Spokane (site of the 1962 World's Fair), Tacoma Valley (with a huge fruit tree industry), and the Columbia River (salmon-counting stations), and then in Oregon went to the state capital, Salem, and back up along the Pacific coast.

On another occasion we traveled into British Columbia to the island of Vancouver and to the city of Vancouver on the mainland. On the island of Vancouver we visited the Bouchart Gardens. These gardens were famous not only for all the hundreds of different flowers and landscaping but also for the fact that the place used to be an industrial mine and the idea of a flower garden was made a reality to beautify the mined-out area and make it a very big success as a tourist attraction for people from all over the world.

I found Vancouver City so interesting, as it has a purely European flavor in its layout and architecture. And I must say that the best *Schweinshaxe* (grilled leg of pork) that I have eaten was in a German restaurant off Robbins Street. Perhaps the reason it was so good was the quality of the meat itself before cooking. On this Robbins Street especially, at that time in the midseventies, I felt like I was in Europe.

While in Vancouver City one afternoon, our small white poodle decided to do what comes natural, and he took off into a small field and never came back to us. Normally he would return without problem. We had looked everywhere, but after an hour or so we gave up and returned to the hotel, about two kilometers away. It was not until the next morning that a commotion was made at the motel door. It was our dog, who let us know that he found his way back to the motel. We were amazed and happy to have him back again.

Putsy had come to us in a rather interesting way. After we had been living in our Bremerton apartment for several months, in the fall of 1975 there appeared at our courtyard a small long-haired and filthy-looking dog, thoroughly soaking wet from a rainstorm hours before. It looked pitiful, and only for that reason I tried to coax it toward me for some food. Eventually this "thing" came close enough that I could see a pair of pleading deep black eyes. It returned the next day and the next. I took this "thing" inside and gave it a bath to find that it was a rather good-looking, now-white, poodle. We took it to a vet, who declared it to be a rather fine animal and that it should be sheared in order to take its place among the other prancing poodles around on the walks. We realized that this was a very special dog, and it became a part of our household. It appeared that someone in the crew of the last aircraft carrier at the shipyard simply left this dog to fend for itself and it became a stray. We had the luck that Putsy strayed into our yard. The unluck was that several months later Putsy was killed by an auto while chasing a motorcycle in Bremerton. Putsy was put to rest under a large pine tree in the wooded area belonging to an old German couple who had taken care of Putsy while we were on a weekend ski trip. Normally this dog never chased vehicles, but it decided to do so while in their care. They were heartbroken and felt much guilt. It took a long time to convince them that it could not have been helped. Putsy simply dashed into harm's way. But it was another case of having a dog problem through the years.

During 1976 I was transferred to and worked at the General Dynamics Pomona Division, Pomona, California, where I had started in 1968, but this time for writing lesson plans to train personnel on automatic test equipment for missile components. This assignment in Pomona was to be a sort of interim placement while the management was making preparations for a contract in Iran and, unknown to me, I was a candidate for the job as in-country manager on a project.

We rented an apartment at the Springdale Apartments, 410 Indian Hill Boulevard, Claremont, California, which is a college town and close to Pomona. In fact, Jim attended Claremont Men's College for two years, 1968–69. Here I had a number of good friends with whom I had previously worked. This rather short several months' stay in the Pomona area was filled with many visits, not only with new friends but also with my brother Bob and his family in San Diego. Christa and I had the opportunity to play tennis and swim in a private facility at the apartment complex, as well as ski in the nearby Big Bear ski area during winter months. Yet there was to be a very sad time here that occurred in the process of adopting a child.

The doctors at the naval hospital in Bremerton had already determined that we were not able to produce a child of our own. We decided to follow up on a tip from friends in Bremerton that there was the possibility of our adopting a four-year-old boy at an orphanage in Linz, Austria. Our next vacation was arranged with a trip to Austria. When we visited the orphanage, there was, sure enough, a very nice-looking blond boy, Peter, whom we could have for adoption. However, according to the rules for an international adoption a study by a social agency of the state of California in Los Angeles would have to be made. Absolutely certain that the adoption would take place during the home study, we prepared a separate room in the apartment for Peter, buying children's furniture, toys, and all that seemed appropriate. The home study appeared to be going well, and the visiting social worker had given us every indication that the adoption would go as planned. After several months' study I got a call from the social office in Los Angeles for an appointment, which we thought was for signing papers for the adoption. Lo and behold, the meeting was all but pleasant. I was informed that we could not have Peter. We were too old; that is, I was told that because our combined ages were over eighty years adoption was not possible. This agency knew from the very beginning that our combined ages were over eighty, actually forty-six and forty-three.

I wondered at the time if some of the answers given to the home study worker had something to do with their decision. For example, when Christa was asked, "How would you feel if the child spilled ketchup or something like that on the table cloth?" the answer was something to the effect: "Naturally I would not like that!" Since the home study worker had always commented positively to our queries, I thought no more about the responses until later, when we were told adoption was not possible. There was to be no further discussion. But it further made us quite bitter to see that even singles were being given adoptions and that in some other states rules varied and adoptions were administered variously, dependent upon the individuals staffing the adoption agencies. While I had had three children, Christa's dream to have a child of her own, albeit one from adoption, was not to be realized.

In February 1977 I was selected for transfer to Tehran, Iran, as the in-country program manager on a project for the Imperial Iranian Navy, to prepare and implement a study on the naval ordnance facilities in Iran. All of our furniture and two cars were put into storage in Riverside, California, because of company rules for overseas assignments in some areas. Iran and the Middle East in general were areas that dictated such a system. At this new overseas location we were given an allowance with which to purchase new, moderately priced items to furnish the apartment we rented. Although this was never intended, all the items in storage, except for the VW, were to stay in storage for the next ten years.

We rented an apartment on the ninth floor at the Behjetabad residential complex in Tehran, which contained fourteen twelve-story buildings that surrounded a large swimming pool. This complex was near Pahlavi and Karimkansan Avenues and across the street from the Khorush department store, a property of the Shah's family. These were some of the more modern high-rise facilities to live in, quite near the city center. The apartments were rather large and air-conditioned and the elevator reliable as long as the power was not interrupted. The problems came when the forces of Khomeini began the revolution, and one of the problems was that the electric power was purposely cut off several times a day and one never knew when it would happen. Therefore, it was no longer wise ever to get in the elevator again for fear of getting stuck in it halfway between floors. Candles were often the only source of light while the entire city of Tehran was without power.

The apartment was another cockroach haven, where I had recollections of my first encounter with these giant cockroach creatures in Corpus Christi, during my first months in the navy. They were everywhere in the Tehran apartment and always active in the dark places. When the lights went on, they scattered into the nearest cracks and holes. They even flew up the sides of the walls outside in the night. One of the worst places was the garbage collection bins located at the ground floor inside of the buildings. In the hallway of each floor there was a small opening in the wall, with a door, into which you had to throw the garbage, which would drop down a common shaft into the garbage bins. The challenge was to be very ready and quick to open and close this door while throwing the garbage into the shaft, before too many of the roaches entered into the hallway on your floor. Some months after moving to Iran the roach problem became secondary as the Khomeini forces gradually began to gain momentum.

Often I had to visit Rasht, and Bandar Pahlavi on the Caspian. In Rasht I learned that it was the people of Rasht about whom jokes were told. Like in every country a certain kind of people are "so stupid that so and so," although not necessarily in reality. Example: A Rashti went on vacation to New York City and was amazed at how big things were. When he returned to Rasht he talked to a group of his friends about how tall the buildings were. "The buildings are so tall that they go high into the clouds. One day a man fell off the top of one of these buildings, and it was so tall that it took four days for him to fall to the ground."

The joke teller continued on with his stories but was interrupted by one of the curious listeners: "But this man, the man who fell from the top of the building, did he die?"

"Of course. Four days without food and water!"

I had an office on the seventh floor of a building rented by the Iranian navy in the middle of Tehran, separate from naval headquarters, located in the north of the city. One unusual feature of the building was that the civilian owner did not like the navy for some reason, perhaps because he did not receive the amount of rent he wanted. In any case, he had the use of the elevator cut off for the entire two years I was there, which meant that I, and all the others on the upper floors, had to climb at least seven floors several times each day. While this was really inconvenient, to say the least, I did acquire considerable exercise, which in the long run was a decided benefit for the skiing season on the great slopes of Dizin, north of the city.

I had two different secretaries over the two years working in this office. The first was Aysha, who was born in Kenya but her grandfather was Iranian and had left Iran years before because of another upheaval in politics and religion. Aysha was raised in Kenya and educated in a Catholic school but was Muslim, and she could speak English, Swahili, and Farsi. Therefore, she was well qualified to perform the work required in my office and in interfacing with the Iranian officers. Aysha was a very nice young lady, but there came the day when, because of the Khomeini forces, she had to leave Iran and go back to Kenya. I met her by chance in Nairobi in 1983 for the only time since Iran. She had married and had two children.

The second "secretary" was Mrs. Darabi. Mrs Darabi was not as accomplished at the job as Aysha, as she struggled to touch each key with one finger, hunt and peck style. It took her forever to get a usable copy of anything that I needed typed. Since it was one of the naval officers who hired the office workers, I could do little to change the situation. I must say, though, that Mrs. Darabi was very pleasant and very punctual, each day at 2:00 P.M. providing me with two peeled and quartered cucumbers. Cucumbers are something that every Iranian eats in much the same way that a Westerner eats an apple or orange. They put cucumbers together with other items in the bowls of fruit.

Along every side of a street in Tehran there are open canals called *jubes* in which water from the mountains in the north flows through the city down to the south of Tehran. Tehran slopes from about six-thousand-feet altitude down to about four thousand feet; therefore the water runs freely, due to gravity, over the terrain and through the *jubes*. These *jubes* are of various sizes, anywhere from a foot wide and deep to double or more that size. The cleanest water of course enters in the north, and it becomes much less clean, let us say dirty, as it reaches the south. I have seen many and various kinds of activities at these *jubes,* from washing pots, pans, and children to draining the oil out of autos.

Every year in Iran the spring is celebrated as the New Year with Now Rooz. It seems that every Iranian family leaves the city and finds open ground near water, or in green parks, to camp out. In these times at certain areas, like along the Caspian Sea, the traffic is worse than a traffic jam en route to Salzburg from Munich or traffic jam from Springfield, Virginia, to Washington, D.C. In the waters of the Caspian you would see hundreds of bathers, including Iranian women with their black clothes on, who appeared like large birds bobbing up and down with the swells of the waves.

Each day everywhere in the world someone is, has been, and always will be taken by the con artist and schemer. All travelers are subject to this phenomenon, but the principal target is the first-time visitor to a foreign land. Just when you think you know all the possible methods of being fleeced, there is always a new experience. While I have seen and experienced a wide variety of schemes, I have been intrigued by the methods of some taxi drivers. There are those who take the circuitous routes for extra fare in most cities around the world, whether it be New York, Tokyo, Paris, or London. A "double rate" sometimes used for evening rides is switched on for daytime fares. There is also the driver who when asked, "How much?" will give a charming smile and say, "As you like," knowing full well that the passenger usually overestimates and will pay more than needed.

I was taken once by an Iranian driver from the airport to Pahlavi Avenue when I was checking in for my assignment in Tehran. The Peykan taxis are small, and one cannot wait to get out of one to stretch after a forty-five-minute ride. The driver stopped his car on the side of a tree-lined street. He purposely stopped where literally thousands of birds were perched. As I emerged from the Peykan, I was summarily greeted with a "white rain" of droppings, as if signaled by the driver. In seconds my suit was quickly covered. In order to make a quick exit from this "shower," I gave the driver the first rial note that I could get my hands on in my wallet and told him to keep the change. His profit was as expected, since the bank notes carried on first trips are often of greater amounts than the price asked. Driver's mission accomplished, or almost.

When I took my suit to the cleaners and picked it up two days later, there was a big hole in the trousers, most probably caused by excessive applications of chemicals. As I was complaining to the shop owner, a local customer standing by explained that I should not complain since this was the best cleaner in the area: "The holes made in the shops around the corner are much bigger!" Birds, I realized, were not only the taxi driver's best friend but also the cleaner's.

Two years later, in the midst of a revolution and death threats, we had to make quick departures. Most of our belongings had to be left behind, including the trousers. And just when I would have paid a million to get to the airport, our driver was in no mood for a scam.

This work in Iran was extremely interesting, especially during the first year, which was peaceful. It involved travel throughout the country in some places that normally were either off-limits, or so remote that no one would have given thought to visiting them. Bandar Abbas, Bushihr, Bandar Pahlavi, Sirjan, Rasht, Abadan, Chahbahar, Kerman, Khorramshahr, and Kharg Island were locations frequented, relative to our project. Visits to Isfahan were for pleasure. The two destroyers that had been overhauled in Philadelphia were now stationed in Bandar Abbas and GD had technicians there to ride these ships when they went to sea for technical support on the Standard Missile Systems during operations. A third destroyer, *Artemis,* was having its weapon system installed while in port at Bushihr. The only telephone available in Bandar Abbas for our people to use to call back to the GD office in Pomona, California, was in a hotel. One had to make a reservation with the hotel operator, who would, in most cases, arrange for a call in the middle of the night. This meant that we had to rent a room in the hotel and wait for the operator to get a call through, typically about 3:00 A.M.

Kharg Island was a primary oil terminal where oil was pumped out to the tankers for shipment to points all over the world, and there was also a refinery there. Several tall stacks were continuously topped with huge flames burning off gas fumes, which could be felt for nearly half a kilometer distant. There was also a naval base on Kharg where we were doing work relative to our naval ordnance facilities contract. We lived on the naval base during this work. The first morning in the men's room I stood at the sink to shave. I turned the faucet handle for water. While I looked out of the window, I saw the stacks with the great flames and became so interested in the amount of fire burning the waste gas that I did not realize there wasn't any water coming out of the faucet. At this same time I felt my feet getting very wet. Instead of water going into the sink, it was going out on the floor. It was quickly obvious that the plumbing was really messed up and also the water was cold. My thoughts were that if they were capable of drawing oil out of the ground, processing it, and sending it out to the tankers, they must surely be able to get water into this sink. And with all that heat from the burning gasses, they should be able to provide hot water for the officers' quarters.

Dinners were more of a joy. Each day the duty officer of the base would send several seamen down to the shores to pick up lobsters, which would be temporarily left high and dry when there was ebb tide. As one would say, "They were just there for the picking."

On the longer trips to the various locations in Iran we were flown with either Iranian air force or Iranian navy aircraft. Once in the general area of our visits, we were then driven in autos by Iranian navy seamen from the airfields to the ammunition storage facilities, ammunition piers, or missile check-out facilities to conduct our surveys. There was one route I really did not like, the road to Sirjan. There was always danger on those very narrow roads, especially with heavy trucks, with chromium ore, coming from the mines at very high speeds down the middle of the road. Our driver would also be in the middle of the road; then at the very last second each driver would steer to his right just barely enough to pass. My boss, ex–navy captain Bob Barnhart, who visited Iran from time to time, had stopped smoking for quite some time, but on one of these trips he got hooked again after a dozen near misses with the drivers "playing chicken." The Iranian navy commander who traveled with us on these surveys would always say, "Well, he didn't take any paint!" Certainly he took some "paint" off of our lives in sweat.

There was always some new experience, it seemed, as Bob and I traveled in all parts of Iran. On these trips to Sirjan we found, along the highway, farmers selling tangerines. But these were not ordinary ones; they were the largest, sweetest tangerines Bob and I had ever seen and tasted, the size of large oranges. I wonder still why they are found only in this area.

In the fall of 1977 we went to Isfahan by auto with my driver Farsola and also accompanied by secretary Aysha, whose uncle owned the Mexican restaurant in Isfahan. Aysha stayed with her uncle, and we lived in the Palace Hotel, which was really a very royal-looking place. The driver said, "I can always find someplace to sleep." When we had a Mexican dinner one night we learned that Anthony Quinn was eating there each day. And of course we wondered why was he there in this desert town. The movie *Caravan* was being filmed in the area around Isfahan and Anthony Quinn was starring in it. It happened on the very next day that we met him in one of the shops in the souk (bazaar). Aysha got his autograph on Christa's passport, as we had no other paper with us.

We had a lot of visitors and attended lots of parties with other expatriates, primarily Americans and Germans, also with Iranians in the beginning, but it became increasingly difficult to socialize with the Iranian military near the end of 1977. They were actually forbidden to attend private functions with us, and if they did, they were called in at security and questioned at length. Even those with whom I had worked in Philadelphia, for instance Rear Admiral Majidi, and had become very close to were not allowed to be with us, by order of the Iranian government. When, in the latter part of 1977, there started to be riots and burning of theaters, et cetera, this social-mingling order became much stronger and dangerous to the participants. And it was then that it was also becoming dangerous to be in certain areas of Tehran and other cities in the country.

In early December 1977 I was starting to have very severe pains around my stomach. We did not know any doctors, but friends told us that the German embassy used a certain doctor and I thought he must be OK if the embassy recommended him. I made several visits to this doctor and he gave me pills, powders, and liquids, but nothing relieved the pains. Then one midnight my pains were so intense I was crying out with pain. I was taken by taxi to the U.S. Army hospital in north Tehran. An Iranian contract doctor came to me out of his sleep and in ten minutes told me I had appendicitis. I was operated on just three hours later on 12 December by the hospital's commanding officer, Colonel Levine. He said that in just a few more hours I would have been in grave condition without an operation.

In a week's time I was out of the hospital and things appeared well enough, so Colonel Levine told me that I could go to Europe on Christmas vacation as planned but not to play tennis or golf or anything strenuous. I still had a two-inch slit on my stomach in a healing process. On the twentieth of December 1977 we went to Kaiserslautern, Germany, to visit my brother John and his wife, Jan, who were stationed at Ramstein Air Force Base. On Christmas Eve I had severe pain from my incision, so Jan drove me to the outpatient clinic at the Landstuhl Army Hospital. There was only a corpsman to be seen, as it was very late evening and during holidays. The corpsman called the medical officer of the day (MOOD), and he came to me as I lay on the treatment table. While he was saying, "This may hurt a little," he was actually cutting into my old incision with the scalpel (without anesthesia), in order to relieve pressure from the infected blood, where a large egg-sized lump had formed. The pain from the scalpel was equal to the pain from infection. He then stuffed about a yard of gauze into the open wound and said that I should two or three times each day soak in a bathtub. The heat would help healing. That was all he told me. For the next week I was in the bathtub at every place visited in Germany.

We continued to meet friends, now Enrico and Kiko Perin, near Venice, Italy. Then in Venice it began again, pain at every step. I could not enjoy any dinner or wine or anything about the visit. In the middle of the night, near Enrico's home, it was necessary to go to a hospital. In this hospital no one spoke any English; therefore, Enrico had to accompany me to translate for the doctors. I lay down on the treatment table. As the doctor removed my bandage and exposed the infected wound, Enrico passed out at the sight of it and was now on the floor. The doctor had to revive Enrico so he could continue as my translator. In the end the doctor said he would put a new bandage on and since I would be back in Tehran two days it would be OK; just keep a hot water bottle on the infection to help healing. No stores were open, naturally, after midnight. Enrico woke an aunt to get her hot water bottle for me to take with me back to Iran, via Athens, where we must first stop overnight.

In Athens we checked in at the Plaka Hotel, which had been recommended by an American friend in Tehran. We made a few visits at the Acropolis and in the Plaka area, but again my pains were so bad, nothing I did was enjoyable. Further, the Plaka Hotel had no hot water to use in the hot water bottle and I could not get anyone to boil some water. A bad hotel recommendation. *Well,* I thought, *tomorrow we are back in Tehran and I will see Colonel Levine, who will surely know what to do.* We arrived by taxi at the Athens International Airport the next morning, which was in the first week of January 1978. A rare snowstorm with high winds was in progress. The airport was closed for at least twenty-four hours. Back to the cold Plaka and one more night to suffer.

The next day I was back in Tehran. Immediately I went to the army hospital and asked for Colonel Levine in person. As I told the whole story to him he had quite a good laugh at what, I thought at the time, was not really so funny. The holiday trip was a disaster. The colonel described to me what had happened. When I went to the Landstuhl Army Hospital, the doctor there had done exactly the right thing for my problem, but he failed to explain to me one important thing. That was that after about five days if the gauze does not ease out of the wound by itself, I should pull it out. The gauze did not come out by itself and by staying inside did not allow the infected blood to properly drain out. The colonel further exclaimed, "It is like opening a good bottle of wine, putting the cork back in, and then trying to pour it out!"

Colonel Levine pulled out the infectious bloody gauze, put on a clean bandage, and then told me to put a hot, wet towel over the wound three times a day and the wound would be closed and healed in seven days. That was exactly what happened. I never did see Colonel Levine again, but I was very grateful to him for the successful operation and the final step in healing when I returned to Tehran. I sure think about him from time to time. I think also about that doctor in Landstuhl who caused my grief, because he did not say, "Be sure to pull out the gauze"!

The first major indication of revolt in Iran was the burning of a theater in Abadan in which several hundred Iranians died. As the months went by into 1978, demonstrations, shootings, and burning became more commonplace. The anti-Shah people regularly shut down the main power stations so that the entire city of Tehran was totally blacked out. Elevators in apartment buildings were made inoperable, and we had to walk in the dark up nine flights of stairs, not knowing whom we would meet along the way up or down.

One day as I was working in my seventh-floor office, an Iranian naval officer, with whom I worked daily, came up and told me I had to leave the building. I said I was not finished with my work. He repeated, "You must leave the building, now!" He would offer no other information as to why. I left what I was doing and quickly ran down the stairway to the main doorway. It was closed with a secondary gate of steel bars like in a jail. The officer said, "I'm going to open this gate and door for you now, and you must leave the building!" It was almost as if he pushed me out, and to my further astonishment I was thrust into the edge of a crowd of thousands of rioters in the street and on the sidewalks. I glanced across the street and noticed that the movie theater was ablaze. I had to take a quick look around to see what the general situation was, and there was rioting as far as I could see up and down the street. I had a stroke of luck in that I was taller than most of the Iranians. Just above the heads in this crowd I saw two arms waving about fifty meters distant. It was my driver, Farsola. I worked my way as quickly as possible toward him alongside the *jubes* to where Farsola had our car parked, just around a corner in a side street. He opened the door, I jumped in, and he drove us safely away to my apartment, a few kilometers away.

Thereafter each day was a new challenge. Farsola, before picking me up each morning, would first cruise the streets to determine the best route to take with a minimum of disturbance. It got to be too dangerous in general to go to the normal office for my work, so I went sometimes to the GD International Corporate Office in the north of Tehran, where there were a few of our people and a small staff of Iranians really loyal to us. Farsola was also extremely loyal to my wife and me throughout the assignment in Iran. He, like many Iranians, was a peaceful man with family and wanted none of this revolution.

On another occasion I received a phone call from Christa at our apartment in central Tehran saying that "there is burning and shooting here, and the Khorush department store next to our building is on fire. They are throwing everything out in the street for burning." Farsola drove me there immediately, as there was urgency in her voice. As we began to approach the downtown area, our roadway ahead was crowded with several thousand rioters wielding various and sundry clubs. There was a tremendous pile of burning material in the main intersection we were approaching. Smoke could also be seen rising out of the center of Tehran from all over. This was the fourth of November 1978. It seemed that the rioters were smashing cars arbitrarily as they ran in between and around all the traffic which was now completely stopped. As they came to our car, Farsola and I ran out into a side street and continued over to my apartment. We ran up the stairs (power was off, therefore no elevators operating), and in our apartment we saw Christa bent over the windowsill, looking at the action below. I pulled her inside, as she was obviously not aware of the possibility of getting shot with stray bullets. She said, "By the way, I meant to tell you to keep the car headlights on, because that means you believe in Khomeini and they won't smash the car." Well, that bit of advice was a little too late and we were once again lucky to avoid serious trouble. We could laugh about this later, but at the time there was obvious danger with each of these demonstrations.

On several occasions, as we walked down some streets, Iranians would spit or throw stones toward us because, we found out later, they thought Christa was an Iranian woman with an American. On other occasions, friends of ours had their tires slashed and hopelessly flattened. Windows of foreigners had been smashed, and some American businessmen were shot dead. Death threats appeared on telex messages to our company. Anyone could have been caught up in the throes of violence at any time.

Near the end of 1978 it became quite obvious that it was really no longer safe, but there were no clear announcements by the embassies until very late in December and early January 1979 when they said that evacuation was necessary.

During the last week of December 1978, I was trying to get a flight out of Tehran for the purpose of going on a business trip to Riyadh, Saudi Arabia. I had tickets for a Pan Am flight out of Tehran to Frankfurt, from whence I planned to travel to Riyahd. Five mornings in a row, just after curfew, which was by now every night until 5:00 A.M., I had Farsola take me to the airport. Each time it was not possible to get out, the first two days because Pan Am refused to land at Tehran and simply overflew the airport. I could not get on other flights, as many Iranians with enough money were paying big amounts extra to buy the seats that were available. Finally my wife, who was working for the Deutsche Bank, was able to arrange a flight with Lufthansa to get me a seat to Frankfurt. In order to carry this act out she covered her head with a scarf and had Farsola drive her to the city center to the Lufthansa office, which at the time was probably the only airline office still not burned out. She told them that I was threatened, as an American, and at this point had to leave. I now had a ticket on a Lufthansa flight for the thirty-first of December 1978. Just before leaving I had gone to the Bank Melli near our apartment, in order to draw out money for my trip. I routinely walked into the bank, as I had during the past two years, to request withdrawal of some money from my account. The two nice ladies who were always there did not greet me in the normal way on this day. In fact, they said nothing at all. Behind these two ladies was a bearded Iranian, with fire in his eyes. He said, "You don't have an account here. Not anymore." Under the circumstances we had been experiencing, I knew exactly what he meant. There was no room for discussion. I left. But I also left the country on that flight to Frankfurt without any cash whatsoever.

It was New Year's Eve, 31 December 1978, as I arrived at the Frankfurt airport at about 2200 hours. As it was a holiday and at night, there were no banks open, and my pockets were empty of cash. Germany on this night was experiencing one of the worst snowstorms in years. What to do? I thought of one friend, Horst Jaeger, in Dietzenbach, whom I knew from working in Tehran. Without money, not a single coin, I could not even call him. Dressed in my usual business attire, a dark suit and brown camel hair overcoat, I was forced to ask a stranger, anyone, in the airport for thirty pfennigs. I wasn't certain of the amount needed but remembered that many persons had often used only that amount. I really do not remember how many times I said, "Bitte dreissig pfennig." To this day, as I write, I cannot believe that I was rejected by so many people when I asked for the equivalent of a few cents to make a phone call. I received the sternest looks, as if I had a sickness. Getting rather desperate, I thought perhaps if I asked for eine Deutsch Mark (100 pfennigs, then about thirty-five cents) there might somehow be better results. I walked into a small bar area where five or six men sat on stools nursing their beer. I said to a man, "I need one Deutsch Mark for telephone, *bitte*" (exact words). He never said a word. He stared at me, and he continued to stare as he hesitantly reached into his pocket and finally drew out one Deutsch Mark. Then he dropped it into my opened palm. I said, "Danke, danke!" I can presume they all stared at my back until I went out of their sight. I was relieved that at least somebody responded. I could only recall that in New York City, in my experience, even a drunk could easily get a quarter from a passerby.

I called Horst, my friend, who answered the telephone. "Yes, Paul, come on out to the house. We already started the New Year's party. I can't come to get you because I already drank too much to drive."

"But, Horst, I don't have the money for a taxi. I had to borrow a mark to call you."

"Paul, just get a cab and come here. I'll pay the driver when you arrive."

It worked out as he said, and immediately I called from Horst's house to Tehran to contact Christa where I knew she would be staying overnight with friends. Amazingly enough the telephone system was still working, and everyone was relieved that I made it out of the country safely.

Because of the snowstorm and various delays in arranging for funds, and the flight to Riyadh, I stayed for three days with Horst and his family.

It was just at this time that the German ambassador announced that all German citizens must leave Iran. This now meant that Christa had to leave, but in the meantime she was pressed with the job of packing what she could carry of our belongings out of the country. The rest of the items had to stay, as there were no means to pack and transport them. Some of the items were given to Iranian friends. In order to get to the airport for her Lufthansa flight out of Tehran, Christa gave some bottles of whiskey to Farsola to trade for gasoline for the car. When he came back he had no gasoline, as it was in extreme short supply, but they had taken the whiskey anyway. Luckily, one of the Iranian naval officers with whom I had worked in both Philadelphia and Tehran, came to the rescue with a couple of liters of gasoline, enough to get her to the airport. And another Iranian, with whom Christa worked, paid a lot of rials to an airport worker in order to get her overweight baggage checked in for the flight. She was packing during nights with candlelight what she felt was of greatest value. Many of our belongings, including most of our clothing, were lost in the shuffle.

With the worsening situation in Iran I was about to begin an earlier than planned assignment in Saudi Arabia and Greece. I never went back to Iran. Our Iranian navy project study was completed but the programs never implemented. After an initial survey of what GD would be doing in Saudi Arabia I made a visit to the GD Mideast Office in Athens. At this uncertain point in time, I was not permanently assigned anywhere, so I had talks with the director of the Mideast Office, Bill Green. I had worked with Bill, fortunately, in Turkey during the shipyard survey in 1972. He knew me and my capabilities and therefore recommended to the corporate office in Saint Louis that I be assigned to work out of the Athens office as a corporate marketing manager with General Dynamics International Corporation (GDIC). So it started that I would spend two weeks out of each month in Saudi Arabia and two weeks in Greece during 1979 and 1980, while having our new residence in Athens. This work involved the marketing of products of all the divisions of GD.

Tavernas and Islands—Prayer Calls and Changes in the Sand (1979–80)
Greece–Saudi Arabia

It became clear from the General Dynamics International Corporation Headquarters that I would be working out of the Mideast Office, Athens, Greece. Our household would be in Athens for two years, but during this time I would spend two weeks out of every month in Athens and two weeks in Saudi Arabia, in the capacity of corporate marketing manager. Hotels would be my home in Saudi at locations wherever the needs of my work took me. We had yet to find an apartment in Athens, but in the meantime we lived in the Athens Hilton. After the first few weeks in the Hilton I got a call from the front desk, where I was told that we had to move out of the hotel because our reservation had run out and the hotel was already booked. The front desk manager insisted there was no recourse. He had no interest in the fact that, just out of Iran with its revolution, we had no place to live and were still looking for an apartment. I asked to see the manager of the hotel, as it was a rather impossible situation for us. With an air of arrogance the front desk manager stated, "Go ahead; it won't do you any good."

I met immediately with the Swiss-born hotel manager, "Rick" Rickenbacher. After I explained the situation including the threat of eviction from the hotel, he said immediately, "You can stay in the hotel as long as you want to." I never have forgotten his understanding and kindness then and during the years that followed.

During the hotel stay we had the opportunity to eat in nearly every restaurant in Athens, as well as having already tried every item on the menu card of the Hilton. At times it became so boring to eat in any restaurant that I would bring a barbecued chicken from a sidewalk shop, along with bread, cheese, and wine, to the hotel room and just eat casually.

One of the favorite places to go out and eat was in Piraeus, where there were about twenty-five or thirty fish restaurants, next to each other, near the water. One could always eat inside in colder months, but when the weather was warm nearly everyone would dine at lunch or in evenings outside, right on the waterfront. A guest in Athens was always taken to Piraeus as one of the points of leisure.

Fish was rather expensive but good and especially enjoyable in the waterfront atmosphere. The fish were always sold by weight, by the kilo. Tourists or newly arrived expatriates as I was in January 1979 so very often did not realize what was happening to their pocketbook until they got the bill. I looked at the fish displayed on the iced trays and said to the waiter, "Two of these and three of those," et cetera. I ordered for four of us, and we thoroughly enjoyed the dinner. But then came the bill. That's when indigestion set in. Only then I realized that, in the future, I would have to take the time and effort to get the fish weighed before ordering. Eventually, though, after several visits, I got used to the weights in kilos and judging cost just by looking at the type and size of these fish.

My thoughts were still geared to memories of the Montauk Fishing Village where fish were available to us just for the asking, and fish that I knew were fresh out of the local waters.

I noted that most all the fish at these restaurants, and others in the downtown area of Athens, came from Morocco. At the air freight terminal each day one could see huge piles of Styrofoam containers with fresh frozen fish. The fish were very good, nothing at all wrong with them. But of course the restaurateurs put these fish on crushed ice in front of their business locations, which was necessary to keep them fresh but also give the tourists the impression that the fish were fresh from the local fishing areas.

We eventually found a large and very nice apartment available in Paleo Faliron, just two blocks from the sea and just west of the international airport. A new international airport was constructed several years later, to the northeast of Athens. Our apartment location was good because of proximity to the airport, which I often used, and the seaside, which was only two blocks away. But there was a downside to the nearness to the airport. Sometimes Paleo Faliron mornings were annoying when there was a west wind. Takeoff and climb-out then were just over our apartment building, only a few hundred meters from the end of the runway. Our entire building, and all its inhabitants, would shudder with the loud roar of the engines, especially the fully fueled and other otherwise loaded 747 aircraft on the flights to New York and other long-distance hauls. The GD office was in the center of Athens, but it was an easy ride along a major road, Syngrou, into the city from the apartment.

We had made quite a number of friends in Iran and many of them had to leave Iran or suffer under the new regime. Some would be killed. Not long after we got settled in Athens we had quite a few of these Iranians visit, and some came to live with us for short periods. One of these couples called us from a cheap unheated hotel and announced that they were there with a newborn baby. "Reza" worked with me in the same office in Tehran. We offered Reza and his wife a room in our apartment. As it turned out, they stayed, and stayed for many weeks without any hint from them about planning to leave. I had orders at this point for transfer to Egypt. Now they had to leave. A small apartment was arranged for them, and our friends even solicited used furniture and kitchen ware. The now-civilian Reza finally found a job as a driver for a rich Saudi, and we thought they were well on their way to freedom and happiness. This was not to be. Reza's wife did not want her husband driving a car for a living. Finally, after talking with Reza, who really was a good friend in Iran and helpful to me at work, I made every effort to help him and arranged for their emigration to Canada, where they could start a new life. They were accepted and flew to Canada in late 1980. After their move and mine, we lost contact. I never heard from them again. I wonder of course what transpired in the meantime and really would like to see them again.

It was usual when renting a house or apartment in Athens that the contract would contain a much lower rent cost than what was actually paid each month to the landlord, obviously of some tax benefit to the landlord. If one wanted to rent, it was the only way. There were some other conditions I found unusual. For example, the heat from the furnace in our multi-story building was turned on about the middle of November and turned off about the middle of March; in both cases it seemed irrespective of outside temperature. Usually it was necessary to have heat before mid-November and after the middle of March as well. There was also the daily problem in that the heat would be turned off about ten o'clock each evening. Just when one might become interested in a TV program or in conversation with guests we found ourselves suddenly starting to "freeze." Therefore one had to purchase other equipment to keep warm, either an electric or gas heater. My initial choice was to obtain a couple of butane gas heaters, which were relatively inexpensive. About one month after using the first butane gas bottle I purchased the second. As I connected the hose between the valve on the butane bottle and the heater elements, flames shot into the air up to the ceiling and I thought the unit would explode. I immediately turned it off. After looking into the situation, I learned that the quality control in maintenance on the gas bottle valves left a whole lot to be desired. I ceased using the gas heaters and found liquid-filled electric-powered radiators. Although more expensive, they were much more efficient and, above all, safer to operate.

It was a surprise to me how cold winters could get in Athens. An overcoat was necessary in midwinter. I had thought from all the vacation posters I had seen in the States that Greece was always sunny and warm. On the other hand, in the summer I found Athens one of the hottest places I had lived. It was welcome, however, always seeing blue skies, without a cloud, from about mid-May until mid-October. This is not to say that there wasn't any pollution; on some mornings there was a very heavy brown layer of the stuff hanging in the air, especially in the direction of Piraeus and the refineries. In fact, driving cars into the center of Athens was restricted to odd-numbered license plates on one day and even-numbered the next. However, many families with two or more cars usually got around this problem.

Air-conditioning was not at all common, despite the very high temperatures in summer. Not a single apartment that I was ever in had air-conditioning. This was cause for a very unusual sight on summer evenings. With such warm weather if you looked up at any given apartment building from the street you would see, on nearly every balcony, a television set in the doorway facing outward and the people sitting on the balcony looking at the TV. Of course not everyone was tuned to the same channel, so you can imagine the mixture of sounds generating pure noise in the entire neighborhood. The warm evenings also encouraged the bike riders to cool off a bit by the air flow in cruising around. Therefore, after going to bed around midnight, because of late dinner hours in Greece, at two and three in the morning there was still the incessant noise of motorcycles on the streets, making a good night's sleep virtually impossible.

Saudi Arabia

My presence in Saudi was aimed at becoming familiar with the land, its people, and the customs, and following market trends and potential business opportunities for GD. My first task was to establish a physical office in Riyadh. This involved the selection of a lawyer who ultimately registered the company's venture with Sheikh Mansour Badr, a fine, relatively young man who was always friendly and cooperative. Sheikh Mansour also had an office in Jeddah, and I would spend some days there as well as in Riyadh during each of my trips to Saudi Arabia. Aside from the routine of the Riyadh and Jeddah offices and marketing work, I was tasked to travel to various locations in order to get firsthand information about certain projects or to learn of company product testing and installation progress.

At the outset I needed furniture for the office space that Sheikh Mansour had provided. He told me to go to a certain store in Riyadh that sold furniture and it would be my choice to determine what was required. "Just go and buy what you need. Here is some money." (What he handed me was a roll of cash amounting to about thirty thousand riyals, then worth about ten thousand dollars.) That in itself already shocked me, the fact that he simply handed me that much money with no accounting whatsoever. I went to the shop, picked out all the furniture items necessary, and calculated that the cost was 23,000 riyals. Then I told the shopkeeper that I added up the costs and it came to 23,000 riyals. He said nothing as I handed him the money, and he also said nothing as he literally threw the 23,000 riyals into the drawer without counting them. I said to him, "Aren't you going to count the money?"

"No," he said. "It is not necessary, I know where your office is located."

This method of handling money would rarely be seen in most any other land. In Saudi if you do anything wrong, including trying to cheat anyone, there is very little chance of getting away with it. When a traveler goes into Saudi Arabia his passport is taken away and not given back until he is ready to depart the kingdom.

My very first trip to Saudi Arabia was with my British-American boss, Bill Green, Director Mideast, General Dynamics International Corporation. I will never forget that first night at the El Kharegi Hotel in Riyadh when I entered my room. A single bare lightbulb hung on its electric cord from the ceiling. As I switched on the light, dozens of giant cockroaches scampered from all directions into a drain hole in the middle of the floor. I had already learned in Corpus Christi, Honolulu, and Tehran that these creatures do not like light. The hanging light stayed on most of the time in the Kharegi. More and very beautiful hotels were being built in Saudi, so on later trips I made certain to stay in one of them.

It was always of interest to me when standing in the international airport customs line upon arrival at Riyadh or Jeddah to see what all the travelers had in their suitcases and to see what the customs agents would take out or throw into the large waste cans, things such as magazines with lightly clad women, Bibles, freshly plucked chickens, liquor, rusty-looking cans with various food contents, and anything at all suggesting political and religious views contrary to life in the kingdom. These lines were, more often than not, long and tiresome. And in winter when the flights landed in darkness it was really cold when you had to stand outside because of the length of the customs line-up. Alcohol was "not allowed" on the Saudi flights; however, I have noticed stewards providing alcohol to certain passengers in the first-class section.

It was extremely interesting especially during the months of the first year working in Saudi, because I had never been there before. During my trips throughout the country I was always keen to observe every facet of life. I worked very long hours, as there was really nothing else for me to do relative to social life. I did get to visit some friends, the Rofalsksi family, who were living in Jeddah, and had dinner with them occasionally. I sometimes snorkeled in the Red Sea. I often made trips to Taif, which is located in the mountains just a few kilometers out of Jeddah. There I enjoyed the souk where I bought an antique Arabic coffeepot. I had planned to stay at the Sheraton Hotel in Taif but learned that it was reserved for the king. Not just a room, but the entire hotel. Taif is the summer home of the Saudi king. The air temperature is a bit cooler there compared to Riyadh, but of course all the important buildings are air-conditioned.

As I got to know the various hotels and restaurants in Riyadh I found the Hotel Al Khozama the nicest in many respects. Although not one of the very large hotels, it was new, very clean, and well managed by Gustar Ltd., a Swiss company. The main dining room, the Windrose Restaurant, was really a superb place to eat and enjoy the evening. As I got to know the staff in this hotel and restaurant, a good relationship developed and this helped create the atmosphere I needed to maintain my sanity in this city. There was a lack of any kind of social entertainment expected by a visitor in a capital city not only of the West but anywhere I had been. The Al Khozama, I believe, had the only piano and pianist in the entire city at that time. After my first night in the Windrose I asked the pianist to play the theme song from *Doctor Zhivago*. Thereafter, every night when I arrived at about nine o'clock and sat at my table, always alone, the pianist played "my song." I felt civilized then, for at least a couple of hours, as my "batteries" were charged listening to my favorite song to carry me through the next day. And then again on the next days, until the end of each two-week stretch in this religiously restricted desert land. Everything inside the hotel was great, but at times something on the outside was quite different. An arrangement of tables was made for the option of evening dining in the garden. Whereas all was beautifully done in terms of table settings, food, flowers, and the like, there was one disruptive aspect to this otherwise exotic setting. This was on days when the grass in this garden was irrigated with processed wastewater from the hotel.

An alternate place for me to stay in the Riyadh area was the new Hotel Khurais Marriott, just north of the city and at the very edge of the desert (at that time). Riyadh continues its expansion into desert land. The Marriott was another of the great modern hotels to be built in Saudi, and I was amazed during my early experiences there just how much elegance was being placed in this otherwise barren and restricted land, elegance in architecture, furnishings, and decoration. A guest in this kind of hotel had a feeling of being in another world. As a matter of fact, it *was* another world. For example, as I sat in the hotel restaurant to order an ordinary meal I observed a waiter rolling out a table upon which was a huge carved block of ice about a foot high. I wondered what this was until it came within range so I could actually see atop this block of ice a very small glass dish filled with Caspian caviar. The cost of this one item shown on the menu, ordered by a man in Saudi dress, was listed as 150 riyals, three times the cost of my whole dinner. After dinner, most of the guests, foreign or Saudi, would sit in fine comfortable chairs arranged along the grand hallway where waiters would pour them Arabic coffee. From the curved spout of the Saudi-type coffeepot, from a height of several inches, the waiters would pour into the very small cup. It was quite a show. I witnessed these pourings many times and never saw the waiters miss the cup, although I supposed that it must happen at times.

After several stays at the Khurais Marriott I began to see a kind of pattern, comparative to the development of Saudi Arabia, as I approached the hotel. It was another extension of a city out into the desert and evidence of changing into a new age out of the sand. There was this beautiful new hotel structure sitting in the desert sands, modern high-tension electric power lines towering over this desert, huge dust clouds churning up from speeding cars on unfinished roads, sheep grazing along the way on something not visible, and wrecked cars along the way. I found recently a sketch that I made of this sight and some verse I thought appropriate while in Saudi on 2 February 1979. The original has been copied for entry here. The Arabic writing near the top of the sketch states: "Khurais Marriott." To the right of the hotel are the location of the Corps of Engineers complex and the International School.

Approach to Riyadh's Khurais Marriott
[Riyadh, 26 February 1979]

Was desert, it is desert
Man comes again—
before with camel but passes on;
Lamb remember—try to hold their place
Did they truly nourish here? Do they now?
For something they look—I see nothing.
The iron camel succumbs with gaping mouth—
both are driven—with hump and wheel;
alas, animal mind supplements the master
no casual iron master stays,
his mount now a monument
to the thoughtless—to the careless.
I continue to follow silica cloud
must be the way
to my desert home—Khurais Marriott.
Yes—power stretching on familiar towers
all the way from Tesla, but did he know
that his Alpine vision
would flow to desert lands,
to the Corps, the International School, or
to the Khurais Marriott?

Two of the most interesting tasks involved the travel to Yanbu and to Jubail. As far as I knew, I was the first from our company to go into these more remote areas, and upon completion of the trips the inevitable "trip report" was written for the corporate headquarters, as information for use by prospective company travelers and of general interest to others. I will de-

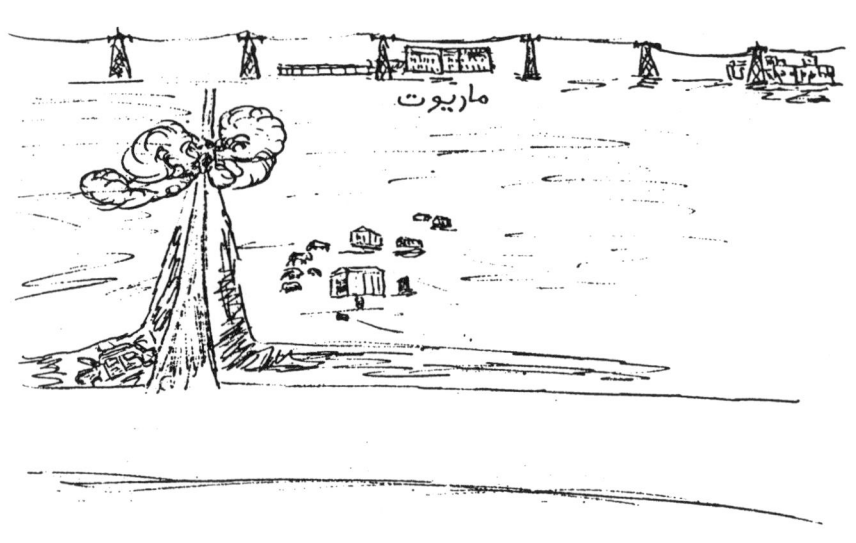

scribe through the use of excerpts from the Yanbu Trip Report the many similarities between this and the trip to Jubail.

Note: The following paragraphs are excerpts of the Yanbu Trip Report and are taken directly from my original reports. Technical aspects of projects have been omitted for obvious reasons.

Yanbu (in 1980)

The following account is on the conditions at Yanbu, Kingdom of Saudi Arabia, and the trip between Jeddah and Yanbu based upon my experience during 19–21 April 1980. A single trip does not make one an instant expert, but these observations may be useful for another traveller on his first venture to Yanbu:

Yanbu is about 350 kilometers north of Jeddah along the Red Sea coastal plains consisting almost entirely of flat sandy ground. It is interrupted occasionally with scattered areas of dry grass, shrubs, and a very few trees of heights no greater than 3 meters (about 10 feet). On the left to the west of the 2 lane, narrow, but rather new road leaving Jeddah, the distance to the Red Sea varies from 1 to several kilometers. On the right to the east there are, at distances varying from 3 to 20 kilometers, all along the way, escarpments of up to perhaps 100 meters (over 300 feet) high, and in a few places small cone-shaped mountains of lava rock, black in appearance. These appear more frequently as we continue northward, 250 kilometers from Jeddah.

Travel by auto on this black-topped road is the only means of transportation to Yanbu. The exception is for those in private aircraft upon request to, and approval from, the Royal Commission for landing at their temporary airstrip, which was intended for exclusive use by the Royal Commission. An operational domestic airport is scheduled at this airstrip site in perhaps two or more years' time. Other transportation for cargo is by ship entering the newly completed port of Yanbu.

One can rent a car and drive alone; however, a "first trip" should be with a driver who speaks English and Arabic, and one who has experience with this run and the village of Yanbu. Although the trip time, one way, is only about four hours, there is little along the way to satisfy thirst, hunger, or auto repair needs. One should inspect the tires of the rental car for newness and ensure that a spare tire, with tools for changing a tire, is in the car. A few bottles of water are recommended to carry. The several small villages on this road may provide some source of nourishment, but the sanitation conditions leave much to be desired.

The speeds at which many drive and the poor judgment of others have produced wreckage along the route of at least one smashed auto every half mile. I witnessed a two-car head-on crash just before us where the occupants became part of the twisted metal, always a sickening sight. A while later, a truck had just overturned. Nearer to Yanbu, two flashing ambulances sped towards us to another incident. With all this, a good driver serves to ease the tension of the passenger, while a poor driver will recycle the reformed smoker. Fortunately, I had an excellent Yemenese driver who maintained a speed of about 110 km/h (about 65 mph).

For reasons of traffic, and at least slightly lower temperatures, it is best to start out early in daylight. Night driving is more dangerous due to not only darkness but also the local drivers' habits of flashing bright lights shortly before approaching in opposing traffic. Others fail often to dim lights altogether. Camel crossings are encountered as well. Although no camels crossed our path, I saw several camel herds along the way within a half kilometer of the road.

There is only one relatively modern hotel in Yanbu, the "Yanbu Hyatt," but it is a nice hotel with good food. Telephones are in each room; however, while I was there, calls could be made only within Yanbu. I could not call anywhere outside of Yanbu. A Hyatt sign is located on the road at the point of turn-off to the hotel on the west side, towards and near the sea. The only other active hotel in Yanbu is the one called the "Middle East" located in the center of the town. Anyone preferring to relive a Peter Lorre–Sidney Greenstreet movie might choose to stay in this hotel, where the clerk was slouched and dozing on a lobby bench. When approached, he lazily brushed away some flies which came in through the open door, along with the heat of the noonday sun. I made this hotel visit as part of my survey of the area. But now came thoughts to inquire about lunch, in a place of local color, and as I reflected on some earlier films I remembered cafe scenes involving Middle East waterfront intrigue, with Peter and Sidney in white suits and Panama hats. On the clerk's third swipe at the persistent flies, he muttered something in Arabic. I was informed by my driver's translation that "it is prayer time, and the best place to eat, in any case, is at the Hyatt, not here." A drive through the town center revealed no other choice of where to eat, at least no place identifiable, in any way, as a restaurant. So it can be said, at this time, there was only one hotel, and only one place to eat: the Hyatt. It should be noted that another hotel is under construction and it is supposed to be operational within the year under a Holiday Inn sign.

As I was casually walking along one of the streets, with a cigarette in hand, I felt a rough tap on my shoulder. I turned around, startled. There was one of the religious police and in his hand a long stick with which he hit my shoulder. He was dressed in galabaya as an ordinary Saudi walking the street. With his arm and hand gestures I learned that smoking in the street is not allowed during Ramadan, and that I must go to the hotel. I had not seen this kind of treatment in Jeddah or Riyadh. I went to the hotel only to find out that smoking was also not allowed in the lobby. In fact, the hotel manager informed me that if I wanted to eat I must order food to my room and eat it there.

After driving through and around Yanbu, I came away with the impression that on every street there were either crumbling buildings or new construction, a town in a state of decay, and yet, almost sudden awakening. Almost any item can be seen for sale in the shops, typical of the Mideast, from brightly colored thermos bottles and Pampers to the endless array of imported electronic gadgets and 5-riyal cassette tapes.

Modern newly installed but non-operational street lamp posts along a few blocks here and there appear almost as partially installed samples. Their tall, downward-curved tops appear to be shepherding a small herd of goats below, grazing, seemingly, on nothing but bare dirt. In the outskirts are a multiple of half-built housing complexes without any sign of activity. A modern highway suddenly commences from our dirt street and we find it leads to the airstrip of the Royal Commission, ten kilometers away. At the waterfront, just north of Yanbu, is a Royal Beach Palace separated from the inquisitive passersby by two parallel cement block walls, not so high that you could not recognize the elegance which identifies its use and user.

Along the coastal limits of the town are dozens of rotting hulls of former fishing boats, handbuilt by the looks of the craftsmanship. Just beyond these high and dry craft, others project out of the shallow water where young and old fishermen are casting out their round throw nets into the Red Sea. Now and then they retrieve batches of small silvery fish, shimmering in the bright sun. This activity is observed between newer small handcrafted boats, in shallow water, with Mercurys and Evinrudes angled up to clear the bottom. On shore nearby, two elderly men in galabayas are stooping over a catch of fish in the hot shade, and viewed by three curious goats. The fish are barely discernible from the hungry flies which mask them. These sights are against the distant backdrop of harbor tugs nudging a large freighter with pipe supplies to carry crude across the Saudi Peninsula to the new Yanbu Petro-Chemical Complex.

The Yanbu that I visited during this three-day trip I found very interesting, a remote, sleepy fishing village becoming the location of a huge, very huge, new petrochemical complex furthering the modern development of a desert kingdom. I was nonetheless relieved to return to Jeddah, a thriving metropolis in comparison.

Just a comment on Jubail, also still considerably archaic at the time, 1980. In one of the hotels, intended for many of the foreigners working in the area, I read this amusing notice: "Fly to Riyadh for a getaway weekend." My thought was if Riyadh was a place for a "getaway," they were really stretching the point.

For people living and working in Saudi, that is, the families, it was customary that wine, beer, and other spirits were made in the house, as long as it was done with discretion. I often heard the comment, "My wife's job is to make the wine in the kitchen." Some proudly announced that they had made some of the best schnapps south of Germany. One can say that the country is not totally dry, but it is difficult, in any case, for the inexperienced to find a drink. On occasions when certain house parties became too loud and boisterous and then attracted outside attention, the authorities would take severe action.

Restaurants were not too plentiful when I was in Saudi, but there were enough, and many foreigners and Saudi men would eat in the hotel restaurants, which were quite good. I almost never saw a Saudi woman in any restaurant. And it was usual for many of the Saudi men to arrange dinners in private rooms, especially for business purposes. Wine was not served in the restaurants of course, but they had very specially made bottles that looked like wine bottles but actually contained juice. The waiters handled the bottles as if they had wine in them in order to give the feeling, perhaps, that you would have at home.

Also interesting was the procedure during prayer call, which occurred five times a day. During my first shopping experience, as I was looking at the wares in a Riyadh shop with electronic items, there happened to be a prayer call. The religious police actually went around to ensure that the customers left, and the shops had to close until after prayer call. The shopkeepers, I noticed on later occasions, did not especially like to close the shop when someone was ready to buy a camera or stereo of significant value, but the police were rather persistent in getting the customers out of the shops. This was every day, not just during Ramadan.

Speaking of prayers, it was during a Saudia takeoff from Riyadh Airport for my two weeks' stay in Athens that I began to pray, spontaneously, as the aircraft rolled down the runway, prayer in earnest, when suddenly just beside my aisle seat was a middle-aged bearded man in galabaya sitting on the deck of the aircraft, legs crossed, pumping a small kerosene stove. It was the size of stove such as those used for camping. It seemed that as quickly as this man had appeared, a teapot was within a circular wall of flames licking up its sides. Most of the passengers probably had no idea what was going on, and this was a lucky thing; otherwise there may have been pandemonium. Yet the others in the immediate area, nearly all Saudis, and some other Mideast nationals, had absolutely no sense of impending danger. I shouted to one of the stewardesses to bring her attention to this flaming stove during takeoff. I could not believe that she did nothing but show me the palms of her hands, indicating, *What can I do?* The man made his tea, and after at least ten or so minutes, while the plane was still climbing out, he shut the stove down and went back to his seat. When we landed with a stopover at Jeddah before going on to Athens, I talked with the stewardess and asked, "How is this? Why didn't you stop him?" She said, "I am a woman and it is not possible for me tell a man to do anything. He would not listen."

During the following year a Pakistani airliner blew up in flight, and also a Saudi Airline aircraft burned to rubble. My thoughts were that it was not beyond the realm of possibility that another "tea maker" had been on board.

When I was in Athens the two weeks per month I had to go to the office on a daily basis, but I did have more time to do other things on the lighter side. Each free weekend we drove to all the possible places of interest in Greece from north to south and east to west. Delphi was one of the first areas to visit, and we took other trips to Arta, Levkas, Agrinion, Kalamata, Yithion, Sparta, Olympia, Tripoli, Navplion, Istiaia, Corinth, Khalkis, Thessaloniki, and all points in between, plus several of the islands, Corfu, Crete, Santorini, and Kefallinia, to name a few. During the week there were often visiting corporate delegations to care for and to help in arranging various marketing meetings.

One warm day after trekking through the Delphi areas of interest we stopped at a restaurant and sat on a patio with a beautiful view to have cool drinks and something to eat. I was in the mood for cake and ice cream along with the drink, so I asked the waiter for "cake à la mode."

"It's not on the menu," he replied.

I asked, "Do you have cake?"

He said, "Yes, of course."

"Do you have ice cream?" I continued.

When he answered affirmatively that he had both cake and ice cream,

I said, "Well, just put some cake and some ice cream on the same dish. I will pay as if it is two separate orders."

"I cannot do that; it is not on the menu."

It ended up that I ordered some cake first and when it was delivered I ordered some ice cream. When the waiter brought the ice cream, I scraped it onto my cake. Finally, I concocted a cake à la mode! I received the handwritten bill, which included: "Cake à la mode 140 drachmas."

I enjoyed the tavernas in Athens and in every small village I drove through. A Greek coffee was a pleasure outside the small restaurants while sitting in the shade of a tree at the waterfront or in the center of the villages where several older men would be engaged in conversation. The villagers were very friendly by comparison to the city dwellers. Numerous ferries were taken from one port to another, often only ten or twenty minutes' travel time, where the scenes were duplicated at the landings. Red and white Domestica wine seemed to be available at every, even the smallest, village. It was not really so bad to my taste, certainly better than the retsina. On more than one occasion we stopped to have something to eat in a very small restaurant in the middle of nowhere. At one memorable stop the menu was "still in the ground and in the water." We sat down as an old lady pulled salad greens from her garden and her man went across the road to his boat. He returned to the kitchen with a pan of small fish. Only after half an hour, fried fish, fresh salad, a Domestica, and "just baked" bread were on the table.

During our time in Greece it was common to find small Greek Orthodox churches in the most remote locations, and they were always open to passersby to enjoy the sanctity and stillness. Only a few years later so many problems were arising from theft and meaningless destruction that these churches were locked up between services. A pity.

Strikes in Greece were held very often; too often, it seemed. They were held by professors, taxi drivers, airport workers, and banks, to name a few. I recall that the banks were so often on strike that it was necessary for me to always have a large sum of money in American Express or Thomas Cook traveler's checks, so that when I was called upon to travel I would be sure to have the necessary funds for the trip. When I finally ended my assignment working out of the Mideast Office, Athens, I remember seeing an article in a prominent business magazine describing cities around the world: "What Cities Businessmen Liked the Most, and the Least." It was no surprise to many who had worked in Athens that businessmen placed

Athens number twenty, the last on the list. But it was declared a great place for touring!

Before leaving Greece finally we made a trip to Bath, England, to visit friends we knew from Iran. It was truly interesting to see Bath and absorb its history. We toured the Roman baths, the Royal Theater, and the like. Also there was a side trip to Wales, where we dined, Middle Ages style, in a real castle with Welsh singing "wenches" with truly great voices. It was said that all people from Wales can sing, that is, they have good voices. Adding to the realism of this ancient atmosphere was a real-live thunderstorm and heavy rain and great bolts of lightning.

In late 1980 I made some familiarization trips to Cairo, Egypt, where I was to be assigned next and where I was about to spend the next six years as the in-country corporate marketing director for General Dynamics International Corporation.

Life and Livelihood on the Nile
(1980–86)

At the outset of my assignment to Egypt, I was very fortunate to have had some assistance of a colleague who had spent several days in Cairo before me. I was introduced by him to our newly hired Egyptian consultant and some Americans who were already established in Cairo. I picked up the responsibility soon afterward, and by the first of 1981 I was "on my own." The consultant, Maj. Gen. Salah Menawi, recently retired from the Egyptian Air Force (EAF), was of the very greatest help initially and throughout the entire next six years in Egypt. He recommended to me the names of persons to hire for positions of expeditor, secretary, driver, and "tea boy" to staff the GD office. An office space was yet to be located, rented, renovated, equipped, and put into operation. In the meantime, in parallel, I was to spend many weeks selecting a place to live. During the months in which these activities were taking place I lived in the Heliopolis Sheraton.

I was the first of GD employees to actually live in Egypt, starting in late 1980, when "my home" was in the Heliopolis Sheraton, before finding an apartment. Later there were to be about a hundred GD families living in Egypt on a contract for training EAF personnel in the F-16 program. Several buildings were rented in Heliopolis to house all these personnel.

Staff Personnel

General Menawi, whom I shall refer to as Salah from here on, was already hired as consultant for Northrup Corporation when he started consulting for GD. However, when it became clear that both companies were competing for the same fighter aircraft for the EAF, Salah had to select one company or the other. He chose General Dynamics Corporation. Later he also became consultant for Westinghouse Defense, which was not a problem since Westinghouse electronics systems (radar) were also in the F-16 Falcon multirole fighter, manufactured by GD in Fort Worth, Texas.

Salah was the operations officer for the EAF during the war with Israel while the commander of the EAF was Maj. Gen. Hosni Mubarak and, therefore, both were very good friends, as well as comrades in arms. Mubarak became president of Egypt after Anwar Sadat was assassinated in 1981 during an anniversary parade of the military in Heliopolis. As a result of this chain of events our consultant in Egypt had an extraordinarily good relationship with the Egyptian president, and also with all the senior officers in the Egyptian military. I had never seen, or became aware of, any underhanded dealings because of this consultant–president relationship, but I must say that this relation did make my job easier at times when certain problems, routine to solve in most developed countries, became real stumbling blocks in Egypt. Two of these problems, for example, involved an electric meter (every house has one to measure electricity consumed) and telephone installations.

During the first few months of 1981 I hired the expeditor, Colonel Rasmy (EAF, Ret.); secretary, Samira; tea boy, Shaaban; and driver, Ibrahim. I found and rented a house for an office on Beirut Street in Heliopolis, which needed renovations, and work got under way. When after several months of work the office was more or less ready to occupy, there were two problems of great significance. In order for the office to really function, there was the need for an electric meter to handle the electrical current for several heater/cooling air conditioners, the telex, a photocopier, computers, typewriters, kitchen appliances, the lighting system, and the like. Prior to the renovation, the house was lived in by a family and the only electricity needed was for electric lighting. This very low capacity meter was still installed and only good for lighting and the telex machine, nothing else. There was no heating available, and it was only during this time that I learned that Cairo in winter months can be very, very cold inside a building. The secretary's fingers were so cold that they could not effectively use the manual typewriters. And the all-important tea and coffee could not be made. No office in Cairo was without tea and coffee and a tea boy. Weeks, then months, slipped by without any trace of an electric meter from the electric department of Heliopolis. Rasmy, the expeditor, had made numerous trips to the department, returning only with promises, "next week" or "as soon as we can."

Then one day Rasmy came back to the office and told me that we could get the proper meter installed if I would give the electric superintendent 1,500 Egyptian pounds "under the table." He had been waiting all this time for his baksheesh. I refused. Then I asked Salah to talk with someone in the government at a higher level, as this office was needed for the development of the Egyptian F-16 program. It was also true that we could not function without a telephone. The whole situation seemed to become impossible. Without a phone I could not even communicate by voice with offices in downtown Cairo. I had to send my driver to deliver messages. In those days a round-trip from Heliopolis would take anywhere from three to four hours.

On a Sunday, a week after talking with Salah, I received a call from the Abdin Palace in downtown Cairo, stating that I was to meet with the director of the office of the president, Major General Shaban. Ibrahim drove me to the gate of the palace. He informed the guards of my name, and they waved us into the courtyard. Another guard met me and pointed to a red-carpeted stairway just inside the palace, which I was to take up to the next floor. Near the top of the stairway I walked into an open doorway and there, immediately, I was greeted with a handshake from General Shaban: "Welcome, Mr. Cook!" I was really taken aback by the casual and friendly character of the man who was the right hand of President Mubarak. I was invited to sit beside the general on a sofa in front of which was a table, with a pitcher of hot water, sugar bowl, tea bags, and two cups with saucers. His first comment was, "Let me show you how Egyptians make a cup of tea, anyway, how I make my tea." The tea bag was put into his cup (I was to follow his moves), hot water was poured into the cup, and then he placed the saucer on top of the cup. "This," he said, "is to contain the aroma and essence of the tea." After four or five minutes the first sip was taken and it appeared to me not unlike any of the tea that was offered so often in the various shops in the souk. But somehow, under the hand of this very kind general, and in the shadow of the Egyptian president, I was impressed with the thought that I certainly must be drinking something special in this particular cup. As a matter of fact, what was to occur very soon led me to believe that this tea had special powers.

"I understand, Mr. Cook, that you have some problems. Tell me these problems and I will try to help you."

I knew at this moment that Salah had really gotten the ear of this general, but he wanted to hear from me. I explained the problems of the meter and the telephones and how absolutely frustrating it had been to get around the obstacles to establish and equip an office. He picked up a telephone and called "someone"; I do not know to this day who it was. But it was a one-way conversation. The general did all the talking. He made a second call to another "someone." Afterward he wrote down the name and address of the person in charge of telephone permits and installations and said that I should see him on Tuesday morning. Also he said, "Tell your expeditor, Rasmy, that he will not have any more problems at the Heliopolis electrical office to get the meter you need." The following week I had three telephone lines installed in the office, a mobile telephone in my car, and a radio transceiver. In addition, the electric meter was installed in the office two days later. The superintendent who had been collecting baksheesh for meters was thrown into jail.

It is a sure bet that in any country, no matter where, shortcuts are made by knowing someone in order to accomplish one thing or another. But the more underdeveloped a country is, the more important it is to have the contacts through which one can accomplish tasks that may be quite routine in many other places. Small amounts of baksheesh, or grease money, are routine in everyday activities in countries like those in the Middle East, but larger amounts get into the way of progress and ethics.

Secretary Samira was an intelligent and very good secretary from the earliest days of her employment and, once past the "cold fingers" days, very productive. She was fluent in English and Arabic, married, Christian, and with a young son at the time of hiring. Some months after the office opened, a second secretary, Sanaa, was hired. She was also very good and with qualities similar to those of Samira. Sanaa, too, was married, Christian, and with a young son. Both Samira and Sanaa learned in just a very few weeks how to operate the new computer, purchased during the first year of office operation, and this served us very well.

Ibrahim, a very reserved Muslim of about thirty years, was my first driver. He was solemn-looking most often and a bit moody, but we got along very well. However, after about one year he left for another driver job. The reason for his leaving was that he could not get along with my wife. Mohammed and Refraat were to follow as drivers later on.

Shaaban, the tea boy, already with a large family, was from upper Egypt, Nubian, and a kind, gentle, and modest young man. Although he was hired as tea boy and cleaner, eventually he made photocopies, answered the telephone when necessary, and did other odd jobs around the office. But he always was able to anticipate one's need for a tea or coffee, and he took good care of office guests in a kind and friendly manner. Some years after I left Egypt I understood that he had a foot amputated because of an infection from a glass cut on the beach. The infection became worse because of his diabetic condition. But he went back to work as tea boy, despite the amputation.

Rasmy, a retired EAF colonel, was hired as expeditor. He was the choice of Salah because Rasmy was his assistant during the war with Israel and could be trusted in all cases. Rasmy arranged for licenses and VIP meetings at the airport, interfaced with EAF officers relative to meeting arrangements, and did such things as following the "meter problem." Rasmy was very polite and very loyal, the traits that stand out in my mind. He was Muslim and, like Salah, Ibrahim, and Shaaban, observed the Ramadan routine of no food or drink during the day. I did not know until later in my time in Cairo that Rasmy was also diabetic. He had to go to the hospital one day after working with us about five years. The result was a leg amputation because of complications from his diabetic condition.. Not long afterward he died, leaving his very nice wife and teenage son.

During my first several weeks and while I was living in the Heliopolis Sheraton, Rasmy was often tasked to pass messages to me or inform me of one thing or another by coming to the hotel, since there were no telephones in the office for several months. On three occasions I was to have received rather useful information but did not. I asked Rasmy whether he came to the Sheraton and he replied in the affirmative. He said that he asked for me, but I was not there. After the third occurrence I got Rasmy in my car, drove to the hotel, and went with him to the front desk. "Now, Rasmy, please tell me just exactly who did you talk to and what did you say."

Rasmy replied, very seriously, "He [pointing to the front desk manager] is the man I talked to. Each time."

"And say exactly what you told him, Rasmy."

"I said that I need to talk with Mr. Ball, and this man said they have no Mr. Ball checked into the hotel, so I went home."

Well of course it then became immediately clear what had happened. In Egypt it is common for an Egyptian to use the first name of almost anyone, preceded by Mister (Madam), and address one as, in my case, Mister Paul. However, most Egyptians find it difficult to say the "p" sound and *Paul* comes out as "Ball." Naturally, this became the subject of good laughs, but it is one of those kinds of things that are all part of the learning process when confronted with an array of cultural differences experienced from one land to another.

When Ibrahim left I found another driver, Mohammed, an older man with a wife and several children who lived in old Cairo, in the south section of the city. Mohammed came on in a friendly manner, but he was squinty-eyed. He could have played a role in a western scene standing up against another cowboy in a gun duel while facing a setting sun.

There was an occasion during the middle of his employment when he invited my wife and me to his house for dinner. That was highly unusual, to say the least, but I did not want to hurt his feelings by refusing. We went. His apartment was in one of the more destitute parts of old Cairo. We entered Mohammed's apartment through a narrow hallway that had a two-burner electric hot plate on a small table, plus various items piled up all along on one side of this hallway. Then through a doorless archway we passed into a room with a table and four chairs in the middle. Off to the left from this space was a room in which, we learned, was a bedroom where all the family slept, father, mother, and four children. Mohammed led us to the one other space in which there were two upholstered chairs and a shadeless floor lamp. Tacked on the walls were several pages torn out of magazines with pictures of landscape. The walls, with the signs of fallen plaster, were green and of various shades, the result of accumulated dirt and fading over time. We were asked to sit while they did something about the food. We sat and wondered, questioning ourselves without words, about how big a mistake we had made. I asked Mohammed if I could wash my hands. As I followed him, I thought, *Better a hot shower or bath.* I was led to the "bathroom." It was not a bathroom, in fact not a room, rather only a few square feet in the corner of the space where the table and chairs were located. The corner was only partially enclosed by a makeshift "cardboard fence" a couple of feet high. In this designated corner about knee-high was a water faucet, such as used for a garden hose. It was near a hole in the floor, the toilet. The sink was also the same hole in the floor, which swallowed everything. A dirty towel hung on a nail in the wall. Beside it was a jagged piece of broken mirror, unframed. I faked a hand wash.

"Mr. Ball!" The call to the table for dinner. The food on the table was recognizable as typical food we had seen in restaurants. However, the sanitary conditions diminished the appetite. They had already put food on our dishes. Mohammed and his wife, with no dishes in front of them, sat only to watch us eat. All four children stood around the table, alternately staring at the food, then our faces. As I began to look for a fork, knife, or spoon, it finally dawned on the hosts that there were none on the table. It became very clear that they had none, as they sent one of the children to a neighbor to borrow two forks. Not to have found a fork, in itself, would have been fine with me, if it meant that I would not have had to eat at all. But almost as challenging as taking in and digesting the food were the attempts to penetrate these offerings with the borrowed forks with completely bent tines. Between the idea of these kids not eating but staring at us from all angles, their silent parents, and the polluted atmosphere, we could barely swallow. It was impossible to finish what they had put on the plates. I wondered what it would take to demolish all these "old Cairo" buildings and replace them with modest but up-to-date facilities. I still wonder.

All the employees were very personable and friendly, including Mohammed. It was a rare case to find an unfriendly Egyptian. Exceptions were the handful of radicals whose actions caused severe consequences from time to time, and they often made news, especially in the foreign press. Mohammed's friendliness, unfortunately, was beset with his urge to try to better his financial situation through his belief that it was OK to take a little off the top when dealing with people who had more than he. This trait I observed of some employees, certainly not all, in other countries.

A simple example of this was when I asked one of the employees in Tehran, in 1978, to fetch me a cola on a hot day in the office. As he delivered the drink requested and I asked how much, invariably he would ask for double the price he had paid. One day I asked him, "Why?"

His answer: "You have a lot more money than I, and you Americans can afford it."

"But do you think this is honest?"

"Mr. Cook, I have a large family. We live in one room with one electric lightbulb and no running water."

The fact is, I would have in any case given him a tip for his effort, even though it was his job to run these errands. But I maintained that this kind of action was dishonest, and I tried to instill in the minds of the employees that it was wrong. It was not the path to becoming a trusted servant for the long run. I felt secure in the knowledge that at least some of these in my employ on that project learned a lesson to their benefit in life.

Mohammed's demise, first of all, was because on several occasions he had driven my wife to "good places to shop." I learned that he had made a deal with the shopkeepers to announce double the price for the items (none of which had prices marked), and Mohammed would take the other half. In another instance, he had said he knew a good carpenter who could make a piece of furniture that I needed for the office. The item was made and Mohammed returned some days later with it and informed me it cost 200 pounds. That sounded like too much money, so I asked Rasmy to check this out. Rasmy asked the carpenter what his work cost and he stated, "One hundred pounds." At this point, I was convinced that the squint in Mohammed's eyes was from something other than the glare of the bright sun of Cairo. I had him fired and informed the staff, in so many words, that anyone who wants to stay employed with us must be loyal and trustworthy at all times.

With Mohammed gone, I had the chore of once again selecting a good driver and hoped that luck would be on my side. As I had already learned well in Iran, and now in Egypt, a driver was really an important part of the expatriate's life. Soon Salah and Rasmy came up with a name, Refraat. They believed he would be a good choice as the next driver. Refraat was married, with children, and he was neat, punctual, and loyal. He came on the scene without fanfare, and the driver situation commenced to settle down.

However, there was yet another incident a couple of years later in which driver Refraat was accused of theft in our apartment. We had gone on a vacation in Kenya and upon our return found that all the gold jewelry, plus DM 5,000 (German marks), was missing from the apartment. The only ones with a key to the apartment were the maid and Refraat. The maid, in our absence, was to maintain the cleanliness, which was especially necessary because of the constant buildup of dust layers. The very fine sand from outside always found its way through the inadequate, and lacking, window seals. Refraat's job was to feed the cat.

One day while I was at work in Heliopolis, the police came to the house to investigate. They had asked my wife whom she thought may have stolen the jewelry. She impulsively answered, "Well, it couldn't have been the maid." My wife had trusted the maid to that extent. Immediately the police arrested Refraat. He was put in jail at the Dokki police station. The jailhouse treatment there is not kind. They hung Refraat upside down from the rafters trying to get him to confess, and he repeatedly denied involvement. In the meantime the rest of the office staff were insisting that Refraat could not have done such a thing. He just would not steal. Since Salah's brother was a senior Interior Ministry official, Salah called on him to get into the act. The number-one investigation squad appeared on the scene and they pored over everything for clues. Columbo could not have done a better job. Since it was beginning to seem less likely that Refraat was guilty, the police turned their attention to the maid, and she was arrested. Now in the Dokki station jail the maid found herself hanging upside down from the rafters. You can perhaps imagine the sight of a short, fat, 200-pound woman hanging by her feet. After ten minutes she confessed that she was the one. The maid then told the police to whom the gold was sold. In another couple of days the police had in their hands all the gold that was stolen. They found it 150 kilometers north of Cairo, in a small village. The DM 5,000 was never recovered.

The maid was taken before a judge who sentenced her to several years in prison. The judge informed my wife that she could now slap the maid's face. This, my wife would not bring herself to do.

Refraat was released and went home. As I did not see him for a couple of days, I assumed he simply needed some rest after his ordeal. I did not think much more about this pause. But he thought I would not want to keep him on as driver, that I would be ashamed of him, and that was why he stayed away. I told Salah to tell Refraat that there was no question in my mind about his honesty. He was a victim of circumstances. Refraat, my third driver, successor to Ibrahim and Mohammed, was always a very good man in all respects. I trusted him implicitly. Refraat was extremely happy that I wanted him back, and he continued his excellent service to me and the company. My wife apologized profusely to Refraat when we left Cairo, as it was her comment about the maid, when questioned by the police at the outset, that had sent him to the Dokki station.

Finding Out About Cairo—Things, People, Places

During the first couple of months in Cairo, while the Heliopolis office space was being sought, then renovated, I had a temporary space in the IBM (International Business Management) facility in Garden City, downtown Cairo on the Nile. An American, Bill Harrison, set up IBM with several office rooms, available for rent to businesspeople without their own office, on either a temporary or permanent basis. It was in this facility that I met June Cosgrove, Jane Foda, and an Egyptian lady who worked together in a real estate business. June Cosgrove was most helpful in finding the first apartment in which we lived. It was a ninth-floor apartment in the Tonsi Building, on Gabalaya Street, Zamalek, on Gesira Island on the Nile River. Many foreigners chose to live in Maadi, south of Cairo, but we wanted to be in the middle of the city, the same way we had lived in Tehran and Athens. A nine-hole golf course was just across the street in the back of our building, and this course was part of the Gesira Sports Club. Other facilities included swimming pools, tennis courts, a restaurant, and the like. We used this club extensively but mostly on the weekends.

It was most interesting for me to learn some of the history of the nine-hole Gesira Golf Course. Prior to Abdul Nasser's rule, there was actually an eighteen-hole course. When, under communism, Nasser came to power, he thought too much land was given up just for the rich to play golf, so he had the course cut in half to provide soccer fields for the lower class.

The woman who owned our apartment had had little money, but she had purchased the apartment before, when the prices were very low. As businesses started to pour into Egypt, good apartments were not easy to find, so the prices shot up in a way that made owners like her become relatively rich overnight. She had not yet finished the apartment for lack of money. When we wanted to rent it she demanded a very large security deposit, so she was then able to hire workers to do the finishing work inside. It was very livable, well located, and with a good view of the Nile as well as the city. We lived here during the first three or four years in Cairo. My wife had always wanted to move to a difficult-to-acquire apartment in the Swissair Building, but there was now another, compelling reason to leave the Tonsi. One day as she opened the door to our ninth-floor service entrance a huge rat appeared at her feet. She quickly slammed the door, as she even more quickly stepped backward, and never again used it. During the following days I witnessed rats, as large as cats, climbing up from the ground level to the ninth floor by way of the various pipes and cables that were attached to the outside walls of the building.

Despite various kinds of problems that one always encounters with rental apartments there is always at least one or more disadvantages to moving away from the problems. That is, the friends made and the bonds built up over the months and years. One couple in particular in the Tonsi Building was the Pipers. Annie and Derek Piper. Derek was a construction manager on various large projects that took him and Annie to many countries in Africa and Asia. But wherever, we remain good friends. They live now in retirement in Cyprus. Really fine people. I look back on the Cairo days and can see Annie riding her rented horse through the desert past the pyramids and then listening to her exhilarating expressions of "flying" through the sands and Derek often talking with pride of his son living in Australia, while we were enjoying drinks and dinner together.

Another motivation to move related to the elevators. More often than not, a relay in the electrical system for the elevators did not function properly. But the *boab* had a fix for this problem. A *boab* is a man who is a sort of "guardian" of a building and usually sleeps somewhere in or near the building entrance. They serve as a security watch guards and in assisting occupants, et cetera. But in the case of the elevators, our *boab* would hold a piece of wire across the terminals of a faulty relay in order to activate it and send the elevator up or down. It was like a gamble in Las Vegas. You could never be sure if the *boab* could hold that wire in the right place for a successful ride. Therefore, it was very often the case that the occupants on our floor walked up or down the nine flights of stairs. This was also a challenge as the stairway lights were nearly always malfunctioning and the floors in the stairwell were not numbered. So even when you had the energy to climb, you could not be certain in the darkness where you were except by counting each of the steps on the stairs. The feeble light of a flickering match or cigarette lighter was more psychological than useful as an aid in the dismal stairwells. After the rat incident it became difficult to concentrate on the number of steps. One had cause to wonder if the imagined noises and scraping sounds were those of rats or shoe scuffles from others, ascending or descending.

Another type situation would occur with the elevator sometimes stopping only at even- or at odd-numbered floors. One never knew. It happened one evening when we had invited about thirty guests that the elevator decided to stop only on the even numbers and we were on the ninth floor. None other than our GD chief executive officer, David "Dave" Lewis, my top boss, was brought to the tenth floor. I had sent my driver, Ibrahim, down purposely to accompany Dave in the problematic elevator, but just seconds before the boab had already sent Dave upward. Then, after a medley of Tonsi Building elevator rides, up and down, he finally found the Cooks' apartment. A tribute to Dave Lewis was that he was completely unshaken and full of humor about the situation as he came through our doorway. Probably his most disturbing moments were when he tried to convince my German wife that she should call him Dave, as in America, instead of addressing him as "Mr. Lewis," by the German method.

We finally had the chance to rent a sixteenth-floor apartment in the Swissair Building on the Nile in Dokki, just a few hundred yards from Sadat's home. The apartments in the Swissair were many times better in size and quality than those in most other apartment buildings at that time, including the Tonsi Building. On the first floor was the best formal restaurant in Cairo, the Swissair Restaurant, and it had waiters serving with white gloves. In addition, in this building there was a Movenpick restaurant of a more casual nature but also with very good food.

We held many formal and informal receptions in our Swissair apartment and had many guests from abroad to visit us. Often after a golf tournament with the German golf group of about twenty-five or so players we gathered at our apartment to eat and drink and discuss the birdies just missed or the ball that got stuck in the palm tree and the like. I played not only with the German golf group but also with the American Embassy Golf Association and the Military Attaché Golfers as well, both at Gezira, and at the Mena House golf courses. The view from our Swissair apartment bar was fantastic. As one sat at the bar, the entire Cairo skyline along the Nile could be seen. The view from the large balcony was equally breathtaking, and from there one could also see the feluccas, silently making their way with ancient hull and sail. Only an occasional prayer call punctuated the atmosphere. Often we had sailed in the feluccas, especially with small groups of friends in the evenings. As I glanced down from our Swissair apartment and privately reminisced about the pleasant conversations with the friends in the breeze from sailing of a warm evening I could not help but reflect as well on the giant cockroaches that scampered over and across the tablelike part of the boat's center where our food and drink rested. These sights during the first experiences on the boat ride would cause untold miseries for many, yet after several months in Egypt you began to wonder if these creatures are also enjoying the sail.

I think the farewell party for Walter and Margrit Paulus of thirty guests at our apartment was one of the most memorable. I am fortunate enough to still be able to view the video made of all the guests, with comments from each, on that evening. George Lefevbre, present with his wife, Rebecca, was generous enough to use his video camera to make the video while I interviewed people with the microphone. We had lived in Tehran at the same time as the Paulus family, then in Cairo, later in Germany. Finally they moved to America because of Walter's work, and now they remain in the States, in Atlanta, Georgia. The Pauluses also had a vacation apartment in the same building as ours for several years in Fischen, Germany. Both of the apartments were sold by the early nineties.

There were so many receptions held in the various hotels hosted by the management of foreign companies, and by the management of the hotels as well, for public relations. Seldom did we have to prepare a dinner at home for ourselves. We were invited to practically all the parties and receptions held in hotels and in many private homes. One of the more exclusive private parties held at the Heliopolis Sheraton when Peter Tischmann was general manager featured Tina Turner. We also had a surprise visitor at our table in the person of Omar Sharif. Everyone immediately thought of *Doctor Zhivago* of course, and he was barraged with comments about the wonderful role he played. It is fair to say that it was not unusual for us to attend three or four receptions nearly every week of the six years we were in Egypt. In summers the very large receptions were held outside, sometimes around the swimming pools, and in winter in the banquet rooms. The Marriott in Zamalek, Nile Hilton, and Ramsys Hilton downtown on the Nile River, the Cairo Sheraton in Dokki, the Gezira Sheraton in Zamalek, the Meridien on the Nile, the Mena House at the Pyramids, and the Sonesta, Movenpick, and Sheraton in Heliopolis were the primary hotels in the Cairo area in which we placed traveling visitors and attended the various parties and receptions. I arranged most of our company's large receptions during visits of GD executives in the Heliopolis Sheraton, the Nile Hilton, the Marriott, and the Mena House and placed most of our company visitors in these hotels as well. As a member of the board of the American Chamber of Commerce in Egypt (AmCham), I was instrumental in acquiring several spaces in the Marriott Hotel to use as offices for AmCham over a ten-year period.

As the senior representative for General Dynamics International Corporation in Egypt, I believed it was appropriate for me to get involved in public service, as was the case for delegates from other major American companies. Several of us formed an organizing committee for the purpose of establishing an American Chamber of Commerce in Egypt. It was so established in 1982, and it became the first AmCham in the Middle East. I was elected as the first executive vice president and remained on the board in various capacities until my departure from Egypt in December 1986. This chamber had tremendous growth upward to about four hundred members in a very few years. The AmCham in Egypt became what might be considered the most prestigious and effective business organization in Egypt. All meetings were conducted in the English language. President Mubarak recognized AmCham as very worthwhile, and in this regard we were invited to his palace offices from time to time for special occasions. Presidents Carter and Ford attended AmCham luncheon meetings in the Marriott, as well as ministers from the Egyptian government on many occasions. The experience gained during this time with AmCham played a role in my election as president of the American German Business Club—Germany, when I was later transferred to an assignment in Bonn, Germany.

I was tasked by the American embassy to be one of the wardens in Cairo for the purpose of passing information down, in a pyramid fashion, to further transmit to others in the event of civil disturbances to "lay low." That was often to state, "Do not venture into the streets today," or "Stay clear of a certain area of the city," et cetera. It was only necessary for the embassy security officer to call the three or four wardens and they would carry out the message to a certain group of about two hundred American families living in the Cairo area. When not in my office in Heliopolis I had a radio in my car and in my home to communicate with all the parties concerned.

Because of my basic assignment and contacts in international marketing, the involvement in AmCham, the warden job, the golfing associations, and the receptions and parties, bringing business to the hotels by the way of hundreds of room-nights each year, it was possible for me to know a great number of people in Cairo, and this of course made my job easier each passing day. Aside from the numerous contacts and friends, one couple who stand out in my mind and helped me immensely to get started and remained very helpful was Paul and Lynn Gelinas. Paul was the manager for Four Winds Moving and Storage Company in Egypt. And wherever they were after the Cairo assignment, continuous contact has kept this friendship alive. After several postings, including the Philippines, California, and Oregon, he became head of Paul Arpin Moving and Storage, International, based in Rhode Island.

Somehow most of the expatriates learned to cope with the everyday problems, i.e., in the household and found ways at times to substitute one thing for another when supplies in the stores were scarce or not at all available for weeks. For example, there were days when it was all but impossible to find a bottle of vegetable oil for cooking in the store where you normally shopped. So the next time a shelf was stocked with oil, the tendency was to buy about five bottles of it, only to realize a few days later that there was no longer a shortage of oil, rather now sugar. And this routine of shortages and hoarding would continue. During one very long period we could not find an onion in the city of Cairo, so one weekend we drove four hours each way over the desert road for a bag of onions in Alexandria, on the Mediterranean. After a few years in Cairo, we learned about the Weasel. The Weasel was a very clever misfit of a person who had the ability to acquire anything, it seemed, that was not normally available in the shops. Whether you wanted fresh frozen chickens from the USA, whiskey, or refined sugar, you name it, he could get it. And he would deliver it to your door for a price less than that in a store. That is, if they ever had it.

Some of the items he sold had a red, white, and blue logo "hands over the sea" from the USA. It was rather obvious that the shipments of goods coming into Egypt did not always arrive at the intended destination.

All the while that I was in Egypt my thoughts about Dad came to mind. He had just turned eighty about the time I was getting started on my assignment in Cairo. We were still corresponding, that is, with Mom doing most of the letter writing. During the previous summer, while I was on a short visit in Montauk, Dad had fallen in the kitchen by tripping somehow when turning around near the refrigerator. This fall resulted in a broken hip. The Montauk Fire Department ambulance carried Dad to the Southampton Hospital, where an operation took place, and then recuperation began. Since it was not possible for Mom at her age to take care of Dad at home he was cared for in a home "up the island" near Patchogue. But then it was necessary to transfer him to a home in Frederick, Maryland, because the home up the island was really not a good, pleasant location and was very poorly appointed. In the home in Frederick, my brother Joe and his wife, Mary, were very near and were able to visit frequently. This seemed at the time a questionable move, since Dad was a long way from Montauk and Mom. On the other hand, Dad had wonderful surroundings in a beautiful nursing home among friendly staff personnel. Of course he communicated via phone with Mom. Mom was not completely alone in that there were always local Montaukers visiting her and we children visited as well, as often as possible. One of the "dubious" benefits of her solitude, relative to Dad's location, was the fact that when Dad did pass away there was a cushion of physical and time separation to soften, to some degree, the loss of her husband of over sixty years.

In 1983, while Dad was still in the nursing home in Frederick, I made an arrangement to visit him, accompanied by Patti and Jim, who had met me in Washington, D.C. We drove there on Thanksgiving Day 1983. There Dad sat, in a normal straight-back chair, fully dressed and wearing a necktie as usual. And on his lap was a round metal box of Danish cookies. With his typical smile, as if looking through his post office service window when greeting each and every customer, he asked, "Would you like to have a cookie?" It was as if a hand from above had touched our shoulders, Jim, Patti, and I, to guide us to Frederick that day for our last visit. Dad died on the twenty-seventh of June 1984.

Traveling to Montauk from Cairo for the funeral during the first week of July 1984 was a case of almost not making it to the church service. When we were halfway out on Long Island, the fog was so thick that it was impossible to continue driving in the evening to Montauk. That meant an overnight in a hotel in Riverhead. The next morning, on the day of the funeral, the heavy fog allowed only crawling traffic. By the time I got to St. Theresa, the mass had already started. Naturally, it was somewhat embarrassing being late, but I had a long ways to travel and, finally, the fog problem. But we did get there and it was so great that Fr. Robert "Bob" Ecker, our Fishing Village boyhood friend and neighbor and a friend of all Montauk's people, said mass. Father Bob had taken leave from the navy and come to Montauk just for this funeral, as he had lived among us in the Fishing Village and was a part of the family.

Medical Problems and Facilities

Probably as a result of almost constant travel in many lands I became immune to the type of bacteria that infected so many visitors suffering from intestinal disorders, resulting, in one form or another, in "Montezuma's Revenge." I was never affected by this during my six years in Egypt. But in 1981, while still temporarily living in a hotel in Heliopolis, I became very ill and a doctor was brought to my room. He declared that I had a case of German measles. How I got it is the question. But then, how does anyone get German measles? The doctor said, "One simply gets it!" My only thought was that maybe it was because I had a German wife. I thought there was as much logic in that as there was in his telling me, "One simply gets it!"

And next, in 1983, came several bouts with kidney stones, for which I needed treatment in a hospital. It was usual, each time in the hospital, for kidney stone patients to carefully use the graduated liter bottles so that measurements of liquid intake and urine discharges could be taken. The first few days on my initial visit were rather hectic for both the doctor and myself because, unknown to us, the nurse's aide was throwing the urine into the toilet before anyone could have the pleasure of analyzing my contribution. I understand that lab technicians placed bets on who would detect the largest of the small calcium stones. The aide said she was just tidying up the room. In any case, I finally got the hang of drinking two liters of water each day, as long as I was in Egypt, to avoid both the pains and the chancy treatment. I recalled hearing my teachers in elementary school always saying that one should drink eight glasses (roughly two liters) of water each day. How right they were. But it is usually only from hard experience, like passing a couple of jagged stones, that one understands why.

In 1984, during a business trip to the States, I had a checkup at a GD medical clinic in San Diego, California. The examining doctor detected a small lump on my throat and suggested it had something to do with my thyroid. During another stateside visit that year, in July, I made an appointment at the Portsmouth Naval Hospital in Portsmouth, Virginia. They did an examination with a needle into my throat and determined that an operation would be necessary to make sure what was happening. I was told to check into the hospital at the earliest possible time, which turned out to be in December 1984. I had already been in the States twice during the month of July.

A surgical operation in mid-December revealed a fibrous growth on my isthmus, a mass of tissue between the left and right thyroid, but it was benign. Following the isthmectomy and a week of recovery in the hospital, I was back in circulation. But while still in the ward after surgery I had a surprise visit from Father Bob, now the chief of chaplains of the Atlantic Fleet but a native and neighbor in the Fishing Village. It was wonderful to see him after so many months, and I was proud to know he thought of me.

I was discharged from the Portsmouth Naval Hospital on the twenty-fourth of December, Christmas Eve. I traveled to New York the same day to catch the evening Lufthansa flight to Frankfurt. I wanted to spend Christmas Day in Germany before returning to Cairo. Hard to believe, but I was the only passenger to check in at JFK for this DC-10 flight. When I checked in at the counter an agent looked at my tickets and said to wait a few minutes. He came out and said, "Merry Christmas! Since you are the only passenger, we put you in the first-class section." For the two inflight meals there were three stewardesses waiting on me, offering everything they had in the line of food and drink. It was an extremely strange feeling during the hours between meals, which was most of the night hours, crossing the Atlantic. Imagine sitting alone in an empty 300-passenger cabin, no one else in sight, also realizing that this aircraft is 30,000 feet over the ocean and you have absolutely no control over the situation. A passenger never has control, of course, even when a plane is full of passengers, but the feeling is eerie when you are alone. Very eerie! A feeling that defies adequate description.

Another medical episode occurred during 1985 in Cairo with chest pains, which over several weeks became more and more severe. After receiving five different diagnoses, in various clinics and hospitals, I had the feeling that I had contracted some rare disease that no one could put his finger on. Then the company's corpsman, trained for handling routine ailments, insisted that it would be best to fly to Frankfurt and then check in at the U.S. Air Force Medical Center in Wiesbaden. When I met the air force doctor who would handle my case, I of course told him the background of my problem and added that I came to Wiesbaden because five different doctors in Cairo gave me five different diagnoses. I showed him the reports. He was highly amused, and with his grinning reaction I already felt somehow better, despite the repeating pain attacks. "Well," he said, "one of them is one hundred percent correct. You need a gallbladder operation." He had determined this in ten minutes with his ultrasound equipment. Although one report of the five Egyptian doctors was totally correct in analysis, it was not possible for me to determine which one, if any, was right. A case of Russian roulette to make a decision with any particular one of them. Following the operation and five days' recovery I was on the street again, minus the pains. Some of the false diagnoses in Cairo included heart attack, dysentery, and "some food that does not agree with you." At one point the pains at night were so severe that Salah, my consultant, had the EAF chief of medicine come to our apartment at midnight. After a cursory examination he suggested that I come into his Heliopolis office in the morning to be examined for possible heart problems. I did. He concluded that my heart was OK but nothing about the source and/or cause of the pains. The next day I was in Wiesbaden.

Lessons learned include: have a plan to handle the eventuality of severe medical problems, especially in places where medical treatment, inclusive of surgery, may be considered questionable at best.

Another outcome of the diagnosis and treatment process was a learning experience gained while recovering in a six-man officers' ward at the air force hospital. A colonel patient, known to be a very heavy cigarette smoker, just had a major operation because of collapsed lungs, in which he was slit down the middle, around his waist, and up his back in order to wire the lungs to his rib cage. Night and day, next to my bed there was a noisy drain pump thumping continuously to drain out the liquids through a garden-sized hose. In addition, because of all the drainage and sweat, a plastic cover was placed between his body and the bed mattress. Between the pumping and the rattling noises of the plastic cover, plus the coughing and various moaning sounds emitted from his wracked body, it was really impossible to sleep or rest.

For ultimately having a successful end to my diagnostic saga I certainly could not complain, but as it was I also could not complain because of loss of sleep. Because, you see, I had lost my habit of smoking cigarettes.

In contrast to the various medical encounters I had experienced in the Mideast area, there was a decidedly bright spot when it came to the problem with my eyes. In Seattle, some thirteen years before my Egyptian assignment, I had been diagnosed as having glaucoma. I was regularly taking Timoptol eye drops (0.5 percent) twice each day. These drops were mandatory and very effective in keeping the interocular pressure (IOP) down to normal levels. But it was necessary for me to get eye exams at regular intervals to check IOP and, importantly, the field of view (FOV). I was informed of an eye doctor in Zamalek, Dr. Ali Mofti. Now in this case of need for special medical care I had the good fortune to have actually not only the best eye doctor in Egypt but a man well known in the United States and Europe. In fact, he studied under the famous eye surgeon Dr. Fitzgerald of Boston and was qualified to perform the most delicate of eye operations. I felt very relieved to be in such good hands. And it was a further blessing. Since the very essential Timoptol eye drops were not always available in the local pharmacy, they were made available to me by Dr. Mofti.

Dr. Ali Mofti's uncle had been the personal physician of former president Abdul Nasser. It is said that Nasser had Ali's uncle killed because he thought the uncle was trying to poison him. I had met Ali's aunt on several occasions. Knowing both Ali and his aunt and the great respect I had for them, I could not imagine that Ali's uncle could have been of such a different character to the extent of trying to take, rather than save someone's life.

Sadat's Assassination

It was generally the case that the expatriates of most foreign companies were more or less required every six months to leave the country for a sort of breather, for rest and recreation, on company expense. One weekend in 1981 my wife and I decided to go to Athens since we knew a lot of folks there and it was within the distance limitation covered by the company. My driver, Ibrahim, was taking us to the international airport, from downtown Cairo to Heliopolis. Along the entire route on both sides of the road, every twenty meters or so, there were soldiers standing in their white uniforms. My wife had made a comment while driving past all these soldiers, "If anyone wanted to kill Sadat, any one of these men, or anyone just dressed like them, could easily do it along the road!" The purpose of all these soldiers was to guard the path of President Sadat's travel to the grandstands for the big 6 October military parade in Heliopolis. When we arrived at the Cairo airport we were informed that the flight was delayed. There was nothing at all unusual about this. We had plenty of experience of this nature. However, after about six hours of waiting in this old airport we realized that this was a very unusual situation of some kind. Finally we were allowed to board our aircraft. The flight departure, and then the arrival at Athens International were quite normal. However, as we disembarked and made our way through customs, we and all the other passengers were besieged with questions from people waiting in the arrival area. What happened in Cairo? Was Sadat dead? I then asked one of the Greek customs officials, "What is going on?"

The answer: "President Sadat was assassinated!" Just then, and only then, did we learn that this was so and that it was the reason we had so long a delay in the Cairo airport. With further thought, I realized that I unwittingly had chosen the right place to be this day. Within a few days Hosni Mubarak became Egypt's president.

One of the other trips we made was to Kenya for a safari. The safari in several parts of Kenya was made among herds of various animals in their natural habitat, and in a treehouse lodge we observed the evening feeding of the animals at a water hole. A visit was even arranged inside one of the Masai villages: a village consisting of perhaps twenty rather large huts inside a compound the size of a football field and surrounded by a very thick fence made of very thorny branches, which would cause very much bleeding if someone or some animal attempted to crawl over it into the compound. At the entrance, a guard of sorts was standing with his long spear. We were summarily told to leave at one point because a man in our small group had taken "too many images" with his large video camera. We absolutely had to go out. There was no arguing the point. But it is a wonder that these people live as long as they do with all the filth and dirt everywhere. And they rub a grease on their bodies with a reddish-orange dye that I suppose keeps various insects from biting them. It seems a wonder they survive. From what I have read later, after this trip, they drink the blood and urine of their cows, which are their wealth.

While in Nairobi, just the day before the safari trip, I was conned. On the way from our hotel to see one of the marketplaces, we were stopped by a young man who called himself Peter. He asked for ten dollars to buy gasoline for his car. Peter said he was sent to the market to buy bananas for the hotel and he ran out of gas. He needed money to buy gas and pay a deposit for the gas can. He sounded so convincing, and he also said that he worked for the hotel where we were staying. I figured I would get the money back when we were back to the hotel. Well, there was no Peter working at the hotel. It was then that I realized I had been taken. I called the police, which was an exercise in futility. Their answer was, "So you met Peter; apparently he is busy on the streets again." Then they said, "You should never give money to a stranger in Nairobi." But nothing at all was done about this. Before hanging up the phone, the policeman said, "If you leave the hotel at night, be sure to take a taxi; it's too dangerous to walk!"

Special Airport Assistance

An important part of my responsibility in Egypt involving services was meeting VIPs from our company, in particular, when they arrived at the Cairo International Airport. The hassle checking into immigration and customs was to be avoided at all costs. Therefore, it was significant to have a planned program for each of these types of arrival. Rasmy, the expeditor, was really great in this matter. He had made the necessary friendly connection with the major in charge of the army security unit in the airport and made the most difficult look so easy with the use of his authority. I was introduced to the major as Rasmy's friend, and he would allow me to sit in his office in the terminal for every official visit of the VIPs. I was informed by the major exactly when the plane would arrive (by his direct contact with the tower) and when the aircraft was landed and parked on the tarmac. Then the major would have a van drive to the aircraft at the bottom of the stairway. The VIPs were then driven privately to the VIP lounge. There we would sit and wait for the baggage, instead of having to go through the immigration and custom process.

After the first several months, when the major became more and more friendly, I was allowed to actually ride in the van to the aircraft, and this was even a greater benefit, because I could easily spot the visitors and they would feel immediately at ease seeing a familiar face. I did not pay any money (baksheesh) to the major. We simply became very friendly as I sat often with him, waiting, having the tea or coffee and a cigarette. Rasmy would translate when necessary, but it seemed that the friendliness just developed through an air of unspoken trust, reading the eyes, more than from what had been said.

The same cooperation was equally helpful for our travelers going to departing flights from Cairo, as the same kind of tedious process was avoided by our arrangements made with the airport's army security unit. In fact, sometimes it was very critical to have this help in making a departure, because of traffic jams during these earlier days in Cairo. I recall one day when our CEO, Dave Lewis, was there for a meeting with the chief of the EAF. This meeting in Heliopolis lasted longer than expected. We were even later because we had first to go to the Nile River downtown, to the Nile Hilton, to pick up the luggage and then backtrack all the way to the airport. The usually bad traffic was even worse this day for many possible reasons. But I was able to call the major's office at the airport with my mobile phone to explain our situation. We agreed on a meeting point near the entrance of the VIP lounge. When we arrived he had a van waiting and whisked Dave and his party directly to the aircraft, making it possible for them to make the scheduled departure. This was one of many instances in which the capabilities of our consultant, Salah and expeditor Rasmy and the support and cooperation of General Shaban of the president's office and the army major in the airport made all the difference, by supporting me in effectively performing the duties for which I was responsible.

The new airport complex was not totally completed before I left Egypt in late 1986, so I hardly had the pleasure of using that modern facility. On the other hand, I sometimes think that I would have missed the storybook character of Egypt, if I had not had the experiences that occurred before the onslaught of more modern developments, including not only the modern flight facilities (civil and military) but also subways, highway flyovers, new industries in desert cities, modern irrigation systems, modern golf courses and newer hotels, et cetera.

Main Projects

The biggest reason for my company's interest in Egypt was the F-16 fighter aircraft and later the M-1 tank, including the service- and training-related options for these items. Other projects discussed for various other company products never had any great value or development.

It happened that the EAF purchased several squadrons of F-16s. The first F-16A/Bs were flown in by U.S. Air Force pilots in 1981 to the air base at Anshas, a desert area northeast of Cairo. The first F-16C/D models were flown into Egypt in October 1986.

A contract was signed on 29 August 1984 for the development of a new tank plant for the Egyptian army. The actual work on construction of this tank plant did not get under way until 1987, after I left the country.

I made several trips to Paris and London for working at the air shows in Le Bourget and Farnborough, respectively. Part of my work involved meeting customers and potential customers as they arrived in the GD chalets on the flight line. Our test pilots flew the F-16 during the air show demonstrations, and of course the chalet locations were ideal for watching the shows. The customers were quite happy with our chalet location, on the flight line, but especially so while drinking wine and eating barbecued beef and all the other good things flown in from Fort Worth, Texas, where the F-16s were manufactured. These kinds of trips were at the height of the perceived need for armaments, so travel money in the defense companies was available for nearly all the international marketers.

The other part of the job for the marketing people was making the potential customers happy during the evenings, as well as in the chalets. Evenings were a bit more expensive, but again, at the time the money was available. I recall vividly my first experience in Paris in the evening when I arranged for dinner shows for about ten persons at the Lido. After a wonderful show and dinner, the waiter was very prompt in handing me the bill, since I had informed him at the outset that these were my guests. I thought that I had read the bill wrong. On this first air show trip to Paris I was very naive about the costs in that city. It was for several thousand French francs and I had only a fourth of the amount needed in cash. The credit card did not allow such a big payment. The only thing that saved me was that our consultant, Salah, was carrying enough dollars with him in cash so that together we managed payment of the bill. This was just another step in the lifelong learning process. My future trips found me carrying a lot of traveler's checks. I enjoyed really doing escort assignments and I think I did well, but I learned to not always be too quick in volunteering.

GD had over one hundred aircraft technicians and staff support, with families, in Egypt for the purpose of training the EAF on the F-16 aircraft. Several buildings were rented in the Heliopolis area for housing these employees during the early eighties at the peak of training at Anshas. In the mideighties emphasis was on training EAF personnel at the Beni Suef EAF Base, southwest of Cairo. Housing for our employees was then provided on base, housing which would be later used by the Beni Suef EAF personnel, upon the completion of in-country training.

Escort Trips to the USA

Incidental to the two major programs, there were several occasions on which I was tasked to escort several of the most senior generals of the air force and army, sometimes accompanied by their wives, to and from the United States. I had to arrange travel (flights, hotels, auto rentals, dinners, et cetera) en route to and from our company or military facilities in San Diego, California; Los Angeles, California; Ogden, Utah; Detroit, Michigan; Lima, Ohio; Fort Worth, Texas; Washington, D.C.; New Hampshire; and Pennsylvania. Naturally these kinds of trips included "cultural" stopovers, between official visits, at such places as Sea World, Universal Studios; Hollywood; New York City; Atlantic City, Las Vegas, and the like.

It was always a lot of work to make various reservations and to be sure that all facilities were suitable and, sometimes, at least adequate. Despite the work, I always enjoyed these trips because of the challenge of making arrangements for such special people and their wholehearted appreciation. The Egyptians were always so grateful for the things that were done for them. It made everything a big pleasure for me, not only in this respect but also due to the special incidents that occurred along the way, such as in the case on one trip with four army generals.

I made a reservation for them in the Polynesian restaurant in the Capitol Hilton, where we were staying while in Washington, D.C. Before the dinner, I had ordered piña coladas for all, but I advised the waiter, privately, that the generals were all Muslims, so please leave out the alcohol, which he did.

The next stop after Washington was Detroit. On the first night, there was a dinner hosted by the marketers from the tank division. All the generals ordered individually from the menus and were served without any problems. However, unknown to anyone else, one of the generals had ordered piña coladas for everyone in the party. During the dinner, all the Egyptians were in full agreement about how much better these piña coladas tasted than the ones they drank in Washington. The general who ordered the drinks at the Detroit dinner did not know that in Washington I had told the waiter to leave out the alcohol. When they realized they got the "real thing" they heartily laughed it off after they understood what had happened. One of them exclaimed, "When a Muslim unknowingly drinks alcohol, it does not go against him!"

While in a hotel in Michigan, just as soon as we had checked into our rooms, one of the generals came running up to me to say, "Gamel needs a doctor, quickly." Because of the urgency in the sound of his voice, I had the hotel manager call the paramedics right away. In not more than five minutes they were in the room, along with three policemen, to check on the ailing General Gamel. He had had what appeared to be a heart attack and was transferred to a hospital immediately. He was well cared for by the doctors there and after a couple of weeks' recovery went back to Egypt to continue work. General Gamel took care to follow the doctor's orders, which included walking four kilometers every day. General Gamel was ever so grateful that I was able to get emergency medical treatment. That sort of thing was just part of what an escort is expected to handle as a routine.

There was another interesting situation that occurred in Washington, D.C., on the same trip with these generals. We were all ready to drive away from our hotel for the airport but realized General Saleh was missing. The porter who had carried the baggage down to the street said he would go to Saleh's room to tell him all the others were waiting.

After about ten minutes the porter came running out to the car very excited. "The general is dead. He must be dead. He's lying on the floor and doesn't move."

All of us immediately went to Saleh's room. General Saleh was quite alive. He just had not yet finished his morning prayers!

Free Time Activities

It was routine during Egyptian weekends, when not playing golf at Gezira or the Mena House courses, to drive to the *souk* or the pyramids through the City of the Dead to watch the typical elaborate Egyptian wedding celebrations in the hotels during the evenings, take felucca rides on the Nile, or venture farther out of the city to Fayum, Ismailia, St.

Catherine's Monastery, or Alexandria. For longer periods, up to a week or so, we traveled to Hurghada, Luxor, or Aswan. Several times with other couples we went into the desert areas and searched for petrified wood, small turquoise statues (or pieces of them), geodes, and the likes. One would sometimes not find anything, but the excitement of possibilities was always there.

While we lived in Egypt there were only three hotels on the beach at Hurghada: the Sheraton, Club Med, and one other whose name I have forgotten. It was very peaceful and pleasant, and especially nice on the patio evenings having dinner. One of the drawbacks then was that water was, in a sense, rationed. You would be lucky to be able to take a shower when water became available. Sometimes there was not a drop when wanted. However, the other pleasantries overshadowed this deficiency.

Our consultant, Salah, had a boat built in Alexandria and moored it at the Sheraton dock in Hurghada on the Red Sea. One evening during a few days' leave in Hurghada, I went out with Salah and his captain to go fishing. I had bought a waterproof light during my last stateside trip, precisely for this fishing trip. Salah had told me that these particular fish were very much attracted to light. As the light was lowered about four or five meters into the water, the fish immediately began to take our baited hooks. This continued for hours. I do not remember the name of these fish, but they looked something like a sea bass and, on average, were about thirty-five centimeters long. I was dead tired from pulling them up into the boat. Because we were catching so many fish we stayed out much longer than planned. Consequently, the folks in the hotel thought something had happened to the boat and were rather desperate to see us finally appear at the dock near daylight. All these fish were given to the local people in the small village of Hurghada, people Salah knew well. Salah took no fish back to Cairo because his wife hated fish, and I had no means to carry any on the flight back. This "night fishing" was not only great sport, but it was also the first time I was able to fish in the Red Sea. I found that a fish is a fish. Whether in Montauk waters or in waters on the other side of the world, "the fisherman waits with bated breath, and a fish is lured to the baited hook."

For a water sport on another occasion I accompanied the German military attaché and his wife to camp on the shore at Ras Mohammed, on the south tip of the Sinai, in order to go snorkeling. It was an extension of previous snorkeling experiences I had when in Jeddah, Saudi Arabia, also on the Red Sea but on the opposite shore of the sea from Egypt. At Ras Mohammed the clear, deep water was so intensely illuminated by the sunshine that one could see from the water's surface down to a hundred feet, it seemed. Thousands of fish of all shapes, sizes, and colors were darting about. Schools of small reddish and silvery fish performed precision ballet movements in and around castles of pink and white coral which appeared as staging for their acts. Some of the larger fish alone would appear and disappear in and out of the sea garden, as if in search of something, all the while steadily and effortlessly moving with only a slight wag of fins and tail to alter their search pattern.

I suppose I began to rationalize that this brightly colored cast of theatrically inclined fish was very special and must by all means be protected from harm's way, but that the general run-of-the-mill fish, like those at Hurghada, were all right to hook and cook. Having been raised in a fishing village, I believed fish were to catch and eat for survival, to catch and ship to a city of hungry folks, to catch and sell to make a living. And of course I still savor a good fish dinner. Millions of people in some nations with few resources must consume the food from their waters to survive. So it becomes a matter of need on the one hand and one man's decision on the other when a decision is taken on viable options and one that is controllable not only in all ocean and sea waters but in inland waters as well. Are only the beautiful fish and unusual mammals, such as whales and dolphins, to be protected? They should be, but not only them. Fish should be caught for food as nourishment, but much more stringent rules should be applied and enforced through international agreements regarding fishing limitations (sizes of catch), elimination of bottom dragging, tanker oil spills, industrial and ships' waste discharges, and other excesses harmful to fish reproduction in general, as well as survival of certain species.

It was always a very interesting view when driving from Cairo to the Sinai just before going through the highway tunnel under the Suez Canal. For the most part one sees stretches of desert land and some dunes along the way, then suddenly there is a large ship "sailing along in the desert," or so it appears. Actually, the ship is sailing in the water of the canal, but all that one can see at a certain point, when still some distance from the canal, is not water but more sand and the slowly moving ship's superstructure.

Directly on the Suez Canal, on the west side, is the pretty town of Ismailia. There one finds a number of houses that were used by those involved in the building of the canal and by personnel of oil companies in years past. On the shore of the canal is a park with restaurant and facilities for bathing in the canal itself. The water is so salty that swimming is effortless, hardly a stroke needed to keep afloat. Because of this, some swimmers venture quite far out into the middle of the canal and have to be watchful for the next ship coming along. Passage of ships through the canal is controlled. Northbound and southbound ships were scheduled, each during certain hours, because of the width limitations of the canal. So at least most of the swimmers knew in which direction to look for oncoming traffic.

The shores of Hurghada and the Mediterranean were much better for pure bathing pleasure, but Ismailia was much more accessible for a drive on the weekend, away from the chaos of Cairo's noisy streets. In addition, in the early eighties one could buy very large fresh shrimp at the equivalent of four dollars a kilo (about two dollars per pound). So altogether the Ismailia trip was worthwhile. A couple of years later prices were twenty dollars a kilo (about ten dollars per pound).

The pyramids were always a fascination for me, particularly at the beginning of my time in Egypt. No matter how many times you see these colossal structures, you have to marvel at the genius of the architects and builders, the accompanying Sphinx, the camel rides available from the insistent Egyptian, the sound and light show each evening, the dust, the sunsets, and the horseback riders flying through the desert sands. I had been there so many times, however, that after five or six years when visitors came I would drive them to the pyramid parking area and say, "There they are. Take your time. If you don't mind, I'll be at the snack bar waiting for you." And the same went for the Memphis visit, a little farther south from the pyramids.

One of the most interesting exhibits, which became available for the first time ever while I was in Egypt, was the sailing ship found very near the pyramids during an excavation. It was a complete ship found dismantled and in perfect condition in a grave, intended for the dead person for his transportation after death. It was rebuilt in the usual form and put on display within an air-conditioned building next to the largest pyramid. Even the original ropes used to tie the planking together were in good shape despite their age of a few thousand years.

The curious always have to see the City of the Dead. It is not a city, and the people who live there are very much alive. The City of the Dead is a very large cemetery area on the east side of Cairo in which, it is said, a million people live. Very poor people live essentially in open "houses," makeshift arrangements around existing cemetery structures. Nearby is the huge waste disposal area, where the donkey wagons are emptied of the garbage collected from all over the city of Cairo. Every scrap of the garbage is sorted out to the last bit for use or sale for recycling: paper, metals, glass, organics, clothing, cloth, wood, et cetera. It is said that those in control of the waste area are relatively rich, despite the destitute look of the area.

I had to make several business trips to Alexandria, "Alex," relative to possible navy projects but also for purposes of sightseeing, purchasing antiques, and having fresh fish lunches at the waterfront. And I don't forget the trips such as those for buying onions in Alex when none could be found in Cairo. A very good Greek-Roman museum located in Alex is worth the trip especially when combined with a meal of fresh fish.

One trip was made one weekend by most of the German golfers just for the purpose of playing on the only eighteen-hole golf course, at the time, in Egypt. A pleasant weekend of golf and sampling some of the Alexandria restaurants. The course in Alex was a nice change in not having to play the same nine holes twice as we had to do, to play eighteen, at the Mena House and Gezira courses in Cairo. One of the things I recall about Alex was that the most rain I ever saw in Egypt was there. In Cairo rain was experienced only a very few hours in any given year.

Upper Egypt

Luxor, Aswan, and Abu Simbel are among the prime places to tour in Egypt. I made several trips to these sights. Each time it seemed to me a marvel, how the tombs were built, how the wall paintings were made, how the giant pillars were perfectly aligned, and how tons of stone slab were erected in places atop the high columns. The unfinished granite obelisk in an Aswan quarry attests to the fact that the several world-famous obelisks surely were of Egyptian origin. This unfinished obelisk was 75 percent completed, but because of a large crack occurring during the quarry work the project was abandoned. The bottom of this horizontally oriented obelisk is still attached in its natural state to the quarry bed. The three exposed sides of the obelisk are perfectly flat and highly polished, as if done with a machine. Then one asks himself, *Just how did the other monstrous granite obelisks ever get lifted onto a boat or raft and on the Nile?* Of course there are a number of explanations given by the Egyptologists. Nevertheless, the feats of the early Egyptians still give one cause to wonder. In addition, every visitor is amazed and in wonder at how the pyramids and the various tombs and temples were constructed with the tools and facilities available centuries ago.

The trip between Luxor and Aswan in either direction on the Nile River is most enjoyable. Peacefully cruising along, one views the tops of mosques above the palm trees and villagers washing their animals on the banks of the Nile. I started to read a book while sitting in a deck chair on the upper deck of the Sheraton cruise ship. I never got past the first chapter, as I was so enthralled by the serenity of the Nile and its bordering landscape. The ship was air-conditioned and clean, and the food was good. In addition each evening, of the four spent on the five-day cruise, there was fun entertainment. In Luxor during one June visit, we got up very early to visit the tombs in the desert, as the noonday temperatures in the summer months are well over one hundred degrees Fahrenheit. Temperature-wise, November and December are the best months to enter the area of Upper Egypt (Luxor, Aswan, and Abu Simbel). There are generally no sandstorms during this time. The temperatures in spring are also comfortable, but then the sandstorms are possible.

After having read Agatha Christie novels you can just feel her presence (her story) with *Death on the Nile* while on the Nile. And very impressive was the afternoon tea when sitting on the veranda of Aswan's Old Cataract Hotel, made famous by the same *Death on the Nile* story.

It used to be that any tourist could, if lucky, find an empty table on the veranda, have a tea, and just dream about being there. Now I am told that only if you are a guest of the Old Cataract can you enjoy this moment of reflection on the Christie novel. There is the New Cataract Hotel nearby for another place to stay.

Fayum

Fayum, about an hour or so west of Cairo in the desert, was a place to visit now and then on a weekend, to either have lunch at the hotel on Lake Fayum, visit the famous irrigation waterwheel in the middle of Fayum, or simply "people watch" in this oasis town where things are set back in time or buy a crate of tomatoes along the roadside. It was always chancy to buy these boxes of tomatoes, because the farmers would not want you to see the bottom layers, where they put the bad ones. However, the tomatoes were so inexpensive that if even half the box was rotten, the rest were still cheaper and tastier than those found in the Cairo market. During my time in Egypt shrimps were available from Lake Fayum. They were smaller than those of the Red Sea but nevertheless good. One always wonders about one thing or another if it is the same as "before." I wonder if shrimps still thrive at Fayum.

St. Catherine's Monastery

St. Catherine's Monastery in south-central Sinai is one of the most inspiring places one can visit, not only in Egypt but probably anywhere that I have been. It is living history! The monastery has been occupied by Orthodox monks since the complex was built in A.D. 300 and survived all the many warring activities through the centuries. When we visited, there were about forty monks still active. This monastery is completely walled in, and the only entrance and exit is a doorway about five feet high. This doorway was controlled for afternoon entrance/exit at 1630 daily. We had been at the monastery before with visitors of ours, and we had lived in nearby hotels. But on one occasion we had the opportunity to actually sleep overnight in the monastery while accompanying the German military attaché and his wife. The men had to sleep in one room and the women in another. Water was available for shaving and showering, but it was very cold water. Food was not available for us, only for the monks. But this was not a point of issue. It was a memorable experience just to have the chance to live a night within the walls of this historic complex. The opportunity came to us because of philanthropic activities by the German government and the fact that we were close friends of the attaché. All of the centuries-old manuscripts in the library of the monastery were microfilmed for the monastery at the University of Thuringen, Germany. In addition, Germany sponsored all the kerosene for the lamps and stoves at the monastery. Consequently these favors, in turn, granted special visiting privileges to the principals at the German embassy.

It is believed that the leafless bush that grows in the middle of the monastery is actually "the" sacred Burning Bush of scriptural accounts. Whether one is a believer or not, it gives you something to deeply ponder over during the days, months, and years that follow a visit here. I was told by a monk at the monastery that many horticulturists have examined this bush and declare there is none other like it in the world. More to ponder over.

Also according to Scriptures, atop the mountains just above St. Catherine's is where Moses had the Ten Commandments revealed at Mount Sinai. Many, many thousands of visitors have climbed up this mountain. It is very heavily visited, particularly on Easter morning. One of the monks told us that the freshwater well within the walls of the monastery has been providing water since the beginning, A.D. 300.

Sinai Holy Wilderness*

In this mountain pass in the Sinai, several kilometers west of Nuweiba, the soft trodding of hooves broke the silence at a thousand meters above the Gulf of Aquaba, barren of plants except for an acacia tree located every few kilometers. The high desert mountains became, nonetheless, more and more beautiful. This beauty manifested itself in a score of colors of the sands and eroding rock formations from ancient volcanic upheavals. Its ruggedness, reaching higher and higher toward the sky, was a sign to be cautious, yet its silence and purity beckoned us to further penetrate this holy wilderness, within the shadows of Moses' mountain (Mount Sinai). Occasionally there was a Bedouin coming, it seemed from nowhere and going seemingly nowhere. Each of us was in his or her own thoughts, a time for reflection. Whatever was on his or her mind could only be intensified, as if being in a medieval cathedral. Here, there was timelessness, stillness, serenity, and closeness among ourselves, to ponder and wonder, as we lurched gently forward and backward, with each step of our camel.

My thoughts wandered back to the mid-thirties, when I was a youngster living in the remote Montauk Fishing Village on Long Island, near the sea and close to nature. Without realizing it then, we had coped with many

---

*The following section tells of my traveling by camel and living with Bedouins in the mountains of Sinai, Egypt, during a week in mid-September 1985 (an account of this experience I wrote in 1986, as one of the participants of this camel trek). The trip started in Nuweiba, Sinai—on the Gulf of Aquaba. Jordan lies to the east of the Sinai on the opposite shore of this Gulf.

hardships but had learned to deal with life. There was no reference for us living in that remote fishing village. Without travel experience I did not know, at the time, what might be a better or worse existence. We did what we had to do to live and, at times, to survive. The catch of the fishermen determined the extent of what there would be to eat. Cutting and chopping wood from the fallen trees in the forest helped to keep us warm in the bone-chilling winters on the Atlantic. Sometimes walking over a mile through the snow to mass on Sundays our family gave thanks for what God had allowed us. I remembered as well, and vividly, the tidal wave of the devastating 1938 hurricane, which carried our house and those of all the neighbors of this fishing village from their foundations in a disarray not to be imagined. Our lives were spared, to experience a variety of heartaches and disappointments but mostly periods of happiness and pleasures in the years to follow. These thoughts were some that went through my mind as we continued in the heat of this mid-September sun.

Our camel safari started with arrangements made in July 1985. Our good friends Col. Eberhard Moeschel, West German defense attaché in Egypt; his wife, Sigrid; Eberhard's brother Rudolf, a dentist practicing in Oberstaufen, Germany; my wife, Christa; and I agreed to rendezvous with the Bedouins, Rima and Anis, on the evening of 15 September 1985 in Nuweiba on the east coast of Sinai. It had been determined at the outset, in the discussion between Eberhard and Anis, that our Bedouin guides would build fires for cooking three times a day and make bread twice a day. We would have to bring food, clothing, sleeping bags, and some water for five days. The amount of clothing and supplies that each of us carried would have to fit into a camel saddle bag, which amounted to a pocket on both sides of the camel, each about the size of a standard sofa cushion. Also, a few smaller satchels could hang from the pommels of the saddle. We talked several times about what we would bring, but we actually had used only imagination in some instances, as none of us had ever been on a camel or ventured into remote desert mountains on a camping trip.

Christa and I had yet to spend the first days of our vacation on a previously planned voyage on a Norwegian coastal steamer from Bergen to the North Pole above the Arctic Circle. This was scheduled from the twenty-sixth of August to the sixth of September. From 7 September we would spend a week in Fischen-Allgau, Germany, then depart for Cairo on 13 September and prepare for the Sinai on 14 September. The coastal voyage became a story in itself. Our 2,400-ton ship, *Polarlys,* on the stormy night of 29 August struck a large rock in the Lofoten Islands, which tore a huge hole in the bottom of the ship. With life jackets donned we stood by the life boats with considerable anxiety. As luck would have it, the captain managed to get the ship to a port thirty minutes away. Suffice it to say, at this time that we survived that trip and were able to rejoin our good friends to experience life in the desert mountains of Sinai.

In the early morning of 15 September we departed in two autos from Cairo en route to Nuweiba via the Suez tunnel, along the Sinai southwest coast nearly to the south tip, then up to St. Catherine's Monastery and proceeded over the mountains to the coast at Nuweiba, arriving in late afternoon. We had stopped twice for snacks and gasoline, in order to top the tanks. One never knows when the next of the very few gas stations may run out of gas supply.

Since it was dusk when we arrived in Nuweiba, we went immediately to locate Rima and Anis, as we would have had great difficulty finding their place in darkness. They appeared pleased to see we had arrived, and the first order of business was to sit around the fire, in front of the small house, and have *chai* (hot tea). Coming in with relatively clean clothes from Cairo and immediately out of our normal environment, we had hesitated to sit on the ground of course. With some muffled comments that we must still check into the hotel to get a good night's sleep, we found ourselves, in any case, sitting down for tea. After what seemed like hours sitting on the ground with crossed legs (it was actually about thirty minutes), Rima announced that we should go to the village. She indicated that we must go to the hotel (about three kilometers away) because the village police had to keep record of the visiting foreigners before we could go into the mountains the next morning. Rima and Anis would be held responsible for us, and the police would want to know where we were in case any problems arose. Rudolf, a bit more adventurous at the outset, slept in the Bedouin's hut at the invitation of Anis and Rima. The Moeschels, Christa, and I spent the night at the Nuweiba Hotel. The site of this hotel was really beautiful; however, the hotel's condition was run-down, and little care, it seems, was given in its maintenance or operation. Yet we did have a good rest and shower, despite having only cold water, and we arose at 4:30 A.M. to meet again at the hut. There we found Rudolf, Anis, and Rima, plus two other Bedouins, already drinking tea and pinching off pieces of freshly made *aish balady* (flat, round bread). We had naturally expected to see several camels standing there with saddles and all in readiness. This was not the case. It was a portent of things to come. Our first lesson in "take it easy; there's time, have your tea first."

It was already 8:00 and we looked in all directions wondering just where these camels would come from. They were to stride in soon from the tiny settlement just to the north of Anis and Rima's "homestead."

While I wondered how all the items that we brought were to be carried on these animals, the third Bedouin, Ahmed, commenced to stuff the saddle bags with our many small canvas and plastic shoulder bags out of the trunk of our car. Two of these shoulder bags each contained about-eight-liter-sized plastic bottles of water. They were slung over the rear pommel, after the loaded saddle bag had been draped over my camel. The two duffel bags containing the sleeping bags we had borrowed from Capt. Roger McPherson (U.S. Naval attaché) and his wife, Cameron, hung from the forward pommel of the saddle. Altogether it appeared as though there were no place at all left for one to sit and ride atop this bulging mass of freight.

In surprisingly short order, after the camels arrived on the scene, all our things had been draped over or tied to the saddle and we were being coaxed to climb upon the kneeling camels in order to get under way. Never having been on a camel in my life, I tried to recall how it was that someone in a movie I had seen had swung himself into riding position. The camel is simply too high to just throw your leg at once over this whole arrangement, particularly with all the baggage mounted. It turned out that it was easiest from the camel's left side for me to sort of kneel first on the top of the saddle with the right knee, then with both hands firmly planted on the forward pommel swing the right leg over the other side of the saddle and baggage, which you are, in fact, sitting on after finally getting in position to ride.

Soon I found myself lurching forward, then backward, as Ahmed had prodded my camel with the toe of his shoe to get her up and moving. Also suddenly it seemed now all five camels, eight persons, and two dogs were on their way in a small caravan heading out from the village of Nuweiba. We rode toward the nearest *wadi* (valley or gorge) that would allow us to commence a gradual climb up into the mountains to the west.

Eberhard, Rudolph (Rudy), Christa, and I each rode our own camel. Sigrid and Rima rode together on the fifth camel, while Anis and Ahmed walked. We didn't realize at the beginning but it was to be these two Bedouin men who would go by foot each step of the way. The two dogs easily kept pace with the camels, and we observed that the shade beneath the camels would provide relief for the dogs from a very hot sun throughout the entire trip.

The first wadi we entered was the site of new highway construction, which would ultimately allow auto traffic directly between Nuweiba and the tunnel under the Suez Canal, located just north of Port Suez. I was imagining the hours to be saved by avoiding the tedious drive from the tunnel into south Sinai, up through the St. Catherine's Monastery area, and into Nuweiba. Quickly following these thoughts, however, I considered the ills of progress. These barren and desolate but yet very beautiful mountains and wadis would probably soon be decimated with abandoned vehicles, spent tires, oil cans, and carelessly thrown garbage from speeding autos. These thoughts were necessarily interrupted by the sudden lurching of my camel, determined to shortcut the intended path of travel down an embankment formed by the buildup of crushed rock for the new highway. It was only a few hours since we had started the camel trek, and I had not yet acquired a very secure feeling on this pitching and swaying mount, over two meters above the ground. The camel's independence was to keep me even more alert, and I began to experiment with the rein to prevent further unnecessary diversions. Exerting gentle but firm pressure with the rein seemed to work, and I had no unusual problems in the days to follow. The first day was to be, in fact, one of experimentation, to learn first of all how to remain stable atop this desert animal, how to "steer" it, and how to make it sit and stand again.

While it soon became obvious how Anis got the camel to stand, with a light toe-kick or hit with a long slender cane stick, I was still trying to figure out how to make my camel sit. After one day, already learning that one's power of concentration comes naturally more intensely in such environment, without all the distractions of modern living, the answer came to me. I observed that Anis did not make any unusual movements at all with hands or feet when the camel went down but made a slight gurgling sound from his throat. My first "gurgle" attempt proved successful, and I felt that now, with basic control of this animal, much of the apprehension of the ride had disappeared. But the only solution to saddle sores of the first day was the passage of time. To alleviate this problem to a great extent, I made bowline loops at each end of the hobbling rope for my camel, then placed it over the forward pommel to use as stirrups. The Bedouins do not use any form of stirrups. Rather, they simply cross their legs and are able to go for many kilometers this way without difficulty.

During the first day's ride we stopped for lunch and rest. It was during the high noon sun under a lone acacia tree, nearly barren of leaves, located in a small canyon off the wadi trail. The camels were set free to roam without their burden of freight and saddles, but their two front feet were hobbled, so that only very short steps could be taken. Nevertheless, after the two hours of our noon rest period they had all wandered about one kilometer away out into the wadi in search of meager pickings of a few dry plants or roots hardly visible to us. It took about thirty minutes on these occasions during noon rests for Anis and Ahmed to round up our camels and another fifteen or twenty minutes for resaddling and repacking before getting under way.

In the afternoon we passed an MFO camp manned by American forces. The MFO, or multinational force and observers, consists of armed forces of various countries participating in the safeguarding of peace in the Sinai as a result of the Camp David accords for part of the settlement between Israel and Egypt. A few kilometers past this MFO camp we approached our first evening's campsite. It was in a very small oasis on a curve of the wadi, where some underground waters allowed about twenty palm trees to flourish. While they afforded us no sort of protection or real usefulness, they were a pretty sight after not having seen anything green all day long.

When we stopped I gave my best gurgling sound to lower my camel. Just as I was about to give myself kudos for accomplishment, I realized that all the camels were also very tired and they all knew it was time to stop. So they automatically and promptly went down anyway. In just moments we had them unloaded, and we carefully stacked the freight of each camel separately, so as to make it easier to reload each one with the same items. The camels were immediately hobbled and allowed to roam again for about an hour or so without burden. Then the camels were led a short distance away from the campfire, perhaps about thirty meters, and made to sit, lie down, where they would remain throughout the night. As they were brought down, feedbags with several handfuls of corn kernels were placed over their heads. There they sat gracefully and happily feeding on their reward for a day's work.

While the camels roamed, we had been busy conjuring up something to eat and determining where best to place our sleeping bags. During this time Rima went out, as she would be doing at each campsite, to find wood (twigs mostly) to make a fire. Rudy would often go with her to help carry the roots, twigs, and branches as available. In the meantime Anis and Ahmed, having walked the entire day, lay down to rest until Rima returned. The very first order of business was to build a fire to make *chai*. Then Ahmed commenced the kneading of flour and water to make bread, as Rima and Anis brewed and served the *chai*. Interestingly enough for me was the prominent red, white, and blue "hands over the sea" logo on the white flour sack clearly indicating that the flour was provided by the United States. I wondered just how many Americans realized the many strange places in the world their food products were being consumed.

Of interest to us all was the fact that Ahmed had accomplished his chores in handling the camels, the dogs, and himself without ever having washed his hands. And the dogs had been previously drinking water out of the aluminum basin in which the bread was kneaded. Our thoughts were the same at this moment: *This bread we will never eat.* We were to change our opinions on this matter that evening, and our tolerance levels were altered drastically as the hours and days passed.

The completed round, flattened bread dough was about one centimeter thick and forty centimeters in diameter. As soon as the *chai* was made, the coals on the fire were spread enough to accommodate the bread dough, which was placed directly on the hot coals. Then hot coals were placed atop the bread as well. After about thirty minutes the bread was tapped with a stick for the proper sound. Sometimes it would go back on the coals for several more minutes, until considered ready, determined through the trained ear of the Bedouin. The blackness of the coals would be scraped off, and when finished the bread appeared quite like that purchased in the bakeries of Cairo. We surmised that anything that would survive that hot fire would surely be safe to eat. We did just that without any further reservations.

On the first night we satisfied ourselves with canned soups and other canned food, requiring only heat for preparation. Whereas we, the foreigners, felt perhaps we would not have enough supplies of each sort, the amount of baggage or freight we carried was clearly ten times more than that of the Bedouins. I had wondered what the differences were, and it was clear at the end of the first day. The Bedouins wore only the simple gallabiya. In contrast, we carried various types, and several changes, of clothes, which we had imagined necessary. This required much more weight and space. Also, the Bedouins were simple in their food needs. They carried only flour, tomato paste, meat, onions, garlic, herbs, and oil. Aside from a knife and a spoon, they needed only three utensils: an aluminum basin, such as those used decades ago for washing dishes, a kettle, and a two-liter pot. The basin was used for washing feet, feeding the dogs, kneading the bread dough, and mixing their one type of dinner, that of bread pieces and a souplike mixture. The kettle was for making hot water or tea. The pot was for cooking the various sauces. Dishes and silver were of no need to the Bedouins. But here again, we had several kilograms more weight to carry and to pack.

One of the sauces made by the Bedouins is of tomato base. I observed Anis making it several times. He poured some vegetable oil to cover the bottom of the pot and sautéed garlic and onions with salt, pepper, and a few herbs. Then he added tomato paste and water and let it simmer. Finally, he would sometimes open a small can of beef, purchased at a government store in Nuweiba, and add the meat after cutting it into small pieces. When finished, the Bedouins would sit crosslegged around the common pot, dip bread pieces into the sauce, and eat with the fingers. We were offered a place to sit with them to eat, which we accepted from time to time, but most of what we ate was from the supplies we had carried. We preferred more variation in our meals, and there would not have been enough, in any case, for everyone to eat from what the Bedouins cooked. We learned that the Bedouins would share any amount of food they might have, even if it meant that each would have only two or three bites. How many people in this world would be so sensitive and generous to others?

This day was to be a sort of test, as there was still time to turn back. That is, it would have been convenient at this point to do so. Rima told us that some of the foreigners would decide to go no farther and she would have to take them back to Nuweiba. On this first camp night, in particular, the wind started up. It caused the sand to fly about, getting into our hair, food, clothes, and bedding. While it was all rather distasteful and discouraging, we felt we must stick it out for the five days. We had done so much talking and planning for the camel trip and made so much preparation that we chose not to think about anything except continuing.

During this evening, a squad of U.S. soldiers on patrol from the MFO camp passed by within a few meters of our camp, gave a friendly wave, then disappeared into the darkness. I thought, *What a terribly lonely duty this must be.* But even worse, it happened that some of these men, and over 200 others, were to die in a plane crash only weeks later on a flight back to the States during Christmas home leave.

Although we had had visions in Cairo of a rather romantic setting under the stars around a campfire, reality played havoc with the dream. By 8:00 P.M. we were all so tired that all anyone could manage was a "good night" and zipping up the sleeping bag. Strangely enough, the thought of a scorpion or snake was furthest from my mind. I suppose that I had subconsciously felt that Anis knew where he was going and what he was doing in this respect, so the thought never bothered me. At any rate, at this point of tiredness I may have simply told the unwelcome creatures to please go away. I counted a few satellites streaking across the heavens, looked at the Milky Way and the Big Dipper, then fell fast asleep.

We were awakened the next morning about four-thirty or five and my first thought was to "turn over." But Ahmed was already working the fire and indicating that we would leave before very long. It seemed there was barely time to make breakfast when we were packing the bags and loading the camels. I had remembered an old breakfast standby in the Boy Scouts and at home in Montauk: oatmeal with raisins. This I made for all of us, as it was substantial, quick, and easy. Unfortunately, Rudy cannot stand to eat oatmeal, but the rest of us ate it for our main breakfast food. After coffee, we ate some dried fruit and nuts, which are very good items to carry on such trips. Then we mounted up and were on our way for our second day into the wadi, still climbing upward.

After a two-hour ride we heard the barking of many dogs. Then up ahead a few hundred meters we saw some Bedouins and their goats taking the meager shelter of three or four leafless acacia trees. The heat of the midmorning sun was growing rapidly. It seemed to us, at first, that this area would be the last place anyone, including Bedouins, would think of staying for even several weeks. It was so barren, desolate, and hot. We learned, however, that there was a small well at the location. That was reason enough for anybody to stay. While we certainly knew that potable water means life, we were to learn even more of its value in the next few days. That we should not take it so much for granted in our own land became more apparent.

It was more interesting each day to realize, too, that our Bedouin friends seemed to know each of the other Bedouins we met in places more remote than the last. Most of them apparently were of the same tribe.

Our noontime rest stop on the second day was in a very wide section of a wadi, where the only shade was from the leafless branches of a lone acacia tree. We did not carry a thermometer, but it was certainly no less than forty degrees centigrade. Food was not so interesting under these conditions, only something to drink. Rima managed to find enough twigs to make fire for the *chai,* which was always made, regardless of location, heat, or other circumstances. Each time it had the same wonderful flavor, their black tea leaves combined with some local herbs and the smoke from the fire. Although very hot, the *chai* seemed to provide a cooling effect under the hot sun. Despite this, each of us clamored for a drink of cool water.

In trying to devise a method to make do under less than desirable conditions I sought to experiment, considering the basic principles of the cooling process of evaporation. I wrapped a wet towel around a liter-sized plastic bottle of water. Even with the slightest of breezes of very hot air, the water became very cool after forty-five minutes through the evaporation of moisture from the towel, which transferred heat from the water in the bottle. A problem one will encounter in this operation is not with the evaporation system but with the supply of water with which to soak the cloth wrapped around the bottle. But with what you would normally be carrying, you can transform a bottle of water, which can be too hot to touch when left in the summer sun, to a cool drink in a reasonably short time with the simple application of the wet cloth. Should you have enough water, there is another practical use of this evaporation system for cooling. After you soak a bandanna, or any similar cloth, in water, it can be draped either over the head or around your neck to generate a comfortably cool feeling in the hottest sun. I recalled the scenes in movies of Foreign Legion troops wearing the unique hats with cloth pieces hanging down to cover the backs of their necks. This is, as I experienced, very practical and effective in such heat and not just a fashionable look for desert troops in films.

The campsite of our second night was a relatively flat horseshoe-shaped area about a hundred meters wide, surrounded by mountains, except for the entrance to the area. From this site we could see the high point of our general area, which was at 1,500 meters. As soon as the camels were unloaded, hobbled, and set free to roam, we staked out our sleeping areas. Rima, with the assistance of Rudy, set out once again in search of material for the fires for that evening and the next morning.

This was to be probably the most welcomed of sites we used because of a water well, developed by the Bedouins. We now had access to plenty of potable water, albeit brackish. But nothing comes free in life. This particular well was continuously swarming with hundreds of wasps. With Rima away in search of wood at the moment and Ahmed busy with the chores around the animals, we sought Anis to inquire of him about the wasp problem at the well. He seemed to have disappeared; a short while later we noticed that he had climbed all the way to the top of the high point, which was several hundred feet above us at a very steep angle. It reminded me of the marketing ad I had seen on television showing a car and person atop an isolated peak in the southwest United States. Even after walking all day in the hot sun, Anis had the energy and fortitude to make this very rapid ascent. He was just a speck as he waved to us down below. As Rima and Rudy returned with the twigs and roots, we learned that Anis had climbed this peak because it was his favorite place for prayer while in this area of the mountains.

With a well potentially at our disposal, we were now thinking not only of potable water but also of using the well water for provisional baths. Had we been alone, the wasps would have easily kept me a respectable distance away forever. I still had memories of a wasp sting in 1940 while I was caddying at Montauk Downs Golf Club. Anis finally returned. He was amused that we let such "tiny creatures" bother us. Anis told us that these wasps would not sting if we moved very slowly. He proved his point by slowly walking through the swarming wasps and taking several buckets of water from the well. I really had great faith in Anis. As a Bedouin living his life in these mountains I thought he must surely know what he was doing. So each of us in this situation carefully but apprehensively entered the swarming area of the well and managed to get our precious water.

Once again it was a long day, and as soon as we arranged our gear, cooked something to eat, and sat for a short while, drinking *chai,* we were all ready for the sleeping bags. The skies were so beautiful each night. Every star in the heavens seemed to be at our fingertips. I fell asleep again looking at the Big Dipper and checking the location of the North Star.

The next morning we went over the ridge to a canyon leading to the slope that would allow us to climb to the same place where Anis had gone to pray the evening before. At the pace we went, it took about an hour to get to the top, but we stopped now and then to take in the sheer beauty of nature all around us. The sandstone was in all colors—deep violet, various shades of yellow, red, green, white, brown, pink, and blue, and mixtures of many of these colors. After we reached the peak I chose to stay on the top ridge to examine the various rocks for their colors while the others continued farther into a canyon on the other side. During the hour alone on this ridge I found what I considered to be thirty or more beautiful rocks of all the colors available. I lined them up for my own satisfaction to admire and for the others to see as well upon their return. Also, I decided to experiment with the sand from these various colored rocks, which were easy to crush. I mixed a bit of water with each of the several colors of fine sand, making a paste of each color. With these I made a design on a clean, flat rock just to see if, in fact, one could paint with it, as I was curious whether this was one method used in ancient times. The wet mixtures dried quickly in the hot sun, but the beautiful hues were prominent on the "rock canvas." Eberhard and I, in a later visit with Rima and Anis in Nuweiba, learned that my "museum of rocks" and the painting were still there after nine months. I am so curious if the paintings still exist.

While returning to the campsite we were fortunate to observe falcons in action against small animals or birds atop some ledges on the side of the mountain. The falcons would fly quite high, then fold their wings inward and dive downward like falling rocks. At the precise moment necessary, their wings unfolded to brake themselves in order to grasp the smaller birds or ground rodents. It was difficult to tell exactly which sort of animal from the distance we stood below. Again we witnessed an example of nature at work and something that, until this day, I had only read about.

Also on the return, Anis showed us a "date cooperative" shared by the Bedouins in the area. It consisted of a rock shelter of four walls but no roof, in which they dried and stored dates after harvesting from various remote locations. I had not noticed any date palms anywhere along our route thus far.

It was noon when we returned to camp and we were hot, sweaty, and thirsty. Our first approach was on the well where we slowly and carefully made our motions, so as not to disturb the wasps, as we drew the buckets of water. The bucket, by the way, was a rusty one-gallon can that was tied to a line consisting of several pieces of string. Someone had acquired this string with great care, as there was no trash or waste anywhere along our route. This bucket and line were always left at the well, and it was understood that no one should remove it.

Because we were without privacy near the well, bathing behind a boulder or two was a delicate but manageable affair among the mix of discreet individuals in the group. We all felt quite good again with clean clothes and the sand washed out of our hair from the sandstorm on the first day. But aside from getting clean, as the sun rose higher we were again melting from the heat. The best relief at this camp was to get one of the others in the group to simply pour a bucket of water over your head, completely dousing each other in turn in order to cool off. This was a super feeling, but it lasted for only thirty minutes at most.

We were told that there would be one more well, on the fourth night of camping, so there was at least something to look forward to, with respect to getting another "shower," as it were. So we were content to fill all our water containers to last two days. We had lost seven plastic bottles of sweet water (Barakat) when these bottles were smashed by a camel walking alongside and bumping into another camel on a narrow trail. This was a lesson learned, that is, not to carry your water supply in the flimsy plastic bottles normally obtained in the supermarket. One should use the heavy plastic five- or ten-gallon containers shaped like jerrycans. Eberhard and Sigrid had an ice chest that had been loaded with bottles of frozen water. These of course were protected inside the ice chest, and they actually had cool water for limited drinking purposes during these first three days with this arrangement. After this point we were primarily on the brackish water from the wasp well. This water was really not so bad to drink as it was, but when used with the Lipton iced tea and lemon powder mixture we brought along it was like a champagne under these conditions.

Like the previous days when the sun had passed its zenith, we started out again to ride most of the afternoon. However, on this day in particular the route we took was so rocky, and with such steep rises and falls, that we had to dismount and lead our camels much of the time. We were by no means any kind of experts with these animals, but we were beginning to at least get familiar enough so as not to be paranoid about their actions, reactions, or sounds. For example, one of the loud, sometimes rather ferocious, gurgling sounds the camel makes is usually a sign that it is uncomfortable, at times because of the wooden saddle frame digging into its back. When this occurred it was necessary to completely unload that camel, readjust the saddle, and place burlap underneath it at the point of irritation before repacking everything. When the camels were happy and comfortable they did not normally utter any sounds.

When we were leading our camels up and down the hills, the proximity of the camels' heads to our own was at first a bit frightening, since we had heard many tales of camels biting people, as well as other camels. As the minutes passed into hours and not one of us had been at all bothered with such a problem, we gained more and more confidence in handling these animals. The camel Sigrid and Rima rode together had a habit of biting another camel but not people. So Anis had told us to always make this one go ahead of the others if in a single file going on a narrow trail.

In spending so many hours in an atmosphere with only the distraction of beautiful scenery and the crashing silence of this pure, clean air, one has time to think. Time to think about good and bad times, to wonder perhaps why this or that happens or what if? It could be a retreat for some, for any cause or purpose. Many thoughts crossed my mind, some uncompleted trains of thought, but those that took my mind back to extremes of pleasure, fear, and anxiety were most vividly recollected. Since these thoughts, expanded, could fill a volume, it is not my purpose really to discuss them here. The point is to say that in such a stark, isolated, silent, but beautiful place one can concentrate, recall, think, imagine, innovate, plan, and do much more. In this environment it can be as well that emotions are intensified to give one tears of happiness, disappointment, or sadness.

I have often heard it said that the older you get the more you think about the past. Well, it's quite natural, because you have so much more past to think back on than someone much younger. So as we grow older we do have many more experiences to recall and this recollection process is started by sensing something now that relates to a past experience. The older we get, the more there is to relate to. Older people are perceived sometimes as wise as the owl. There is some truth in this because they can draw from the longer list of real-life experiences with which to make comparisons. And when we have a lot of time on our hands in a quiet place there is a tendency to become more philosophical. There is the solitude to think more clearly and the opportunity to run the current circumstances we are experiencing against all the similar circumstances of our past. Through a lifelong process of recollecting and comparing we establish a bank of data upon which we continuously develop our capacity for sound judgement and in a wider range of topics.

Since a unique environment such as this mountainous desert provides conditions of emotional stimulus, the solitude of this experience can certainly have as much effect on a human, although not as potentially destructive, as the experience of a seaman on a ship tossing about in a hurricane. On the desert mountain one has the time to logically think out why one should take a certain action that may affect oneself or those close to oneself. On the tossing ship one makes the promise to observe a higher moral stand if his life is spared through this storm. I believe that the person who thinks out the problem situation in the desert mountain would be more realistic and true to himself in a decision, whereas the seaman comes to a decision as result of fear, with a promise to his Maker. The desert provides the positive environment for thoughts, discussion, and decisions relative to personal relationships in particular. More often than not, I believe, a decision or the promise of a personal nature made under the stress of potential disaster is weak of foundation and destined in many instances to be short-lived or with a broken promise. This is an example, in brief, of the many thought processes that I had gone through during the camel trek.

We had several times discussed among ourselves just how well suited this fine animal, the camel, was to the desert. God has surely "designed" the camel for such a dry, barren, and rough environment. We all agreed that the face of the camel has a serene and royal appearance. Despite that serene facial appearance, of course, there were those moments of fit, for whatever reason, when the camel fills the air with loud gurgles of displeasure. We had also observed that the surefootedness of the camel while walking the rocky trail was most interesting. For the many hours I watched the feet of the camel in front of me I never saw a misstep. Always each foot would come down ever so gently and precisely between the rocks, almost never on top of the rocks, where it may slide off, and this seemed an exceptional feat (no pun intended). After a long time I came to a conclusion as to how I think this is possible. Logically and first of all, if I want to be sure where I am stepping I will naturally look down at my feet. So I looked at the camel's eyes. The eyes of the camel, already extended on a long neck, are bulging out to both the left and right sides of its head. It is quite clear then to notice that these eyes are so positioned as to have line of sight to all four feet.

We are reminded, as we ride along, that tomorrow night we will come upon the next well. We will fill the water containers and take "showers." During this third afternoon we are still nursing the water carried from the wasp well for drinking and cooking along the way. There is some sort of comfort in knowing that up ahead there will be a life-giving well and, with that, a certain feeling of confidence that we can afford to take yet another swallow of the water taken from the wasp well. It continues to be quite hot and there can be little relief from the heat of this sun. Christa has some solution for herself to this problem, as she has brought along the umbrella from her golf bag. While not the whole answer to the heat problem, as she has to hold it continuously, the umbrella does reduce the temperature a few degrees.

Finally, at about five in the late afternoon we arrived at an area on a high plateau but with mountains rising nearby on two sides of the intended campsite. There is to be a discussion here between Rima and Anis for the first time, that we noticed, as to the best place to actually make camp. The two did not see eye-to-eye on this matter at all. This was the first time we saw tears on Rima's face. Anis insisted, although very calmly and politely, that we should proceed around the bend a few hundred more meters. The choice of Anis was in the middle of a wide, flat area that was really not very appealing. We felt that perhaps Rima may have been right, but Anis may have had some very practical reasons for his choice. In any case, Anis was the final authority. Since Rima was not terribly happy at the moment and this site did not look good, there were tense moments as we commenced to unload the camels. In order to keep things on an even keel we went about our chores to set up camp as if nothing had happened. When completed, just prior to the preparation of evening meal, I set up my *Tragbare Bar*. This is a German expression for "portable bar," and mine consisted of a number of small one-serving bottles of the various drinks for our "cocktail hour." We had done this each previous night actually and also had some canned sardines, and the like, to have a few minutes of relaxation. We had some fun joking about our cocktails in the desert mountains. Tonight, the eighteenth of September, was a night of celebration because it was Sigrid's birthday. We had brought, especially for Sigrid, as a surprise for this night in the desert, two bottles of schnapps from the Allgäu in South Germany. On this evening we were to talk more at the campfire after we had eaten and made all our things ready for the night. We got to know more about Rima and Anis and, I think about this time, we developed an even closer bond of friendship between us.

I recall that also on this evening, in particular, I had made special observations of the camels after dark. From the campfire location I directed my flashlight on each of the camels, which were lying about twenty meters away and encircling us. Strangely enough, to me at any rate, was the fact that each of them was headed in the same direction. At one time while they were eating their corn I watched as they came to the end of their corn supply, when only two or three kernels were left in the feed bag over their heads. They would turn over on their backs, kicking their feet wildly in a desperate attempt to get the very last kernel. After this bit of excitement, they got back in kneeling position, eventually laid their long necks flat on the ground, and went to sleep until about four the next morning.

Another interesting point about the camels is that they knew exactly where the corn was kept in the burlap feed sack. Several times while we were busy setting up camp at various sites we would have to watch the camels very closely. If they got to the corn supply, they would completely consume all their feed at once. They took little or no water most of the five-day trip but had their corn ration each evening before sleeping.

On the morning of the fourth day, after riding for only a short distance, we came to the place where the camels could not pass. At this point, Ahmed and Anis led all five camels around the area and we were to continue through a very difficult pass by foot. We were to rendezvous with them two hours later. Then Rima led us through some very difficult trails up and down ridges and gulleys, with much of the surface consisting of sliding rocks under each step. This brought us to an incredibly deep cut, a sort of canyon about two meters wide and with rock walls, going almost straight up to about one hundred meters. It was like walking down a narrow hall with a sand floor and extremely high walls.

But to enter this narrow canyon was most interesting and required a bit of care. One had to go through a hole in the rock formation and sort of slide down a steep slope a few meters to the sand floor below. Each of us gradually made our way to the bottom and commenced to proceed through this amazing cut. But one of the dogs decided to follow us. We realized that he had remained above and was frightened to drop through the hole. He commenced to whine and nervously pace back and forth so as to gain all the sympathy and pity possible. We supported Rudy's footing to get him as high up as possible on the slanted chute beneath the hole. Then using Rudy's body as an intermediate step, the dog made his leap to freedom. We were all very much relieved to be able to proceed on through this beautiful sculpture of nature, which must have been formed many thousands of years ago.

Surely only a very few people had ever made their way through here. Considering the extremely small population of the Sinai, I expect that only a very few Bedouins even know this canyon exists. We made our way through it because Anis had discovered it and believed that his visiting friends would find it fascinating. We did and it was unforgettable.

We stopped midway in this passage to rest in a spot of shade provided by a bend in the walls. Since it was near noontime by now the sun was directly overhead; therefore shade was difficult to find anywhere. Besides the enjoyment now of the inevitable sip of "wasp" water, Rudy and I had a few extra moments of serenity with a new pipeful of tobacco. As I puffed my Captain Black, I thought this was in the class of one of the most remote, quiet, and serene and perhaps safest places in the whole world. It was certainly one of the several moments most vivid in my recollections of this trip into the mountains of Sinai.

Having immensely enjoyed this venture through the passage we came out, eventually, into a wide wadi, appearing much as you would think the moon's surface would. Now we still had to walk for over an hour in very hot sun. Sometimes, as we approached any vertical rock formation we stood in the tiniest spots of shade it might afford. It was more psychologically helpful than it was cooler. There is really no escape from the intense heat when the sun is directly overhead. Only during the early morning or late afternoon, with a lower sun angle, can one realize some shade near the base of a large rock or mountain formation. On the other hand, in mid-September we found that during the evening hours it was necessary to use a light sleeping bag, as the temperature drop was considerable, yet comfortable for sleeping.

As we continued to walk through this hot, open wadi, I thought, probably for the first time since the sandstorm on the first night, *Why are we doing this?* But as we experience in life generally, there are those good and bad days and we must accept all that comes. Finally, we were much relieved to see Anis and Ahmed with our camels. Just before this point, we came upon several very green plants, about knee-high, in the middle of this barren wadi area. Each plant had green fruits, about five centimeters in diameter, that Rima said were very good to eat. Some of the fruit was picked, and each of us tasted them with varied reaction. To me the taste was absolutely terrible.

The noon camp of this day was also very hot, like the others, and nothing special can be said, except that we wished the high sun would pass quickly to a lower angle in the sky. The dried fruit and nuts became more welcomed along with whatever we could drink; it was too much of a chore to cook any food at noontime.

We started out once more on the camels to proceed to the long-awaited evening campsite where we expected to see the next well. All the afternoon we continued to plod onward in heat that had seemed greater each day. All the while we were taking in the wonderful landscape, each independent in thought. Few words were spoken along the trail while mounted, as the camels were very often not so close together and we would have to sort of shout out to talk to each other. And at times there was no desire to talk perhaps because of heat or because we just wanted peace and quiet to think and ponder. Since Rima and Sigrid were mounted on the same camel, they talked together much of the way.

Ahmed spoke only Arabic. Anis speaks English and Arabic. Rima speaks Arabic, English, and German (because she is Swiss).

Rima came to the Sinai on a visit several years ago during the occupation of the Sinai by the Israelis. She liked the Sinai very much, and when the Sinai reverted back to the Egyptians all non-Bedouins and non-Egyptians had to leave the peninsula. Rima and Anis found each other, fell in love, and married, so Rima stayed. Rima became a Bedouin and lives every part of the life of the Bedouins in Nuweiba and in the mountains nearby. Rima and Anis have a small homestead in Nuweiba a few hundred meters from the shores of Aquaba where they grow a variety of vegetables and some fruit trees and have goats and chickens as well. Rima has almost single-handedly built a small shop where she also sells handmade Bedouin jewelry, animal trappings, dresses, and the like. They arrange and conduct the camel treks I am now describing. Some people go to Nuweiba and want to ride only for a day, some for five, and others for six or seven days into the mountains. The arrangements can only be made by driving to their place in Nuweiba and then, at the agreed-upon date, returning to Nuweiba to start the trip. They have no phone of course where they live, and postal service is, for all practical purposes, nonexistent for them.

So we finally come to our campsite for the long-anticipated "bath" on the fourth night. After provisionally setting up camp at about five o'clock, Rima tells us to get our soap, towels, and containers for water. She said it was a "little way" over the top of the mountain to which she points. After half an hour we are still climbing up and trudging down some very difficult hills with many sections of sliding rocks under our feet. It is still very warm and we are very dirty, but we are somehow happy inside that we are about to get "bathed" and obtain more water to drink, water to carry us through the day today and all of the next. After nearly an hour we finally arrive in a canyon and look up to see a few palm trees sort of sprouting out of the mountainside nearly 100 meters above us. Rima tells us that the well is there, at a small flat spot near the palms.

As we climbed for the last time to the water source, we found to our utter dismay only about one gallon of water. This was in a concave part of a large flat area and with the bottom full of green fungus. From the crack in the side of the mountain where the water came from there were only drops of water seeping into this well. We could not have been more disappointed. Rima scooped off what water she could without disturbing the mucky green bottom, and she half-filled a two-gallon plastic jerrycan. The smell of this water was absolutely horrible, like sulphur and something rotten, but Rima insisted that the water was safe to drink. We did and no one had any problems with this. Our total water supply now was a meager four quarts for the next twenty-four hours. It was consumed sparingly and handled with great care during the remainder of the trip.

But we had yet to walk back to the campsite over the same mountainous route we took to the empty well. We were now so very tired. Just the thought of the walk back to camp, especially without the water, was really very depressing. At one point while on a ridge with a narrow catwalklike path, Christa lost her footing and nearly fell down the steep slope leading far below into a canyon. With the fatigue, this near miss, and little water found, she could only sit and cry from nervousness. Everything came together. We managed to calm her and, after some time to rest, continued ever so slowly on back to camp.

We looked about to find a good spot to put our sleeping bags, as was usual each night, and at this site there were some inviting sand slopes at the base of a mountainside about twenty meters away from the campfire. After arranging the sleeping bags we prepared something to eat, which in the evening consisted mostly of soup and some prepared canned food requiring only heat. Always there was tea or coffee to sip before and after eating and sometimes during discussions at the fire or perhaps while watching Ahmed knead the dough for our bread.

Once again we were to fall asleep quickly, but not before "touching" the stars and gazing at the Milky Way or other known feature of the night sky.

On this night, not long after falling asleep, the long run of a zipper on a sleeping bag had awakened me. Curious, I asked Christa what was happening and she replied that she was too warm. *Fair enough,* I thought, and fell asleep. Again I heard the same noise; now she was getting cold. A third time, too warm. I got to see the sky again at any rate, the Milky Way had shifted to my right several degrees, and again to sleep. I was again awakened and noticed the Milky Way now overhead with probably one or two hours of position change. What was happening now? I asked Christa. She said that the sand was too hard and she could not sleep. Her sleeping bag was sliding down the slope because of the nylon cover on the foam rubber pad under the nylon-covered sleeping bag. Finally the tiredness won out and neither zipper noise nor sliding bags could deprive me of sleep until Ahmed called us once more to get our breakfast and pack up.

Contrary to what we had heard in many discussions prior to our trip about desert snakes and scorpions, we had in fact seen only one black scorpion during the entire trek. This is not to say that they do not exist there. We did not experience more. On the other hand, and perhaps more annoying at times, were the wasps, not only at the "wasp well" but in the high rocky peaks, and the flies, which appeared to be everywhere. There were also scores of lizards seen each day scampering about whenever disturbed by our intrusion through their particular area. But I viewed the lizards as I do small mice in the house. You don't really want them too close around you, but they sort of fit in their respective environment. While they simply peer at you from around a corner or from underneath their protective hideaway, they seem perfectly harmless and evoke my sympathies, rather than generate chilling reactions at the sight of them.

It was extremely interesting to watch a demonstration of the reaction of a black scorpion when put to a test by Anis. He made a flat mound of dirt about twenty centimeters in diameter in the center of the campfire, and the scorpion was dropped in the center of the dirt mound. It was therefore surrounded by fire. The scorpion scrambled to the edge of the mound and, sensing the danger of fire, went back to the center of the mound. It then went out to the edge on a different radial, returned to mound center, and repeated this action several times covering all possible directions for escape. Finally, with fire all around, the scorpion then ran so as to leap in desperation from the mound, into the fire, committing suicide. Anis said that of the hundreds of times he had witnessed this, the scorpion would perform consistently in the same manner. With some patience of course, since the fire would eventually burn out, the scorpion could have crawled calmly and safely out of the dilemma. Another lesson for human society I suppose can be drawn from this observation, is that patience and reason most generally produce solutions to many of life's problems.

We thought again about getting water at the "wasp well." We were taught in that instance that with care, patience, and calm and an understanding of things natural we could intermingle with the wasps and suffer no more than a bit of anxiety during activity in a potentially dangerous environment. Panic and flailing arms would have caused no end of grief through a mass of painful stings. Could we not learn to tread more carefully in life? Patience, finesse, and understanding are essentials in these troubled times as man, more than ever before, must learn to cope and intermingle without disturbing his neighbor or those of customs and beliefs different from his own.

Mostly I recall the fifth day of our very long camel ride to complete the last leg of this trip. It roughly followed a clockwise circular path, beginning and ending at Nuweiba. All together among us there were now only two or three quarts of very brackish water remaining. The fact that there was so little water seemed to add kilometers more to the ride as I could begin to imagine what it would be like had we exhausted the supply. Once again, however, I thought that Anis surely was aware and he wouldn't have allowed us to get into a desperate situation. It is very difficult but essential to fight off the instinct to take just another sip when the going seems rough. In this instance we were not in any danger, but it was one of great discomfort in any case.

Thoughts came to me many times, but I pondered, now profusely, on Moses, as well as Mary with Jesus, in their own times trekking through such barren lands as in Sinai. With very little imagination one could compare their lives in this environment with the lives of these very Bedouins with whom we traveled. Consider that they necessarily had no more than a camel or donkey, some goats, and a few meager belongings such as the clothes they wore and perhaps grain flour, some spices, oil, and vegetables and fruit as available from place to place. While the five days we traveled seemed at times an eternity, their weeks and months of travel into this then virtually unknown territory must have been indeed endured with severe hardship and ever-present danger.

I do not know precisely the weather pattern in this area, but rain is a rarity. In my experience living six years in Cairo and near the eastern desert I witnessed a total of only a few hours' rain. This generally occurred just during the December–February time frame. But the past seven years, according to Anis, there had been virtually no rain at all in South Sinai. That was the reason, apparently, the last well yielded only a few liters of very odorous water. When the rain does fall in these mountains, there are actually rivers, for limited periods, flowing down the slopes. The water gouges the wadis and causes sand and rocks to form patterns of nature along their downhill paths.

Just thinking about it, I wondered if people in the time of Moses, for example, were informed of the weather patterns from experienced travelers and made their journeys, accordingly, during the rainy season or in springtime, when well water might have been in abundance. At St. Catherine's Monastery itself, not so far from where we were riding and very near where Moses received the Ten Commandments, there is a sweet water well that has existed since the monastery was constructed many centuries ago. We were to drink of this well the next day, during a visit at St. Catherine's.

When there is plenty of everything one usually gives it little thought. When there is nothing, when you have no water, you think of it a lot. This was our state of mind as we continued on, this last day.

In midafternoon we approached a large herd of goats tended by a young woman perhaps only in her early teens sitting on her camel. What the goats were busily gnawing at was really difficult to assess, as there appeared to me nothing at all. However, it had to be that there were roots available, which only a hungry goat or camel could manage to find. It was odd for us to see this girl, alone, so calmly attentive to her duties in this barren wadi. I suppose that many would consider her a lonely creature, cruelly tasked to tend the animals. Yet it brought to mind a comparison in another flashback to my own youth in Montauk where, I might repeat, I wish that every child could have had the good fortune to live. There were many days when I found myself walking in all sorts of weather, long distances, remote and alone on the ocean beach, in the woods, in the grassy hills, or rowing a small boat far out into the bay waters from the village shores. I had never a feeling of loneliness or fear but that of being a part of the environment in which I lived. We had nothing to fear, as the surroundings were beautiful and we lived as a part of nature. Far from being barren, on the contrary, life in all forms was in abundance. As fishing was the livelihood of the village, there was an abundance of fish, plus many types of wild berries, grapes, beach plums, and garden fruits and vegetables. But I remember the visiting "city folks" would say, "My God! What a barren and remote place! How could anyone ever live here?" I never understood why they said this, because I suppose I never grasped, then, the real meaning of their comments. Montauk was the only place I ever knew. It was naturally comfortable, because I was born and raised there. Only when I started high school in the nearest large town of East Hampton, fourteen miles away, did I begin to realize the meaning of the words *remote* and *isolated*. Then I had a means to compare and began to understand why those visitors thought as they did.

I am quite certain that this young girl could never have been in any village greater than the size of Nuweiba, which is, by far, smaller than Montauk of the 1930s. She doesn't know "barren." She doesn't know the meaning of *isolated* or *remote,* as I also did not know then. So she is content and quite happy, alone as I was on the outer limits of my village. Every day this Bedouin girl drinks goat milk. I ate fish. The only difference is what sustained us. I rode on past, knowing that she was at peace and to be more envied than pitied.

It was about noon of the last day when I noticed a camel and its rider quickly approaching from a distance on our left quarter. As they came much nearer and into sharper focus, there was a sight before us that gave me a feeling of being cast in *A Thousand and One Nights*. Atop this magnificent camel, draped with brightly colored trappings, was a Bedouin man of perhaps forty years, wearing the typical turban of wrapped cloth and a long black coat over a gallabiya. In photos, books, and magazines and in theatrical films I had seen numerous scenes of deserts, tribesmen, horsemen, and camels. But just before me, at this very moment, was a genuine Bedouin tribesman in all his splendor, now in an easy gallop approaching our small caravan. Words cannot adequately describe, nor can any photograph properly depict, in any way this scene and the accompanying excitement as this Bedouin reined his camel alongside Anis. It became apparent that Mohammed, the rider, and Anis were longtime friends. But it seemed a bit strange that their greeting was so casual, as if they had seen each other just moments ago.

I had noticed this trait a few days before. While squatting and making tea one evening at the campfire, Anis was conscientiously observing his steeping elixir when yet another Bedouin had come out of the darkness into our camp, as if he were one of us, and squatted beside Anis. I had been startled to suddenly see this total stranger come "out of nowhere." But it was clearly two or three minutes, before Anis even turned his head to look at the visitor. Yet words were calmly exchanged between them, as they had been with Mohammed, like they had been together during the past four days. I thought that this was a marvelous indication of the tremendous faith held by Anis, in particular, and perhaps all these Bedouins in their desert home. I believe that Anis's faith in his God is so real and deep-seated, his philosophy of life so pure, clear, and simple, and his mind so well disciplined that he would not flinch for a moment or hesitate for fear in the face of any danger. I sense that he could have sad moments, but not from fear or danger. Rather, as he was very human and sensitive, any measure of sadness or happiness in Anis would be affected only by personal feelings between him and Rima or his friends. I believe that his love for Rima and their companionship are his salvation on this earth and that his faith in God is his pass to the endless heavens above, which beckon nightly before each sleep.

It was only a short while after our visitor, Mohammed, joined us that we stopped for midday camp. As on the previous day, the heat of the noon sun was rather fierce. Therefore, the very thought of getting everything together to conjure up a meal, over a hot fire, was something less than inviting. The result was that we commenced to munch on nuts and dried fruit and sip the *chai* made by Anis and Rima. In the meantime, without discussion or any words now, Mohammed had untied his flour sack from the rear pommel of his saddle. Ahmed, also without words, brought his aluminum basin over to Mohammed, who dumped flour into it and started to mix the flour with the water Ahmed was pouring. Steadily, with experienced hands, Mohammed continued to knead the dough mixture until satisfied that it had the right consistency. As I watched, I imagined that there must be a custom among these Bedouins imposing an implicit rule of the desert to share their material possessions, as well as their labor, as contribution toward dividends from use of the end product. I recalled that Mohammed had also gone in search of roots and twigs to make a fire. Having found so very little to burn, he climbed a leafless acacia tree and with a large rock in hand broke sections of dried-out branches to help make this fire. Well, this is really not so different. My non-Bedouin friends and I would also help in every way. We would all join in to help one another. It came clear to me now that the major difference was the silence with which these chores were performed by them. The needs were so basic, the daily actions so repetitive in the process of survival, that words actually were unnecessary. They chose, more often than not, to do things quietly. But did it somehow have a religious connotation?

In moments as this, and when riding or facing the stars just before sleep, it was not unlike the stillness at St. Theresa not only during but also before and after masses I had served. When one felt compelled to communicate, it was done in whispers so as not to disturb the serenity and to show respect in a house of worship. I had witnessed during my travels that same respect in many churches and cathedrals whether in America, Brazil, or Spain or those of Italy and Norway. Even in different countries and cities, people of varied origins and faiths almost always preserve the sanctity of holy space by respecting the unwritten code of silence. Moments of my navy travels came into focus as I recalled seeking that extra measure of peace and serenity. I found those precious moments in entering cathedrals in Recife and Toledo and in Rome. I recall a very stormy winter night in Kodiak, Alaska, when I had the urge to seek some peace of mind from the rigors of flying patrols in some of the worst weather conditions. In freezing and howling winds I made my way to the tiny chapel that was always open. There was no one there as I entered. The only lights were those of the votive candles and the red candlelight denoting the presence of the Blessed Sacrament in the tabernacle. It meant more to me, as a Catholic, than it might to those of other faiths, yet anyone there at that moment would necessarily have felt inspired and have a greater sense of well-being if for no other reason than the serenity afforded there. When one dwells on emotion-yielding experiences in an atmosphere such as that, the feelings from good experiences are strengthened and feelings from the bad can be dampened or diminished. Through successive immersions in the votive-lit chapel or, as I see now, in remote desert mountains free of distractions, one is inspired. It is my thought that the Bedouins, at least in large part, if not completely, for this reason have the feeling that in their desert they are in a holy wilderness. I have the idea that these people are in their church. Their quiet manner and humility are out of respect for this tremendous mountain desert House of God.

I Did Not Want to Leave Egypt

In the fall of 1986 I was informed that I would be transferred to Germany and work in Ottobrunn, just south of Munich, where the German company MBB had its headquarters. MBB was one of the German companies, along with AEG, Diehl, and BGT, involved with the Rolling Airframe Missile (RAM), for which GD had the lead in design and manufacture. Eventually various phases of development and manufacture would be shared among the companies. The German companies formed a separate company, RAMSYS, to specifically handle the RAM. RAMSYS would interface with GD throughout the program until it became operational aboard the ships of the U.S. and German navies. I was to be the representative for GD in an office at RAMSYS near Munich.

I can say that I was not so happy to hear the news for transfer because I wanted to stay in Egypt. But a decision had been made at the corporate headquarters that I go to Germany and that was it. As things turned out, however, I never regretted the effects of the transfer and it became an opportunity for promotion.

But before I left Egypt, there were some unfinished personal plans to complete. One of them was to visit Rome and really take in all the sights and to visit Popoli, Italy, where my mother's parents lived, before immigrating to the States about 1900. Another was to make a trip around the world, at leisure and, finally, to spend Christmas week in Aswan, Upper Egypt, with our friends German military attaché Colonel Moeschel and his wife, Sigrid, and Dutch military attaché Colonel Zweegman and his wife, Martha.

I was very much impressed with all the history and sights at Vatican City, especially the tremendous artwork of paintings, sculptures, and architecture. Attending a blessing by the pope in Vatican Square with literally tens of thousands of people was very special. And of course I sent a nice card from the Vatican to my mother, which was a treat for her. I always sent postcards of special cathedrals and interesting places, which she liked. Visiting the fountain that was made even more famous by the song "Three Coins in the Fountain," the Spanish Steps, the Colosseum, all one expects to see and more, was a great experience.

I had seriously planned for the visit to Popoli, east of Rome. The very morning to go I was so sick from something eaten the night before, I had to stay in bed for next two days. The owner of the small hotel, Sitea, not far from the Spanish Steps, brought me rice soup from the hotel kitchen twice a day. I never made it to Popoli. A few years later, Anne Dinizio, Bob Cook's wife, made the trip to Popoli, since her parents also came from this very village. Of interest is that Aunt Sue's husband, Peter Piccozzi, had parents who came from Popoli as well.

Our round-the-world trip, starting the first week of December 1986, was not as fast as my nine-minute experience around the world at the North Pole. However, for the distance covered in this three-week trip it was a real whirlwind tour. The itinerary, in short, was Krefeld, Germany; New York City; Montauk; Washington, D.C.; Saint Louis; San Francisco; Honolulu; Tokyo Airport; Hong Kong; Singapore; Bangkok; New Delhi; Agra; Japuir; Bombay; and back to Cairo.

The stops made, in the order shown, up through San Francisco, were stopovers for visits to family and friends. From Hawaii on through to the Indian cities the stopovers were all for leisure and sightseeing. I had lived in Hawaii in 1951–52, but it was the first time there for Christa. I think of all the places visited I was most impressed with Hong Kong for its efficiency, cleanliness, and orderliness. The language used in Hong Kong being English was a plus for me. The mention of Bangkok today reminds me of the hours spent in the jewelry shops where Christa had more interest than I. However, I did come away with one item I still have and use occasionally, a rather heavy solid gold ring with a ruby encased in the face. The ruby is the traditional birthstone for those born in July.

Agra was special for the sight of the Taj Mahal, and Japuir for all the pink buildings and the castle, which we visited atop an elephant. The Rambagh Palace Hotel sends one back into yesteryear with thoughts of the wealthy maharajas and all their splendor. The British influence remains strong with the pronounced accents. All the people we met seemed very friendly, but too many, it appears, are poor, the latter most prominently visible where we traveled in Bombay. Not far from the airport and en route to downtown Bombay there were dozens of very young and naked children meandering through widespread piles of garbage. It was actually difficult for me to enjoy the luxury of the hotel in which we stayed and the enormous spread of food provided us. As we had traveled through the country by car and passed through a lot of farm areas, it seemed that life in these areas would have been more normal or bearable. Yet one wonders about those under more destitute conditions whose numbers are constantly growing among the over 1 billion population of India now in 2001.

We returned back to Egypt to meet friends in Aswan just a few days before Christmas of 1986. The idea of an Egyptian location for Christmas was out of a historical thought. At some point in my life I began to think about all the twinkle and sparkle, the snow-covered rooftops, Santa and Saint Nick, fancily wrapped gifts, Dancer and Prancer, and even the stirless mouse in the house on the eve of Christmas. If only I could turn back the pages of time and live at least for a moment as it was without the commercial frills and fanfare. I thought of how it might, or even must, have been to experience the occasion of Christmas in the atmosphere of an earlier-century version and in the Middle East area where Anno Domini began.

I had occasion, in fact, to get a feeling of such an experience in a remote section of Aswan, in Upper Egypt. Only the sand, not a tree or wrapping in sight, no jingle of bells or sounds of Crosby and Como. I had ample time to recall my camel trek earlier through the barren Sinai Desert several days with Bedouins and realize how very difficult it must have been for the Holy Family traveling through this and even saving the Christ child from the terrorism of Herod. Free of all extraneous sounds and distractions one can dwell upon what we believe is the real meaning of Christmas. It was a most peaceful, enjoyable, and inspiring "Silent Night" in Aswan, even nearly 2,000 years after the birth of Christ.

After having experienced that Christmas in Aswan I did a little research in various references about the historical aspects of this great event in order to round out my thoughts on this theme. The date of the birth of Christ on which we celebrate Christmas was established as the reference for a system of computing time and has been almost universally accepted. We live now in the year 2000, this many years after his birth, or A.D. 2000 (*Anno Domini*, meaning "year of our Lord"). This system was introduced by an early Christian monk, Dionysius Exiguus of Scythia, who placed Christ's birth in the 754th year after the founding of the city of Rome, or 754 A.U.C.** It was years later determined that the Nativity occurred no later than 750 A.U.C. and could have been even earlier, by 746 A.U.C.

**A.U.C. is the abbreviation of *Ab Urbe Condita,* Latin for "from the founding of the City" (of Rome). From the earliest days of powerful Rome, the Latin word *urbe* meant not only "urban" or "city" but also *the city: Rome.* In some documents instead of B.C. (*Before Christ*), A.C. (*Ante Christum*), Latin for "before Christ," is used.

Dionysius dated the beginning of the Christian Era several years too late. The only notable consequence of his calculations resulted in the absurdity that Christ was born sometime between 8 and 4 B.C.

The date of Christmas, 25 December, varied until the fourth century in the Western Church, the fifth century in the Eastern Church. Early Christianity regarded the birth of Christ as a significant moment, important for the understanding of his person. Despite the beliefs about him expressed in the Gospels, the church did not observe a festival for the celebration of the event until the fourth century. This period was chosen to counter the pagan festivities connected with the winter solstice.

In medieval Europe, the folk customs connected with the winter solstice were perpetuated together with the church celebration. The Christmas tree became the major decorative object in the celebration of Christmas. The symbolic use of evergreens has its roots in ancient times, especially in the Egyptian, Hebrew, and Chinese cultures, in which it signified eternal life. When Christianity became widespread in Europe during the Middle Ages, the pagan custom of tree worship nevertheless lived on. By the eighteenth century the custom of the Christmas tree was common in Germany, and, in fact, German settlers had already introduced the practice into North America as early as the seventeenth century. The tree's use as the decorative focal point of Christmas celebration has not waned. Electric lights, candy canes, shiny ornaments, religious symbols, cranberries or popcorn beaded on thread, angels, and apples adorn the trees in homes and offices, and as we have all seen, they appear in spectacular fashion in the commercial arena.

One Eye Laughing, One Eye Crying

Just before departing Egypt I attended my last AmCham Luncheon, which was in the Marriott Hotel, Zamalek. As a longtime member of the board and one of the founders, I was handed an appreciation certificate on papyrus and expected to say a few words. Over 200 members and guests were present, including a few of the ministers of the Egyptian government. I reviewed several of the accomplishments from AmCham's beginning in Cairo, gave my thanks to all my colleagues, and wished them all well. And I added the reason that I had spent my Christmas in Egypt at Aswan and not in my home country. It was for the thoughts as just described. The Egyptians were so elated at this that they gave a long and rousing round of applause, which I had not experienced in my years there.

I left Cairo with "one eye laughing and one eye crying," as they say. I did not want to leave, yet they made it such a memorable day for me that it was somehow made a bit easier to depart the land to which I had become so attached.

The Wurst Is Yet to Come!
Germany (1987–2002)

One of the biggest difficulties in the departure, aside from the fact that I did not want to leave the Cairo scene, was the shipment of my 1971 Volkswagen Bug to Germany. This VW was allowed into Egypt from Athens, Greece, without customs duty, by my agreement with the Egyptian government that I take the car out of the country when I leave. So the VW had to go out or I would have to pay $4,000 customs duty, regardless of the current worth of the car. Its worth was essentially nothing after fifteen years on the road, six years of which were in Egypt.

The other options were to pay some ship's captain 500 Egyptian pounds under the table and have him dump the VW into the Mediterranean, or pay a moving company $2,000 for transport to the port of entry closest to Munich, Germany. The VW, purchased in Cherry Hill, New Jersey, where it was imported new from Germany and built to U.S. standards, cost only $1,900 when new. GD paid the least price, of the legal methods available, by shipping the car to Munich.

But then I could not use the VW right away on the German highways because the lighting system did not conform to the German regulations. The VW's lighting system conversion, back to the German standards, plus heater system repairs, cost me DM 2,000 (about eight hundred dollars at the time). I finally sold the VW, after some weeks, to a young German man for DM 1,000.

Although the arrival in Germany on the second of January 1987 was a whole lot simpler than the departure from Egypt, the test for AIDS required by Germany was rather shocking and, I thought, demeaning. I was thinking that, if the requirement was because I came from Egypt, why aren't all Germans who have toured Egypt, or certain other countries, also AIDS-tested?

During the search for an apartment in Munich we lived in the Arabella Haus near the Sheraton Munich. That January was the coldest for a decade, and during this period we still did not have an operable car. We had to walk around the freezing streets looking for addresses of advertised apartments and not always knowing where we were going. We learned that one cannot "hail" a taxi in Germany like in many countries. You have to go to a taxi stand or call a taxi company by phone. If you do not know the taxi stand locations you have a problem, and if you do not know where you are it's difficult to explain via telephone to the cab company where to pick you up. A really difficult time. We did finally find a place in northeast Munich after two months, near the Englische Garten, at the Isar River.

While we were deep in the process of installing drapes, kitchen equipment, and lighting fixtures I received a call in February from my boss, Joe Pennisi, in Pomona, who asked if I wanted to go to Bonn for assignment. At first, this sounded preposterous. We had just arrived from Egypt several weeks prior and had gone through so much acquiring an apartment. But then my senses started to work. Victor Warriner, Captain, U.S. Navy (Ret.), who had been stationed already a few years in Bonn as the European Deputy for the RAM program, had just died from cancer. A replacement was urgently needed and it would be a promotion for me, so I said yes. Luckily, our household effects had not yet arrived in Germany. The ship that had our household goods had to return to Port Said, Egypt, for repairs. Now the goods could eventually be sent directly to Bonn, Germany, instead of Munich after arriving at a port in Italy.

In February 1987 I made my first official trip to Bonn, not only to attend funeral services but also to get acquainted with the office and the people where I would be working. Soon after, we moved into temporary quarters in the Eden Hotel in Bad Godesberg and eventually settled in a nearby area.

I bought a used Mercedes 380 for a few thousand Deutsch Marks as a temporary measure. This was an older model but one of the bigger Mercedes and very comfortable. I even drove it down to Spain and through the country without problems. Then one day, in order to remove the Spanish dust and highway grime, I drove the 380 into a car wash in Bad Godesberg. This new, imported, automatic "California" car wash system had just been installed a couple of months earlier. When my car was about halfway through the wash there was a jolt and the whole car wash system came to a halt. The problem was that the width of this big old Mercedes 380 was wider than the recent models, also wider than the car wash tracks. The wheels on the right side of the 380 ran off the tracking device, the side of the car was smashed in, and the garage insurance company had to pay damages for both the car and the California car wash system. Needless to say, the owner of the car wash paid "special attention" thereafter, to the older, larger-width cars. "Special attention" meant no more big old Mercedes were allowed in.

Soon after this little catastrophe, I bought a new 1988 Mercedes 230E. As of this writing, it has over 230,000 kilometers (138,000 miles) and is still running smoothly.

German Atmosphere

In Germany, where it seemed that all was quiet, orderly, clean, and efficient, "the something about life that I experienced in the developing countries" was missing. Probably the excitement, for one thing, the exotic sights and sounds, even though amid chaotic streets with their constant noise of traffic, peddler shouts, and prayer calls from a multitude of minarets. Moreover, another kind of anomaly entered into the equation. It became easier in many ways to accomplish work in Germany, but it has been a constant learning process coping with the cultural differences in various situations at work and in the social environment. There were of course cultural differences, which I experienced in all other lands. But there people responded, more often than not, with a friendly smile at the newly arrived foreigner, rather than an intolerant frown. My learning process of the German culture began within days after arrival in this country. Unfriendly treatment in shops was most noticeable at the outset.

Incidents with Language

I knew very little German in the beginning, but I wanted, and was willing, to learn. I started with a language course at Goethe Institute. Even during my early learning process I tried to use German whenever possible.

Early on, in Bonn, I was tending to something on my car near the street in front of our apartment. A little old lady walked the street with her dog, typically to find some yard other than her own for her dog to do its thing. I thought, *This is a chance to exercise my skills.* "Hallo!" I said, with what I thought was a pleasant look on my face. There was absolutely no answer. The lady simply kept on walking, and without a hint of a glance in my direction. Afterward, I commented to my wife that this woman was not at all friendly.

"What did you say to her?"

I said, "Hallo."

"Well, people do not say 'Hallo' here; it's 'Guten Tag'!"

A few days later I was again at the street in front of the house and another little old lady was walking by. "Guten Tag," I said to her.

With a stern look on her face she glanced at her watch, jerked her head upward, then further jerked her head toward me only to say, "Guten *Abend*!" With her nose in the air, she continued on.

I went immediately into the house and exclaimed, "I said exactly what you told me, 'Guten Tag,' and the rather disturbed lady said, 'Guten Abend.'"

My wife responded, "Well what time was it?"

I said, "What difference does it make what time it was? I suppose about six P.M."

Her answer: "Naturally when it is later in the day, like evening, you must say 'Guten Abend.'"

Subsequently I began to look at my watch before ever giving a greeting. After some months, I further learned that Germans hardly ever looked at their watches but seemed to have an inborn sense to come up with the correct expression. To this day I am sometimes on the wrong frequency, as it has now and then happened when I said "Guten Abend," after a quick observation of a darkening sky, the response from the passerby was, "Guten Tag."

I became aware of the fact that Germans in different parts of the country may act quite differently. For example, in my experience, when walking in the woods on a hiking trail in North Rhine Westphalen most of the people walking in the opposite direction never say anything at all to each other. And when I would say, "Guten Tag," even at high noon, some people answered and some not. On the other hand, in Bavaria on a hiking trail in the woods or on a mountainside I was always given a friendly greeting, every time, in the Bavarian style: "Grüss Gott."

Private Telephoning

In any of the other countries where I lived I never thought of the time of day when dialing a phone number of a friend or acquaintance. But in

Germany it is a general rule, among most of the people I know, that one does not make calls to private homes between 1:00 and 3:00 P.M., before 9:00 A.M., or after 9:00 P.M.. I had learned this early on, when one party I called in the evening never answered the phone. The next day, the individual told me he was home, but 9:30 P.M. was too late to talk on the phone. In early afternoon the folks are often taking a siesta and want no noise of any kind to bother them.

Closed Office Doors and Working Hours/Days

During my very first weeks working in the Ottobrunn, Munich, area, I was assigned to an office in a building of one of the German contractors, MBB, with whom we shared space. I experienced several things so different from my work in the United States that the impressions are everlasting. First noticed was the fact that every one of the approximately thirty office spaces had the doors to the office always closed. When seeking a colleague one would have to either phone him or knock on several doors to know where he was or if he was in. When I had to go to several offices to look for a person I lost a lot of time because along the way there was always someone who decided to converse about one thing or another. So it happened on a number of occasions that half an hour would pass and I still could not find the person I was looking for. My work environment in the United States was such that simply looking out over the heads of dozens of engineers in a large space I could see immediately whom I wanted. The doors of department heads' offices were mostly left open. Rarely a closed door. This Ottobrunn situation was frustrating to me especially on a Friday afternoon, at which time I learned yet another feature of German habits. On Friday when I needed someone, instead of calling or knocking on doors I found out that if I immediately went down into the underground garage I could see at a glance who was still in the building by checking whose car was still there. If I saw the car I would know the man I wanted was still "somewhere" in the building. On Friday afternoon, after twelve, it was most usually the case that nearly everyone had already gone home to start their weekend, leaving only a few cars to identify. And even on a "normal" workday it was a rare case to find anyone in the office after five. I recall my days in GD where I worked, the clock meant little if there was unfinished work.

On this theme of work and off hours, it seemed to be the case that every time I talked to a German he talked about either his last vacation trip or the vacation trip he was planning. And I began to realize that vacations were on the minds of most people because in Germany six weeks of vacation a year are the norm, plus all the individual holidays and the "sick days" usually taken. And of course it is also usual that most employees are given a "thirteenth-month pay" bonus at the end of the year.

Birthdays

Birthdays are taken very seriously in Germany. It seems that a party "must" be held and gifts given, especially for all children. When one is older, there are usually telephone calls the day long from friends and relatives wishing good health, everything good in the future, that all wishes come true, et cetera, et cetera, and everybody seems to say the same words. I have received these calls a hundred times over the past several years. And when a person reaches a "round" birthday, i.e., forty, fifty, sixty, et cetera, there is really a big celebration, except for some women who do not want to expose their age.

Birthday Celebrations in Offices, with Beer and Wine

Whenever someone in the offices in Ottobrunn had a birthday I could expect an office party, that is, with everybody participating. All work stopped. Typical fare was *Sekt* (champagne), wine or beer, and either *Brötchen* (rolls) sandwiches and/or cake and cookies. At first this appeared to me to be absolutely contrary to a good business atmosphere and it was something that I had never experienced, yet it seemed not to seriously affect progress on the various projects. It was absolutely unheard of, in my previous experience, to consume alcoholic drinks in the workplace. Alcohol, primarily beer, was commonplace in the company's cafeterias in Bavaria.

The Welcoming Sekt and Wine at Dinner

Welcoming drinks and wine at the dinner table deserve some mention for the newcomer in Germany. And once again my comments stem from my experiences early on after arrival here in residence. When entering into the German home for dinner it is common to receive a glass of *Sekt* as a welcome drink. On all previous occasions, in other countries, such a welcoming drink would be given and normally the first sip taken at one's leisure. Not in Germany. As I started to sip the *Sekt* during my first dinner invitation, I was told by another guest next to me that the host has not yet toasted. My reaction, in thought, at the time was, *So what?* But I waited, and waited, until a few more guests arrived and now there were a circle of standing guests facing inward, each holding a glass of *Sekt*. Eventually the host entered the circle, once again repeating his welcome to each and every one and stating the reason for this dinner with a rather lengthy dissertation. Then the moment came when the host finally sipped on his *Sekt*. By this time, after such a long introduction, my own thirst demanded more than just a sip and my glass was nearly emptied in one go. Over time I had acquired the necessary patience for this inevitable ceremony.

Then when you are seated at the dinner table there is invariably white or red wine poured depending upon the food served. Again it is the custom for no one to take a sip of this wine until the host or hostess first offers a toast and partakes of the wine him- or herself. At each dinner one can observe that some one or more persons at the table will commence to reach for their wine but then hesitate, trying to remember whether the host already toasted. Or they will keep their hands on or quite near their wineglasses in an attempt to prompt the host to make his toast, thinking, *Dear host, please say what you're going to say so I can take a sip!*

Gift Giving

In America it is not unusual for a guest to bring a token gift to the home of the host and hostess, however I would say that it is very traditional and "necessary" to do so in Germany. Mostly *Blumen* (flowers) are the gifts brought by guests, but other items such as homemade *Marmelade* (fruit preserves or jam), *Pralinen* (a box of chocolates), or *Flaschen* (bottles of wine or other alcoholic drink) are also well accepted. This practice of gift giving therefore could require a significant amount of your money if you were invited very often each month of the year.

Noisy, Lengthy Meetings

During my fifteen years to date in Germany I have attended very many of all kinds of meetings. I think it is safe to say that at every single meeting, whether an important business meeting, a social meeting, or a small or large meeting of the membership of a golf club, every time a speaker has the floor two or three or four persons commence side conversations and with enough volume so as to disturb others in attendance. I become very annoyed at this practice still to this day. I see it as being rude. I have commented on this point many times to friends after various meetings and they say, "Well, that's the way it is here." And if an attendee wants to comment on what the speaker has said, he does not usually state a question or give a comment in a precise manner. Rather, he may take ten minutes to expound on a subject as if he is wanting to simply be heard by the masses at the meeting. When there is a discussion it winds up with several persons all talking at the same time and nobody knows what the other is saying. This is so aggravating to me because I was trained always to wait until the other person was finished before I said my piece.

Addressing a German

It is well known that in America, and many other places in the world, people are called by their first names. For the American, especially, it is always difficult to get around the problem of having to learn the *Sie* (formal for "you") and *du* (informal for "you") and the *Herr* ("Mr.") Müller or *Frau* ("Mrs.") Dr. Schwarz and the like. I heard during my early days in Germany, "You must say 'Herr Müller,' not simply his first name, like Fritz. And address the lady doctor as 'Frau Doktor Schwarz,' not just 'Doktor.' And you must say '*Sie*' to someone you do not know well, not '*du.*' *Sie* is formal and *du* only for close friends."

Another form of confusion came to me on the golf course. After I had been a member of the Bonn Godesberg Golf Club a couple of years, certain members began to tell me I should call them Werner, Jürgen, Wilhelm, Marianne, or Inge, as the case might be. They now knew me well enough to "allow" me to use the first name. Well, I thought this was really a great day that they accepted me. Since I was now using first names I assumed it proper to use the form *du* (not *Sie* anymore) and therefore began to speak like the German friends of these men and women. One day I said to

Marianne, "Spielst du morgen mit mir?" (Do you play with me tomorrow?) I was informed by my wife that I cannot say that. I told her that Marianne said I should call her by her first name. "Yes, but you cannot say 'du' just because you can use her first name! You must become *very* good friends, not only well acquainted, to say 'du.' It is necessary to perform the little ceremony of *Brudershaft* where the German, in your case, offers this to you."

Well, of course my point is to say that it can be somewhat complicated to understand all of the little rules, and even when you finally understand them you wonder if it has to be. Since many Germans think that Americans are more or less ignorant about the world outside of their own backyard, I have sometimes taken advantage of that perk in order to avoid a lot of discussion and simply said, "My friends call me Paul," when asked my name at the golf course. Most of the time they answer saying, "You can call me Wilhelm" (or whatever). And we tee off for a good game of golf without the language and grammar barriers.

My spacious office in Bonn was located in the center of Bad Godesberg. It was necessarily large, 2,000 square feet, because each year there were several meetings in Bonn with forty attendees from company, government, and military representatives out of Germany, the United States, and Denmark.

During the years 1987 to 1992 as the European deputy for the RAM program it was my task to make personal contacts with many government and European company officials, arrange for meetings, respond to various requests from companies participating in the RAM program, and escort visiting company executives around Germany, Denmark, and Switzerland. Besides traveling often to the stateside locations (Washington, San Diego, and Pomona) I made numerous trips within Europe to Munich, Nurenberg, Uberlingen, Nabern, Hamburg, Koblenz, Kassel, Bremen, Ottobrunn, Ulm, Paderborn, Zurich, Copenhagen, Stockholm, and Brussels. Regular weekly, sometimes daily, visits were made to the U.S. embassy and the German ministry of defense.

The wall came down between East and West Germany in November 1989 (Germany reunified in 1990), signifying the end of the cold war. Defense business was decreasing, in general, all over the world to the point that thousands of employees were being laid off. The GD office in Bonn was closed in 1992, and it went the way of many other American companies. In fact, the CEO of GD, Mr. Anders, a former astronaut, held to his philosophy, "If we can't be number one in any of our divisions, we will sell, and we will buy to be number one!" All but two (Tanks and Submarines) of the fourteen divisions were sold. A few years later GD bought Bath Iron Works (a destroyer shipyard) in Maine. GD is currently number one in these three specialties: army tanks, nuclear submarines, and naval destroyers

The fortunate ones, like myself in 1992, had the option to take early retirement. I was just eligible for early retirement at sixty-two years of age. Therefore, GD, it seemed, was doing me a favor asking if I wanted to take early retirement. But I really did not have a choice. At age sixty-two people are not hired in defense or practically any other business. But I did arrange a little consulting with GD for about one year. I found it to be not worth all the time and energy. GD paid me only for the hours to develop a report, but I was not paid for all the hours and days I had to spend to keep up with the contacts and making a lot of visits to keep abreast of what was going on. Also, because I was in retired status as far as the U.S. government was concerned and now again receiving additional income, my Social Security pension was decreased, so I wound up working almost for nothing. I went into full retirement in 1993. Some Social Security rules on this subject have been modified in recent years for the benefit of the older-than-seventy retirees.

Already we had bought an apartment at Jaegerweg 16a, Bonn-Bad Godesberg and moved there from Muffendorf in June 1992. The "holiday apartment" that we had for several years in Fischen, Bavaria, was sold in order to purchase the apartment at Jaegerweg 16a, Bonn-Bad Godesberg. I was always happy to be able to use this Fischen apartment, as it was very comfortable and in a picturesque location. After moving to Germany from Egypt, in the years before it was sold my wife insisted on renting it out because she said we were not using it much. I did not want this to happen, but in about 1988 she rented it anyway, to a young couple who eventually failed to pay the rent. There were then more problems getting them out of the place. For several years I missed the potential joy of using the apartment myself. It had been a rather happy period for me to be in the mountains. Now this disagreeable situation started to work on my feelings further, to a point that it was instrumental in making a real impact on our domestic life.

Full retirement did not mean, "doing nothing." I had been elected president of the American German Business Club, AGBC-Bonn, in 1990, and by 1992 the club already began to grow in leaps and bounds from one to, ultimately, ten chapters throughout Germany. I was national president of the AGBC-Germany, all chapters in Germany, since 1990. I decided to resign as national president in November 2001. For the foreseeable future I will probably remain involved as president of the AGBC-Bonn Chapter. Despite all the work and responsibilities with my volunteer positions with AGBC, I have found great satisfaction in seeing the organization grow and doing well. But after ten long years of this voluntary work, I was inspired to divert some of my attentions to another hobby, perhaps artistic painting, in addition to my favorite one, golf.

I had my eyes operated on because of cataracts and the accompanying reduction in vision in the spring of 1995. Artificial (silicon) lenses were installed, and I regained full vision, now needing only reading glasses. But there was a stitch on one eye that was bothering me very much. The doctor said he could not yet remove it. It was at this very time my mother was losing her strength and expected to live but some days. I should already be traveling to see her at our home in Montauk, but the doctor declared it to be too risky for me. Well, just four days before she passed away, which was on 26 June 1995, I was able to make the trip. As I arrived at the house, with all the rest of our family already there, Mom was asleep. But a couple of hours later she awoke and asked, "Where's Paul?" I went immediately into the bedroom where she lay, on a hospital-type bed. She still found the strength to raise her arms and hug my neck, saying my name. Thereafter she slowly but steadily faded. She died peacefully in her sleep. She is surely in heaven with the life she led, always with God and family in her thoughts and actions.

I played my first golf when a caddy in 1939 in Montauk, but I never had so many chances to play often until in Cairo and now in Bonn. I have been playing since 1987 as a member of the Golf Club Bonn-Godesberg. Most of the golf competition is in seasonal golf weather, but recently during winter as well I play each week with a small group of men, even at times when there is a light snow on the ground. During the normal golf season I play as a member of the Herrengolf group: about sixty men of the club gather every Wednesday afternoon for tournaments. I am also a member of the Golf Senioren Gesellschaft (GSG), which schedules over twenty-five tournaments each year in different cities throughout Germany. Members can choose which tournaments to play. Then once each year, since 1988, I have been a member of a ten-man group traveling to various countries outside Germany for private golf tournaments. Scotland, France,

Spain, and the United States are countries we have played in, as well as several times in France and Spain.

High-Profile Courses and High School Reunion

One of the highlights during my life in Germany was my annual trip to the States in 1996. Besides visiting son Jim and daughter Patti, it was to play especially on the following golf courses: Maidstone, East Hampton; Atlantic, Bridgehampton; Shinnecock Hills, Southampton; Gardiner's Bay, Shelter Island; and Montauk Downs, Montauk, and to attend my fiftieth high school class reunion. The games on these golf courses were organized by Dick White Jr. of Montauk and Bob Osborne of East Hampton. Our golf group consisted of nine men: Matthias Venker, Horst Gundelach, Jürgen Assmann, Rüdiger Gustke, Karl-Heinz Happel, Herbert Huck, Helmuth Niederhoff, Tony Panek, and I, all members of Bonn-Godesberg Golf Club, Bonn, Germany. We stayed at Gurney's Inn, Montauk, during our Eastern Long Island Golf Tour, which was one of the most exciting tours of all those played in the past several years. Dinners at Gurney's Inn, Gosman's Dock, and the Lobster Inn in Southampton were memorable in enjoyment of all the fresh fish and lobsters. Even for the van trip on the Long Island Expressway to Manhattan for a Broadway show (*Les Miserables*) and sightseeing we were provided a fresh lobster box lunch by the staff at Gurney's Inn.

Coincidentally, the high school class of 1946 reunion was scheduled in the same month, on the twenty-eighth of September, so I stayed on to attend this gala affair held at the Waterside, Noyak (near Sag Harbor). It was great to meet members of the class after so many, many years. But it was very sad to learn that fifteen of the graduating class of about forty had already passed away. The average age of those present was about sixty-seven years, which meant that most of those who had died were relatively young when they had passed on.

What I have written about my stay in Germany so far is rather concise and with fewer incidents of special interest, mainly because of a less exciting atmosphere compared to all the locations where I had been previously assigned. However, one of the situations occurring in this country had the most profound effect on my personal life, cultural differences and language problems on the one hand and the long-term effects of differences in my personal, married life on the other.

During assignments in Greece, Iran, Saudi Arabia, and Egypt my attentions were so focused on important projects and dealing with proportionally greater responsibilities that any anomalies in my married relationship, although growing, were pretty much in my peripheral vision. My wife was quite involved with guests from abroad, receptions, often several times a week, taking trips, and her own family matters. Many of the guests she dealt with were the wives of company and customer business travelers, and her social efforts were well received. She liked to control all aspects of the events. My attention and efforts as in-country director of marketing for GD were focused upon making sure everything with respect to business, as well as large receptions, was properly arranged so that my colleagues in GD and other defense firms and the various military and government counterparts came together in productive and successful business meetings.

After arriving in Germany I became much more aware of the differences in our temperaments and their telling effects on many issues, especially after full retirement. I became less and less tolerant of the incompatibility. There was no one single incident that caused the separation from my wife. It had been kind of like the river that flows over the years and gradually, over a long time, wears away the earth, rocks, and gravel, the very ground upon which it flows. The effects of the flow cannot be seen each day or each month, but you eventually come to realize it.

Despite any and all negative comments stemming from actions in my personal life, I always hold my door open to any of my friends, family, and relatives, if and when they feel the desire to enter.

It was never ever my intent or desire to be searching, or to be "on the lookout" for another partner in life, nor was that the case for Ursula. It just happened. Ursula was the catalyst, not the root cause, of the general situation. I found our dispositions and character to be so much alike, both basically easygoing, quiet, and very compatible.

Although I felt I was reasonably successful during all the fifty-six years of career and volunteer work with the U.S. Navy, General Dynamics Corporation, and the American German Business Club, respectively, only after fifty years of married life was I able to reach a plateau of compatible domestic partnership. It has often been stated by some during my life, that "two opposites" attract in a marriage and are better. "Variety is the spice of life." After lifelong experiences, I cannot subscribe to that philosophy at all. Rather, I learned that two persons in marriage must have a whole lot more in common, in all aspects, including similar temperaments and compatible religious leanings, in order to live a peaceful and happy life.

The *Wurst* is over!

Epilogue

I still revel about the past, my life in the Montauk Fishing Village. There is nothing that can take the memories away, but I do recognize those things declared as progress. As one advances in years one is prone to look back on situations and conditions, which may have been the height of discomfort, and relive the good feelings and romanticism of his formative days of yesteryear. When I see a steam locomotive today, even if only in pictures, there is immediate recall of our Cannonball Express approaching or departing the Fishing Village, the blowing whistle in the woods near Rocky Point announcing its arrival, and the great columns of black cinderous smoke trailing the stack of the locomotive, then the stop at the station, the very last stop of the Long Island Railroad, at Montauk, as the loc engineer noisily releases huge white billows of excess steam from the boilers. As soon as the mail and passengers depart, the loc takes on water from the old wooden water tower not far from the stationhouse. With some switching of tracks and using the "turnaround" the trains's direction is being readied for the westward run, back to New York City. But first, to the very large coal bin, where coal is taken and piled high on the tender. We villagers are hoping during the winter months that the coal is piled so high that the slightest shake of the bouncing train will dislodge enough coal to the ground alongside the tracks that we can gather enough to last a few more days for the stoves to warm our homes. Now another departure. Such a load for the locomotive, from standstill, requires yet another touch by the engineer to overcome the lack of traction between the huge loc wheels and the rails. A "shot" of sand on the rails, a rapid spinning of the wheels. Finally, there is enough forward motion, and the train moves slowly outbound. The whistle announces its departure as it disappears into the woods toward Hither Hills.

But as I recognize the need for progress I was at the same time very pleased to see the shiny new diesel-driven trains standing at the Montauk Rail Station during my visit to Montauk in June 2000. *What a contrast,* was my very first thought. Then, the steam train reminiscing.

But I also think about the relationship between the Fishing Village and the Montauk Manor. Those who lived in the manor in the 1930s era looked down upon the village and most probably thought about what they saw as "picturesque." For my very first time I stayed a few days in the manor, sixty years later, after my leaving the Fishing Village. I looked out of my hotel window, facing Fort Pond Bay, with a feeling of "one eye laughing and one eye crying." There was no Montauk Fishing Village, yet I saw it and relived that life.

Paul Cook, Ted Cook, Richard White Sr., and Edward Edwards celebrate Paul's enlistment in the U.S. Navy in February 1947.

Paul completes boot camp and is dressed for travel, 1947.

Paul Cook, back row second from the left, poses with the other crewmembers of Aircraft 137890 before departing for Med deployment to Malta during the Lebanese Crisis in 1958.

In 1961, Paul Cook was promoted to Lieutenant Senior Grade. Later, in dress blues, he was thrown into the cold waters of Patuxent River for initiation.

The U.S.S. *Norton Sound (AVM-1)* tied up at the pier in Baltimore. At time of *AVM-1* re-commissioning in 1965, Paul was assigned as Electronics Officer and as Assistant Combat Information Center Officer.

The retirement ceremony for Lieutenant Commander Paul T. Cook was held aboard the U.S.S. *Norton Sound (AVM-1)* on 1 September 1968.

Lieutenant Commander Paul T. Cook addresses the full ship's company on the hangar deck of the U.S.S. *Norton Sound (AVM-1)* on the occasion of his retirement.

James "Jim" Anthony Cook was born on 28 March 1950 in Memphis Naval Hospital in Millington, Tennessee. Husband of Ellen Campbell and father of Theo and Lila, Jim is an art professor at the University of Arizona.

David "Dave" Paul Cook was born 2 February 1952 in Tripler Army Hospital in Honolulu, Oahu, Territory of Hawaii.

The Lord is my shepherd; I shall not want.
He maketh me to lie down in green pastures:
 He leadeth me beside the still waters.
He restoreth my soul: He leadeth me in the
 paths of righteousness for His name's sake.
Yea, though I walk through the valley of
 the shadow of death, I will fear no evil:
for thou art with me; Thy rod and
 thy staff they comfort me.
Thou preparest a table before me in the presence
 of mine enemies: thou anointest my head
 with oil; my cup runneth over.
Surely goodness and mercy shall follow me
 all the days of my life; and I will
 dwell in the house of the Lord forever.
 — Twenty-third Psalm

In Loving Memory of

DAVID PAUL COOK

Died October 7, 1972

Funeral Services

Wednesday October 11, 1972

11:00 A. M.

Southwood Baptist Church
Greenfields

Woodbury, New Jersey

Officiating

Rev. George A. Huber

Interment

Woodbury Memorial Cemetery

Victim of a drug prank in Simi, California
Died a violent death in Woodbury, New Jersey
7 October 1972

David, the victim of a drug prank in Simi, California, died a violent death on 7 October 1972.

Patricia "Patti" Anne Cook Moss was born on 18 January 1954 in Memphis Naval Hospital in Millington, Tennessee. Wife of Jimmy Moss and mother of Dallas and Zachary, Patti is a Licensed Professional Counselor.

From the left: EAF Retired Major General Salah Menawi (GenDyn Consultant), Major General Shaaban (Commander EAF), Paul Cook (Director of Marketing, Egypt), and Otto Glasser (GenDyn International Director) are seen at Air Show Paris in the early 1980s.

Paul Cook with his Mideast boss, Bill Green, and an unknown name at the Farnborough Air Show in England during the mid 1980s.

Egyptian President Hosni Mubarak; Paul Cook, In-country Director of Marketing for General Dynamics International Corporation, AmCham's first Executive Vice President, elected in 1982; and other AmCham Board Members from American companies Alex Shalaby, AT&T; and Khalil Nougaim, Morgan Grenfell/CPF meet at the Heliopolis Palace after the founding of the American Chamber of Commerce, Egypt.

American Chamber of Commerce Egypt board members meet with President Hosni Mubarak at the Heliopolis Palace in 1984. Pictured in the front row, left to right, are Khalil Nougaim, M. Shafik Gabr, Ashraf Ghorbal, President Mubarak, Sam Zavatti, Ahmed Shawki, and I.N. "Alex" Shalaby. Pictured in the back row, left to right, are Paul Cook, Elhamy El Zayat, and Hisham Fahmy.

Paul (left) unloads his camel during his camel trek through the desert mountains of the Sinai Peninsula between the Gulf of Suez and the Gulf of Aqaba in September of 1986.

A typical scene during Paul's mountain desert trek in September 1986.

A private golfing group from Bonn-Godesberg Golf Club pose on one of their international golf tournaments in Prestwick, Scotland, in September 1989. *(Author Cook is fourth from left in white top.)*

Dr. Elke Leonhard, Member of Parliament; Paul Cook, President, AGBC-Bonn; United States Ambassador Daniel R. Coats; and Mayor Bärbel Dieckmann at a luncheon in the historic "Alte Rathaus," Bonn, Germany in November 2002. *Photo courtesy of Bonner Rundschau-Germany.*

April 23 1995

Dear Paul,
Yes I received postal cards and letter you sent. Only wish I could be here to see the beautiful churchs they have, at 92 can't do much if I were younger and in good health, I would love to visit all those churches. Some days I don't feel to good, and can't write nice, my hands are shaking. You and Christa are in my daily prayers. I read a small piece about St Paul, about how beautiful the church is Glad your name was Paul.
Paul wish I could write more. so I better stop.

    Love & Prayers
    Mother.

I only have maria to talk to. She's very good to me.

This letter is the last letter that my mother wrote to me and it may be the very last letter that she wrote to anyone. She passed away in June 1995.

The last letter Paul received from his mother and possibly the last letter Beatrice wrote before her death in June 1995.

Appendixes

Appendix 1
A Cathedral of Holy Wilderness

We stand in awe, inspired at the sight of the world's great cathedrals because of their massive and magnificent structures and the genius of their architects, the domes, the spires and sculptures all beautifully dignifying their individual existence as houses of worship for their intended believers. Yet there exist, in and of this world, special places, likened to these famous architectural wonders, that are in themselves houses of worship but enveloped by invisible walls and roofless save for the sky above, such as in Egypt's Sinai. As I recall the lurching and swaying approach on camel into the desert mountains of Sinai, there was eventually visible a profusion of brilliant colors on the sloping mountainsides. There were no stained-glass windows. Instead, nature had painted the mountains as if her light had been refracted and dispersed all the colors of the spectrum permanently into their sides. There was a deafening awareness of silence except for the padlike hooves plodding through the wadi. We had just entered one of those special places, albeit without a door; we knew that we were inside a cathedral of greatest dimensions and the shining sun was the light of all candles for eternity.

After a week of almost monastic life in this barren but nevertheless beautiful and peaceful area it was clear that one could absorb more of life's meaning and have more of the mysteries of life unraveled than from hundreds of sermons from the pulpits of the aforementioned architectural wonders. This does not take away from the inspirations generated by the product of a human designer who trod this earth before us. It is to say that in this time living with the Bedouins, immersed in the wadis of the Sinai mountain desert, within the reaches of Mount Moses, it is as a house of worship for one of any faith, the Bedouins themselves going about with deliberate motions, speaking quietly to one another, as if it might be in the sanctity of a cathedral. Their modest subsistence, more often than not, of tea and bread, which they patiently made three times a day over the fires of scarce twigs and roots, speaks of their fortitude and staying power. Their pew for prayer throughout the day in this expansive house of worship varied from the sand at camp level to a remote ledge on the side of a mountain peak, the latter, it seems, corresponding to the reach of a cathedral spire to the heavens.

At night as you lay on the sand bed before sleeping you observe the crystal clear skies emphasizing each star in the heavens as if touchable. Then you ponder the depths of the universe and wonder. The serenity of these moments is quietly shattered by the light reflected off a satellite racing through the sky and appearing to be among the much more distant stars. As you know full well the many contributions by satellite given man, implied dangers for the future lurk in the mind. The satellite passes out of sight; serenity returns. Thoughts come and go about incidents along the way, thankful that Anis, our Bedouin leader, spotted the black scorpion near us while sitting on the sand around the fire. We learned yesterday how to shore up courage to safely retrieve some water from a brackish well infested with hundreds of wasps. Today's tiny water source from the crack in the side of a mountain gave only two liters of sulfurous water to last twenty-four hours for the eight of us. There's the Big Dipper, which tells me the direction of north. There are more thoughts about Moses and Mount Sinai and the Holy Family, which we were taught traversed this very land. More thoughts about the creation of this universe, its incalculable dimensions. And now, if not fortifying your beliefs, perhaps you begin to believe. The eyes become heavy from thoughts and the body gives in from fatigue on the long hot ride in the serenity of this Cathedral of Holy Wilderness.

Appendix 2
Naturalistic *Observations*

Witness the death of a tree
after a storm, perhaps a very heavy rain,
as invaders in the night,
striking swiftly and with heedless warnings.
Or at times in the bright sun
the potential house, once a gem in the forest,
its length submitted to the quadrant fall.
Once beautiful coat, the bark,
bears ugly scars but reveals
the solid trunk of year layers.
We ponder, "Why *this* tree?"
further, "Why this mighty natural wonder?"
Passing curiosity goes not beneath its coat.
The seeker, loving or appreciative of nature,
pauses to examine, to analyze, to discover.
This fibrous cadaver will become its own grave,
but, "Why *this* tree?" again heard by unconcerned boughs.
Environment for trees, not unlike that of man,
reveals soft soil at the precious point

where once the roots of life had nurtured.
It drank of thirst freely, never in want
from shallow water table, short to reach.
Troubled times from air, not even gusts
had swayed a branch
or dropped a seed of holiday adornment.
Unconditioned in this habitat
to the rigors of a storm,
certain of the population in this stand
fall, unprepared, some not even knowing.
Observe some others in the stand still reaching
to the sky for enlightenment,
towards Earth's center for nutrient,
reaching, ever reaching not in waiting.
Tall and straight from the heavenly reach,
as the hundreds of fingers work
into the depths of soil toward drink and food, elusive
yet available, to the tireless
and deserving, these trees still grow,
still live to provide, to share
their usefulness and beauty.
How often now we mortals
also fall from stunted root,
awaiting care that never comes
from undernourished, or overtended, earth.
Without strong root, a whisper of breeze
becomes as if a mighty storm,
unable to sway and flex, as boughs
in health.
Some fold and droop, prerequisite
to eternity, as if a tree without its ground.

Appendix 3
Think and Complain No More

This day is dull, nothing happens;
at least it seems to be the case.
No quakes, less golf ball hail, not even
the wailing of mercy wagons upon the ears.
No holiday population changes, not
a passing friend to change the mood
of this altogether lackluster life.
But I begin to consider now, beyond complacent,
beyond apathetic reactions to the stimuli.
In a moment, suppose man without
taste *buds* of the tongue, a bite of cane,
a sip of Margarita or Manhattan, perhaps a lime.
Without the *buds, no tastes at all.*

Pine away the hours of the day
as you sip your salt-rimmed glass.
Without your tastes, all drinks the same.
Nerve endings in your olfactory epithelium,
without receptors filled no message to the brain.
No cooking smells, no flowers sweet,
not even putrid odor of the pulp mills
that identify your location, Tacoma or Brunswick.

It's sure you'd be much more alive
after drops of Chanel No. 5.
So now combine the thought
of the drinks and the tantalizing perfume.
Is not your day now somehow less dull?

Hair cells of organ of Corti, now I begin
to think of you, more as I sense loss of sweet and sour,
and since no longer do I respond to the magic
of the whale sperm with roses.
What would awaken me of sleep, no alarm
to hear, no sweet sounds of my love
with morning greetings.
Once pleasant tones of music or
voice of world events no longer.
To be capable of stimulating the cells of Corti.
What to do, where to turn
if now no flavors, odors, tones.
I shall have to feel and observe
by skin and retina, respectively.
Each remaining sense now becoming
so terribly more significant.

Standing at Nedick's on 42nd Street
I see my ordered specialty, orange,
as signaled by my cones, and I know
by memory, of the flavor unnecessarily present.
Although the clinks of ice chips escape,
my sense of touch allows me that cold prevails.
Mixed blessing though on this occasion,
since by me pass honking horns,
the roar of rails below, and "Whadda ya wan'?"
As I reflected on those years past, also the taste
of Nedick's juice, it's as well my buds are gone.
The tube steak, though, I wish for active tongue.
Now envision the senses oblivious to all—
molecules of soluble and volatile substance,
to energy mechanical and other,
waves of heat, of light and sound.

Left only the sensations of bodily motion
and of balance, movement in part
of muscles in space, no astronaut without,
reflect in the moment, your presence,
irrespective of surrounding, just within.

Without flutter of the sparrow, the splash of the fountain,
the tacky release of summer heat on highway pitch,
the rustle of drying leaves on windblown branches,
Doppler changes of approaching and departing whistles
and even the footsteps of a stranger through the doorway.
How without the sights and sounds, changing lights of man or nature,
without view of golden hills or white of snow,
a lovely face, the pleasant honesty of our loved ones, or
the panorama of city skyline on moving clouds
can we ever know the mood of our world?
Dullness will you know when you no longer taste,
when you no longer sense the whale's contribution
to her neck and lobes.

Appendix 4
Emotions

Emotions *Various*

No show of fear, this is a man,
we learn this as a child,
that girls should cry and shed the tears—
of man you are beguiled.

The engines roar, the turn is made
the runway long appears.
I wonder if the pilot feels, as I
request, two beers.

Our ship sets sail upon the waves,
the winds commence to blow.
"Where are my pills of Dramamine?"
Now down below I go.

"How large they are, your eyes tonight!"
"My dear, what did you see?"
"Your other love, I saw tonight,
you *were* my chickadee!"

"It must be love, your heart pounds fast,"
I told my dame last night.
"But no!" she said. "He's got a gun!"
"My man don't think it's right!"

The *bell does ring* at Pavlov's house.
There's no one at the door.
An aid to science as *juices flow,*
and Rover eats no more!

The flames are leaping from the room,
their mother hears them cry.
She dashes in without a thought,
for life you cannot buy!

Emotions *Dental*

The palms again are wet with sweat,
you're in the waiting room.
The dentist calls, "I'm ready now,"
it is the voice of doom.

Once in the chair you tell yourself,
I'm really not afraid,
as wet hands from the chair arms do slip,
At home I wish I'd stayed!

The needle now is in the gums,
at least it's meant to be.
It seems it went through all my head,
for this I pay a fee?

He says, "Relax, it will not hurt."
Impressions are my need.
"Breathe through your nose a little while,
please, on my hand don't feed!"

Again I hear, because I gagged,
"Please, sir, breathe through your nose!"
His understanding wouldn't come
if *he* were in *my* pose!

To calm his patient now he says,
"I know what I will do.
I'll raise my fees to twice the rate,
unless you help me through."

At this, my anger rose above
the fear of gag or pain.
My hands went up, the mold came out,
and the sound waves cleaned all stain.

No longer do I go in fear
to the dental office now.
I take along a case of beer,
contented as a cow!

Emotions *Reality*

My pulse begins to change in count
like votes on polling days
when she tells me how much she loves
the manner of my ways.

"Why do you scratch your head and nose?"
she asks me as I squirm.
I never realized that I act
the motions of a worm.

Off came her cape and there they were,
I'll fight for love and glory.
But on the floor fell *pads* and *wig,*
no battles in *this* story!

And when the *facts* became so bare
I must be sure to state
my hair stood up like a Halloween cat's
as I said, "It's getting late!"

My scratching stopped, as did my squirm,
no longer had I time.
My body turned and made a start
like the race car *on a dime.*

Of purpose did I run so fast,
and oh, how I did jump!
I cleared two cars and a six-foot fence
as adrenaline went to pump.

Appendix 5
What Is Smart?

A test today for your IQ
is not like that they used to do.
My two-year-child knows mouth and ear,
at four says nights are dark.
When nine years old he talks in rhyme,
and cars adults can park.

Compare now this with ages past,
when people few and distance vast.
The princess beauty in the tower,
her prince on journey travels.
Along the way he slays a beast,
and now her heart unravels.

We look these days for mental age
and use a test of Binet—sage.
Test props are many to use for child,
photos galore to stymie.
For adults they use a Wechsler Scale,
the blocks with clocks defy me.

"Boy is to trousers as girl is to *what*?"
Well, *dress,* is sure the answer.
Otis-Lennon would be proud of me
for all the smarts I got.

Atop the vinculum you put MA,
below chronological age.
Now multiply a hundred
and you see that I'm a sage.

Now Pinter says of a little girl,
"What's missing from the rooster?"
Since *leg* is gone, the child says,
"He *lost* it when he *goosed* her."

High school students take an SAT,
standard for the grades.
Six hundred is a real good score,
Three hundred you're in the *trades*.

One-eighteen as a freshman in,
grads one-twenty-three to go.
And if you want a Ph.D.
under one-four-one too low!

IQ tests, they seem to favor
the *middle-upper* class.
So let's improve achievements,
then the *skills* will also pass.

Intelligence allows one to adjust,
new info will you learn.
From experience one will profit,
and in pockets will you earn.

Appendix 6
The Way the Twig Is Bent

If knowing what I am is self-identity and what I do and how I do it is the role I play, well, so much for the academics. It seems that I necessarily associate the terms and phrases relating to "identity" with words of those persons who say they have not found themselves. To me it is inconceivable that one cannot "find himself" or that he or she does not know why he or she is here. Perhaps, I think, at times these are expressions of those who have found "an out" from taking part in their share of the load in their city, state, or country, because it has become fashionable to expound on such thoughts. I think further and ask, "When did these kinds of thoughts become fashionable?"

As I passed through early years of life, having entered this world in 1929, as far back as I can remember, I knew who I was and what I had to do. I did not falter in wonder at my identity or my "role" in life. Of course we are all imitators of sorts just as instinctively as the animals that roam through the forest or pace a cage in the zoological gardens. Maybe it became a goal of mine at a childhood age to achieve the qualities of perseverance and dedication and to learn the talents of my father. I recall that I was always aware of this although I never became restless or lost in thoughts about this naturally imitative relationship. I did not want to be like him because I thought I *had* to be or that I *should* be, rather because I *wanted* to be. Even at such a young age (about eight to twelve), and I realize that "age" is relative, I believed in his way of being, implicitly. And those "fuzzy" aspects of life as relate to the "before" and the "hereafter," the *why and how* of the "beginning," the orderliness of nature and its source, never presented a problem to me.

The few hundred population of the village where I lived, along the sea from which the fish that nourished came, were God-fearing, and in the most positive sense. The reiterations of liturgical mysteries and pulpit gospels at mass provided each and every one with the strength to respect man and the stormy sea. There was balance in the thoughts, decisions, and deeds of the men and women just as that balance existed in the purest settings of nature, untouched by the ill thoughts and greed of the expansionists. Each family had its own home, a shack but a home in the real sense. Respect and dignity penetrated the then rubberized cloth of the men on the sea. Each, it seemed, was a carpenter, machinist, humanist, and humorist, as well as catcher of fish. The sale of fish to the "drummers" (agents of fish markets such as Fulton Fish Market, New York) provided for the material necessities and food for the asking by the neighbors in the village. What a bond among the villagers and what a culture!

There were no outlets to plug in a refrigerator. There was no refrigerator, except for the box containing a continually melting block of ice from springtime to the beginning of cold weather. Then, in winter, the window box was used to store the food by the freezing or near-freezing outside temperatures. The ice man came with the ice that was sawed out from the local pond in winter and stored in the large wooden house with insulating layers of straw for preservation until use in summer. An exchange of news and humor was made with each delivery. If no one was at home, the ice man came into the house, always unlocked in those days, and laid the twenty-five pounds of block ice in the "icebox." For respect of the family, a knock was always in order for entrance. If no response came, deliveries were made whether of ice or any other items expected. These men who brought their goods to the Fishing Village from the "outside world" were ambassadors of the highest level.

The sea itself was teacher as well as provider. To learn with care is a lesson not always easily learned. Consider the moment when my "ship" commenced to sink, the ship I had built from scrap lumber at the age of seven and eight. Quality control was not a course in school but a factor learned by doing, trial and error. One does not forget these trials, and one always remembers, very clearly, the error. The launch of a scrap lumber ship, whose cracks were tarred with the waste tar from the fishermen's nets, along the sand and pebbled shores of Fort Pond Bay was a delight like that displayed by a new father. I departed the shore using my driftwood paddle, my eyes affixed to the trawlers at mooring piles in the inner bay. *I am now one of them,* I thought with my head high. I was to hold it higher still as my ship began to sink because of defective caulking. Water had slowly but steadily poured in as the various principles of Archimedes were now being exercised. I was to learn, more formally in school of later years, that my ship would remain afloat only so long as it displaced an amount of water equal to its weight. There was at this moment zero displacement, as the weight of my body far exceeded the capacity of the waterfilled craft. As I was yet unable to swim, my recognition of a need for this talent was immediate. A yell for help was instinctively bellowed out and it echoed off the buoys and boat hulls. Fatefully, my father was sculling about in his sharpie on this Sunday afternoon and heard my plea. He sculled some hundred feet in record time, it seemed, to pull me from an almost certain finish in the water at five fathoms' depth. My respect for the sea heightened dramatically as I learned man must be in constant awareness of his environment. The sea was our friend but a potential enemy as well. It is essential to be aware of the mood of the sea and at times, irrespective of its mood, approach this awesome body with an appropriate and respectful attitude.

It became my belief, through this series of trials and errors like that of my ship and the bay, whether it be in an environment of sea, on the ground, in the air, or among people, that respect supersedes material claims. What can we say about which society or which culture is better than another? Conceivably any culture can be better than another for the people within a certain grouping. If the people of a fishing village are, within themselves, living in harmony and happy and contented who is to say that they need a social revolution? Even if the contentment of these villagers was in large part contrived from the need for survival through long hours in harsh circumstances, isn't it better that camaraderie prevails? Fights, theft, and murder were topics only read in city newspapers. In the village, a good catch, the birth of a child, a marriage, and the Cannon Ball Express puffing into the rail station were foremost in their minds. There is nothing in my recollection of artificial talk or actions. Just as the devices of the trade on the sea were uncomplicated, so lived the people in everyday life.

In a not so simple society, where greed and disrespect more often seem to prevail, we oftentimes see the sullen reflection of a troubled inner mechanism as difficult to observe as a hermetically sealed modern contrivance. The more difficulties that we have to cope with from our own undoing, the more difficult the task of soothing their ill effects.

At one end of a two-man timber saw, on a blustery winter day cutting lengths of fallen trees in the forest for the kitchen stove, one had the chance to ponder. The thoughts primary in the mind were again of a survival nature or of getting out of the cold wind. Then the splitting of logs welcomed the desire to be close to the hot ashes of yesterday's cuttings, to be near the smells of the rising bread loaves just kneaded, at the back of the stove.

These are but a few thoughts of my early environment, which molded my way of thinking, my character, and my philosophy of life to be lived. The inherently impressionable youngster following parental actions and also imitating the general character of the people of the village, I feel, made me whatever I am today. I think I have changed very little until now in middle life years, not just because I believe "things were better in the old days." It is because with respect to my own set of molded traits I sincerely feel that the life I lived and observations made my childhood far more beneficial to the inner self. And it was collectively far more beneficial to the society of the time in the village than the more "civilized" and "advanced" societies of the world today. I am quite certain that the type of childhood environment I described still exists in many places in the world that support "village societies," yet, unfortunately, it is diminishing on a grand scale due to encroachment by profit seekers and politicians.

I took on the role of a navy man at a young age, seventeen, as I was accustomed to the sea and its accompanying features, additionally because the navy offered me educational benefits. University or college was not affordable for my family. I wanted ultimately to be like the naval officers that I observed on the naval ships at anchor in Fort Pond Bay. These officers, standing on the ships' decks, so neat and clean in their white summer uniforms, represented the more sophisticated sea life that challenged my whole being. So in my efforts to one day become a naval officer I did everything to perform in the very best way I knew while still an enlisted petty officer. I saw these officers as responsible and friendly role models, along with my parents and the other villagers. I like to believe that these associations helped to instill in me those same qualities I had liked and consciously recognized as a youngster.

Also during my various positions of leadership responsibilities, later in life, I was conscious of the need for dealing with people in as sincere, kind, and positive a manner as had been demonstrated to me. All the people of the village did not have to try to be the way they were. They were simply the kind of people they were as a result of the nature of the culture developed there. Some of the basic factors contributing to this wonderful culture included hard work, exposure to and respect for the elements, little idle time, respect for people and their personal rights, and the recognition of God.

A code of common decency is essential at the outset in life, and this involves very basic concepts of morality. Morality these days seems to be so nonexistent in the more academic environment that it is not at all surprising that increasing numbers of people within its grip falter and slide from efficiency, neatness, respect, and decency. These words of my thoughts, my beliefs, are based upon what I have lived, what I observe, what I know, see, and hear, and above all what I feel.

My obligation in life primarily involves living in a style as closely as possible to my impressions in the Fishing Village during my childhood. I have always hoped for myself, "the way the twig is bent, the tree is inclined."

Appendix 7
Tax-Supported Health Care

The amount, and quality, of medical treatment to each person should not be a function of his or her ability to pay.

Because of a wide separation in the abilities of people to pay for any given service, I believe we should have tax-supported hospitals and health care just as we have tax-supported (public) schools. Our education system, for the most part, comprises public schools, and it was established to guarantee every American a substantial education. Equally or perhaps more important is a need to make available to each and every American the complete range of medical facilities irrespective of the role held in society, socially or economically.

While there exist some of the most modern facilities and a relatively extensive source of facilities and people in medicine in America, it remains all too often the case that the degree of service attainable is directly proportional to the "thickness of the wallet." Doctors who are especially talented know that they can establish a fancy office on a Park Avenue site and expect the higher fee. The upper-level-salaried patients, and those *born* wealthy, will obviously find their way to this realm of service. The low- and middle-income or hourly wage worker must necessarily settle for the average medical talent and limited hospital confinement because of his lack of ability to pay high insurance rates or direct medical service charges. Even if the latter submits to the higher-cost route, which may be desperately needed or maybe morally appropriate, there always remains for him the worrisome and awesome financial burden for years after the services are rendered.

If laws can be written providing our citizens tax-supported education, it is not unreasonable to consider tax support providing these same people with proper health care. Some people will say or argue, perhaps, that they are never sick and then they would be just paying for other people's problems. Maybe they argue that "my health insurance payments take care of my needs, so why should I pay more for greater taxes?" Well, when a family sends a child to a private school they still have to pay school taxes in any case, as one always has to pay school tax regardless of having children or not. There will probably always be some inequity in any sort of plan designed for the masses. Yet these inequities are small with respect to the very great advantages that are provided for the large majority of the people. There are many who not only do not have sufficient money to pay a hospital bill but also do not have money to pay for an insurance premium for total medical service. If the level of education a person received was commensurate with his ability to pay there would be millions of people in this country with no more than a grade school education. Only tax-supported schools allow for the chance to educate everyone through the high school level. Likewise for public hospitals there ought to be a tax-supported system that will ensure all people the comfort of hospital and health care without the additional burden of worrying where the money will come from to pay the bill.

It would be a morally corrupt philosophy to believe that it is proper for a rich man to receive more intensive medical care and better treatment than one less financially fortunate. A person who enters a hospital should not be confronted with the routine and untimely question of how he will pay the bill. Too often only the "well off" have an answer comforting to themselves. On the other hand, there are certainly many who are turned away at the hospital door for lack of money or, at best, receive minimal care because they, or their inadequate level of insurance, will not allow another day more at the hospital. I feel sure that a large number of folks do not even entertain the thought of going to a hospital to improve their condition because there is no way they could find sufficient funds to defray expenses.

Everyone needs medical attention at one time or another in his or her life. Just as it is in the best interest of our society to properly educate each and every American, it is certainly in our best interest to properly care for the physical and mental health of all citizens.

It would behoove all of us to talk or write to the senators and members of Congress of our districts to support action at a national level for the development of a national health plan. Through this action all Americans, irrespective of financial standing will at least be able to enjoy one less burden and at a time when this burden, relieved, would hasten one's medical recovery.

Appendix 8
Is a Good Education Essential for Success in Our Society?

The standard for acquiring success in our society is not merely the level of education one receives. It has been customary in the many past years to suggest that because a person graduated from an institution of higher learning such as Harvard or Yale and then became president of a bank or a senator he was very successful. Certainly this person was generally considered of high esteem. Still today a person will, generally, not be considered for a position as, let us say, a cabinet member or ambassador without a higher level of college education. But what is success? Is it achieved by attainment of a goal in the public eye or in the credit column of a ledger?

All too often, society or some factions of our society place the value of success alongside the headline, title, or dollar sign. If we fall back to regroup and at least open our mind to all the definitions of *success* as per *Merriam-Webster,* they include "a favorable termination of a venture."

A neighbor friend of mine in New Jersey started on a venture to become a contractor building houses. He had not completed high school and, in fact, he usually frowned at a technical approach to any problem in his trade. Today he has reached that point in life where he has favorably terminated his venture. He is very happy. He has a comfortable new home, considerable savings in the bank, and a wonderful wife. In my estimation this man is quite as successful as any college graduate and perhaps happier than the "magna cum laude." This is not to suggest that all educated people are not successful or happy; rather, education is not necessarily a prerequisite to success.

In another instance there is the case of an employment trend in a division of a large corporation in the defense industry. Of over 3,000 engineers employed in 1969, 1,200 were laid off due to contract cutbacks. All these men were graduate engineers, some with doctorate degrees. On the other hand, there were about 20 nonengineers (without college degrees) maintained on the employment rolls because of their specific abilities accumulated through experience in life. This experience, as opposed to formal education, meant the difference between a paycheck and a "pink slip" (loss of job). In this instance, the 20 men were successful; the 1,200, unsuccessful.

Success is highly dependent upon one's point of view and current station in life. At the moment I feel I have attained success in that I am healthy, employed [1975], and married to a wonderful woman. Another person's success may be a venture that he still seeks, as he breathes his last breath, highly educated.

Appendix 9
Perception: "It seems to be that way"

my "yacht"
vor 60 Jahre
Jetzt wirchlich
mein yacht,
mit Dir drinnen.

The Sport Fisherman

How large your fish it matters not;
just use your camera quite a lot.
Eat your catch before you say
about the one that got away.
Before the feast here's what to do:
just hold the fish out front of you.
Your friends will think how smart you are
to hook this huge and mighty gar.
They'll wonder where you found the hole
from which you caught the fish with pole.
"What kind of bait?" they're bound to ask.
"It surely must have been a task
to find the kind for giant to lure!"
"How did you get him through the door?"
You do not have to tell your friends
your fish is that which Kodak sends.
The tiny Dolly Varden trout
in front of you held two feet out.

The Cloud Watcher

On back I lie, with sky above,
that cloud appears just like a dove.
Also I see a face of man,
on other days a moving van.
The air is quiet, so change is slight,
but comes a wind and shapes delight.
Let your pure imagination run,
it's always nice to have some fun.
At times they're real, almost to touch,
those figures in the clouds are such.
Years have passed since that day when
I saw John Hancock with his pen.
So real this scene, I had to think,
He's sure to leave if I do blink.
And with a twitch I lost this sight,
but wait, two cowboys in a fight.
Which one would win I could not say,
because the wind blew them away.

The Skier

On weekends here the skiers flock,
no need to even wind the clock.
Up and at 'em is the cry,
the snow is falling from the sky.
We'll be first when we suit up now,
hurry, hurry, I'll show you how.
Into the long johns and double knits,
and don't forget to bring your mitts.
Buckle your boots and carry your skis
to the base of the hill and pay your fees.
Now here we are, all in the line,
awaiting the lift is not so fine.
We fidget and poke our poles in the snow
and see all the people in wait for tow.
While shuffling forward on eager wax
you sometimes stop assembling facts.
For all you know is what you see,
a mile of people in front of thee.

Finally on top, on skis and snow,
you see the mountains and far below.
Beginner and novice on bunny runs
appear like ants on sugared buns.
The nearby mountains are cold, you see,
a coat around them like you and me.
What coat is this? you ask yourself,
just like those on the sport goods shelf.
It's herringbone, the pattern's clear,
but would it be if we were near?
Let's start our run on down the hill
and keep our view without a spill.
As fiberglass now cuts new a trail
it seems the mountain coat a sail.
Nearing the bottom, it's not herringbone
but countless boughs of pine with cone.

Appendix 10
Modern Communication Methods

Remember the good old days when you dialed a number of a company, for one reason or another, and you got an answer (yes, a real-live someone actually talked to you): "Hello, Blue Grass Weevil Exterminators, Mary Lou Snodgrass speaking, may I help you?"

"Yes, this is John Frantic. I would like to know the proper spray for a stink beetle, please."

"I will mail you a brochure, John, with information for all weevils and the appropriate insecticide today."

"Many thanks, Mary Lou."

On observing an advertisement in a magazine for "Best and Cheapest Life Insurance Company" John Frantic dials the given phone number in the USA from his home in Oberhochberg. Some voice answers John, telling him that he will be charged for the 800 call. If he does not want to be charged, he should hang up now. John is perturbed, but he gives in and stays on the line. The phone at "Best and Cheapest" rings.

"Welcome to Best and Cheapest Life Insurance Company. If you know the last four digits of the party you wish to speak to, press two." John does not know the last four or any of the digits, because he does not know who he should be talking to in the first place. He only knows the company name. The voice continues, "If you do not know the last four digits, press one." John does not know. He presses 1. That voice comes on again: "Press * to begin again." John presses * and he hears, "Thank you for calling Best and Cheapest Life Insurance Company; call us at any time for any of your insurance needs." John has not talked to anyone at the B and C LI Co., so he talks to his neighbor in Oberhochberg. John does not want to let on that he failed to complete his call to the States, so he goes around the issue, tactfully asking if the neighbor has had any problems with his telephone. "No," replies the neighbor. "Just last week we had a new phone installed because my wife wanted a green telephone instead of that old black kind.

The phone man said that now we have a "touch-tone phone." John now thought that "touch tone" was a shade of green and let it pass.

But the neighbor carried on with John's problem. "John, when you press the buttons on your phone be sure to press them firmly and then the system will respond better to the audio frequency that you hear when you press them."

Well, John thought, *I will go home and try the call again, being sure to press firmly.*

But John did not hear anything. Nothing at all.

John goes to the phone repair shop and explains to the man that he hears no sounds when he pushes the buttons. "You have an analog phone, Mr. Frantic. What you need for this, unless you buy a new phone with touch tone, is a touch-tone generator." John has immediate thoughts of his auto generator as he has no clue about the availability of these small handheld gadgets with buttons to generate the necessary tones of different frequencies for the phone systems. After a painful period of searching he finally finds a shop in the nearest larger town that sells tone generators.

John, happier than ever, is now ready to make his call again to B and C LI Co. He dials, ignores the operator telling him he has to be charged for the stateside 800 call, and waits for the phone to ring and be answered. "Welcome to Best and Cheapest Life Insurance Company. If you know the last four digits of the person you want to speak to, press two." By now, John knowingly presses 1 while holding the tone generator against the mouthpiece, to continue, because he does not know to whom he should speak. He is happy to hear another voice, but it is asking him to be prepared to provide his Social Security Number (SSN). John did not realize he would need this number. It is not at hand. He must hang up and look for the SSN in his files.

John repeats all steps as before on a new call and works his way down to the same point of the Social Security number reminder from the voice, which continues, "If you want to get information about saving policies, press one. If you want to be sent application forms, press two. If you want term insurance information, press three. If you want directions to our headquarters, press four. If you want to apply directly for a savings plan policy now, press five. If you need to talk with someone in any other area, please press zero and stay on the line. The next available agent will be with you as soon as possible."

John optimistically presses 0. Strains of the first few bars of Beethoven's Fifth are repeated every minute, with interruptions of: "Please have patience; someone will be with you shortly." After John waits for ten minutes, his patience is exhausted. He hangs up.

The next night, John begins the entire process all over again. When he hears the voice for the first time on this call attempt, "Press one," which he now knows he must do, nothing happens. John forgot to turn the tone generator switch to the "off" position; the battery is dead. John goes to the nearest *Stübchen* (German pub) to recharge his battery.

Appendix 11
Ancestry Charts

English Ancestors of Paul T. Cook (Native of Montauk, N.Y.) ....
one of whom (William Wells) played a prominent role in the establishment of the Southold Settlement in Eastern Long Island, N.Y., claimed by Southold to be the oldest English Settlement (1640) in the State of New York.

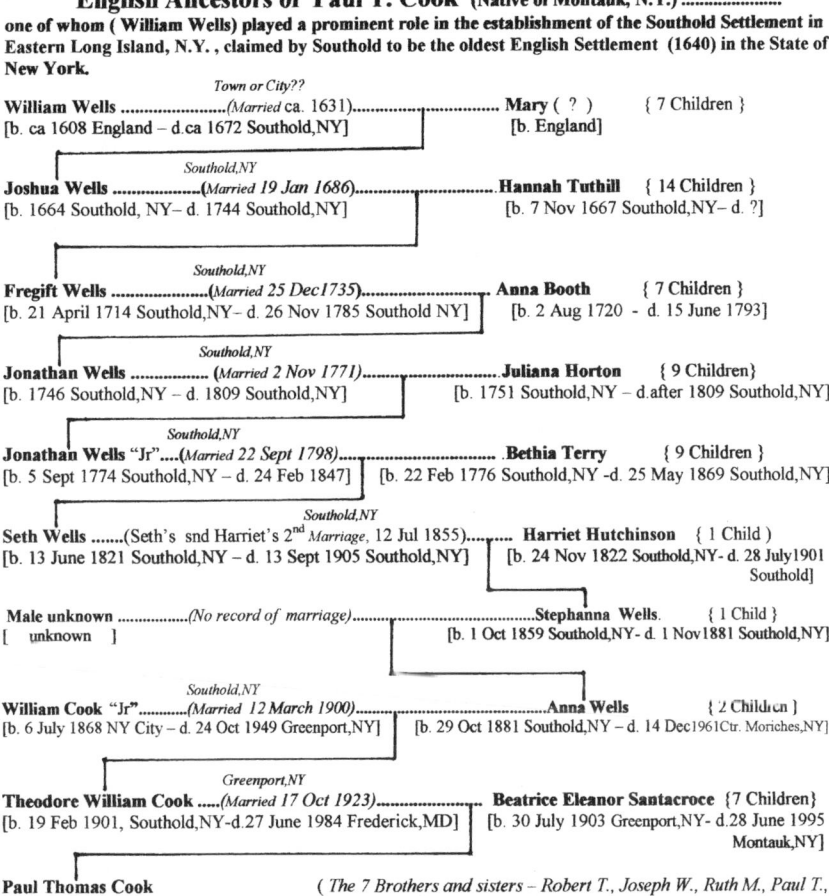

Town or City??
William Wells ....(*Married* ca. 1631).........................**Mary** (?)   { 7 Children }
[b. ca 1608 England – d.ca 1672 Southold,NY]   [b. England]

Southold,NY
Joshua Wells ....(*Married 19 Jan 1686*).........................**Hannah Tuthill**   { 14 Children }
[b. 1664 Southold, NY– d. 1744 Southold,NY]   [b. 7 Nov 1667 Southold,NY– d. ?]

Southold,NY
Fregift Wells ....(*Married 25 Dec1735*).....................**Anna Booth**   { 7 Children }
[b. 21 April 1714 Southold,NY– d. 26 Nov 1785 Southold NY]   [b. 2 Aug 1720 - d. 15 June 1793]

Southold,NY
Jonathan Wells .... (*Married 2 Nov 1771*).....................**Juliana Horton**   { 9 Children}
[b. 1746 Southold,NY – d. 1809 Southold,NY]   [b. 1751 Southold,NY – d.after 1809 Southold,NY]

Southold,NY
Jonathan Wells "Jr".....(*Married 22 Sept 1798*)...................**Bethia Terry**   { 9 Children }
[b. 5 Sept 1774 Southold,NY – d. 24 Feb 1847]   [b. 22 Feb 1776 Southold,NY –d. 25 May 1869 Southold,NY]

Southold,NY
Seth Wells ....(Seth's snd Harriet's 2nd *Marriage*, 12 Jul 1855).........**Harriet Hutchinson**   { 1 Child)
[b. 13 June 1821 Southold,NY – d. 13 Sept 1905 Southold,NY]   [b. 24 Nov 1822 Southold,NY- d. 28 July1901 Southold]

Male unknown ....(*No record of marriage*)..........................**Stephanna Wells**.   { 1 Child }
[unknown]   [b. 1 Oct 1859 Southold,NY- d. 1 Nov1881 Southold,NY]

Southold,NY
William Cook "Jr"............(*Married 12 March 1900*).....................**Anna Wells**   { 2 Children }
[b. 6 July 1868 NY City – d. 24 Oct 1949 Greenport,NY]   [b. 29 Oct 1881 Southold,NY – d. 14 Dec1961Ctr. Moriches,NY]

Greenport,NY
Theodore William Cook .....(*Married 17 Oct 1923*)...................**Beatrice Eleanor Santacroce** {7 Children}
[b. 19 Feb 1901, Southold,NY–d.27 June 1984 Frederick,MD]   [b. 30 July 1903 Greenport,NY- d.28 June 1995 Montauk,NY]

Paul Thomas Cook   (*The 7 Brothers and sisters – Robert T., Joseph W., Ruth M., Paul T.,*
[b. 16 Jul 1929 Southampton Hospital, NY -]   *Gladys J., Joan C. and John A. Cook)*

    Paul T. Cook *(& other siblings of Theodore and Beatrice)* are 10th generation descendants of **William Wells**, one of the **original English Puritan settlers** in the group from Southwold and Hingham, England, who further migrated to Southold from the New Haven Colony in the period 1635 – 1640. William Wells was one of the prominent settlers of Southold and is buried next to the First Presbyterian Church in **Southold,NY**. in **"The Old Burial Ground"**. The oldest stones that can be dated in this cemetery are those of **Rev. John Youngs** (organizer of this 1640 settlement),and **William Wells**, both of whom died in 1672. They are in two, of the only nine, graves in the cemetery which are marked with raised, horizontal table stones marking the locations of **prominent settlers**. Southhold claims to be the oldest English Settlement in the **state of New York**, however, Southampton makes a similar claim. But the cemetery was officially designated as the "oldest burial grounds" in the State of New York.[Paul says that with his father born in Southold, and he born in Southampton, he has a pretty solid relationship with Eastern Long Island, but his childhood memories of life in the Montauk Fishing Village are most prominent and everlasting in his mind.]
    Through the marriage of **Harriet Hutchinson** to **Seth Wells** on 12 July 1855, g-g-grandparents of **Paul T. Cook** *(& other siblings)*, Paul is also a 10th generation **descendant of Nathaniel Dominy (1st)** and **Sarah Edwards** (married 25 Dec 1669) of **East Hampton, NY.** East Hampton's **Mary Dominy** (grand-daughter of **Nathaniel Dominy 1st**), married in Southold on 8 July 1731 to **Benjamin Hutchinson** of Southold. **Harriet** is the great-grand-daughter of **Mary Dominy** and **Benjamin Hutchinson**. The latter couple, **Mary and Benjamin**, and their children in the following 4 generations, **died in Southold.**

Italian Ancestors *(Santacroce Family)* **of Paul T. Cook** (Native of Montauk, N.Y.) ....
My Italian grandparents, and all their ancestors were born and married in Popoli, Italy (a poor farming area, located about 75 km east of Rome). Grandparents, Vincenzo and Anna Santacroce, emigrated from Italy and settled in New York (ultimately in Greenport, L.I.) in 1898. 5 of their 9 children were born in Popoli, and 4 in Greenport. 2 of the children born in Popoli died early, perhaps at birth. Anna could not read or write. Although Vincenzo had been a laborer, he could read and write and after settling in Greenport he developed a grocery business catering to the Italian population in the area by importing items from Italy, among other things specialities like cheese, salamis, & black cigars. Each year in the fall, Vincenzo, would buy crates of grapes and with the help of his close Italian men friends, produce enough red wine to last through the following year. They not only had a very successful grocery store business but accumulated some real estate properties as well.

Joseph Santacroce .... [?]
[b. (?)   Popoli   d. before 1803 Popoli]

Pasquale Santacroce ....Mattia Trasoli (or Frasoli)
[b. ca 1738 Popoli d. Oct 1803 Popoli]   [b. (?) Popoli   d. before 1836 Popoli]

Francesco Santacroce ....Anna delle Ville   (5 Children)
[b. ca 1756 Popoli d. 22 Sept 1836 Popoli]   [b. (?) Popoli   d. after 1836 Popoli]

Pelino Santacroce ....Anna Rose Damiani
[b. ca 1790-1793 Popoli   d. 1 May 1818 Popoli]   [b. ca 1791-1795 Popoli   d. 18 Oct 1836 Popoli]

Giuseppe Santacroce ....(Married 1854 or 1855)....................Filomena de Felice   (2 Children)
[b. 24 Nov 1817 Popoli   d. (?) Popoli]   [b. 13 Aug 1835 Popoli   d. (?) Popoli]

Vincenzo Santacroce ....(Married 12 July 1887).............................Anna Ciccarelli   (9 Children)
[b. 2 Feb 1863 Popoli d. 13 Mar 1942 Greenport,NY]   [b. 1 Dec 1864 Popoli d. 12 Apr 1941 Greenport , NY]

Theodore William Cook .... (Married 17 Oct 1923)............Beatrice Eleanor Santacroce   (7 Children)
[b. 19 Feb 1901 Southold, NY d. 27 June 1984 Frederick,MD]   [b. 30 July 1903 Greenport,NY d. 26 June 1995 Montauk,NY]

Paul Thomas Cook
[b. 16 July 1929 Southampton Hospital,NY

(The 7 - COOK brothers and sisters   –   Robert Theodore., Joseph William., Ruth Marie., Paul Thomas., Gladys Jane., Joan Cecelia., and John Anthony Cook)